尾田栄一郎

Talking about boogers is gross, so instead I'll use the word "honey" below.

I asked this question to one of the staff: "Chairs at school always have honey stuck on the bottom of them, right?" He said, "Huh?!" To which I replied, "Huh?!" So what do people do with all the honey they harvest during class? Flick 'em?! *That's crazy!!*

  –Eiichiro Oda, 2004

E iichiro Oda began his manga career at the age of 17, when his one-shot cowboy manga **Wanted!** won second place in the coveted Tezuka manga awards. Oda went on to work as an assistant to some of the biggest manga artists in the industry, including Nobuhiro Watsuki, before winning the Hop Step Award for new artists. His pirate adventure **One Piece**, which debuted in **Weekly Shonen Jump** in 1997, quickly became one of the most popular manga in Japan.

ONE PIECE VOL. 33
WATER SEVEN PART 2

SHONEN JUMP Manga Edition

STORY AND ART BY EIICHIRO ODA

English Adaptation/Megan Bates
Translation/John Werry
Touch-up Art & Lettering/Elena Diaz
Design/Sean Lee
Supervising Editor/Yuki Murashige
Editor/Alexis Kirsch

VP, Production/Alvin Lu
VP, Sales & Product Marketing/Gonzalo Ferreyra
VP, Creative/Linda Espinosa
Publisher/Hyoe Narita

ONE PIECE © 1997 by Eiichiro Oda. All rights reserved.
First published in Japan in 1997 by SHUEISHA Inc., Tokyo.
English translation rights arranged by SHUEISHA Inc.

Printed in the U.S.A.

Published by VIZ Media, LLC
P.O. Box 77010
San Francisco, CA 94107

10 9 8 7 6 5 4 3 2 1
First printing, February 2010

www.viz.com

THE WORLD'S
MOST POPULAR MANGA
www.shonenjump.com

SHONEN JUMP MANGA

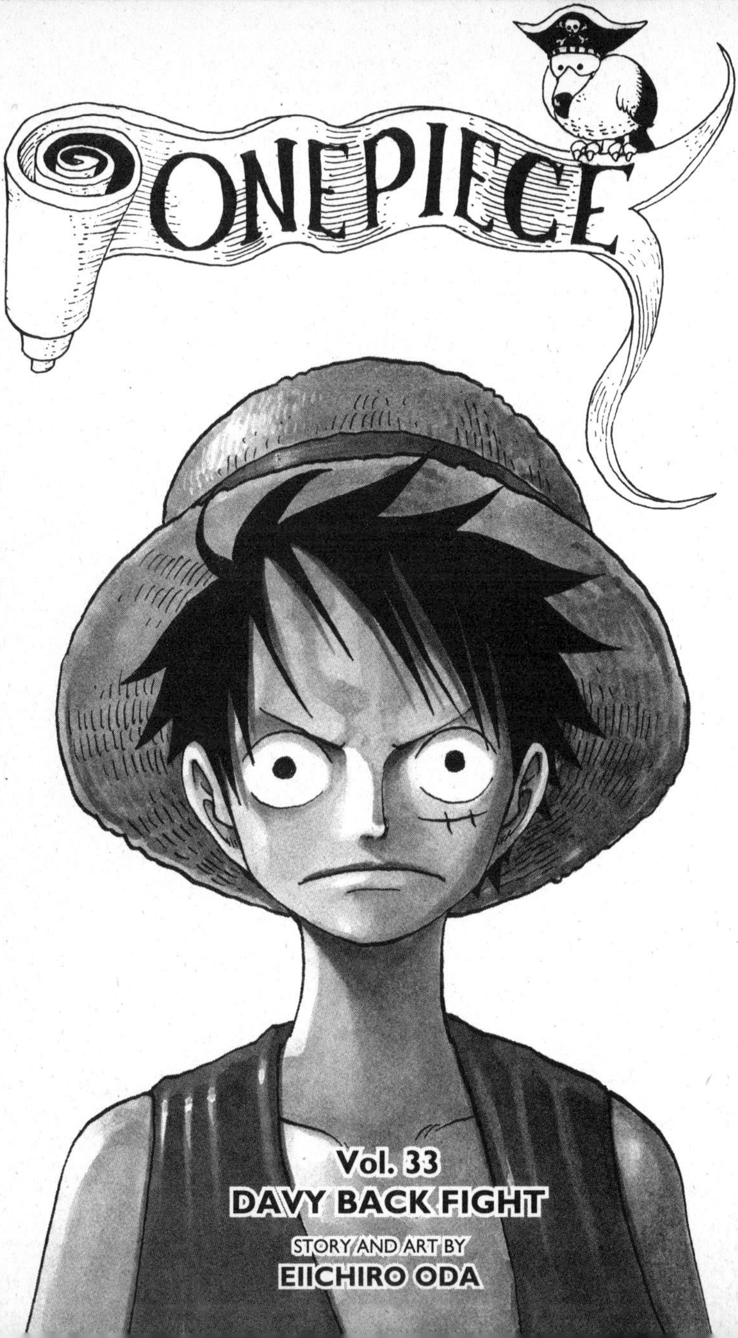
ONE PIECE

Vol. 33
DAVY BACK FIGHT

STORY AND ART BY
EIICHIRO ODA

The Straw Hats

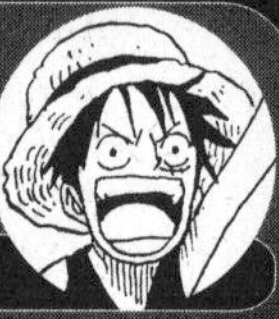

Boundlessly optimistic and able to stretch like rubber, he is determined to become King of the Pirates.

Monkey D. Luffy

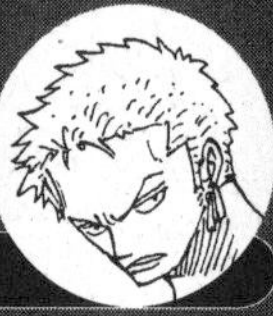

A former bounty hunter and master of the "three-sword" style. He aspires to be the world's greatest swordsman.

Roronoa Zolo

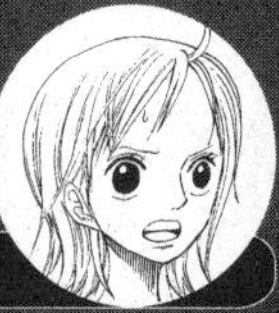

A thief who specializes in robbing pirates. Nami hates pirates, but Luffy convinced her to be his navigator.

Nami

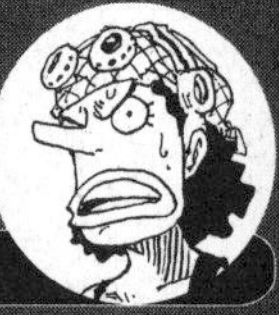

A village boy with a talent for telling tall tales. His father, Yasopp, is a member of Shanks's crew.

Usopp

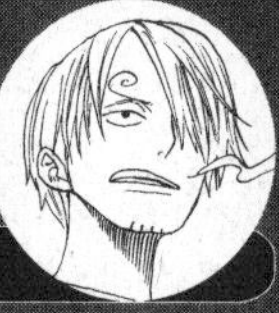

The big-hearted cook (and ladies' man) whose dream is to find the legendary sea, the "All Blue."

Sanji

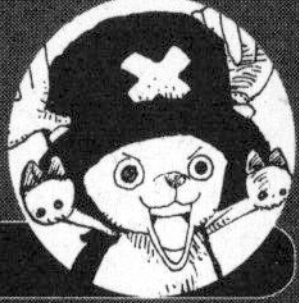

A blue-nosed man-reindeer and the ship's doctor.

Tony Tony Chopper

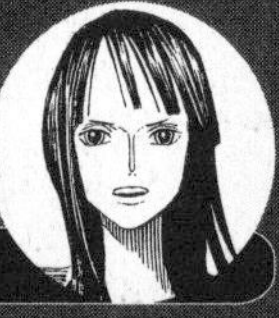

A mysterious woman in search of the Poneglyff on which true history is recorded.

Nico Robin

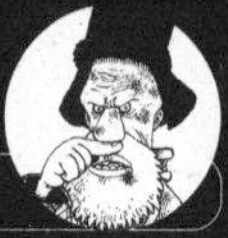

Tonjit

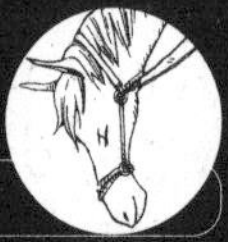

Sherry

THE STORY OF ONE PIECE

Volume 33

Monkey D. Luffy started out as just a kid with a dream—to become the greatest pirate in history! Stirred by the tales of pirate "Red-Haired" Shanks, Luffy vowed to become a pirate himself. That was before the enchanted Devil Fruit gave Luffy the power to stretch like rubber, at the cost of being unable to swim—a serious handicap for an aspiring sea dog. Undeterred, Luffy set out to sea and recruited some crewmates—master swordsman Zolo; treasure-hunting thief Nami; lying sharpshooter Usopp; the high-kicking chef Sanji; Chopper, the walkin' talkin' reindeer doctor; and Robin, the cool and crafty archaeologist.

The Straw Hat pirates reach Sky Island, where they seek the golden treasure and Great Bell said to be found in the ancient city of El Dorado. However, they soon become enmeshed in a three-way battle for survival with Eneru, a despotic ruler, and the Shandians, a group of natives fighting to recapture the island. One by one, warriors fall before Eneru's enormous power, but when Luffy enters the fray, a grueling battle ensues. As the resonant tones of the Great Bell ring out, the Straw Hat pirates leave Sky Island behind.

While seeking a carpenter to repair their ship, Luffy and his crew pass a mysterious ship with no captain or navigator. They soon arrive at an island and meet up with the Foxy Pirates, a goofy group of ruthless seafarers who challenge them to a dreadful game in which their very comrades are at stake...the Davy Back Fight!!

The Foxy Pirates

This crew's motto is "We take what we want!"

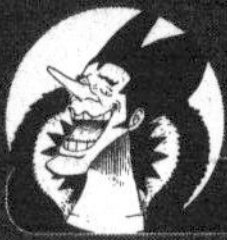

Captain

Foxy the Silver Fox

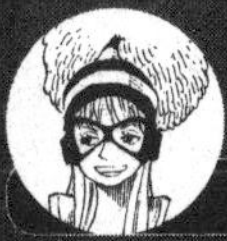

Warrior

Porche

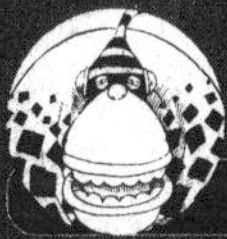

Warrior

Hamburg

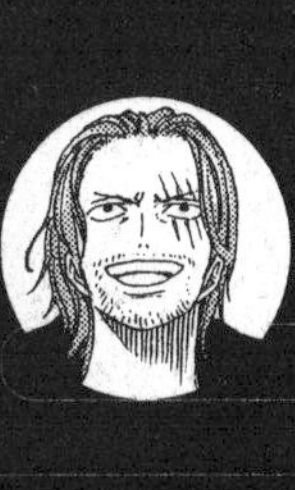

A pirate that Luffy idolizes. Shanks gave Luffy his trademark straw hat.

"Red-Haired" Shanks

Vol. 33
Davy Back Fight

CONTENTS

Chapter 306:
DONUT RACE

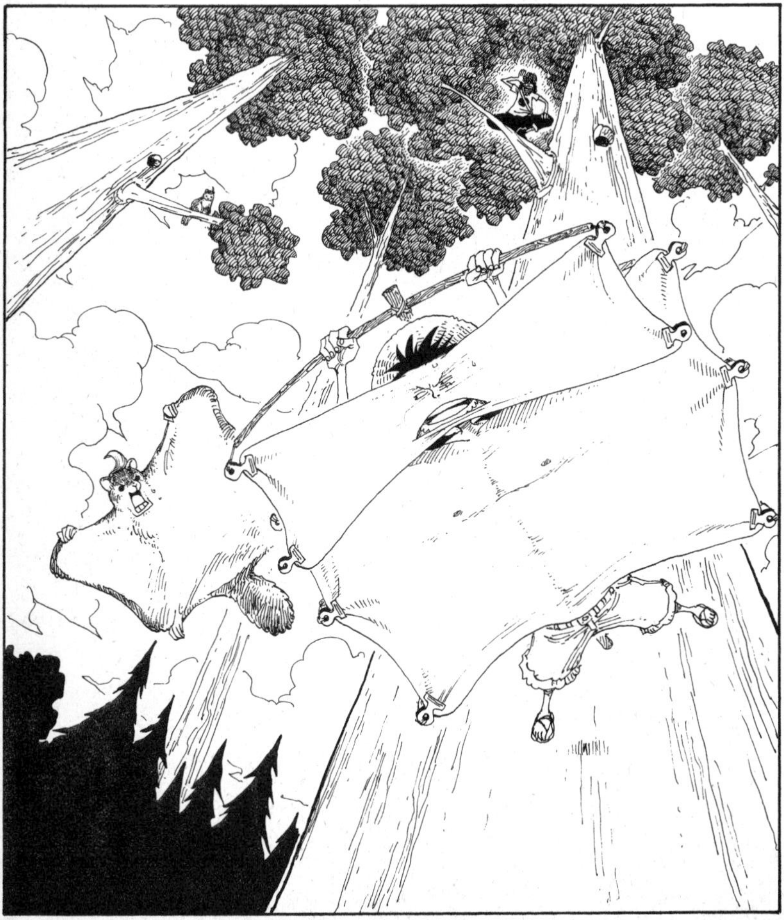

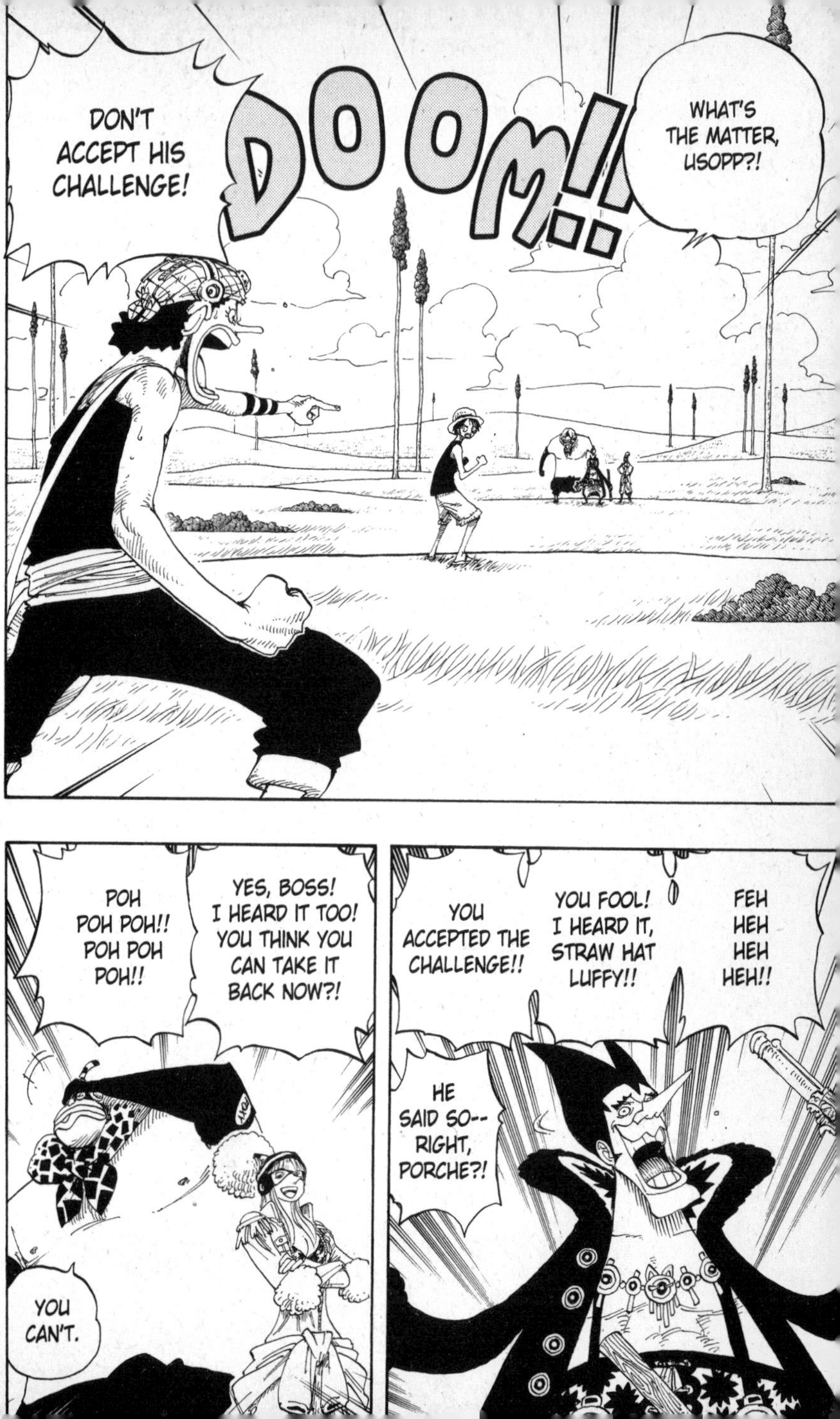
WHAT'S THE MATTER, USOPP?!
DOOM!!
DON'T ACCEPT HIS CHALLENGE!
FEH HEH HEH HEH!!
YOU FOOL! I HEARD IT, STRAW HAT LUFFY!!
YOU ACCEPTED THE CHALLENGE!!
HE SAID SO-- RIGHT, PORCHE?!
YES, BOSS! I HEARD IT TOO! YOU THINK YOU CAN TAKE IT BACK NOW?!
POH POH POH!! POH POH POH!!
YOU CAN'T.

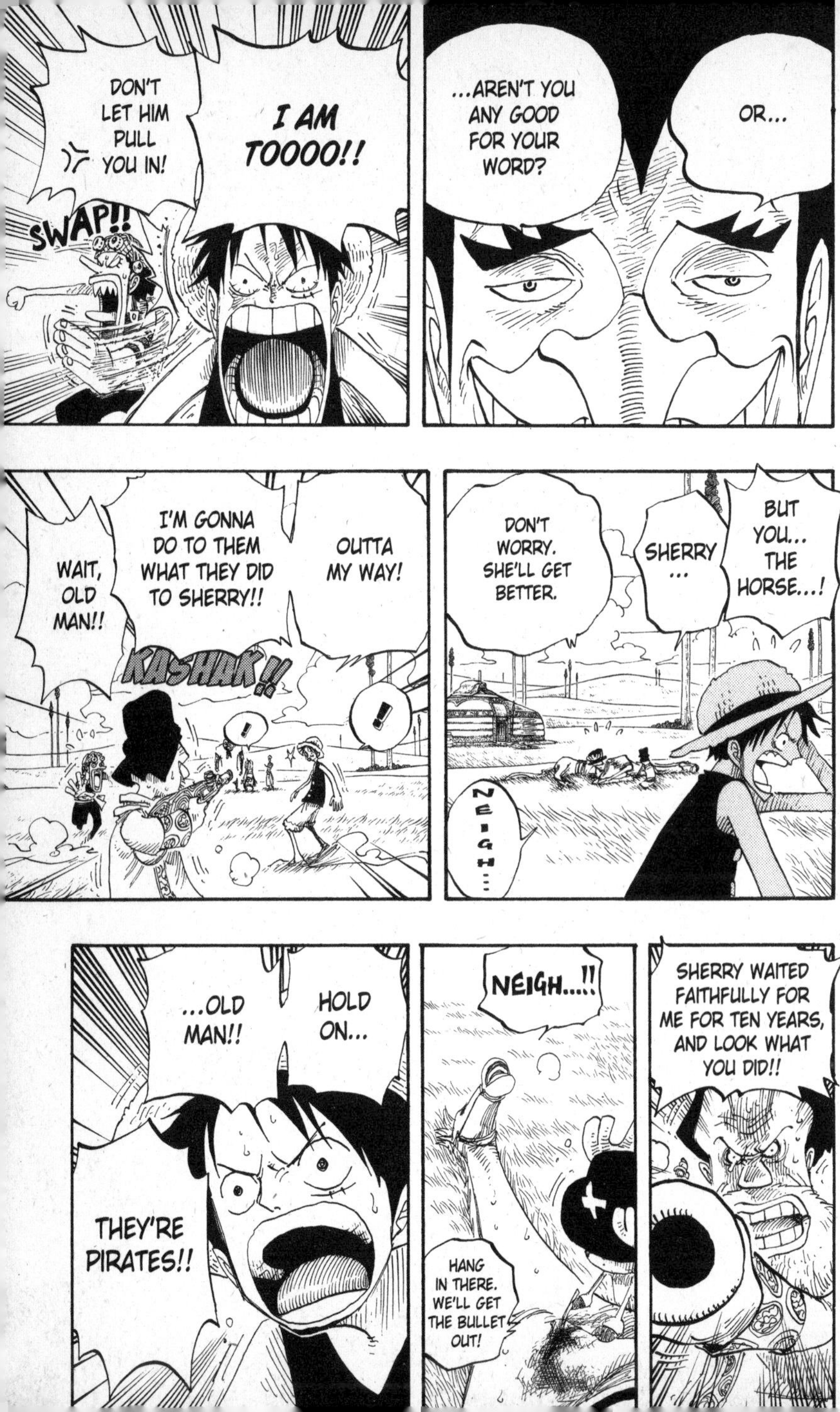
OR...
...AREN'T YOU ANY GOOD FOR YOUR WORD?
I AM TOOOO!!
DON'T LET HIM PULL YOU IN!
SWAP!!
BUT YOU... THE HORSE...!
SHERRY ...
DON'T WORRY. SHE'LL GET BETTER.
NEIGH...
OUTTA MY WAY!
I'M GONNA DO TO THEM WHAT THEY DID TO SHERRY!!
WAIT, OLD MAN!!
KASHAK!!
!
!
SHERRY WAITED FAITHFULLY FOR ME FOR TEN YEARS, AND LOOK WHAT YOU DID!!
NEIGH...!!
HANG IN THERE. WE'LL GET THE BULLET OUT!
HOLD ON...
...OLD MAN!!
THEY'RE PIRATES!!

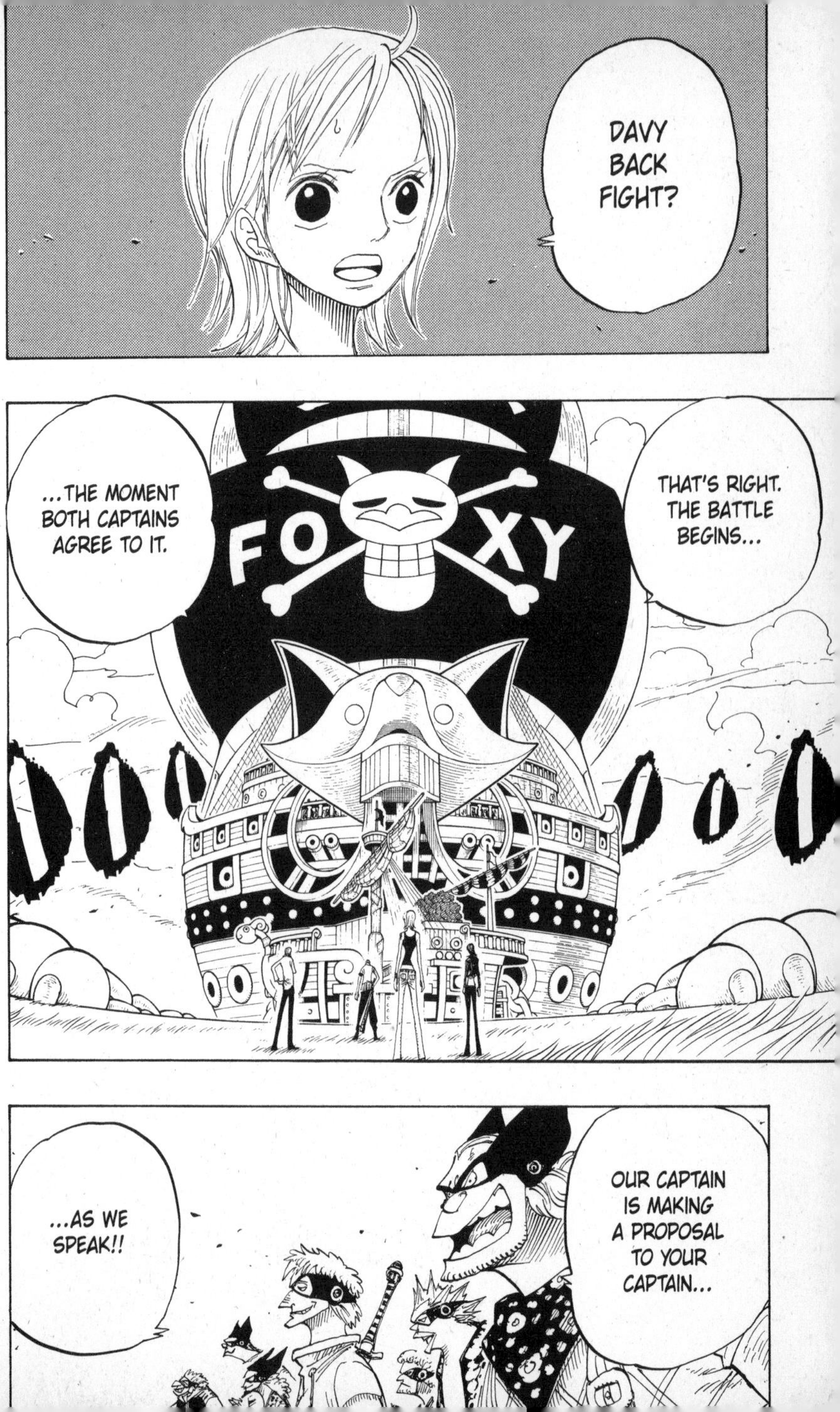
DAVY BACK FIGHT?
THAT'S RIGHT. THE BATTLE BEGINS...
...THE MOMENT BOTH CAPTAINS AGREE TO IT.
OUR CAPTAIN IS MAKING A PROPOSAL TO YOUR CAPTAIN...
...AS WE SPEAK!!

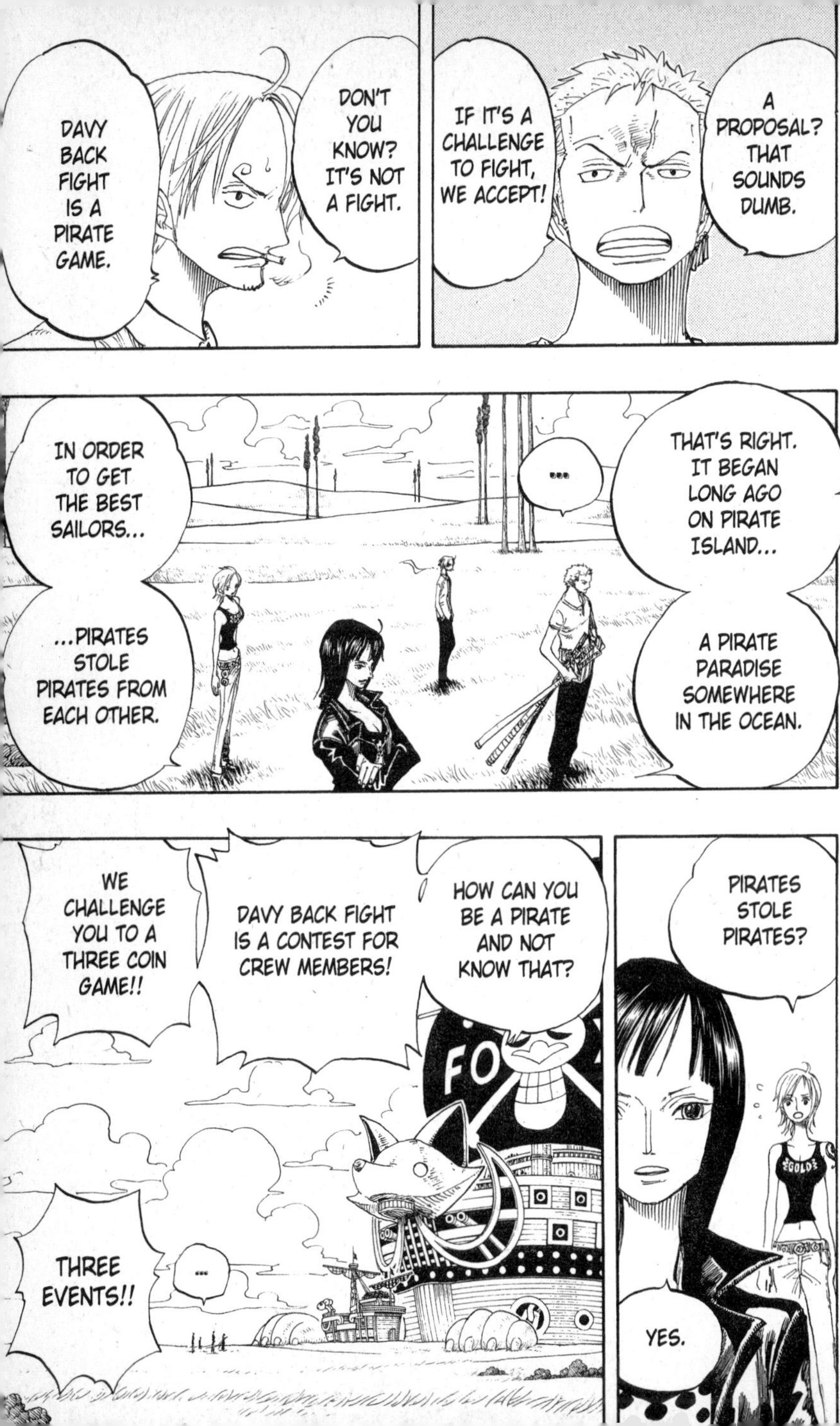
A PROPOSAL? THAT SOUNDS DUMB.
IF IT'S A CHALLENGE TO FIGHT, WE ACCEPT!
DON'T YOU KNOW? IT'S NOT A FIGHT.
DAVY BACK FIGHT IS A PIRATE GAME.
THAT'S RIGHT. IT BEGAN LONG AGO ON PIRATE ISLAND...
A PIRATE PARADISE SOMEWHERE IN THE OCEAN.
...
IN ORDER TO GET THE BEST SAILORS...
...PIRATES STOLE PIRATES FROM EACH OTHER.
PIRATES STOLE PIRATES?
GOLD
YES.
HOW CAN YOU BE A PIRATE AND NOT KNOW THAT?
DAVY BACK FIGHT IS A CONTEST FOR CREW MEMBERS!
WE CHALLENGE YOU TO A THREE COIN GAME!!
...
THREE EVENTS!!

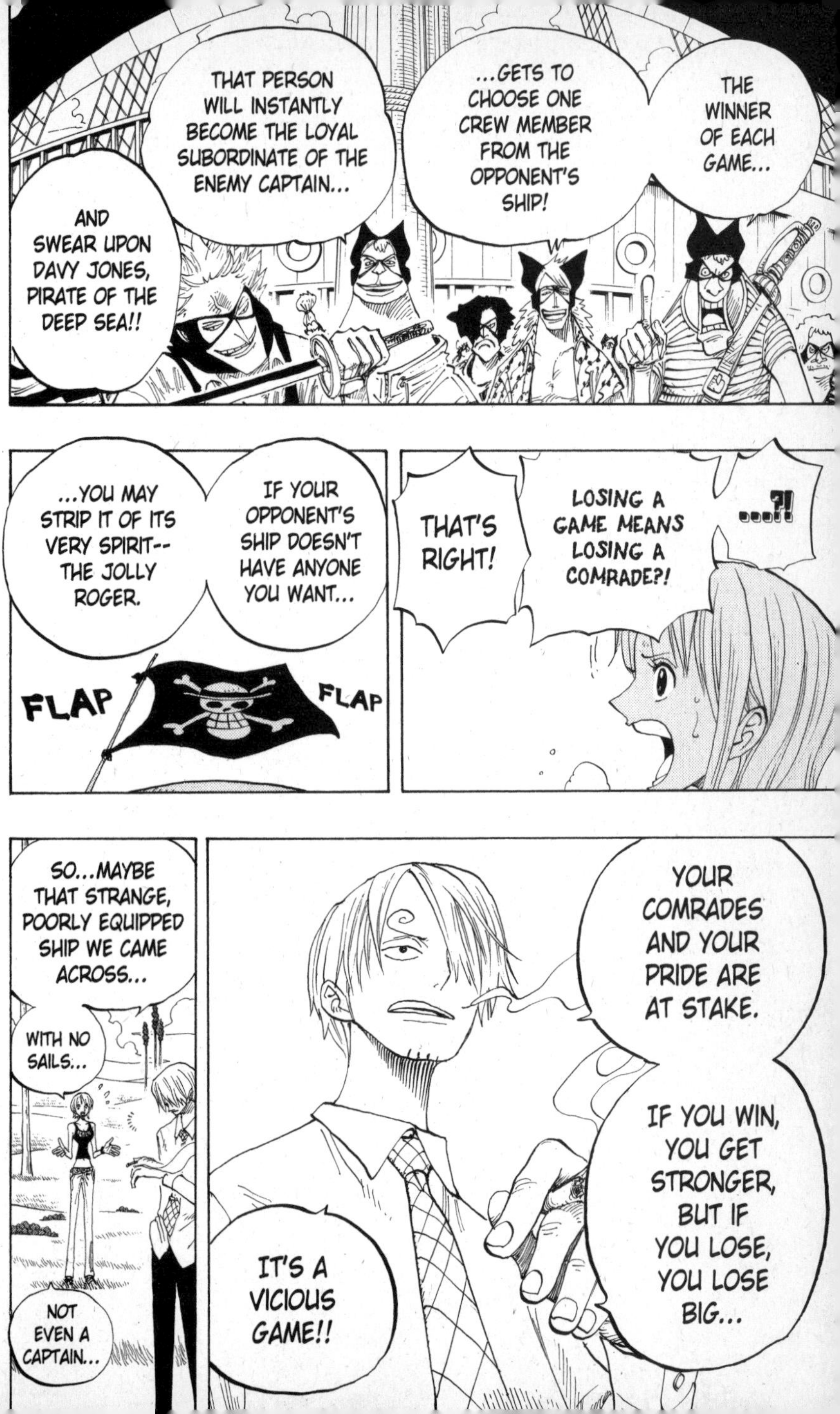
THE WINNER OF EACH GAME...
...GETS TO CHOOSE ONE CREW MEMBER FROM THE OPPONENT'S SHIP!
THAT PERSON WILL INSTANTLY BECOME THE LOYAL SUBORDINATE OF THE ENEMY CAPTAIN...
AND SWEAR UPON DAVY JONES, PIRATE OF THE DEEP SEA!!
...?!
LOSING A GAME MEANS LOSING A COMRADE?!
THAT'S RIGHT!
IF YOUR OPPONENT'S SHIP DOESN'T HAVE ANYONE YOU WANT...
...YOU MAY STRIP IT OF ITS VERY SPIRIT-- THE JOLLY ROGER.
FLAP
FLAP
YOUR COMRADES AND YOUR PRIDE ARE AT STAKE.
IF YOU WIN, YOU GET STRONGER, BUT IF YOU LOSE, YOU LOSE BIG...
IT'S A VICIOUS GAME!!
SO...MAYBE THAT STRANGE, POORLY EQUIPPED SHIP WE CAME ACROSS...
WITH NO SAILS...
NOT EVEN A CAPTAIN...

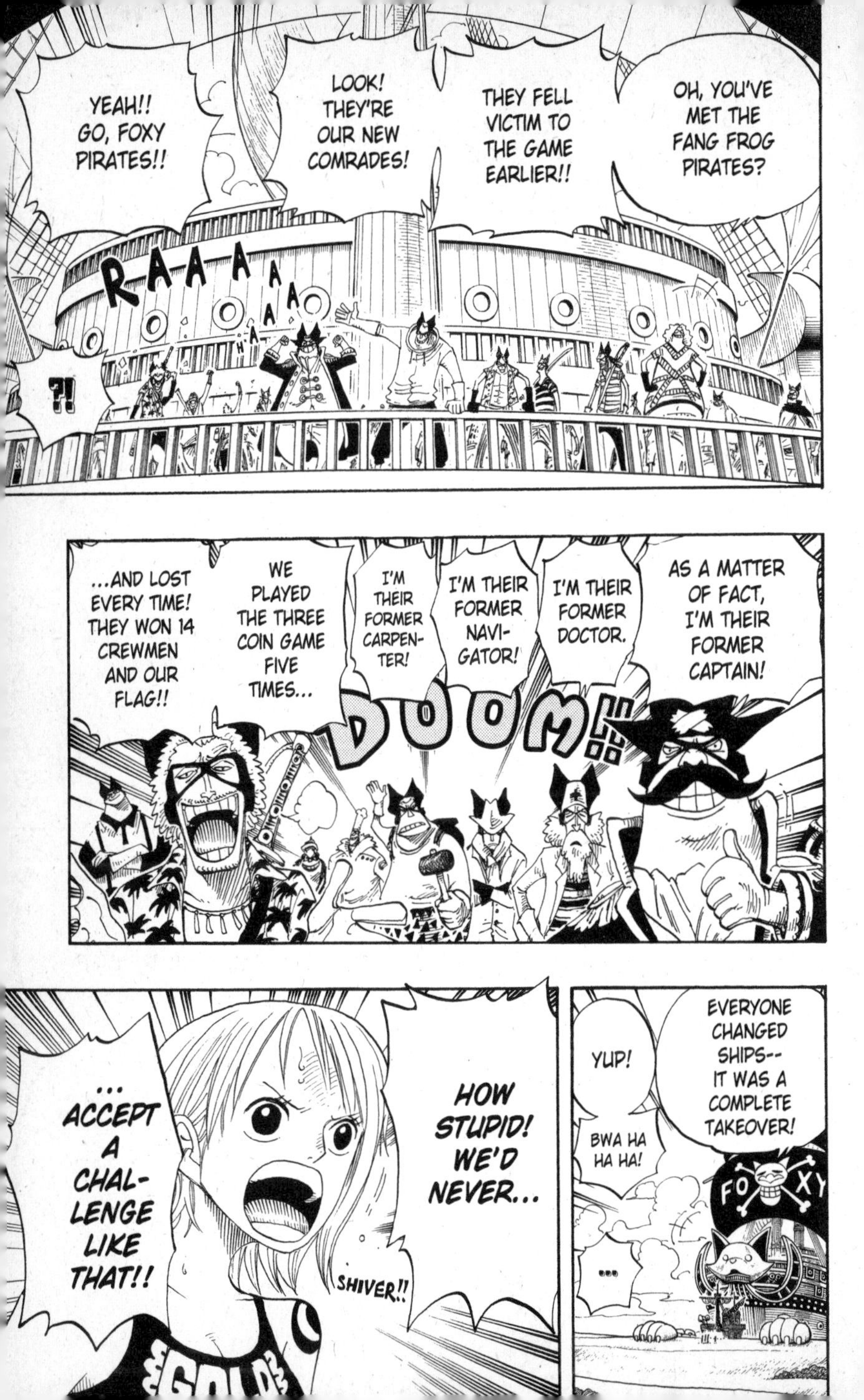
OH, YOU'VE MET THE FANG FROG PIRATES?
THEY FELL VICTIM TO THE GAME EARLIER!!
LOOK! THEY'RE OUR NEW COMRADES!
YEAH!! GO, FOXY PIRATES!!
RAAAAAAHA
?!
AS A MATTER OF FACT, I'M THEIR FORMER CAPTAIN!
I'M THEIR FORMER DOCTOR.
I'M THEIR FORMER NAVIGATOR!
I'M THEIR FORMER CARPENTER!
WE PLAYED THE THREE COIN GAME FIVE TIMES...
...AND LOST EVERY TIME! THEY WON 14 CREWMEN AND OUR FLAG!!
DOOM!!
EVERYONE CHANGED SHIPS-- IT WAS A COMPLETE TAKEOVER!
YUP!
BWA HA HA HA!
FOXY
...
HOW STUPID! WE'D NEVER...
SHIVER!!
... ACCEPT A CHALLENGE LIKE THAT!!
GOLD

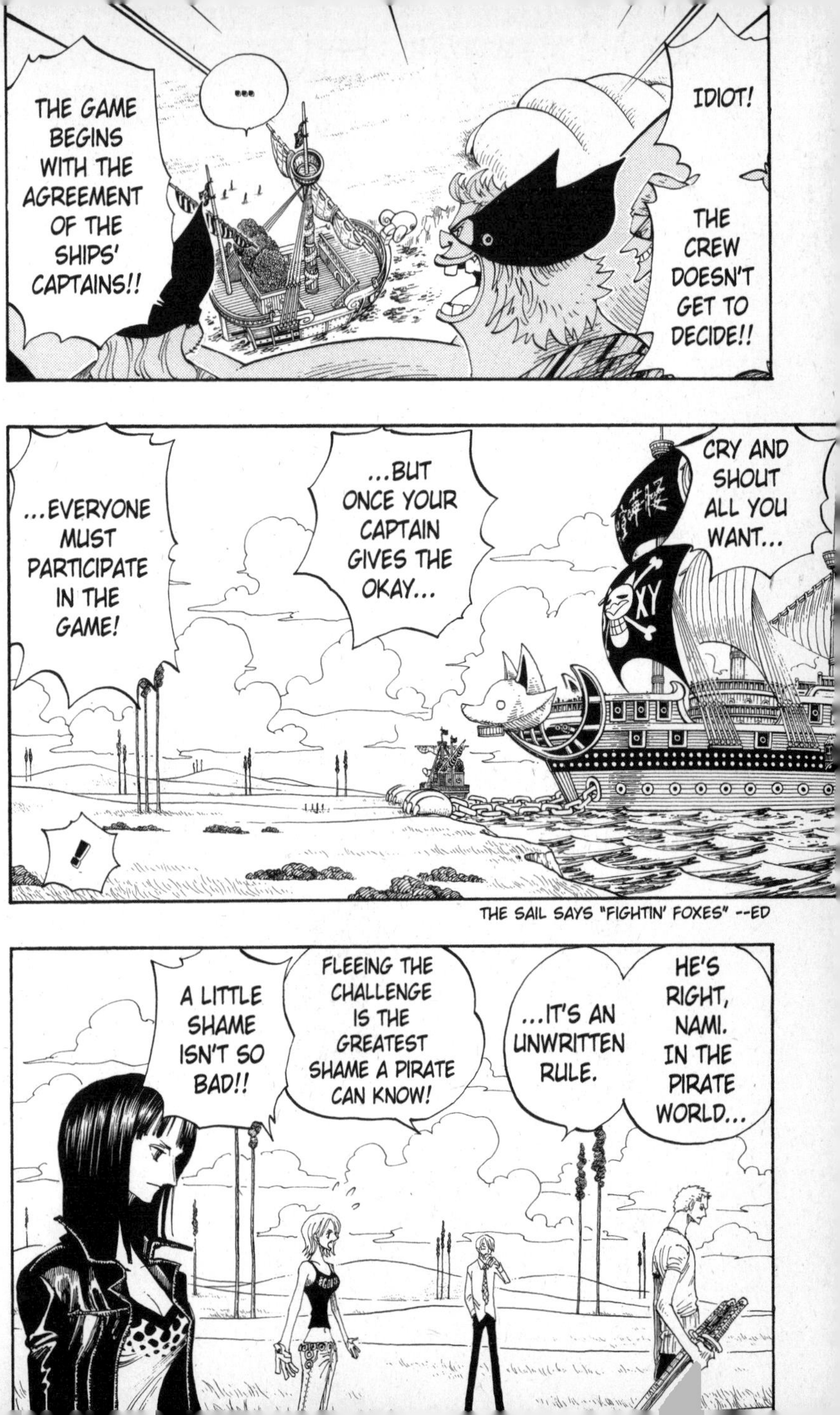
IDIOT!
THE CREW DOESN'T GET TO DECIDE!!
...
THE GAME BEGINS WITH THE AGREEMENT OF THE SHIPS' CAPTAINS!!
CRY AND SHOUT ALL YOU WANT...
...BUT ONCE YOUR CAPTAIN GIVES THE OKAY...
...EVERYONE MUST PARTICIPATE IN THE GAME!
!
HE'S RIGHT, NAMI. IN THE PIRATE WORLD...
...IT'S AN UNWRITTEN RULE.
FLEEING THE CHALLENGE IS THE GREATEST SHAME A PIRATE CAN KNOW!
A LITTLE SHAME ISN'T SO BAD!!

THE SAIL SAYS "FIGHTIN' FOXES" --ED

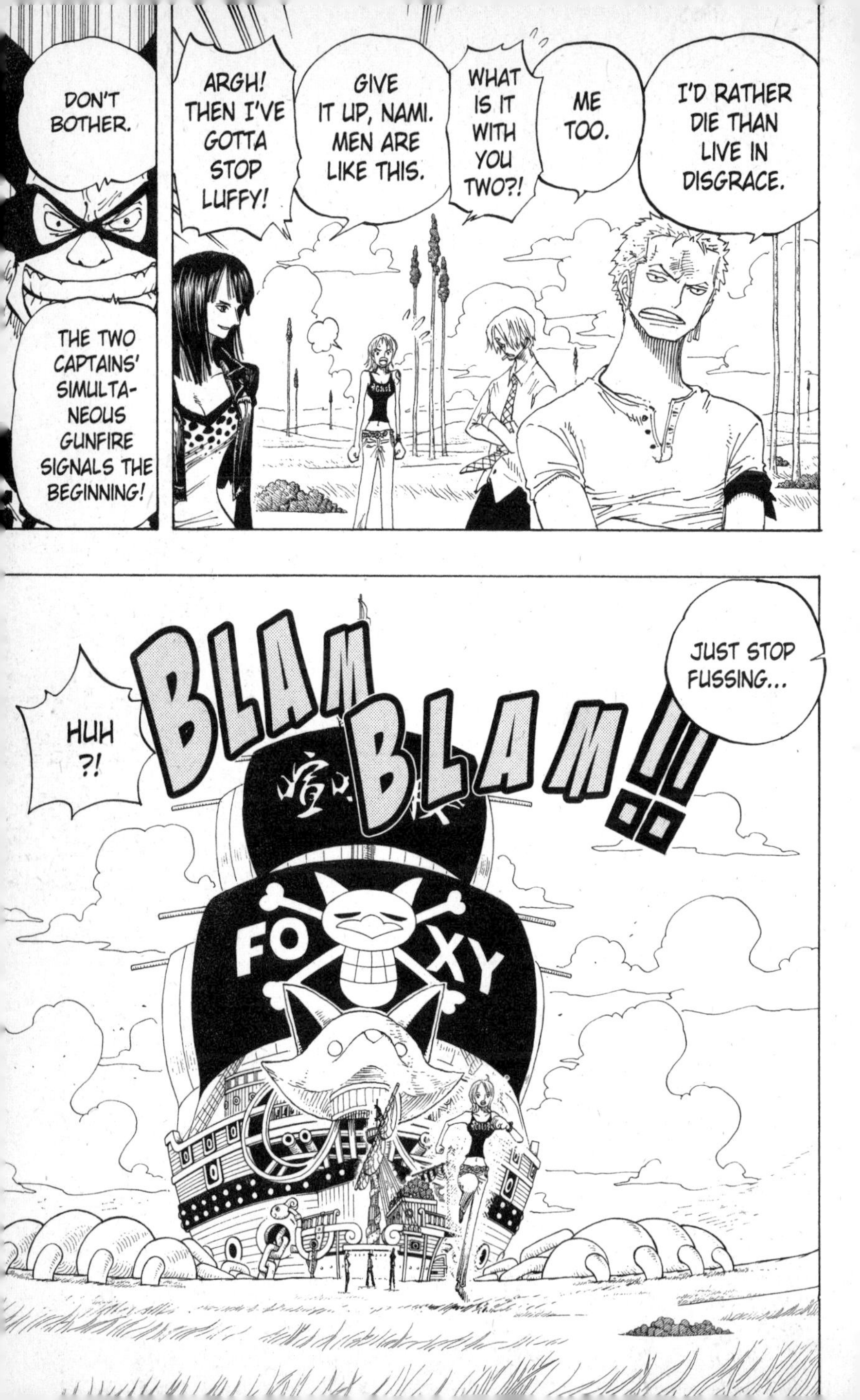
I'D RATHER DIE THAN LIVE IN DISGRACE.
ME TOO.
WHAT IS IT WITH YOU TWO?!
GIVE IT UP, NAMI. MEN ARE LIKE THIS.
ARGH! THEN I'VE GOTTA STOP LUFFY!
DON'T BOTHER.
THE TWO CAPTAINS' SIMULTANEOUS GUNFIRE SIGNALS THE BEGINNING!
JUST STOP FUSSING...
BLAM BLAM!!
HUH ?!
FOXY

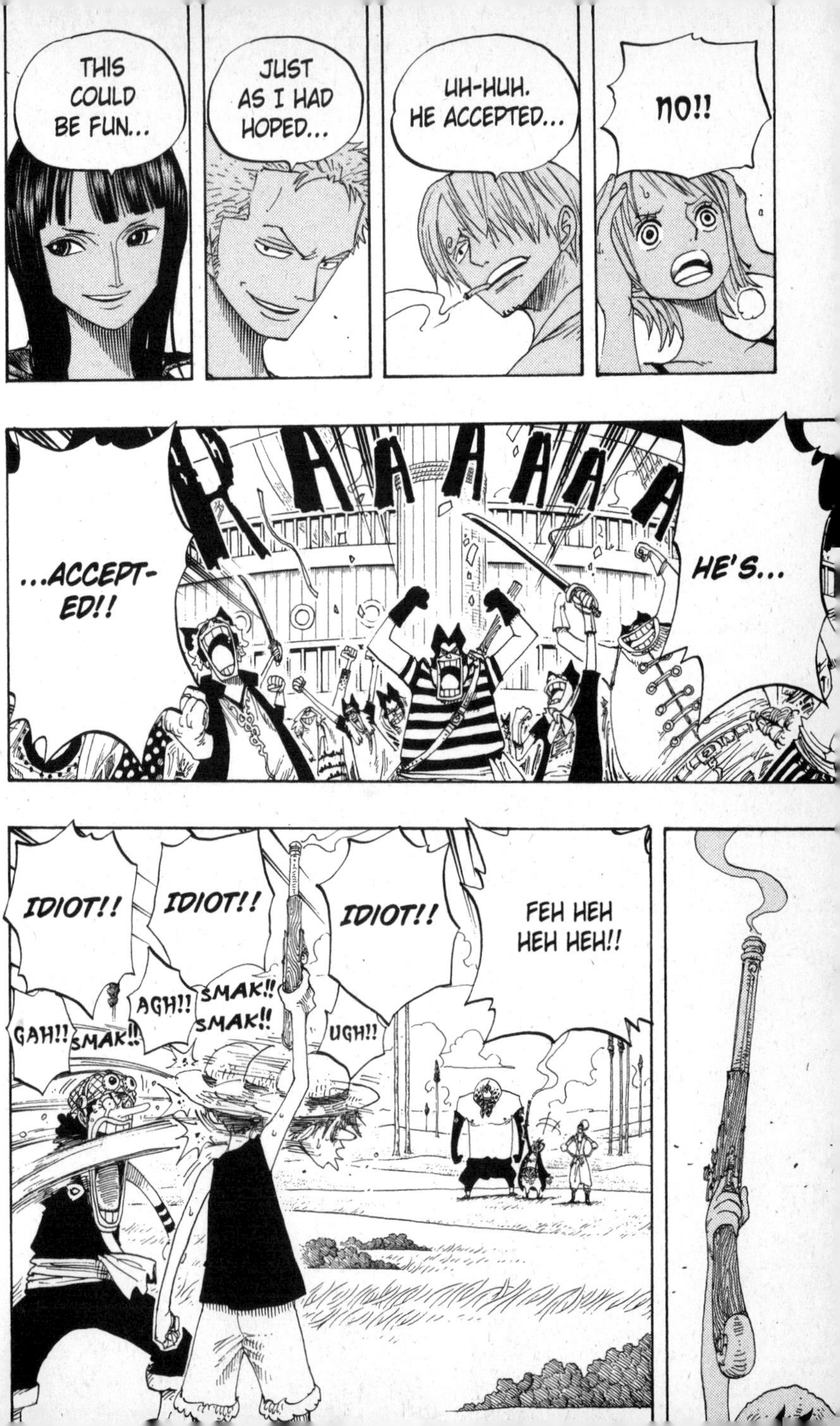
NO!!
UH-HUH. HE ACCEPTED...
JUST AS I HAD HOPED...
THIS COULD BE FUN...
HE'S...
...ACCEPT-ED!!
FEH HEH HEH HEH!!
IDIOT!!
UGH!!
IDIOT!!
SMAK!! SMAK!!
AGH!!
IDIOT!!
SMAK!!
GAH!!

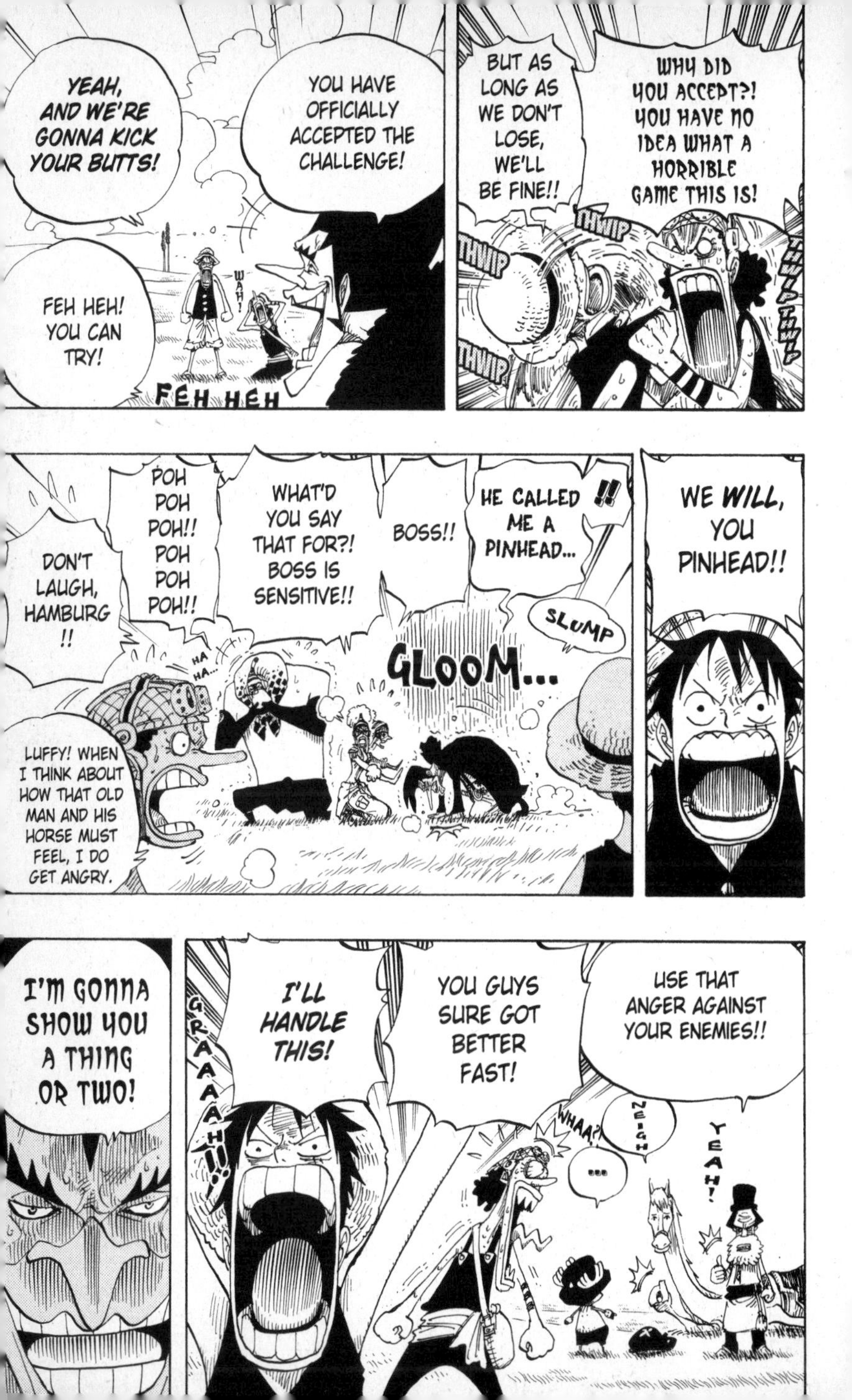
WHY DID YOU ACCEPT?! YOU HAVE NO IDEA WHAT A HORRIBLE GAME THIS IS!
BUT AS LONG AS WE DON'T LOSE, WE'LL BE FINE!!
THWIP THWIP THWIP THWIP THWIP
YOU HAVE OFFICIALLY ACCEPTED THE CHALLENGE!
YEAH, AND WE'RE GONNA KICK YOUR BUTTS!
WAH!
FEH HEH! YOU CAN TRY!
FEH HEH
WE WILL, YOU PINHEAD!!
HE CALLED ME A PINHEAD...!!
BOSS!!
WHAT'D YOU SAY THAT FOR?! BOSS IS SENSITIVE!!
POH POH POH!! POH POH POH!!
DON'T LAUGH, HAMBURG!!
SLUMP
GLOOM...
HA HA...
LUFFY! WHEN I THINK ABOUT HOW THAT OLD MAN AND HIS HORSE MUST FEEL, I DO GET ANGRY.
USE THAT ANGER AGAINST YOUR ENEMIES!!
YOU GUYS SURE GOT BETTER FAST!
YEAH!
NEIGH
WHAA?
...
I'LL HANDLE THIS!
GRAAAAAH!!
I'M GONNA SHOW YOU A THING OR TWO!

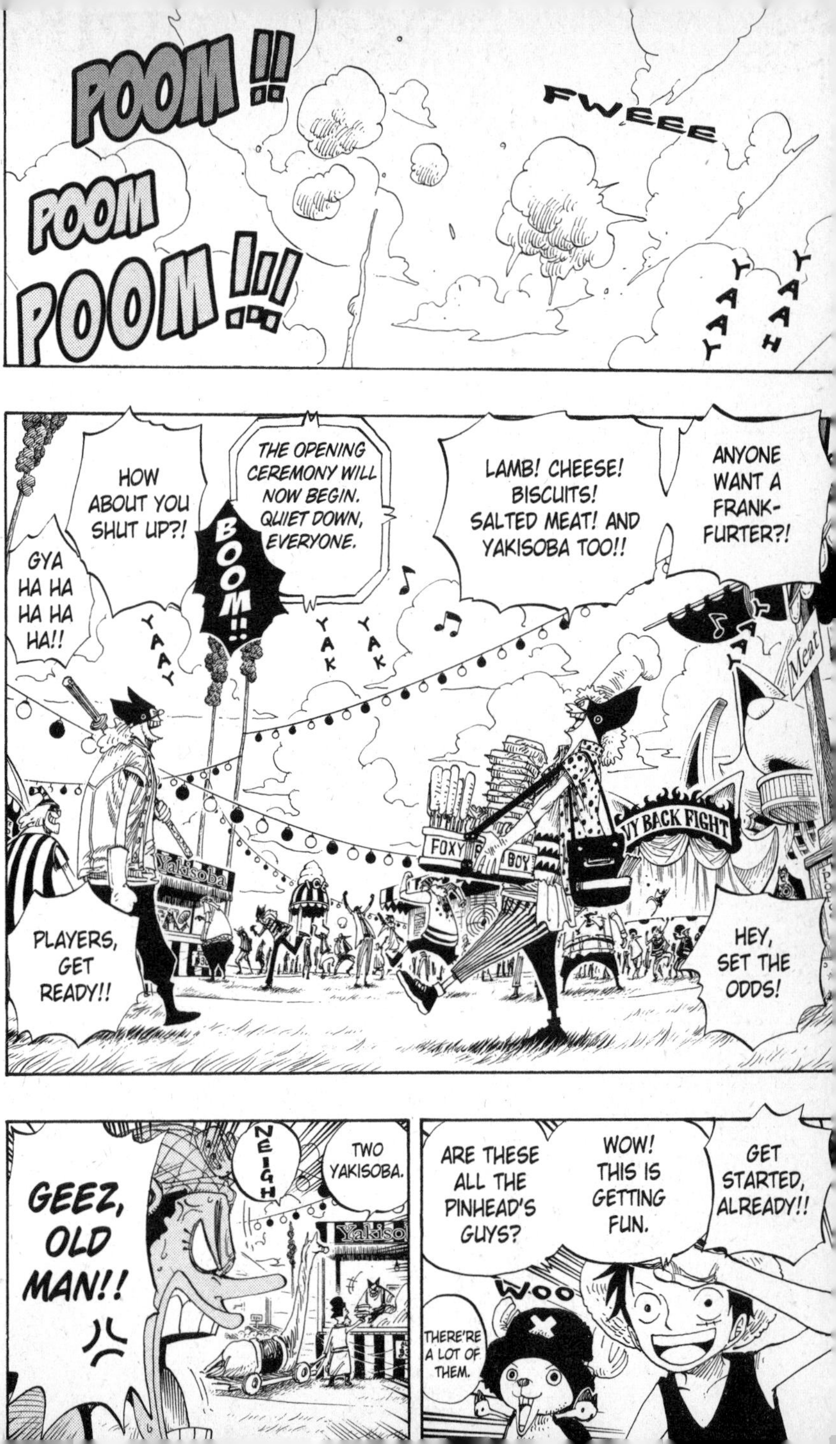
YAAAH
YAAAY
FWEEE
POOM!!
POOM
POOM!!!
ANYONE WANT A FRANK-FURTER?!
LAMB! CHEESE! BISCUITS! SALTED MEAT! AND YAKISOBA TOO!!
THE OPENING CEREMONY WILL NOW BEGIN. QUIET DOWN, EVERYONE.
BOOM!!
HOW ABOUT YOU SHUT UP?!
GYA HA HA HA HA HA!!
YAAY
YAK YAK
YAAY
Meat
BACK FIGHT
FOXY BOY
Yakisoba
HEY, SET THE ODDS!
PLAYERS, GET READY!!
GET STARTED, ALREADY!!
WOW! THIS IS GETTING FUN.
ARE THESE ALL THE PINHEAD'S GUYS?
WOO
THERE'RE A LOT OF THEM.
TWO YAKISOBA.
NEIGH
GEEZ, OLD MAN!!

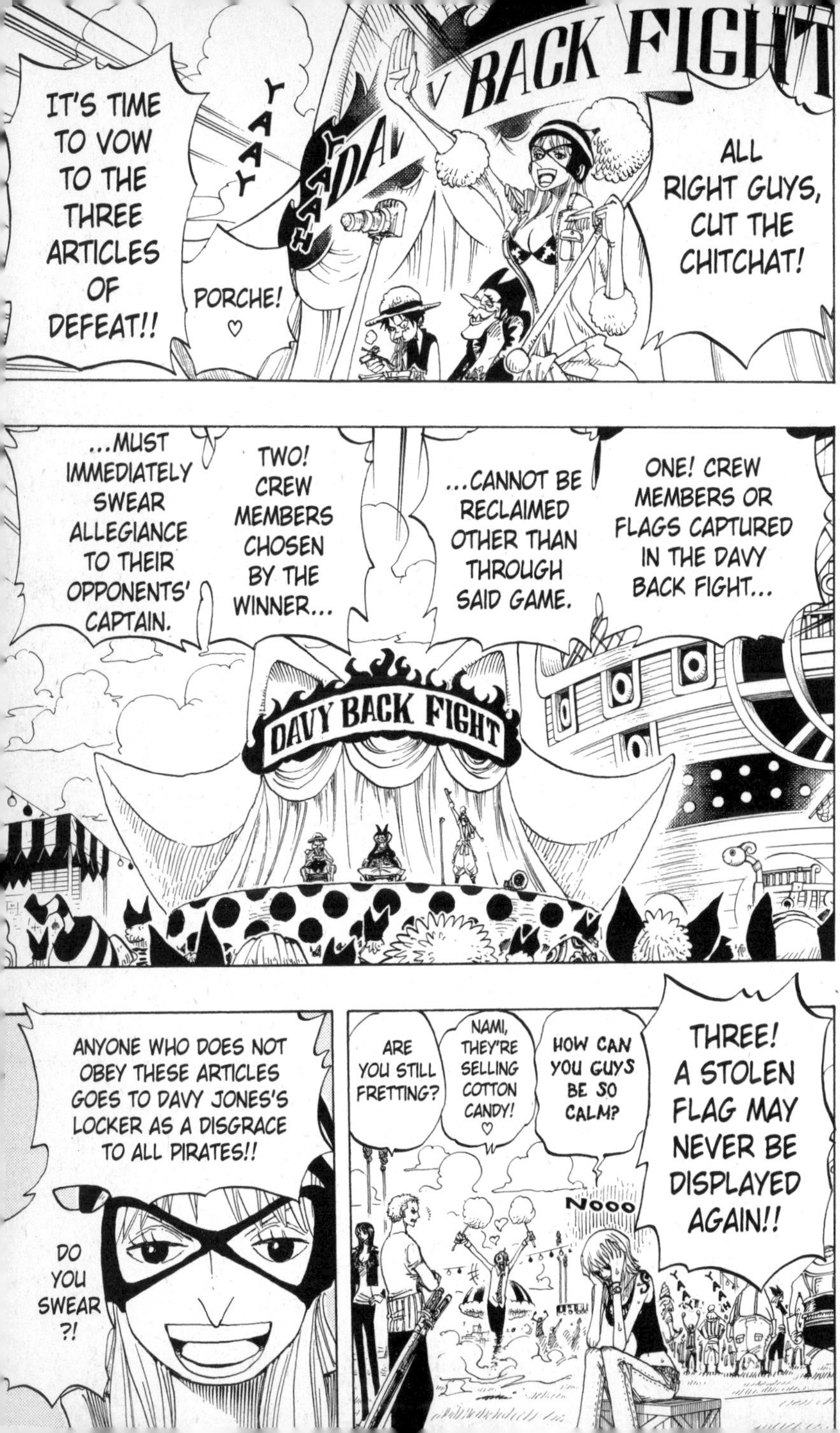
ALL RIGHT GUYS, CUT THE CHITCHAT!
DAV BACK FIGHT
YAAAAH
YAAAY
PORCHE! ♡
IT'S TIME TO VOW TO THE THREE ARTICLES OF DEFEAT!!
ONE! CREW MEMBERS OR FLAGS CAPTURED IN THE DAVY BACK FIGHT...
...CANNOT BE RECLAIMED OTHER THAN THROUGH SAID GAME.
TWO! CREW MEMBERS CHOSEN BY THE WINNER...
...MUST IMMEDIATELY SWEAR ALLEGIANCE TO THEIR OPPONENTS' CAPTAIN.
DAVY BACK FIGHT
THREE! A STOLEN FLAG MAY NEVER BE DISPLAYED AGAIN!!
HOW CAN YOU GUYS BE SO CALM?
NOOO
NAMI, THEY'RE SELLING COTTON CANDY! ♡
ARE YOU STILL FRETTING?
ANYONE WHO DOES NOT OBEY THESE ARTICLES GOES TO DAVY JONES'S LOCKER AS A DISGRACE TO ALL PIRATES!!
DO YOU SWEAR?!

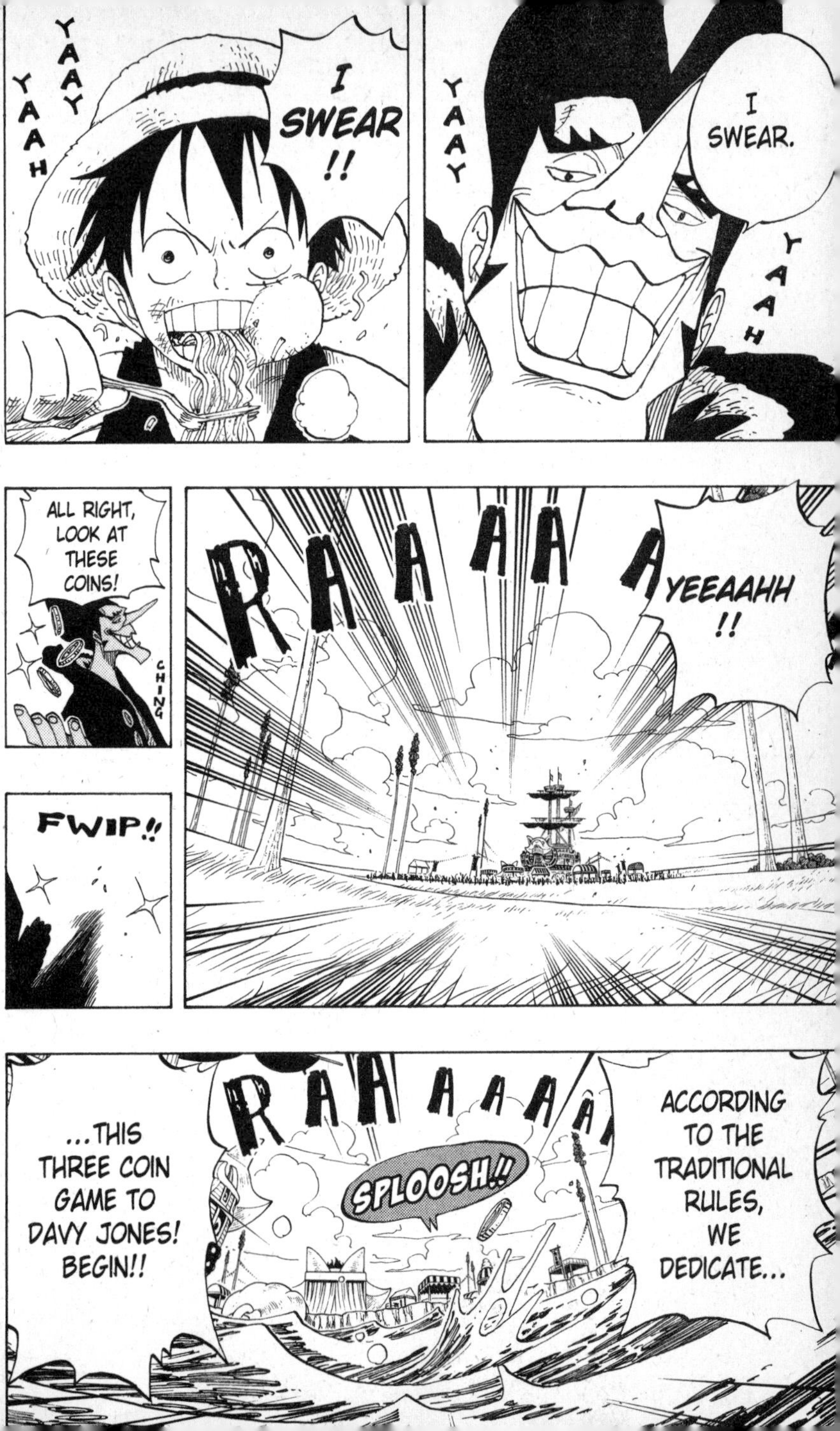
I SWEAR.
YAAH
YAAY
I SWEAR!!
YAAY
YAAH
RAAAAA
YEEAAHH!!
ALL RIGHT, LOOK AT THESE COINS!
CHING
FWIP!!
RAAAAAA
ACCORDING TO THE TRADITIONAL RULES, WE DEDICATE...
SPLOOSH!!
...THIS THREE COIN GAME TO DAVY JONES! BEGIN!!

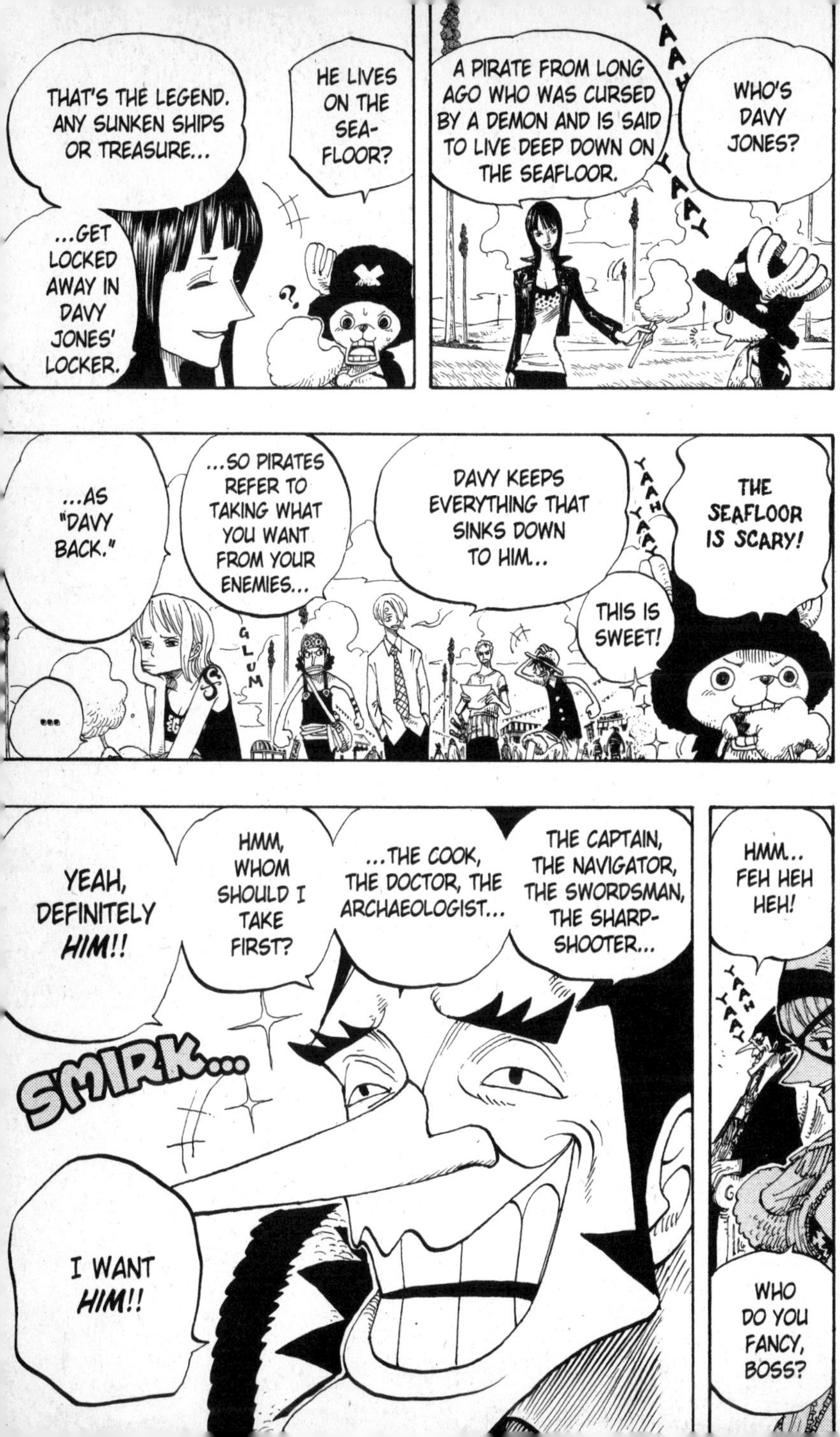
WHO'S DAVY JONES?
YAAH YAAY
A PIRATE FROM LONG AGO WHO WAS CURSED BY A DEMON AND IS SAID TO LIVE DEEP DOWN ON THE SEAFLOOR.
HE LIVES ON THE SEA-FLOOR?
THAT'S THE LEGEND. ANY SUNKEN SHIPS OR TREASURE...
...GET LOCKED AWAY IN DAVY JONES' LOCKER.
THE SEAFLOOR IS SCARY!
YAAH YAAY
DAVY KEEPS EVERYTHING THAT SINKS DOWN TO HIM...
THIS IS SWEET!
...SO PIRATES REFER TO TAKING WHAT YOU WANT FROM YOUR ENEMIES...
...AS "DAVY BACK."
GLUM
...
HMM... FEH HEH HEH!
YAAH YAAY
WHO DO YOU FANCY, BOSS?
THE CAPTAIN, THE NAVIGATOR, THE SWORDSMAN, THE SHARP-SHOOTER...
...THE COOK, THE DOCTOR, THE ARCHAEOLOGIST...
HMM, WHOM SHOULD I TAKE FIRST?
YEAH, DEFINITELY *HIM!!*
SMIRK...
I WANT *HIM!!*

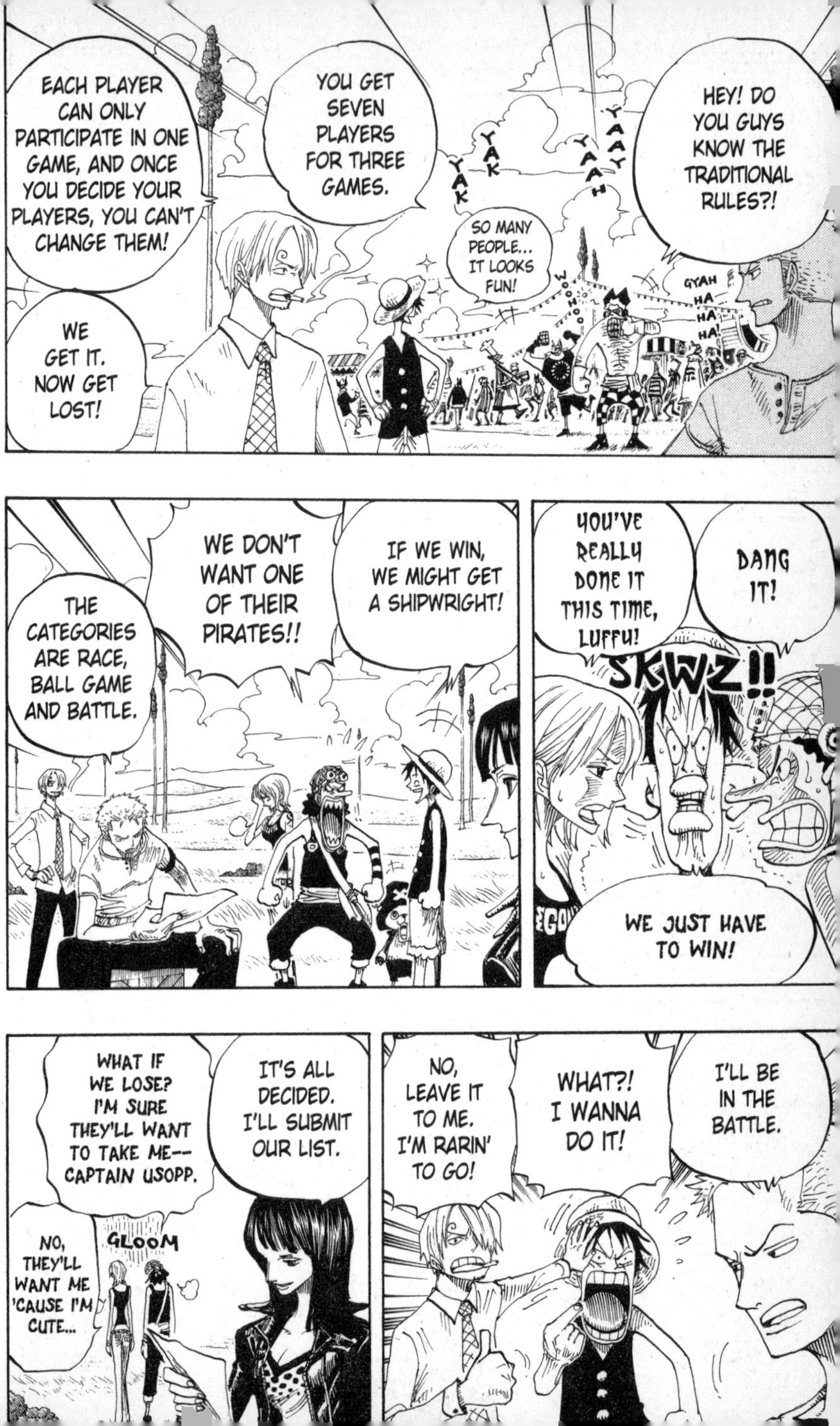
HEY! DO YOU GUYS KNOW THE TRADITIONAL RULES?!
GYAH HA HA HA!
YAAAY
YAAAH
SO MANY PEOPLE... IT LOOKS FUN!
WOOHOO
YAK YAK
YOU GET SEVEN PLAYERS FOR THREE GAMES.
EACH PLAYER CAN ONLY PARTICIPATE IN ONE GAME, AND ONCE YOU DECIDE YOUR PLAYERS, YOU CAN'T CHANGE THEM!
WE GET IT. NOW GET LOST!
DANG IT!
YOU'VE REALLY DONE IT THIS TIME, LUFFY!
SKWZ!!
WE JUST HAVE TO WIN!
IF WE WIN, WE MIGHT GET A SHIPWRIGHT!
WE DON'T WANT ONE OF THEIR PIRATES!!
THE CATEGORIES ARE RACE, BALL GAME AND BATTLE.
I'LL BE IN THE BATTLE.
WHAT?! I WANNA DO IT!
NO, LEAVE IT TO ME. I'M RARIN' TO GO!
IT'S ALL DECIDED. I'LL SUBMIT OUR LIST.
WHAT IF WE LOSE? I'M SURE THEY'LL WANT TO TAKE ME-- CAPTAIN USOPP.
GLOOM
NO, THEY'LL WANT ME 'CAUSE I'M CUTE...

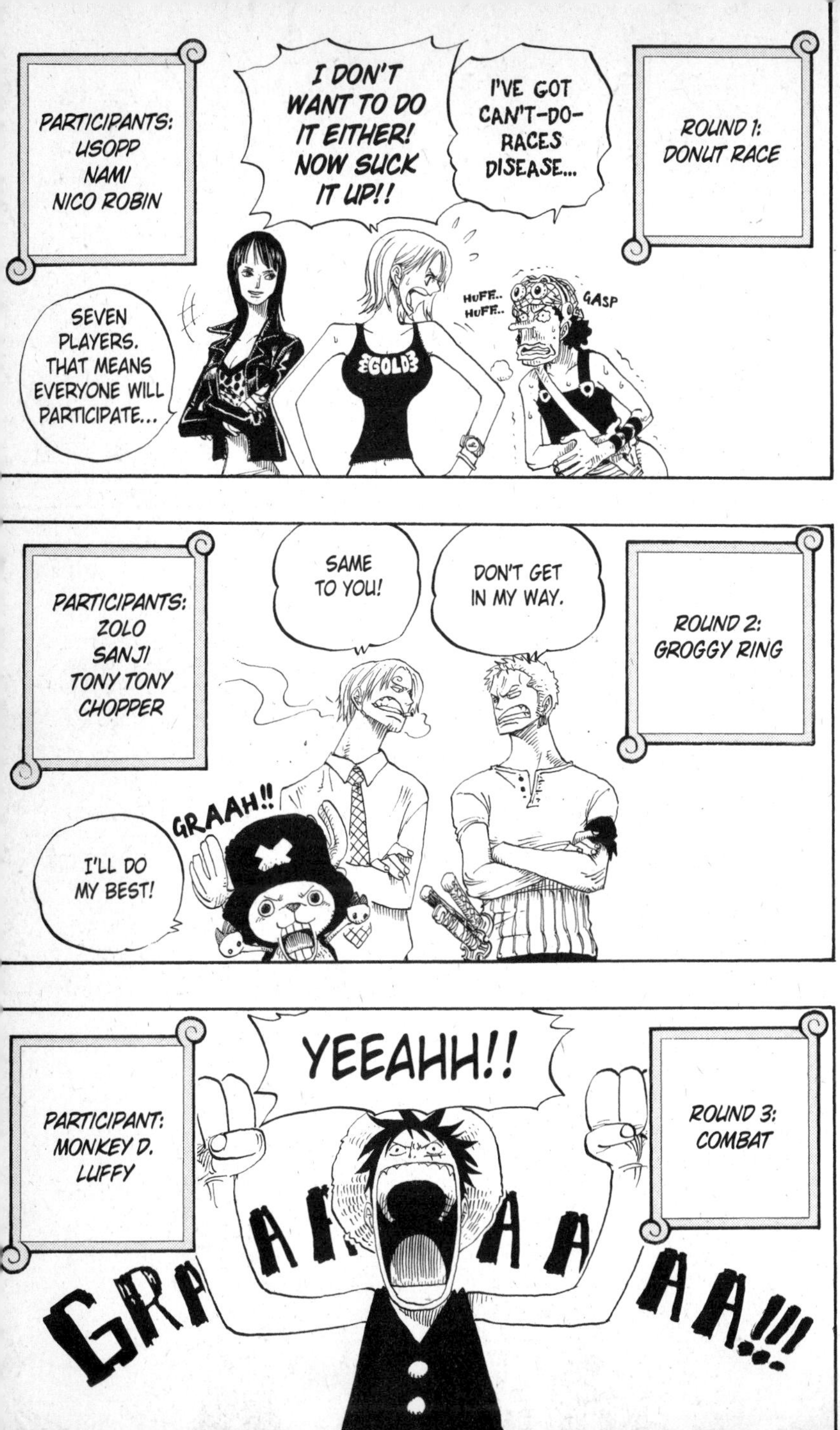
ROUND 1: DONUT RACE
I'VE GOT CAN'T-DO-RACES DISEASE...
I DON'T WANT TO DO IT EITHER! NOW SUCK IT UP!!
GASP
HUFF.. HUFF..
PARTICIPANTS: USOPP NAMI NICO ROBIN
SEVEN PLAYERS. THAT MEANS EVERYONE WILL PARTICIPATE...
ROUND 2: GROGGY RING
DON'T GET IN MY WAY.
SAME TO YOU!
PARTICIPANTS: ZOLO SANJI TONY TONY CHOPPER
GRAAH!!
I'LL DO MY BEST!
ROUND 3: COMBAT
YEEAHH!!
PARTICIPANT: MONKEY D. LUFFY
GRAAAAAA!!!

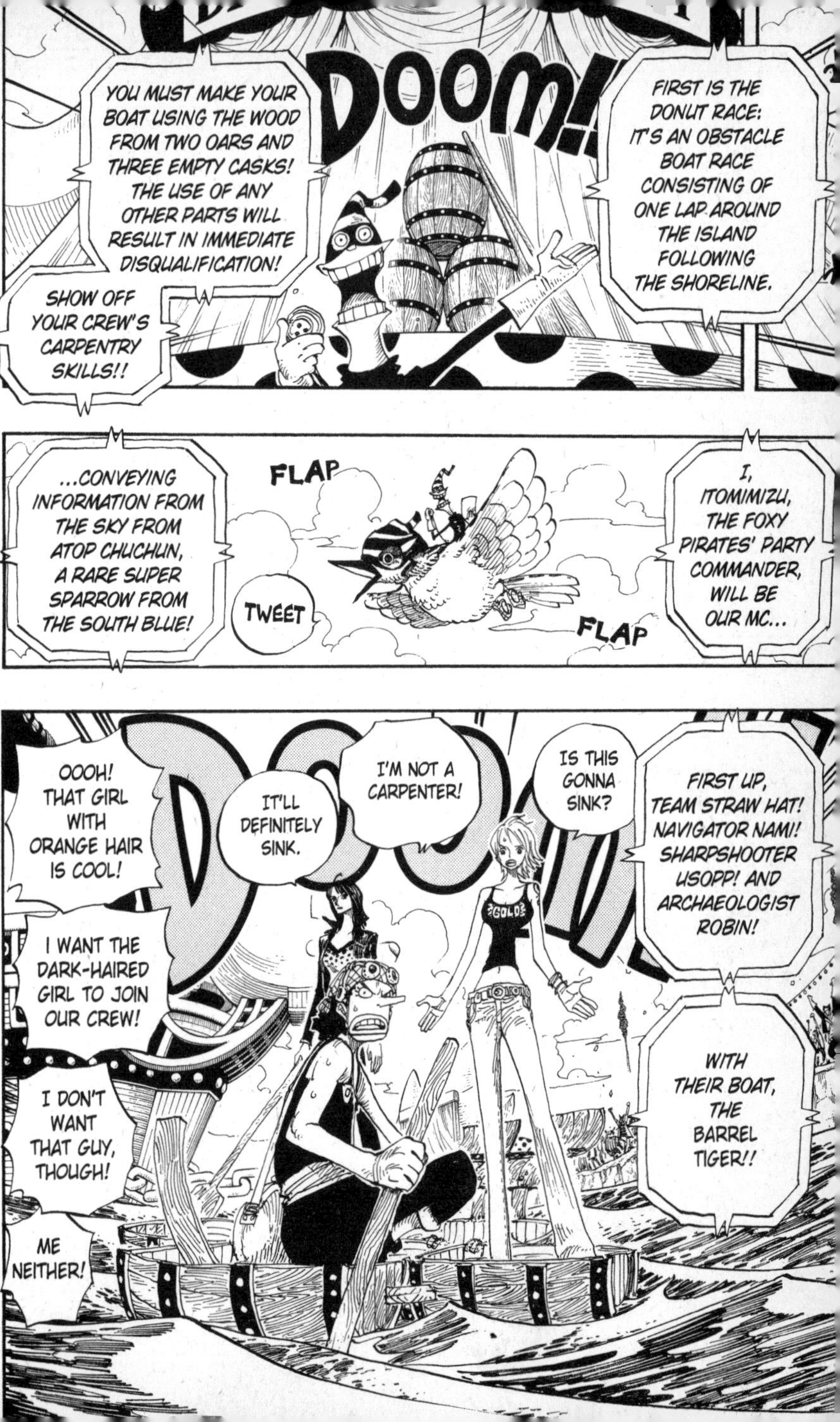
FIRST IS THE DONUT RACE: IT'S AN OBSTACLE BOAT RACE CONSISTING OF ONE LAP AROUND THE ISLAND FOLLOWING THE SHORELINE.
DOOM!!
YOU MUST MAKE YOUR BOAT USING THE WOOD FROM TWO OARS AND THREE EMPTY CASKS! THE USE OF ANY OTHER PARTS WILL RESULT IN IMMEDIATE DISQUALIFICATION!
SHOW OFF YOUR CREW'S CARPENTRY SKILLS!!
I, ITOMIMIZU, THE FOXY PIRATES' PARTY COMMANDER, WILL BE OUR MC...
FLAP
FLAP
TWEET
...CONVEYING INFORMATION FROM THE SKY FROM ATOP CHUCHUN, A RARE SUPER SPARROW FROM THE SOUTH BLUE!
FIRST UP, TEAM STRAW HAT! NAVIGATOR NAMI! SHARPSHOOTER USOPP! AND ARCHAEOLOGIST ROBIN!
WITH THEIR BOAT, THE BARREL TIGER!!
IS THIS GONNA SINK?
I'M NOT A CARPENTER!
IT'LL DEFINITELY SINK.
OOOH! THAT GIRL WITH ORANGE HAIR IS COOL!
I WANT THE DARK-HAIRED GIRL TO JOIN OUR CREW!
I DON'T WANT THAT GUY, THOUGH!
ME NEITHER!

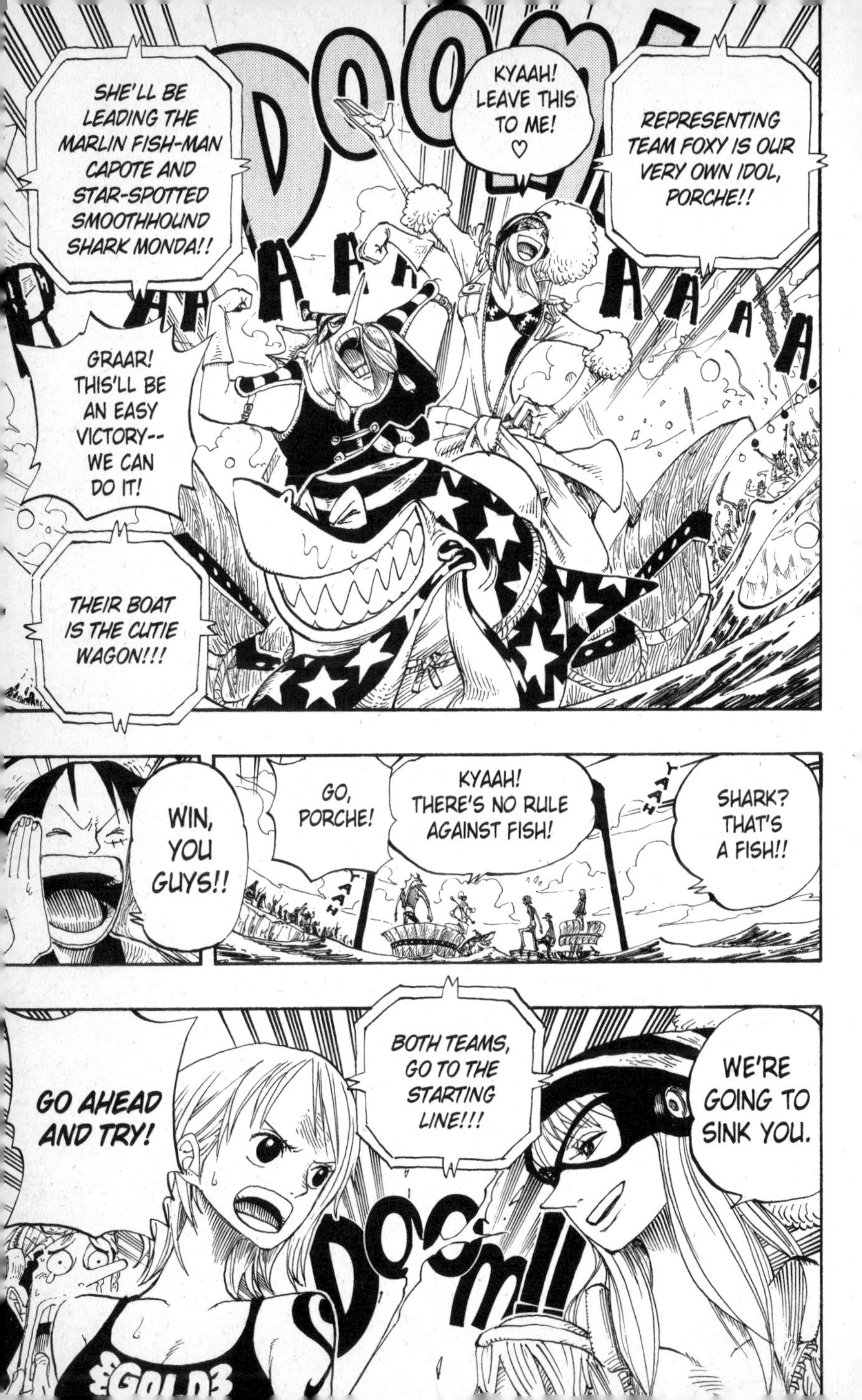
REPRESENTING TEAM FOXY IS OUR VERY OWN IDOL, PORCHE!!
KYAAH! LEAVE THIS TO ME! ♡
SHE'LL BE LEADING THE MARLIN FISH-MAN CAPOTE AND STAR-SPOTTED SMOOTHHOUND SHARK MONDA!!
GRAAR! THIS'LL BE AN EASY VICTORY-- WE CAN DO IT!
THEIR BOAT IS THE CUTIE WAGON!!!
SHARK? THAT'S A FISH!!
KYAAH! THERE'S NO RULE AGAINST FISH!
GO, PORCHE!
WIN, YOU GUYS!!
WE'RE GOING TO SINK YOU.
BOTH TEAMS, GO TO THE STARTING LINE!!!
GO AHEAD AND TRY!
DOOM!!

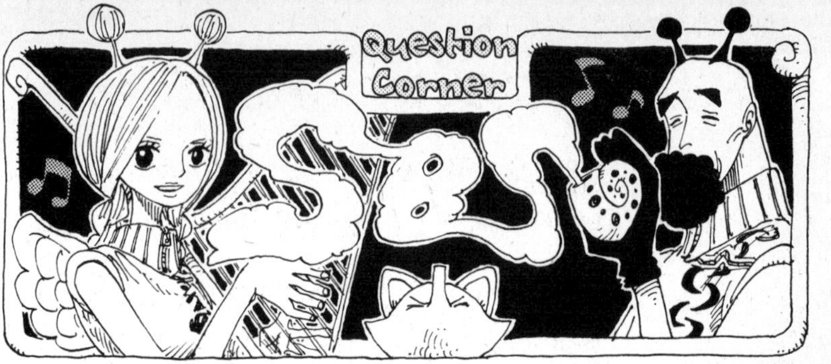
Question Corner
SBS

Reader: Hiya, Oda(T)! I always enjoy reading *One Piece* ♡ ! (And the Question Corner.) So I'd like to be the one to utter that popular phrase! ♡ But, wait! Oda(T) isn'there. Oh, well. Let's begin the Question Corner! ♡ Yes!! ♡ I said it! Sorry, Oda(T). ♡

--Chairman, Friends of *One Piece*

Oda: Whoa... So many hearts! It's cute, so I'll forgive you! ♡ I got up early and was all lined up and ready to go, but I'll forgive you! ♡

Reader: Hello, Oda Sensei! *One Piece* always cheers me up, makes me laugh and gives me hope. Thank you.
Take this!! Oda!! (…Sensei) Usopp Voodoo!! (DOOM)
"Ink spilled on the finished manuscript!" SPLASH!
"All the assistants are unable to come in today!" SILENCE
"After the manuscript was turned in, three blank pages fell out!" FWAP
What do you think?

--Hokuto Hyakuretsuken

Oda: That'll never work on me. THUD...!!

Reader: Hello, Oda Sensei, you with the bright smile! I always enjoy reading *One Piece*. I tried my hardest…even skipping meals…to count all the appearances of Panda Man (who could be your clone) in the Skypiea storyline. I gave it everything I had. And the result?! Panda Man appeared…DADADADADUM...17 times! Am I right?

--Hikari

Reader: Oda Sensei!! I looked for Panda Man throughout volumes 5 to 31 and found him 92 times!! Try for 100!!

--Panda Man 2

Oda: Good work, everyone. But I can't tell you the right answer. (←Actually I don't remember it.)

Chapter 307:
READY, SET, DONUT!

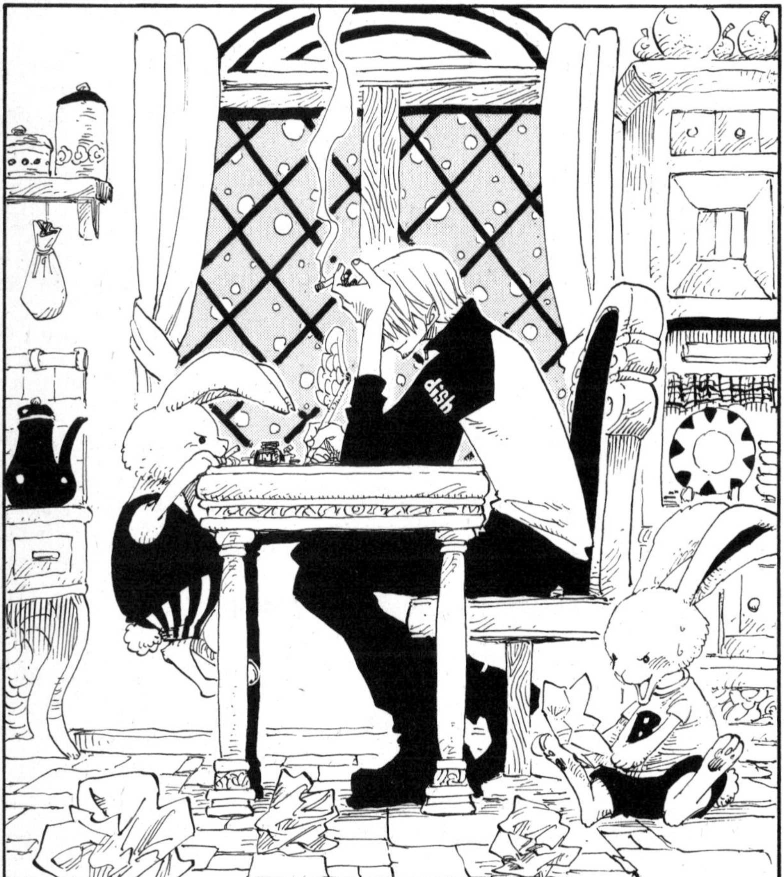
dish

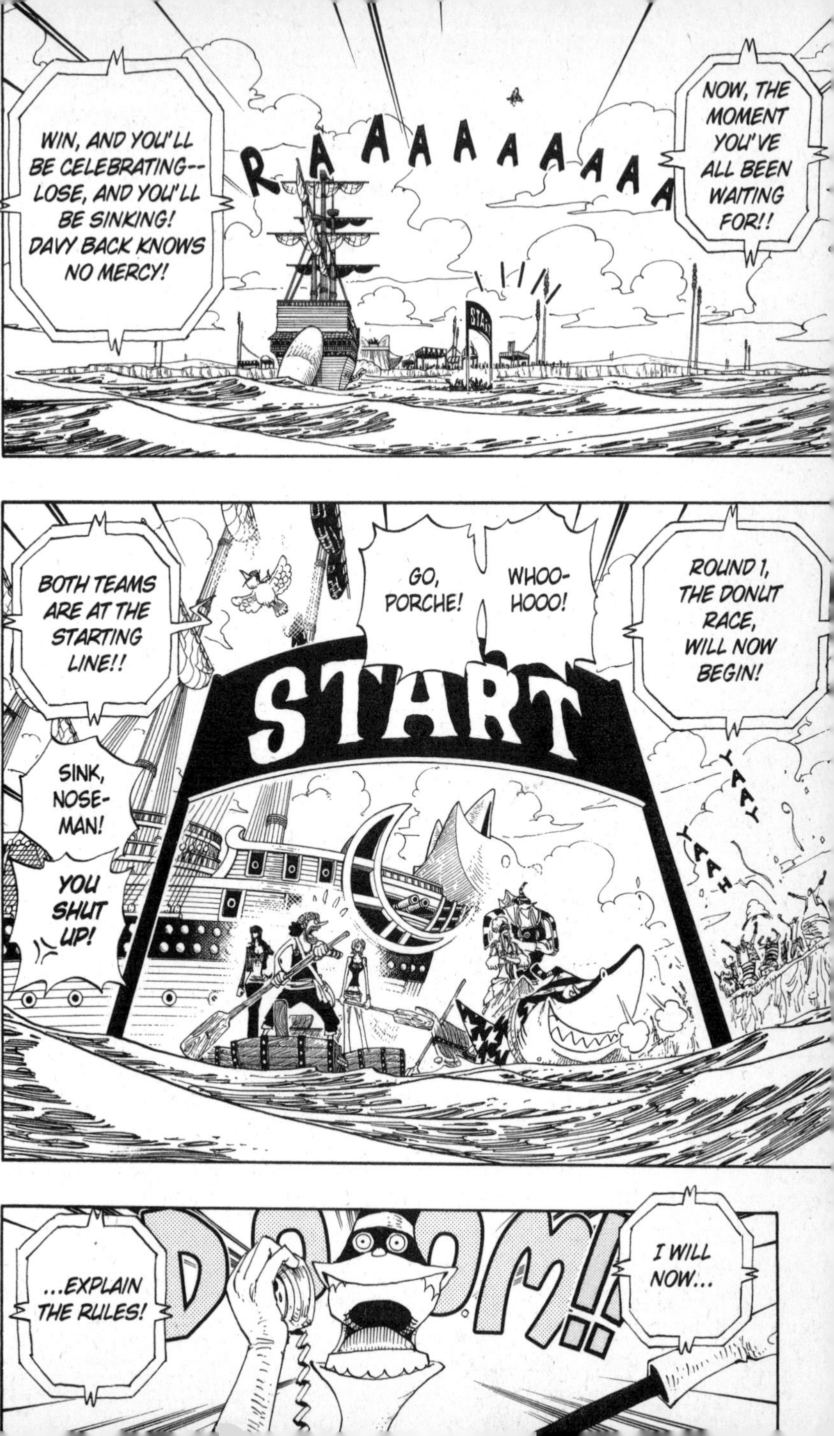
NOW, THE MOMENT YOU'VE ALL BEEN WAITING FOR!!
RAAAAAAAAA
WIN, AND YOU'LL BE CELEBRATING-- LOSE, AND YOU'LL BE SINKING! DAVY BACK KNOWS NO MERCY!
ROUND 1, THE DONUT RACE, WILL NOW BEGIN!
WHOO-HOOO!
GO, PORCHE!
START
YAAAY
YAAAH
BOTH TEAMS ARE AT THE STARTING LINE!!
SINK, NOSE-MAN!
YOU SHUT UP!
I WILL NOW...
DOOM!!
...EXPLAIN THE RULES!

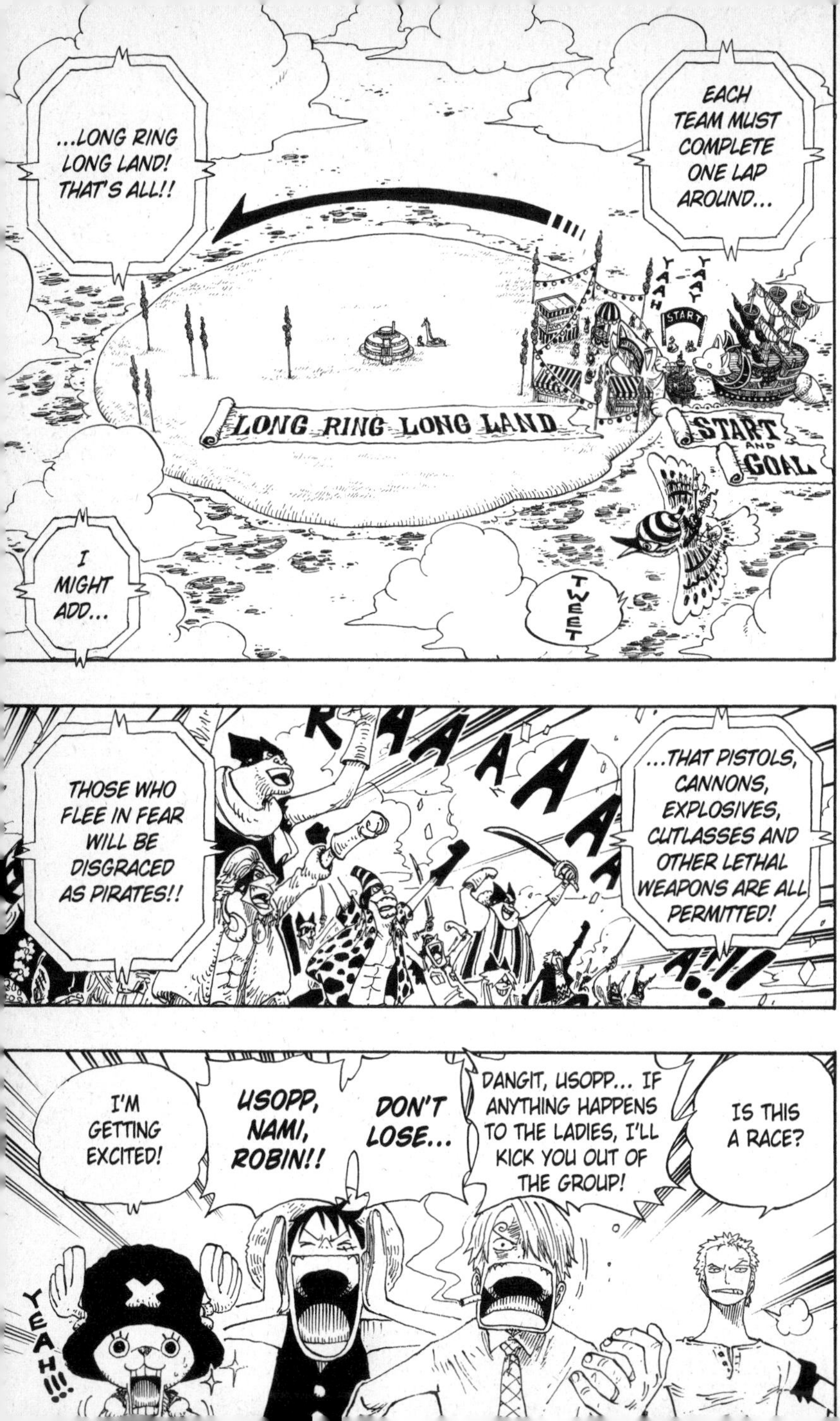
EACH TEAM MUST COMPLETE ONE LAP AROUND...
YAAAH
YAAAY
START
...LONG RING LONG LAND! THAT'S ALL!!
LONG RING LONG LAND
START AND GOAL
TWEET
I MIGHT ADD...
...THAT PISTOLS, CANNONS, EXPLOSIVES, CUTLASSES AND OTHER LETHAL WEAPONS ARE ALL PERMITTED!
RAAAAAAAAA!!!
THOSE WHO FLEE IN FEAR WILL BE DISGRACED AS PIRATES!!
IS THIS A RACE?
DANGIT, USOPP... IF ANYTHING HAPPENS TO THE LADIES, I'LL KICK YOU OUT OF THE GROUP!
DON'T LOSE...
USOPP, NAMI, ROBIN!!
I'M GETTING EXCITED!
YEAH!!!

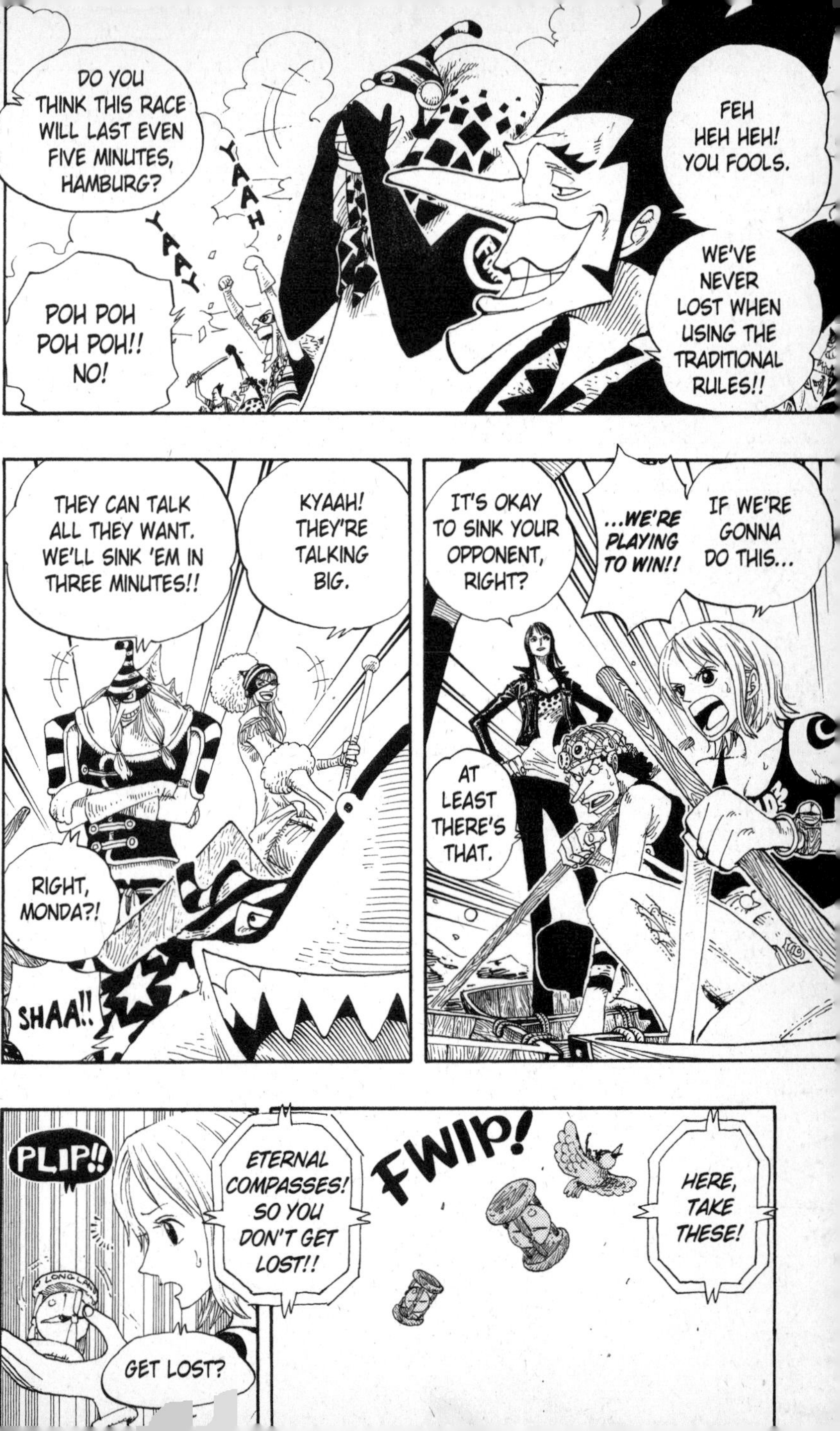
FEH HEH HEH! YOU FOOLS.
WE'VE NEVER LOST WHEN USING THE TRADITIONAL RULES!!
YAAAH
DO YOU THINK THIS RACE WILL LAST EVEN FIVE MINUTES, HAMBURG?
YAAY
POH POH POH POH!! NO!
IF WE'RE GONNA DO THIS...
...WE'RE PLAYING TO WIN!!
IT'S OKAY TO SINK YOUR OPPONENT, RIGHT?
AT LEAST THERE'S THAT.
KYAAH! THEY'RE TALKING BIG.
THEY CAN TALK ALL THEY WANT. WE'LL SINK 'EM IN THREE MINUTES!!
RIGHT, MONDA?!
SHAA!!
HERE, TAKE THESE!
FWIP!
ETERNAL COMPASSES! SO YOU DON'T GET LOST!!
PLIP!!
GET LOST?

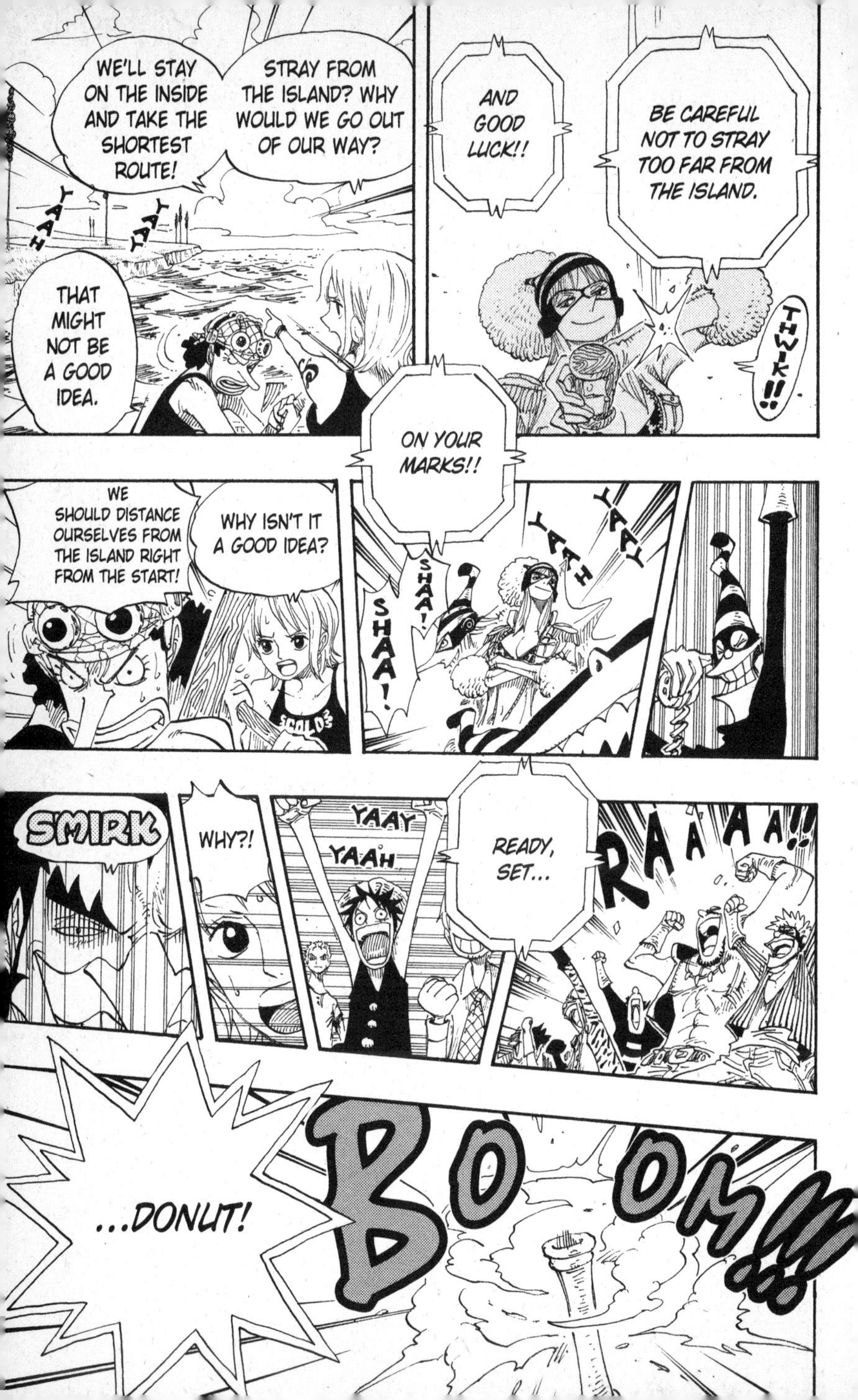
BE CAREFUL NOT TO STRAY TOO FAR FROM THE ISLAND.
AND GOOD LUCK!!
THWIK!!
STRAY FROM THE ISLAND? WHY WOULD WE GO OUT OF OUR WAY?
WE'LL STAY ON THE INSIDE AND TAKE THE SHORTEST ROUTE!
YAAY
YAAH
THAT MIGHT NOT BE A GOOD IDEA.
ON YOUR MARKS!!
YAAY
YAAH
SHAA!
SHAA!
WHY ISN'T IT A GOOD IDEA?
WE SHOULD DISTANCE OURSELVES FROM THE ISLAND RIGHT FROM THE START!
READY, SET...
RAAAAA!!
YAAY
YAAH
WHY?!
SMIRK
BOOM!!
...DONUT!

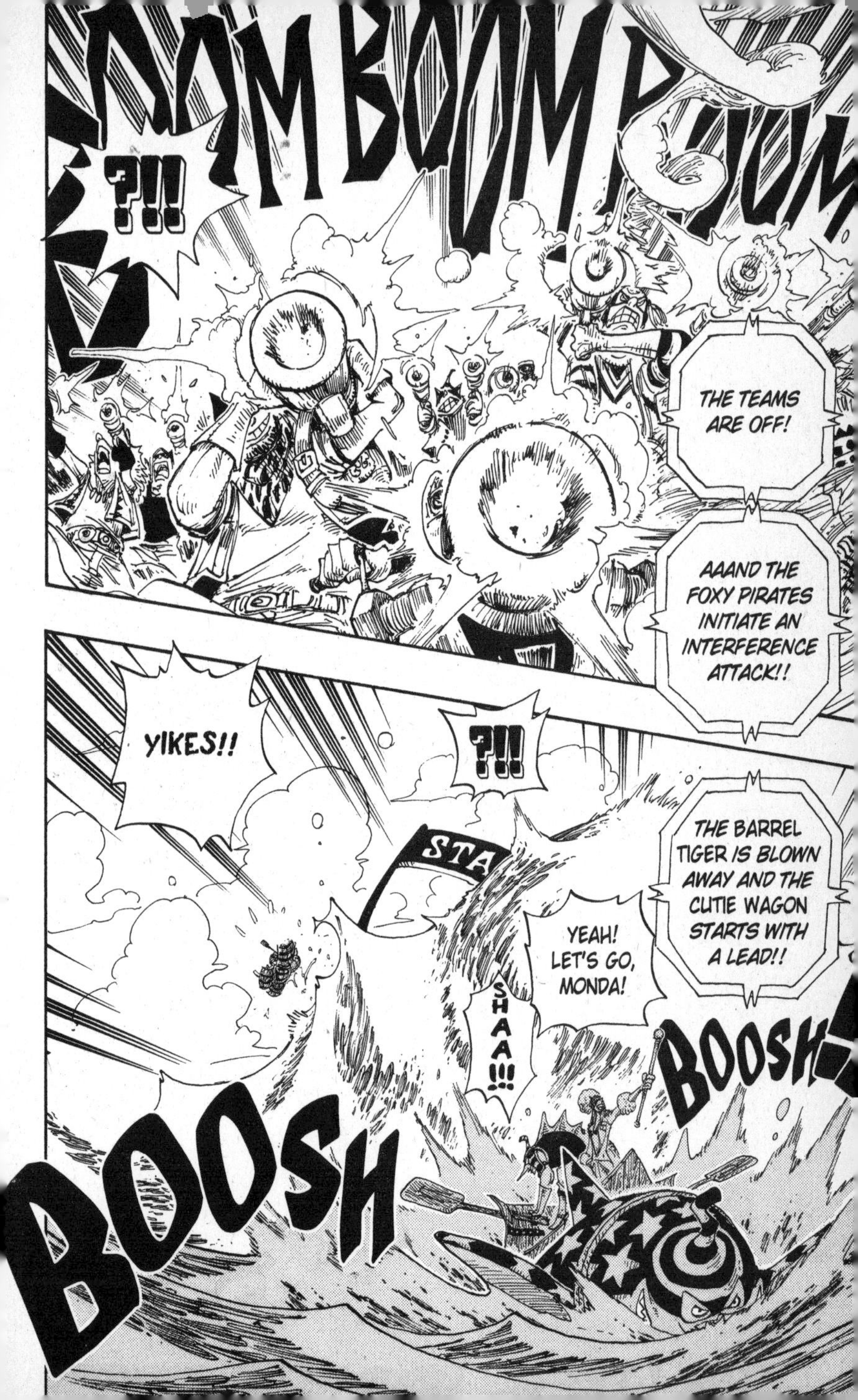
THE TEAMS ARE OFF!
AAAND THE FOXY PIRATES INITIATE AN INTERFERENCE ATTACK!!
BOOM BOOM BOOM
?!!
THE BARREL TIGER IS BLOWN AWAY AND THE CUTIE WAGON STARTS WITH A LEAD!!
BOOSH
YEAH! LET'S GO, MONDA!
SHAAA!!!
?!!
STA
YIKES!!
BOOSH

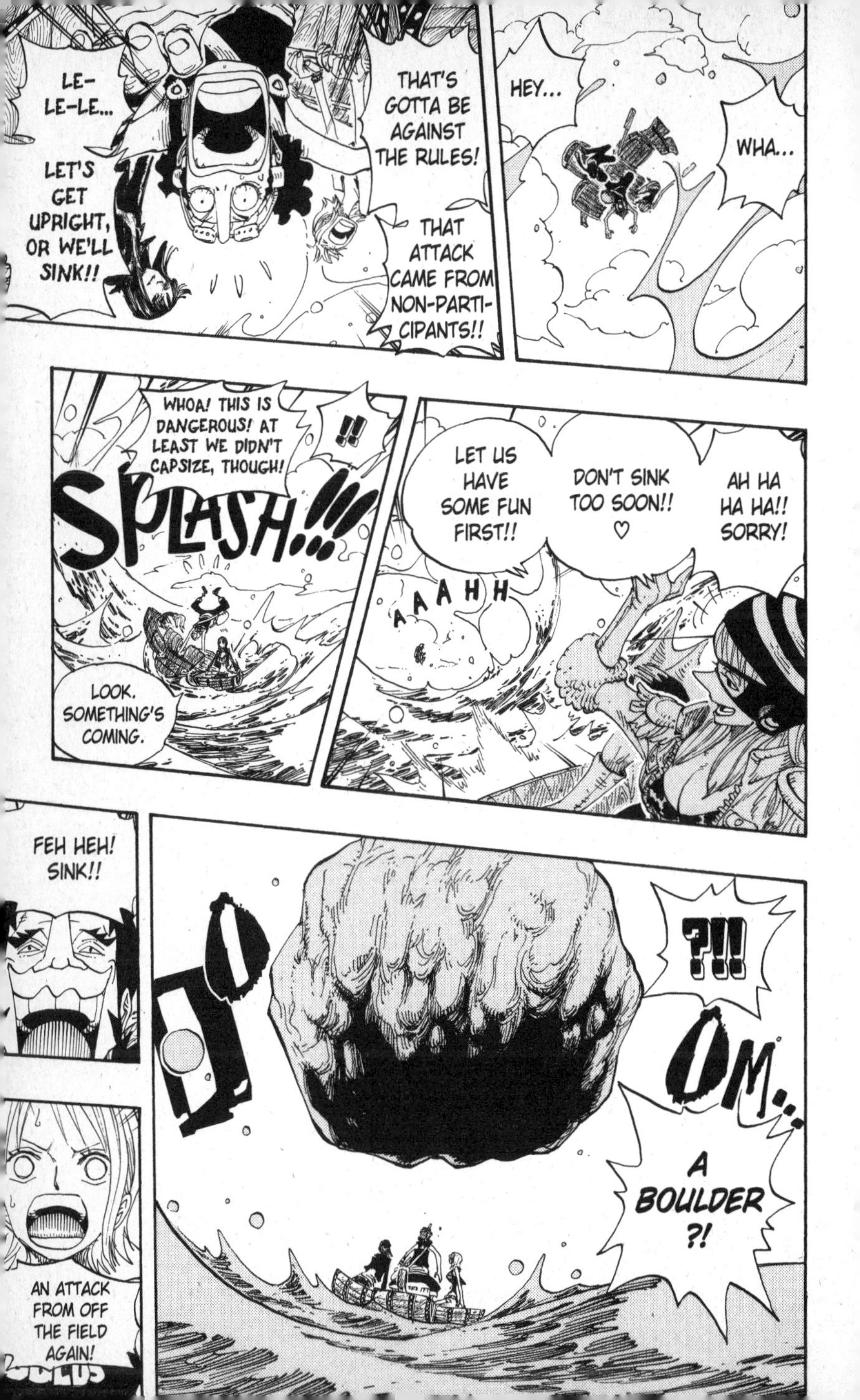
HEY...
WHA...
THAT'S GOTTA BE AGAINST THE RULES!
THAT ATTACK CAME FROM NON-PARTI-CIPANTS!!
LE-LE-LE...
LET'S GET UPRIGHT, OR WE'LL SINK!!
AH HA HA HA!! SORRY!
DON'T SINK TOO SOON!! ♡
LET US HAVE SOME FUN FIRST!!
AAAHH
!!
WHOA! THIS IS DANGEROUS! AT LEAST WE DIDN'T CAPSIZE, THOUGH!
SPLASH!!!
LOOK. SOMETHING'S COMING.
?!!
OM...
A BOULDER ?!
FEH HEH! SINK!!
AN ATTACK FROM OFF THE FIELD AGAIN!

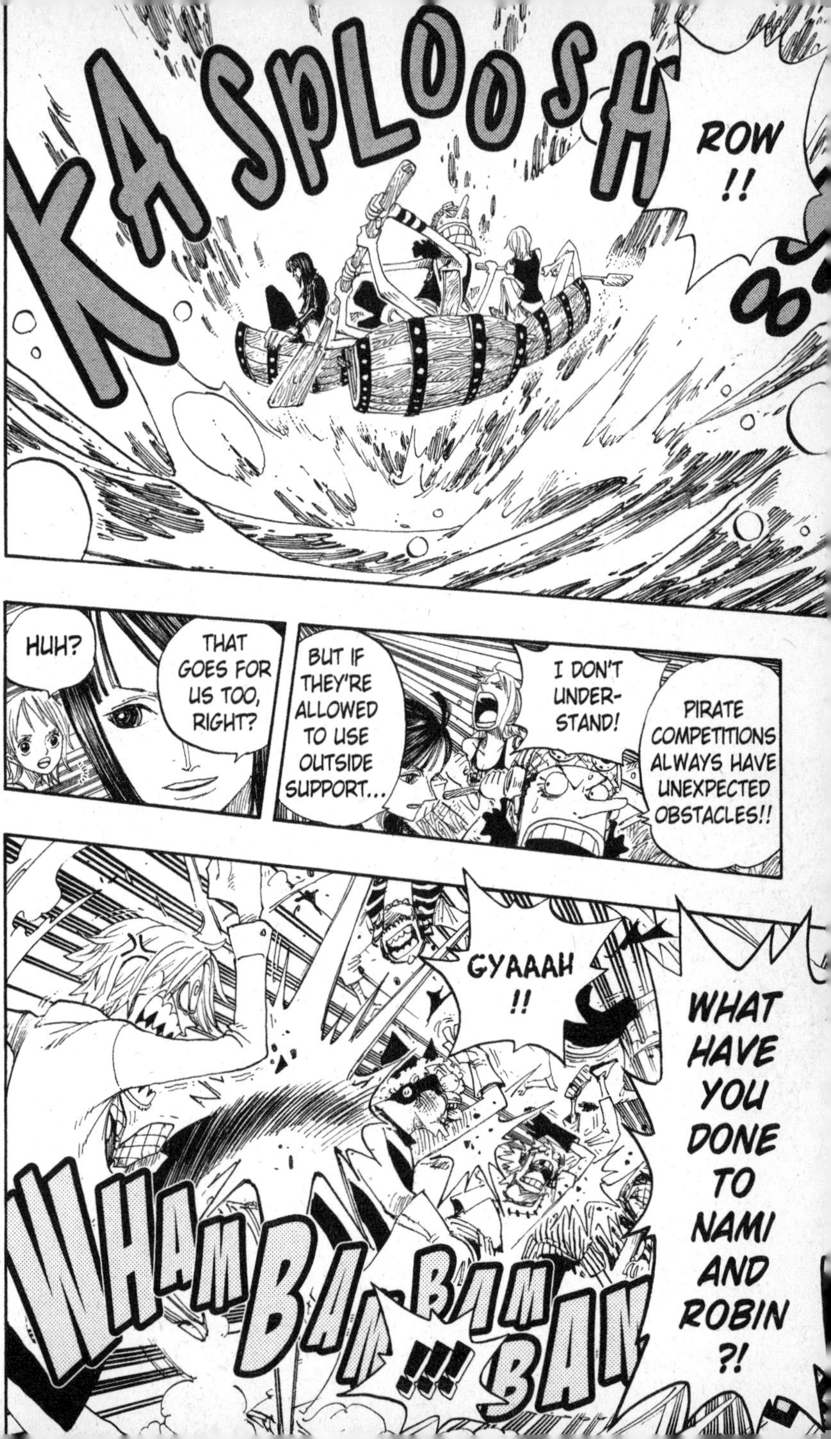
ROW!!
KASPLOOSH
PIRATE COMPETITIONS ALWAYS HAVE UNEXPECTED OBSTACLES!!
I DON'T UNDER-STAND!
BUT IF THEY'RE ALLOWED TO USE OUTSIDE SUPPORT...
THAT GOES FOR US TOO, RIGHT?
HUH?
WHAT HAVE YOU DONE TO NAMI AND ROBIN ?!
GYAAAH!!
WHAM BAM BAM!!! BAM

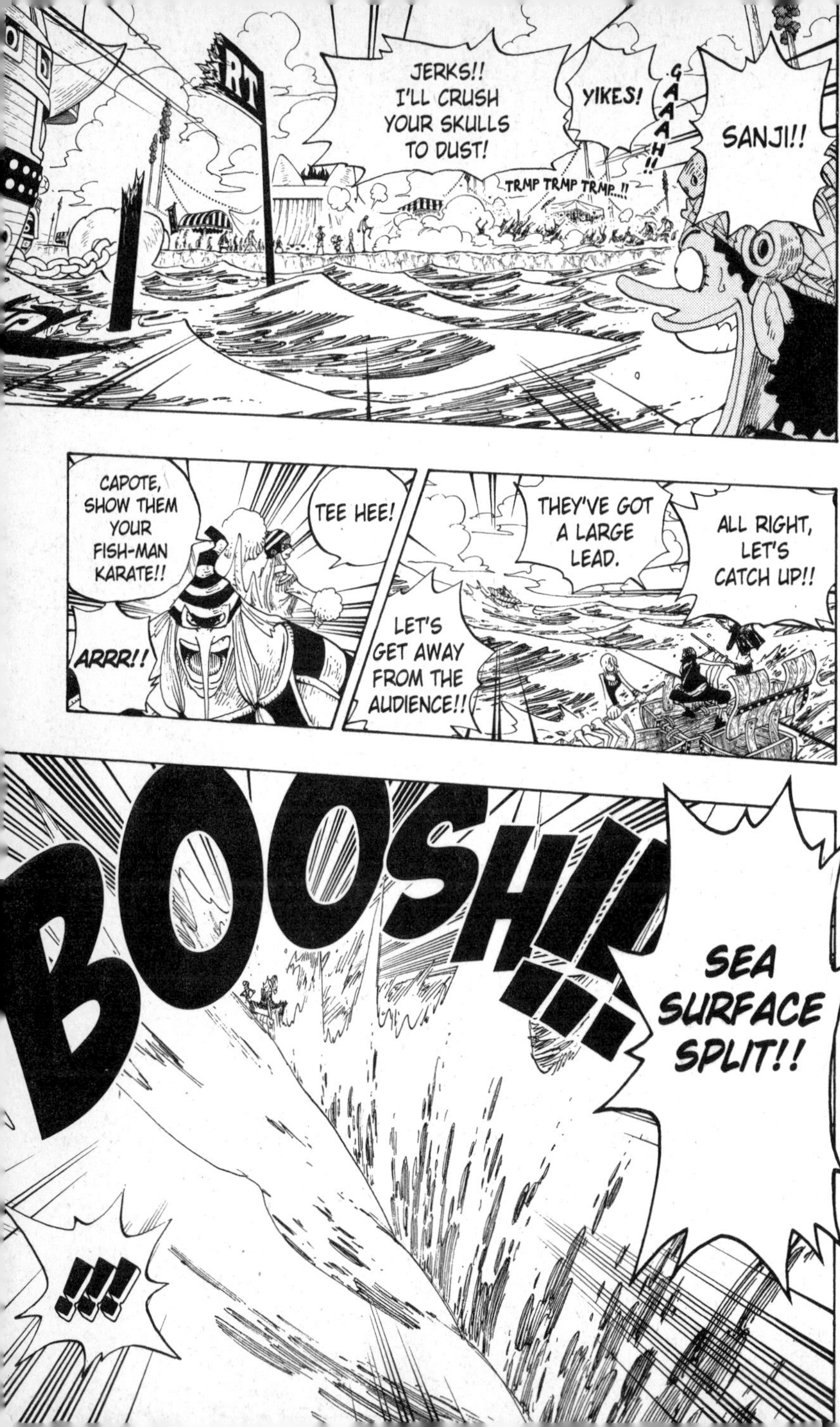
SANJI!!
GAAAH!!
YIKES!
JERKS!! I'LL CRUSH YOUR SKULLS TO DUST!
TRMP TRMP TRMP..!!
ALL RIGHT, LET'S CATCH UP!!
THEY'VE GOT A LARGE LEAD.
LET'S GET AWAY FROM THE AUDIENCE!!
TEE HEE!
CAPOTE, SHOW THEM YOUR FISH-MAN KARATE!!
ARRR!!
SEA SURFACE SPLIT!!
BOOSH!!
!!!

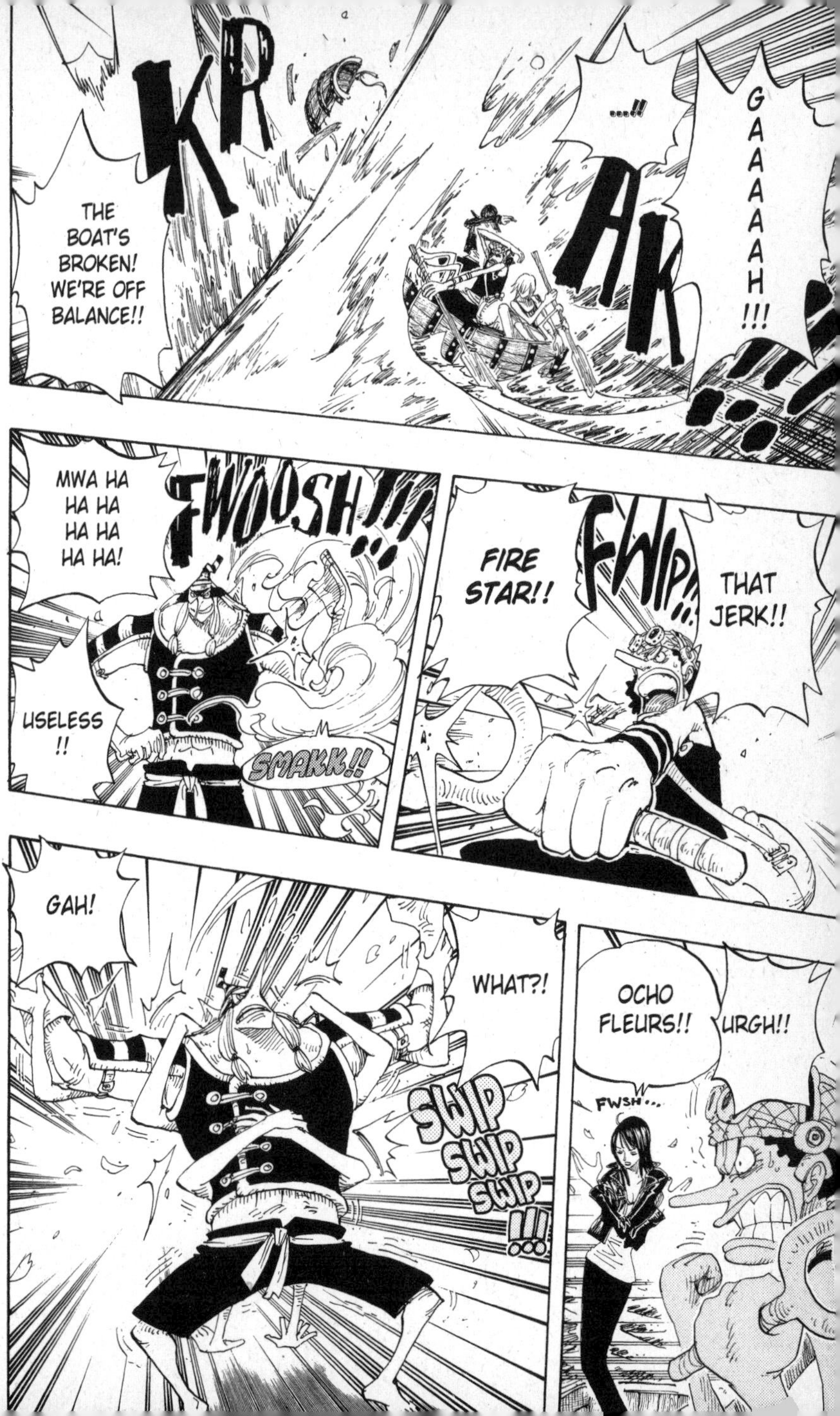
GAAAAAH!!!
...!!
AK
KR
THE BOAT'S BROKEN! WE'RE OFF BALANCE!!
THAT JERK!!
FWIP!!
FIRE STAR!!
FWOOSH!!!
MWA HA HA HA HA HA HA HA!
USELESS!!
SMAKK!!
URGH!!
OCHO FLEURS!!
FWSH...
WHAT?!
GAH!
SWIP SWIP SWIP!!!

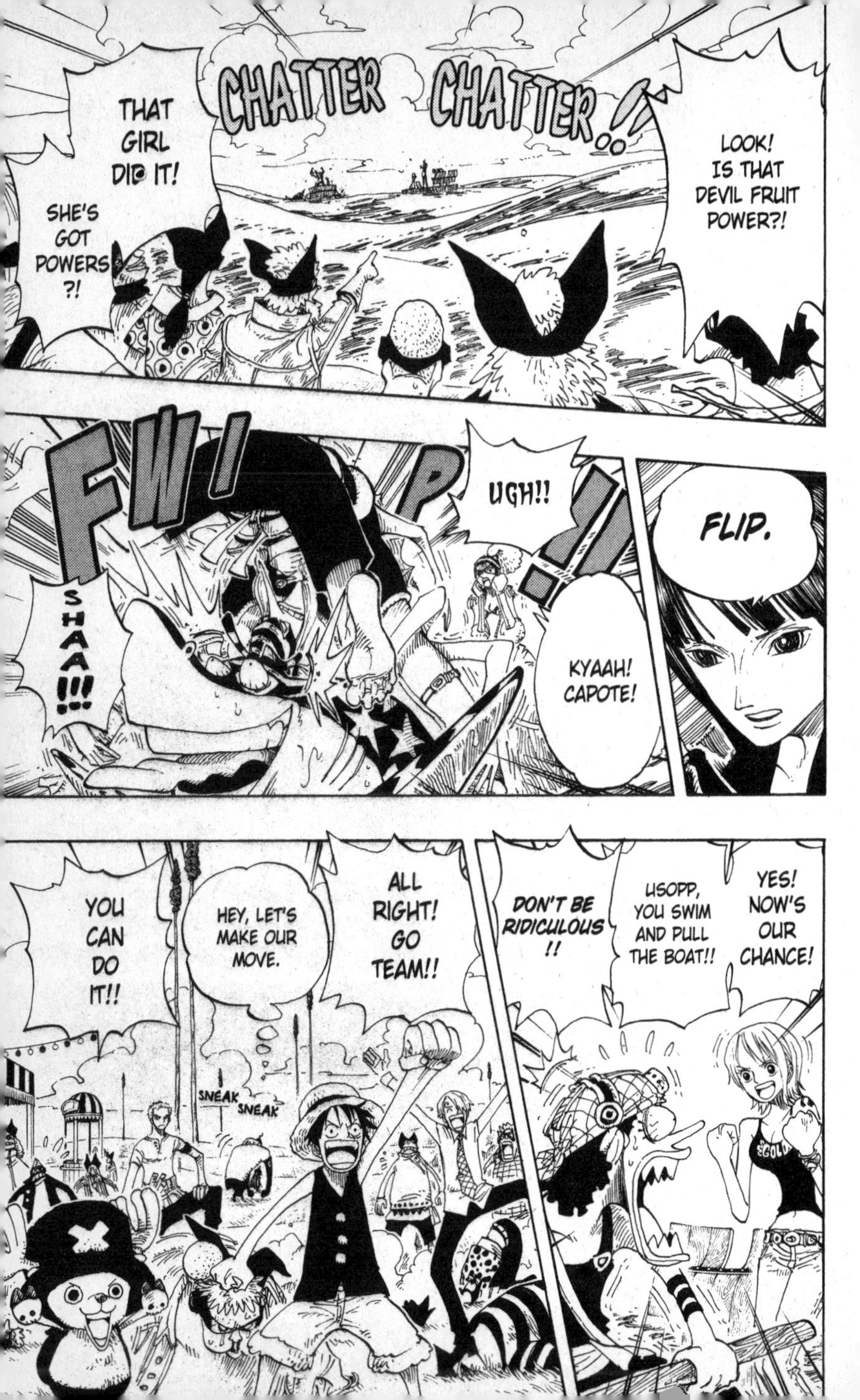
LOOK! IS THAT DEVIL FRUIT POWER?!
CHATTER CHATTER!!
THAT GIRL DID IT!
SHE'S GOT POWERS?!
FLIP.
UGH!!
FWIP!!
KYAAH! CAPOTE!
SHAAA!!!
YES! NOW'S OUR CHANCE!
USOPP, YOU SWIM AND PULL THE BOAT!!
DON'T BE RIDICULOUS!!
ALL RIGHT! GO TEAM!!
HEY, LET'S MAKE OUR MOVE.
YOU CAN DO IT!!
SNEAK SNEAK

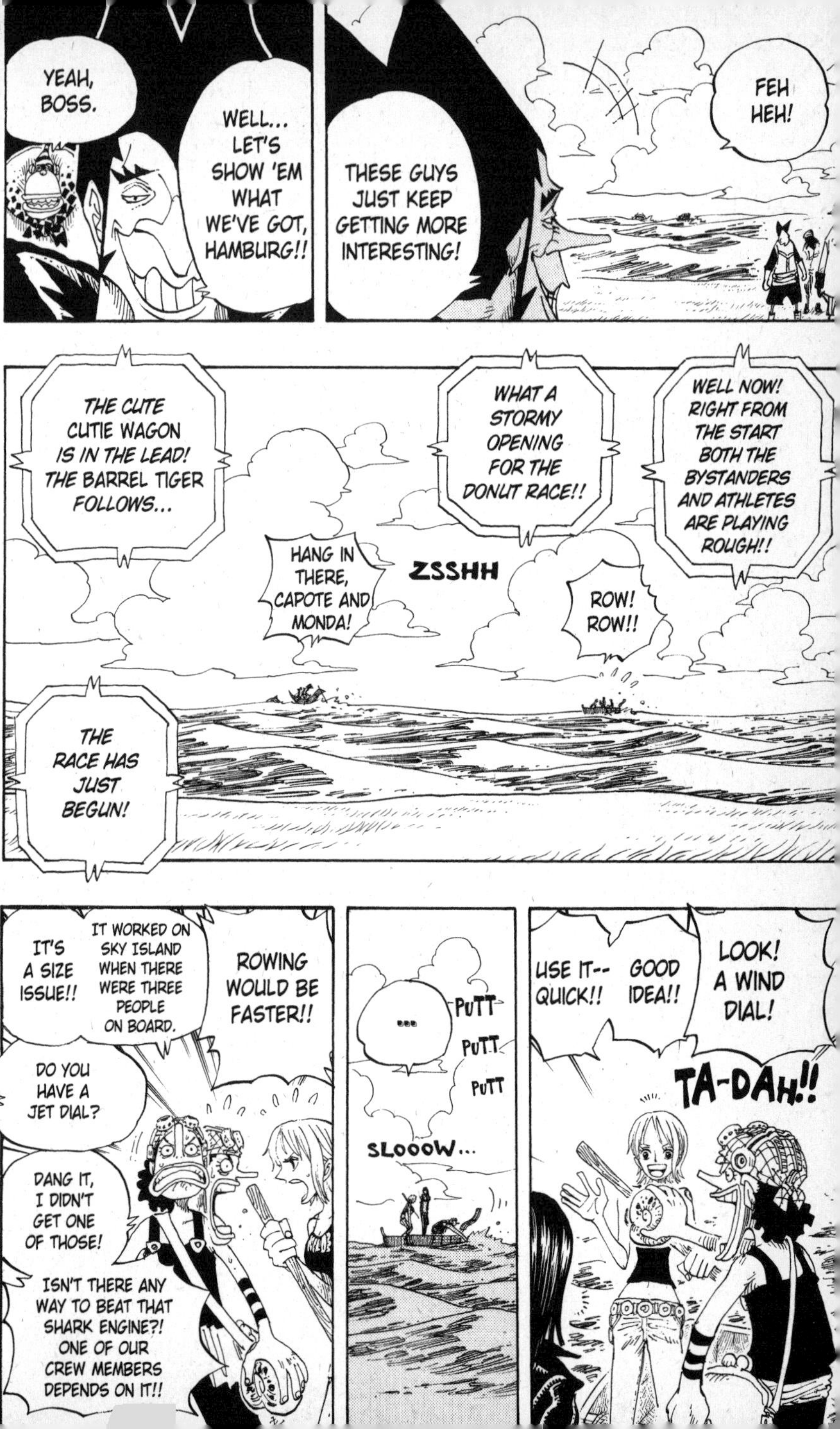
FEH HEH!
THESE GUYS JUST KEEP GETTING MORE INTERESTING!
WELL... LET'S SHOW 'EM WHAT WE'VE GOT, HAMBURG!!
YEAH, BOSS.
WELL NOW! RIGHT FROM THE START BOTH THE BYSTANDERS AND ATHLETES ARE PLAYING ROUGH!!
WHAT A STORMY OPENING FOR THE DONUT RACE!!
THE CUTE CUTIE WAGON IS IN THE LEAD! THE BARREL TIGER FOLLOWS...
ROW! ROW!!
ZSSHH
HANG IN THERE, CAPOTE AND MONDA!
THE RACE HAS JUST BEGUN!
LOOK! A WIND DIAL!
GOOD IDEA!!
USE IT-- QUICK!!
TA-DAH!!
...
PUTT
PUTT
PUTT
SLOOOW...
ROWING WOULD BE FASTER!!
IT WORKED ON SKY ISLAND WHEN THERE WERE THREE PEOPLE ON BOARD.
IT'S A SIZE ISSUE!!
DO YOU HAVE A JET DIAL?
DANG IT, I DIDN'T GET ONE OF THOSE!
ISN'T THERE ANY WAY TO BEAT THAT SHARK ENGINE?! ONE OF OUR CREW MEMBERS DEPENDS ON IT!!

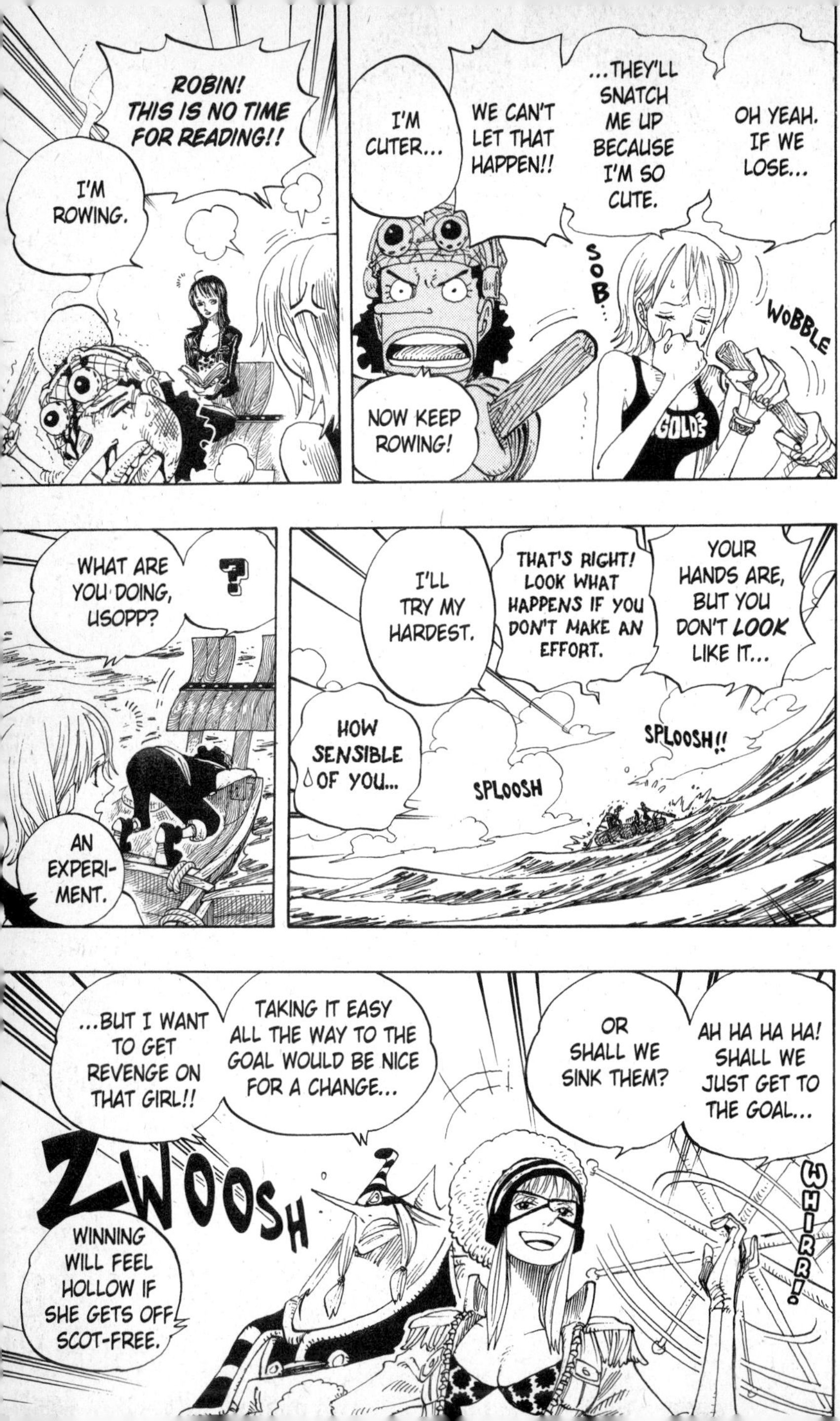
OH YEAH. IF WE LOSE...
...THEY'LL SNATCH ME UP BECAUSE I'M SO CUTE.
WE CAN'T LET THAT HAPPEN!!
I'M CUTER...
SOB...
WOBBLE
NOW KEEP ROWING!
ROBIN! THIS IS NO TIME FOR READING!!
I'M ROWING.
YOUR HANDS ARE, BUT YOU DON'T *LOOK* LIKE IT...
THAT'S RIGHT! LOOK WHAT HAPPENS IF YOU DON'T MAKE AN EFFORT.
I'LL TRY MY HARDEST.
SPLOOSH!!
HOW SENSIBLE OF YOU...
SPLOOSH
WHAT ARE YOU DOING, USOPP?
?
AN EXPERIMENT.
AH HA HA HA! SHALL WE JUST GET TO THE GOAL...
OR SHALL WE SINK THEM?
WHIRR!
TAKING IT EASY ALL THE WAY TO THE GOAL WOULD BE NICE FOR A CHANGE...
...BUT I WANT TO GET REVENGE ON THAT GIRL!!
ZWOOSH
WINNING WILL FEEL HOLLOW IF SHE GETS OFF SCOT-FREE.

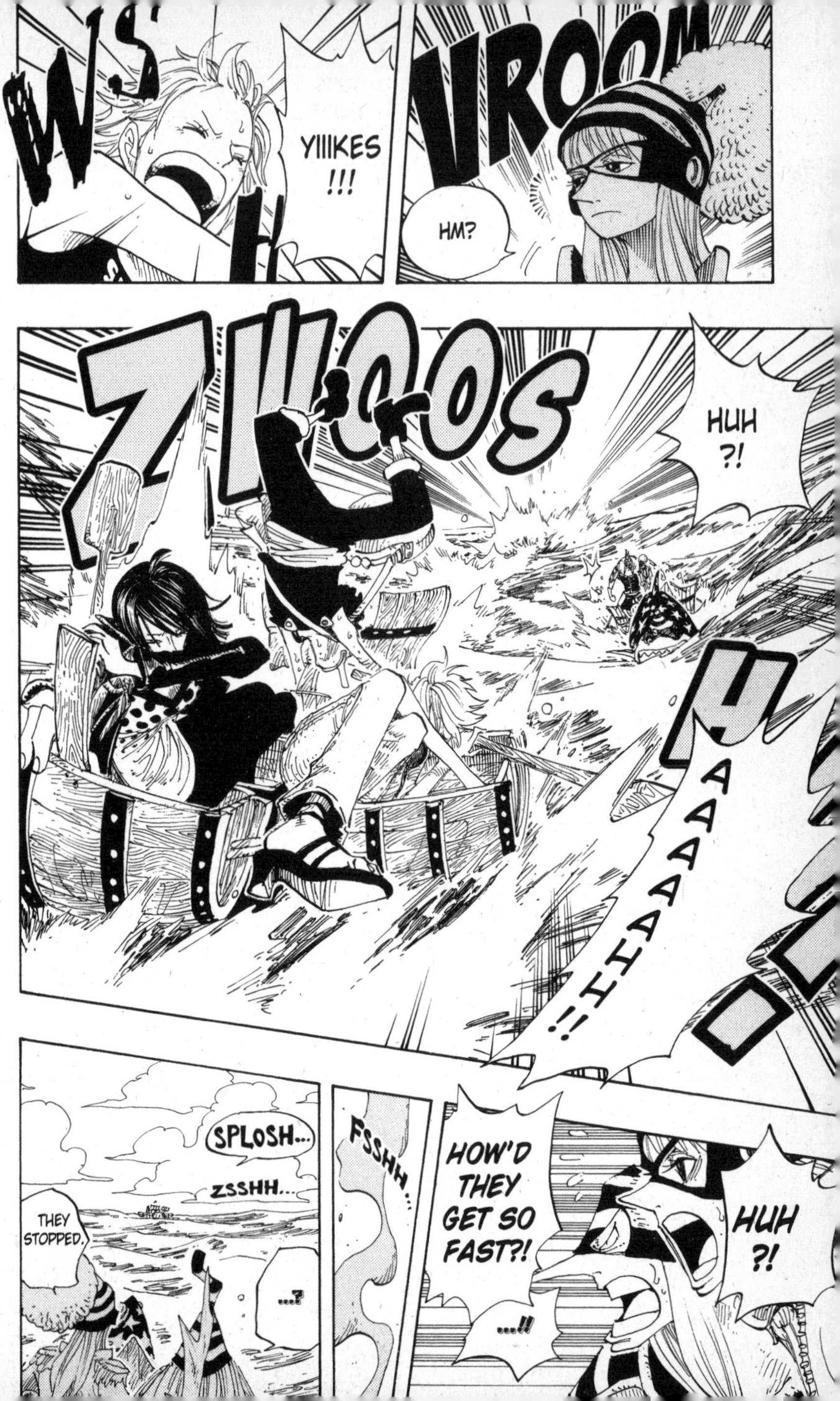
VROOM
HM?
WSH
YIIIKES !!!
ZHOOS
HUH ?!
AAAAAAAHH!!
HUH ?!
HOW'D THEY GET SO FAST?!
...!!
FSSHH...
SPLOSH...
ZSSHH...
THEY STOPPED.
...?

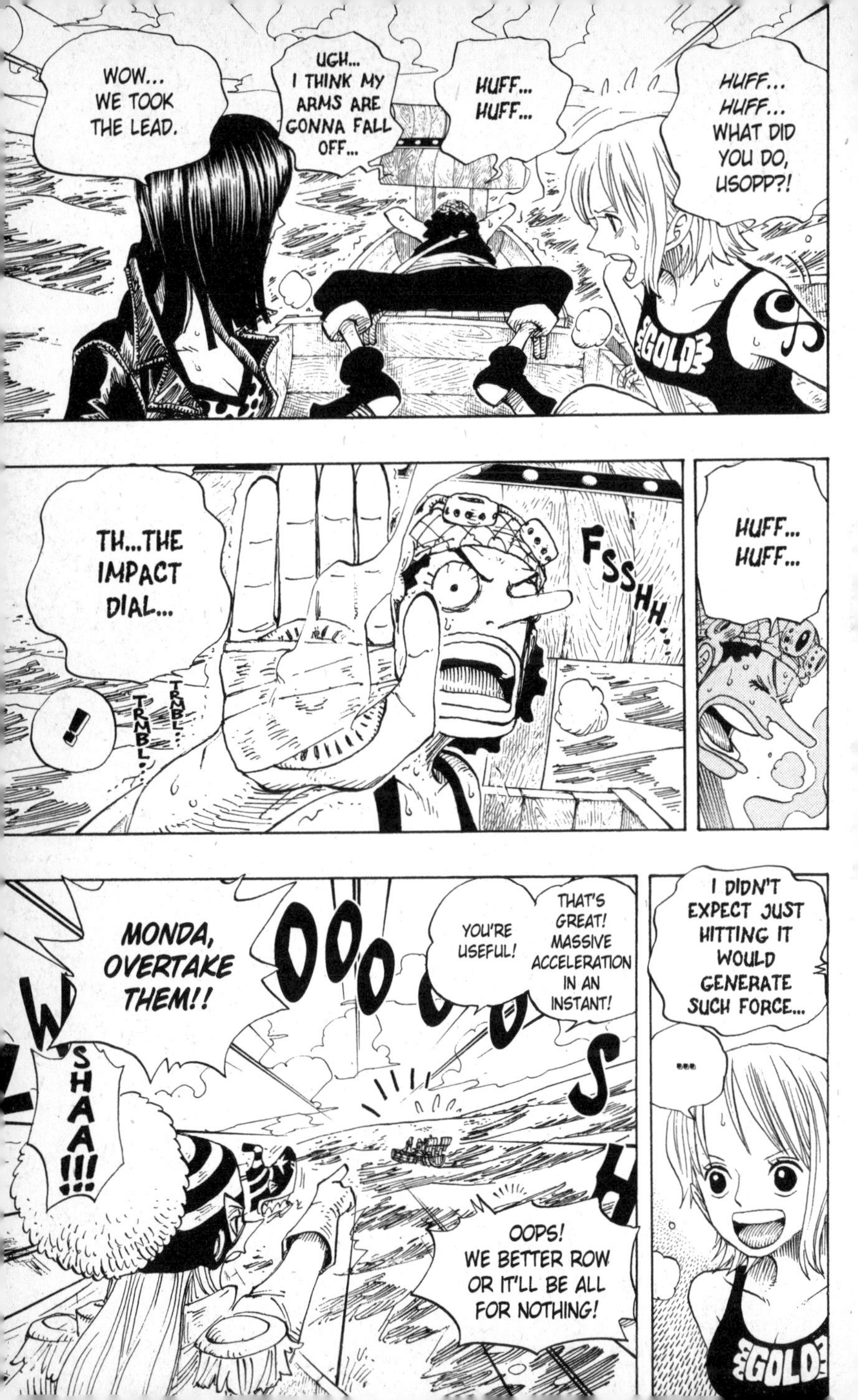
HUFF... HUFF... WHAT DID YOU DO, USOPP?!
HUFF... HUFF...
UGH... I THINK MY ARMS ARE GONNA FALL OFF...
WOW... WE TOOK THE LEAD.
HUFF... HUFF...
FSSHH
TH...THE IMPACT DIAL...
TRMBL...
TRMBL...
!
I DIDN'T EXPECT JUST HITTING IT WOULD GENERATE SUCH FORCE...
...
THAT'S GREAT! MASSIVE ACCELERATION IN AN INSTANT!
YOU'RE USEFUL!
OOOOOSH
MONDA, OVERTAKE THEM!!
WSHAA!!!
OOPS! WE BETTER ROW OR IT'LL BE ALL FOR NOTHING!

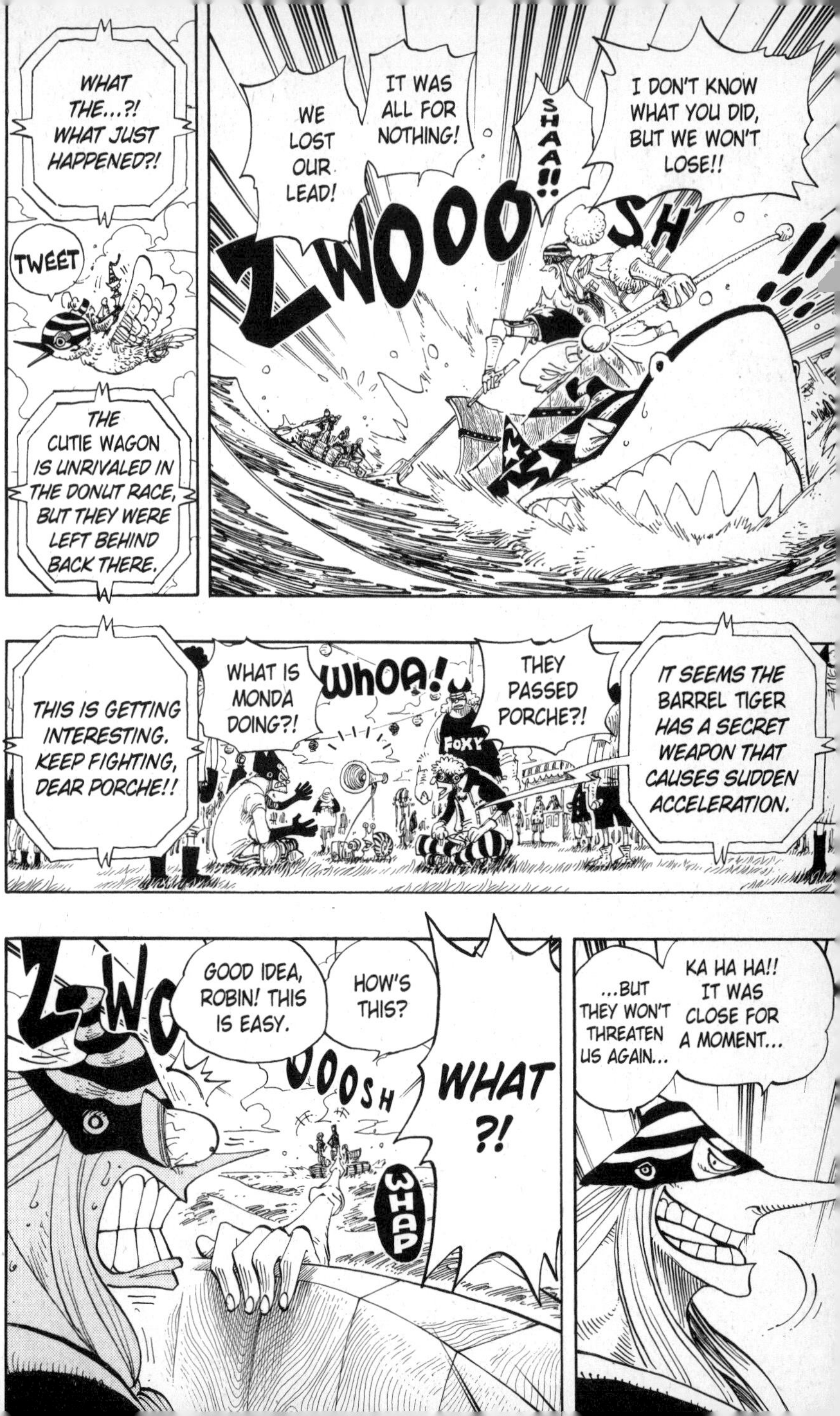
I DON'T KNOW WHAT YOU DID, BUT WE WON'T LOSE!!
SHAAA!!
IT WAS ALL FOR NOTHING!
WE LOST OUR LEAD!
ZWOOOOSH!!!
WHAT THE...?! WHAT JUST HAPPENED?!
TWEET
THE CUTIE WAGON IS UNRIVALED IN THE DONUT RACE, BUT THEY WERE LEFT BEHIND BACK THERE.
IT SEEMS THE BARREL TIGER HAS A SECRET WEAPON THAT CAUSES SUDDEN ACCELERATION.
THEY PASSED PORCHE?!
WHOA!
FOXY
WHAT IS MONDA DOING?!
THIS IS GETTING INTERESTING. KEEP FIGHTING, DEAR PORCHE!!
KA HA HA!! IT WAS CLOSE FOR A MOMENT...
...BUT THEY WON'T THREATEN US AGAIN...
WHAT ?!
HOW'S THIS?
GOOD IDEA, ROBIN! THIS IS EASY.
ZWOOOOSH
WHAP

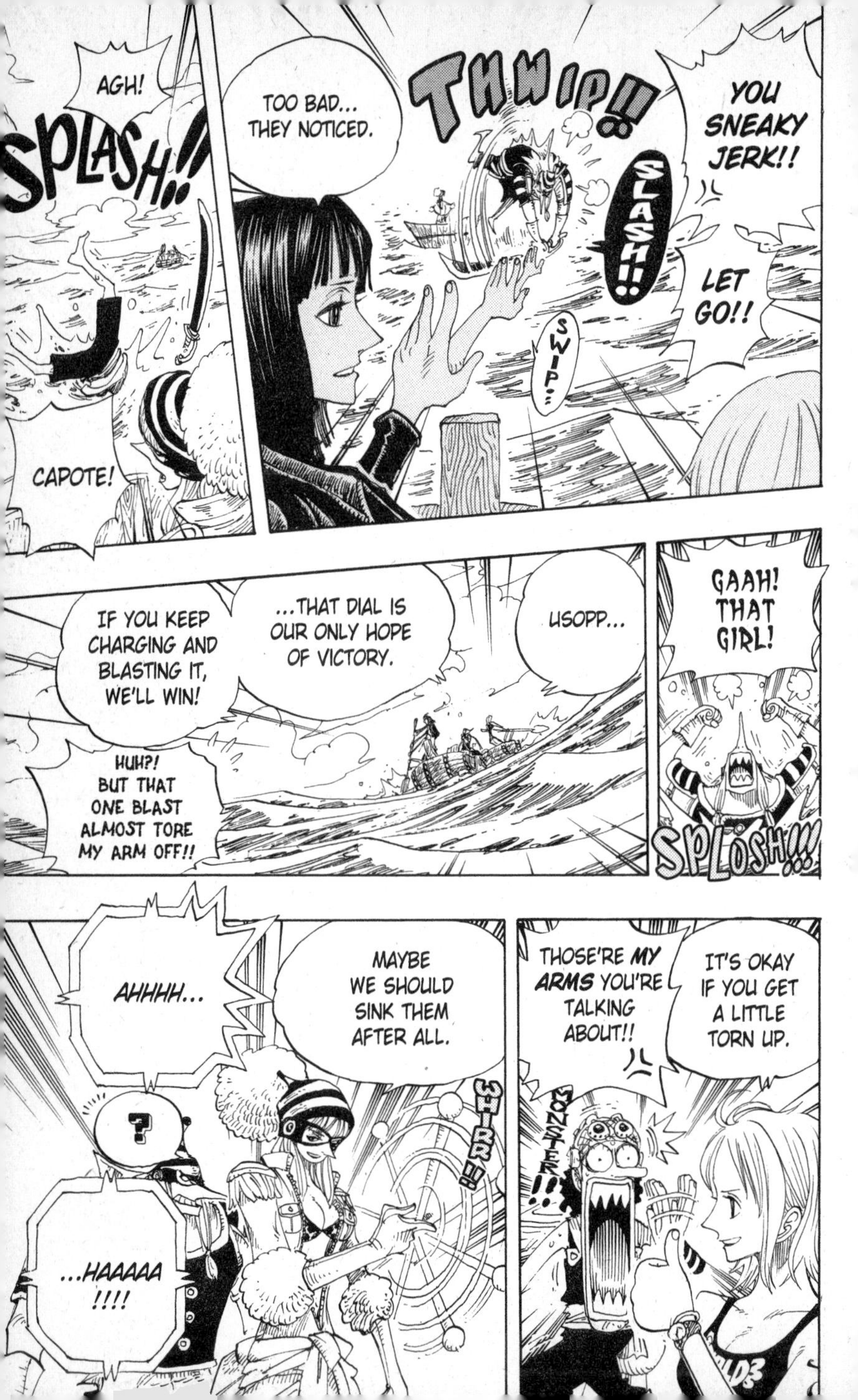
THWIP!!
YOU SNEAKY JERK!!
SLASH!!
LET GO!!
SWIP!!
TOO BAD... THEY NOTICED.
AGH!
SPLASH!!
CAPOTE!
GAAH! THAT GIRL!
SPLOSH!!!
USOPP...
...THAT DIAL IS OUR ONLY HOPE OF VICTORY.
IF YOU KEEP CHARGING AND BLASTING IT, WE'LL WIN!
HUH?! BUT THAT ONE BLAST ALMOST TORE MY ARM OFF!!
IT'S OKAY IF YOU GET A LITTLE TORN UP.
THOSE'RE **MY ARMS** YOU'RE TALKING ABOUT!!
MONSTER!!
MAYBE WE SHOULD SINK THEM AFTER ALL.
WHIRR!!
AHHHH...
?
...HAAAAA !!!!

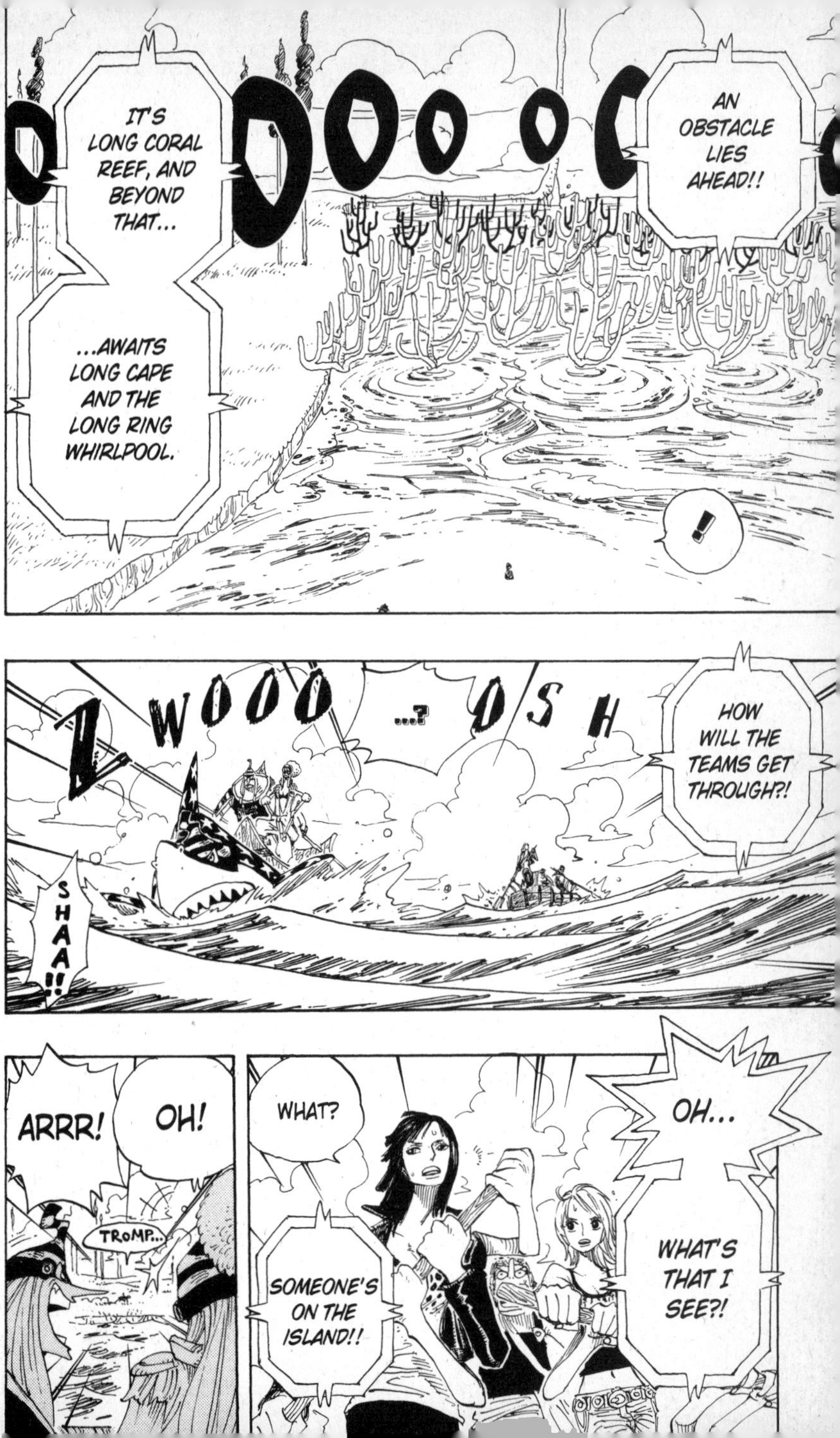
AN OBSTACLE LIES AHEAD!!
DOOOO
IT'S LONG CORAL REEF, AND BEYOND THAT...
...AWAITS LONG CAPE AND THE LONG RING WHIRLPOOL.
!
HOW WILL THE TEAMS GET THROUGH?!
ZWOOOOSH
...?
SHAA!!
OH... WHAT'S THAT I SEE?!
WHAT?
SOMEONE'S ON THE ISLAND!!
OH!
ARRR!
TROMP...

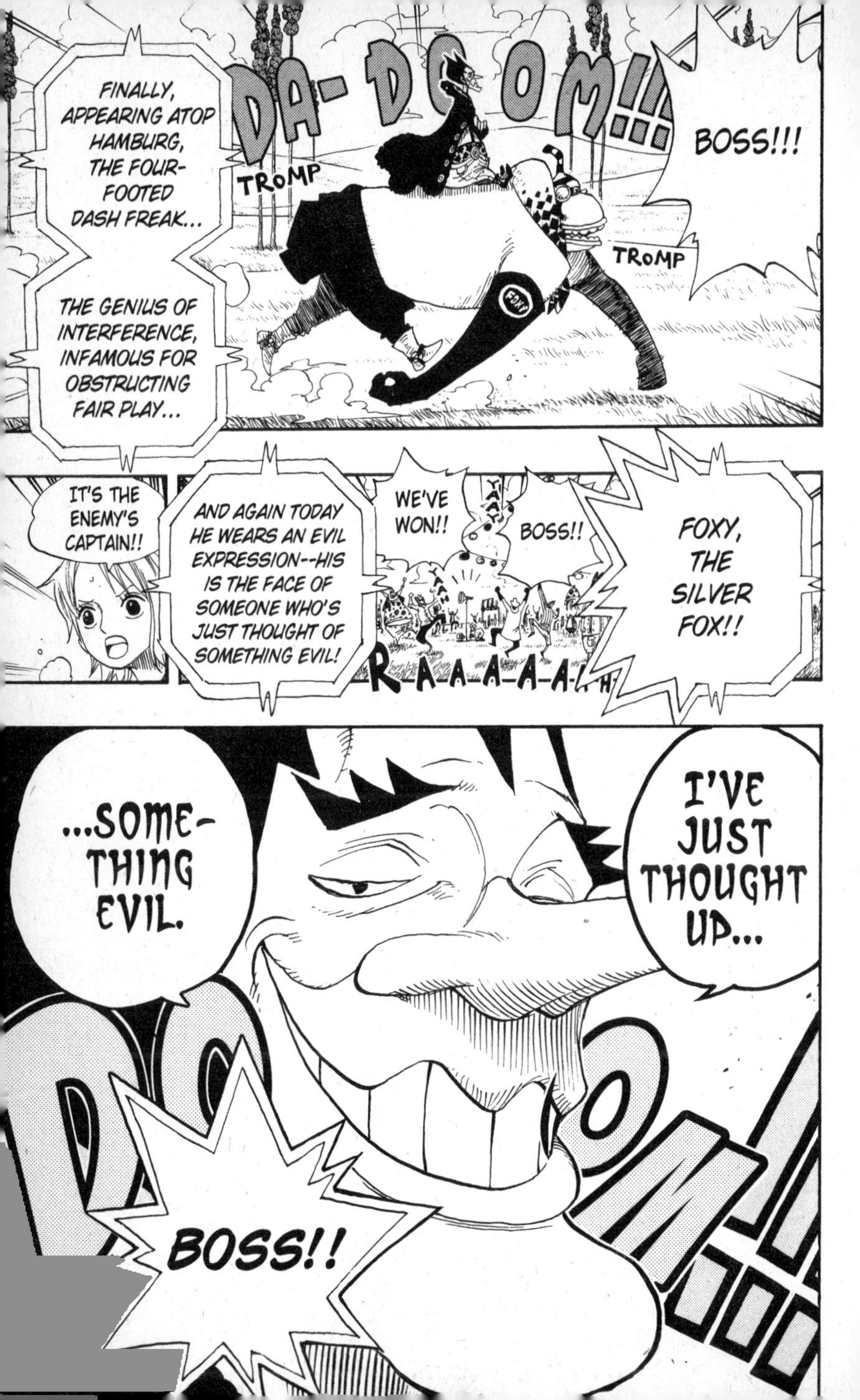
BOSS!!!
DA-DOOM!!!
TROMP
FINALLY, APPEARING ATOP HAMBURG, THE FOUR-FOOTED DASH FREAK...
TROMP
THE GENIUS OF INTERFERENCE, INFAMOUS FOR OBSTRUCTING FAIR PLAY...
FOXY, THE SILVER FOX!!
BOSS!!
YAAAH
WE'VE WON!!
YAAAH
AND AGAIN TODAY HE WEARS AN EVIL EXPRESSION--HIS IS THE FACE OF SOMEONE WHO'S JUST THOUGHT OF SOMETHING EVIL!
RAAAAAAH
IT'S THE ENEMY'S CAPTAIN!!
I'VE JUST THOUGHT UP...
...SOMETHING EVIL.
BOSS!!

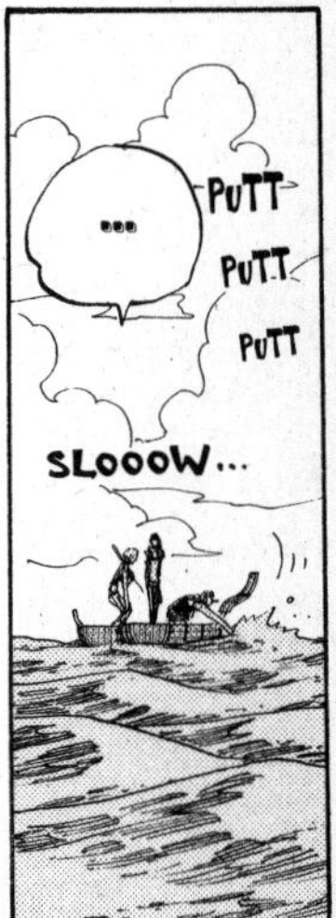
...
PUTT
PUTT
PUTT
SLOOOW...

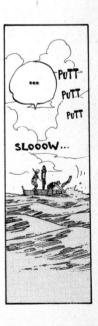

Chapter 308:
OBSTRUCTIVE TACTICS

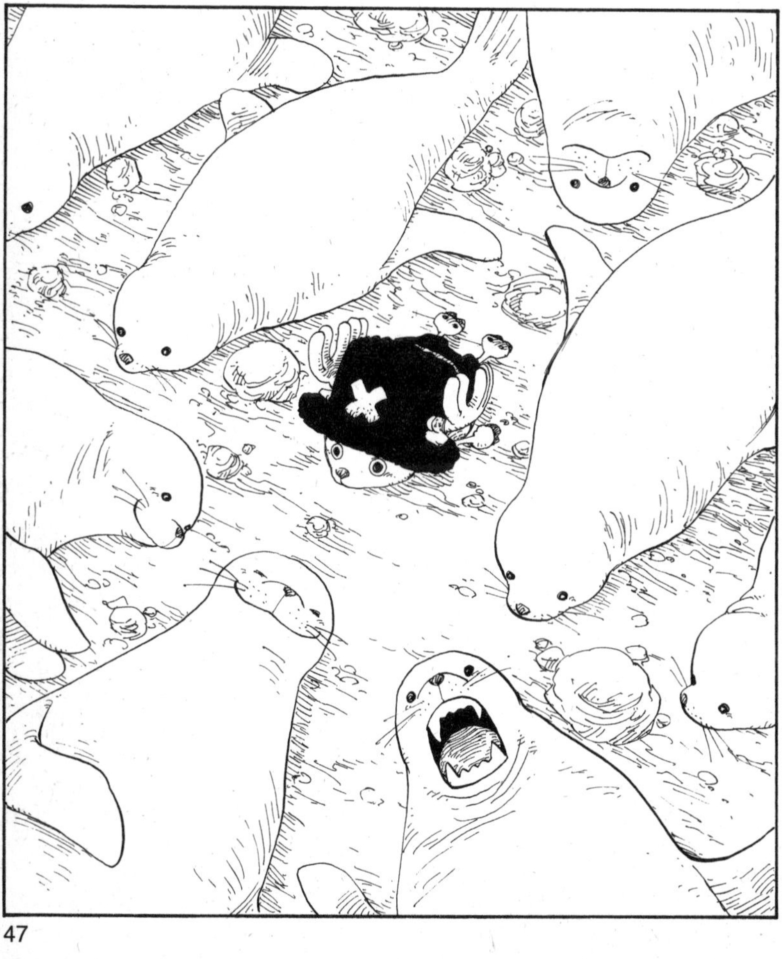

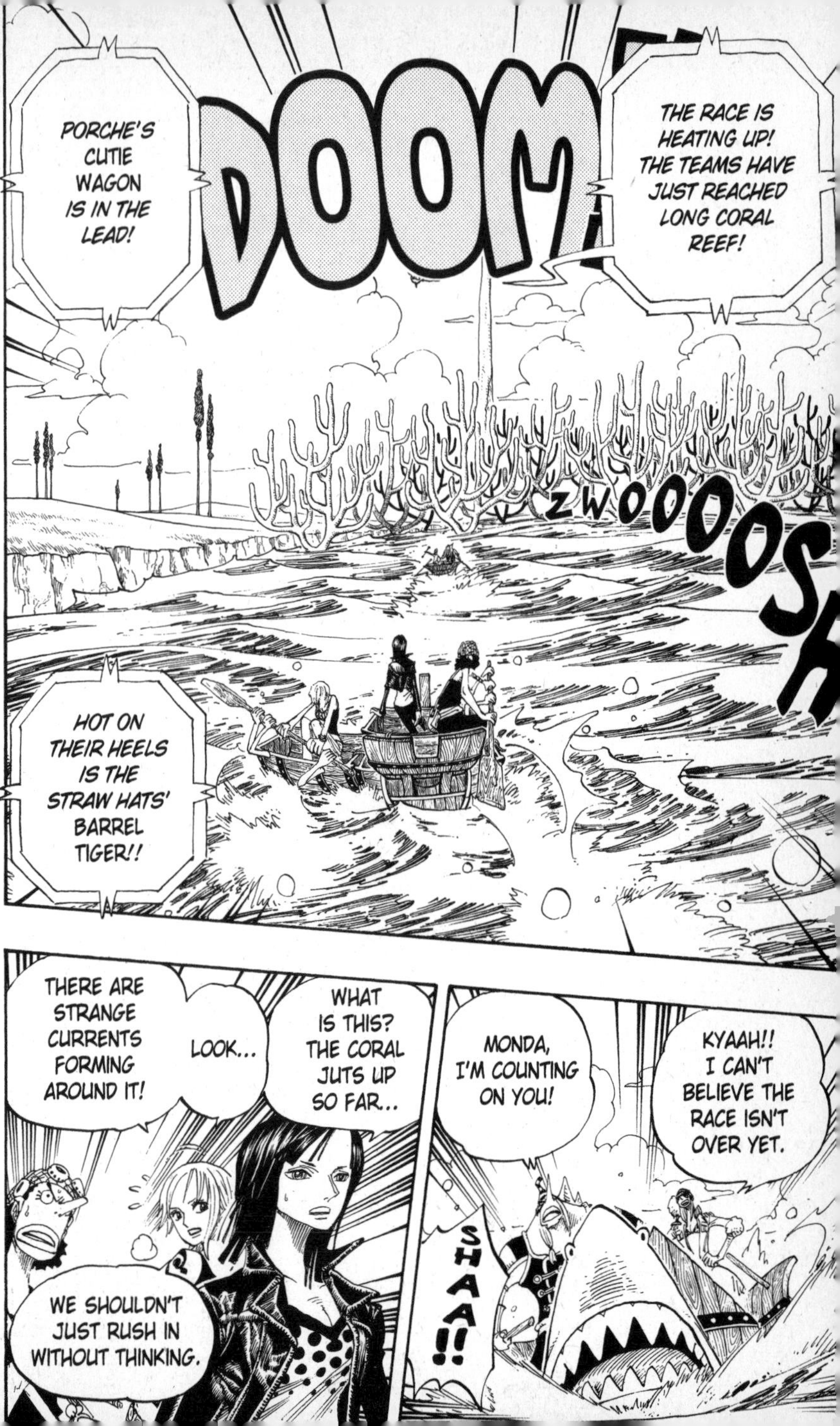
THE RACE IS HEATING UP! THE TEAMS HAVE JUST REACHED LONG CORAL REEF!
DOOM
PORCHE'S CUTIE WAGON IS IN THE LEAD!
ZWOOOOSH
HOT ON THEIR HEELS IS THE STRAW HATS' BARREL TIGER!!
KYAAH!! I CAN'T BELIEVE THE RACE ISN'T OVER YET.
MONDA, I'M COUNTING ON YOU!
SHAA!!
WHAT IS THIS? THE CORAL JUTS UP SO FAR...
LOOK...
THERE ARE STRANGE CURRENTS FORMING AROUND IT!
WE SHOULDN'T JUST RUSH IN WITHOUT THINKING.

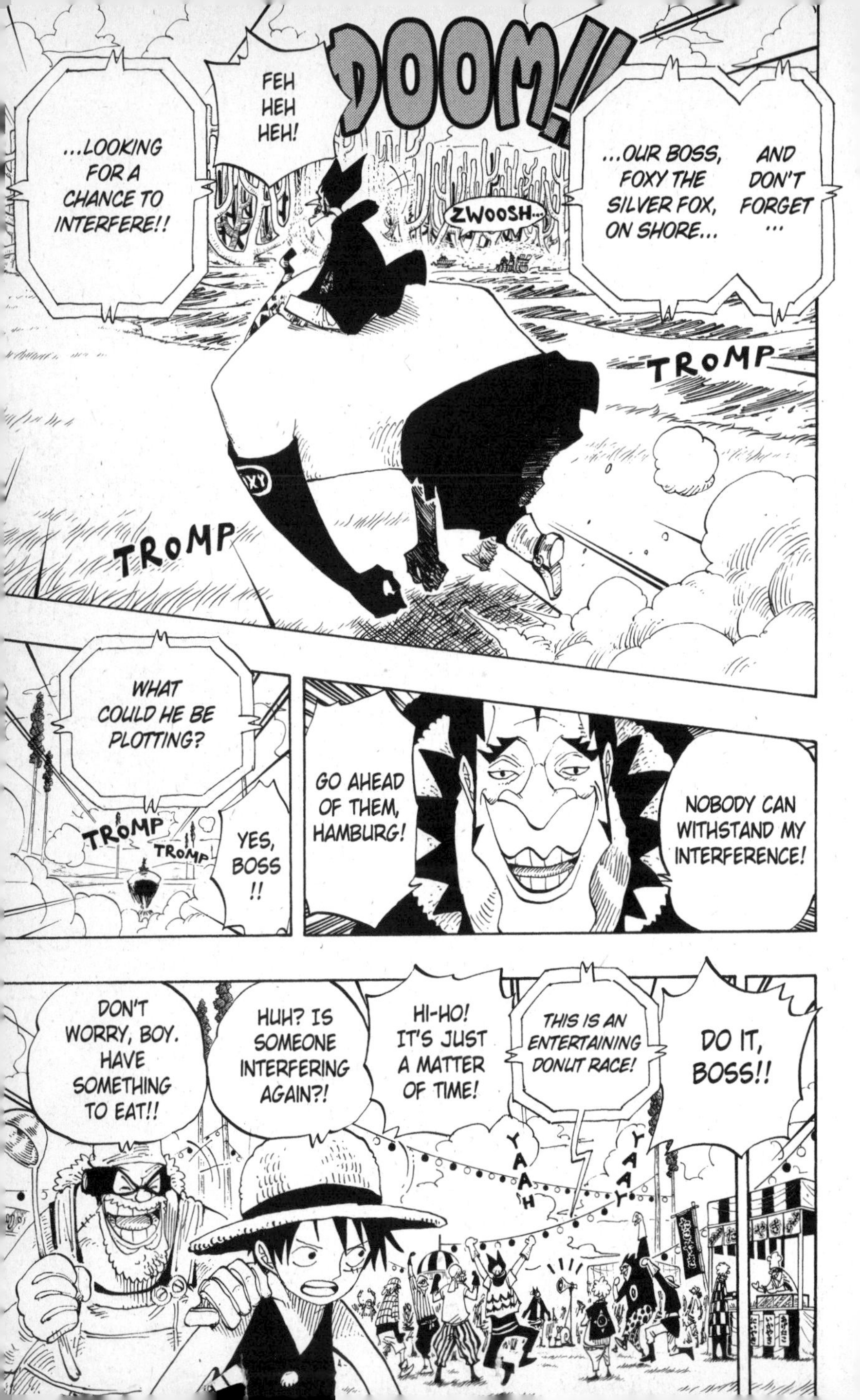

AND DON'T FORGET ...
...OUR BOSS, FOXY THE SILVER FOX, ON SHORE...
DOOM!!
ZWOOSH...
FEH HEH HEH!
...LOOKING FOR A CHANCE TO INTERFERE!!
TROMP
TROMP
NOBODY CAN WITHSTAND MY INTERFERENCE!
GO AHEAD OF THEM, HAMBURG!
WHAT COULD HE BE PLOTTING?
YES, BOSS!!
TROMP
TROMP
DO IT, BOSS!!
YAAAY
THIS IS AN ENTERTAINING DONUT RACE!
YAAAH
HI-HO! IT'S JUST A MATTER OF TIME!
HUH? IS SOMEONE INTERFERING AGAIN?!
DON'T WORRY, BOY. HAVE SOMETHING TO EAT!!

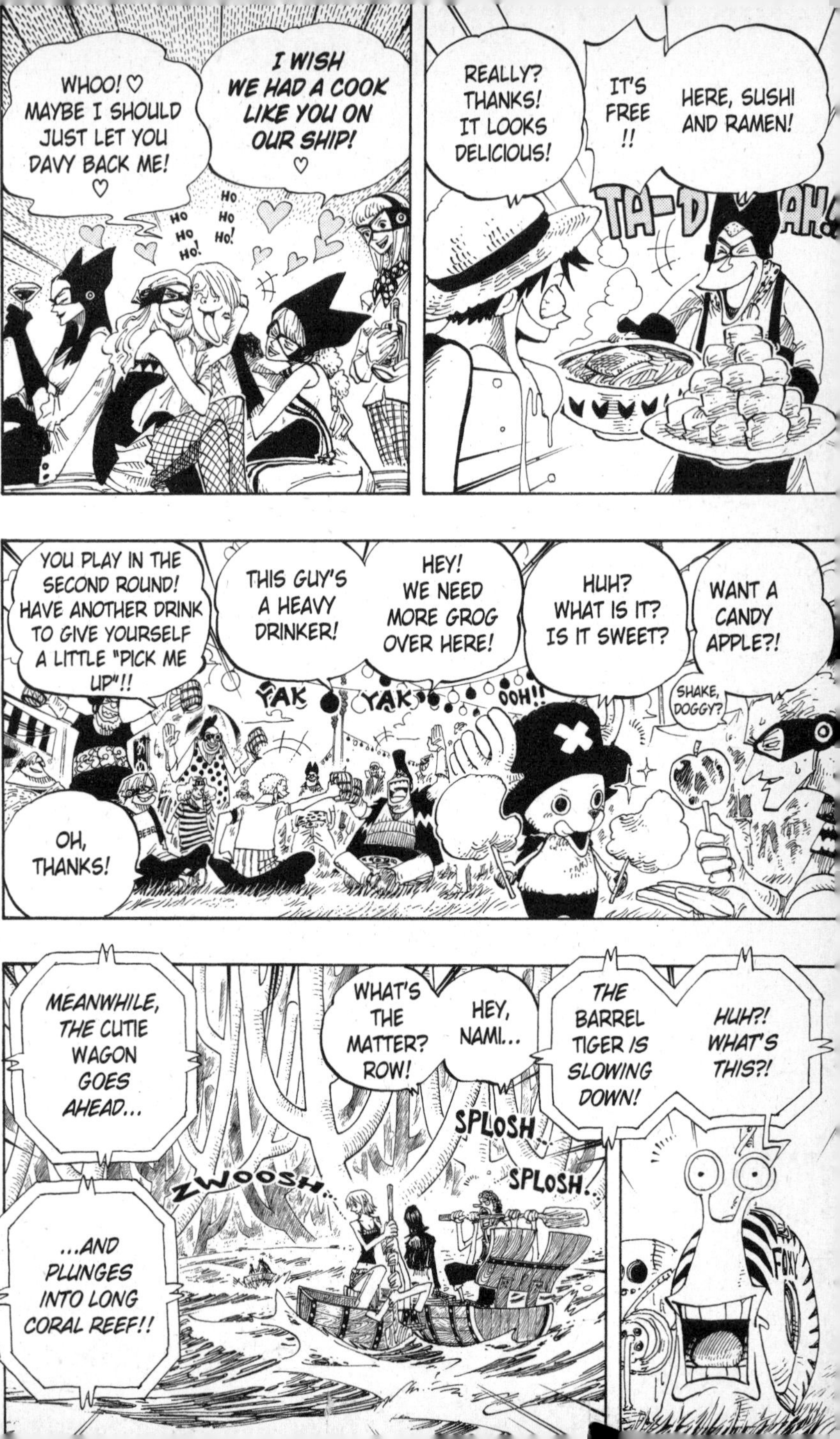

HERE, SUSHI AND RAMEN!
IT'S FREE !!
REALLY? THANKS! IT LOOKS DELICIOUS!
I WISH WE HAD A COOK LIKE YOU ON OUR SHIP! ♡
WHOO! ♡ MAYBE I SHOULD JUST LET YOU DAVY BACK ME! ♡
HO HO HO!
HO HO HO!
WANT A CANDY APPLE?!
SHAKE, DOGGY?
HUH? WHAT IS IT? IS IT SWEET?
OOH!!
HEY! WE NEED MORE GROG OVER HERE!
YAK
YAK
THIS GUY'S A HEAVY DRINKER!
YOU PLAY IN THE SECOND ROUND! HAVE ANOTHER DRINK TO GIVE YOURSELF A LITTLE "PICK ME UP"!!
OH, THANKS!
HUH?! WHAT'S THIS?!
THE BARREL TIGER IS SLOWING DOWN!
HEY, NAMI...
WHAT'S THE MATTER? ROW!
SPLOSH...
SPLOSH...
ZWOOSH...
MEANWHILE, THE CUTIE WAGON GOES AHEAD...
...AND PLUNGES INTO LONG CORAL REEF!!

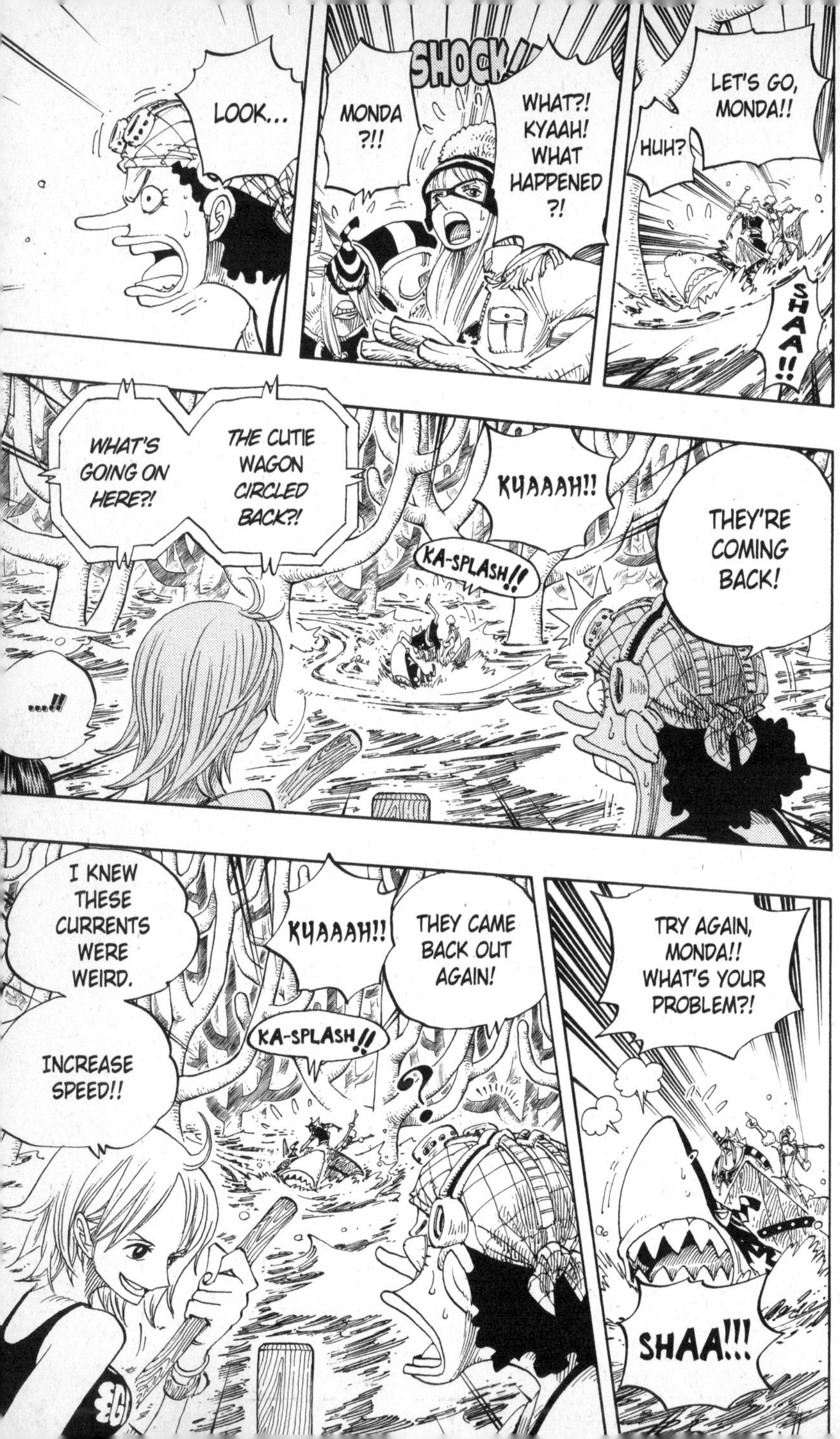
LET'S GO, MONDA!!
HUH?
SHAA!!
SHOCK!!
WHAT?! KYAAH! WHAT HAPPENED ?!
MONDA ?!!
LOOK...
THEY'RE COMING BACK!
KYAAAH!!
THE CUTIE WAGON CIRCLED BACK?!
WHAT'S GOING ON HERE?!
KA-SPLASH!!
...!!
TRY AGAIN, MONDA!! WHAT'S YOUR PROBLEM?!
SHAA!!!
THEY CAME BACK OUT AGAIN!
KYAAAH!!
I KNEW THESE CURRENTS WERE WEIRD.
KA-SPLASH!!
INCREASE SPEED!!

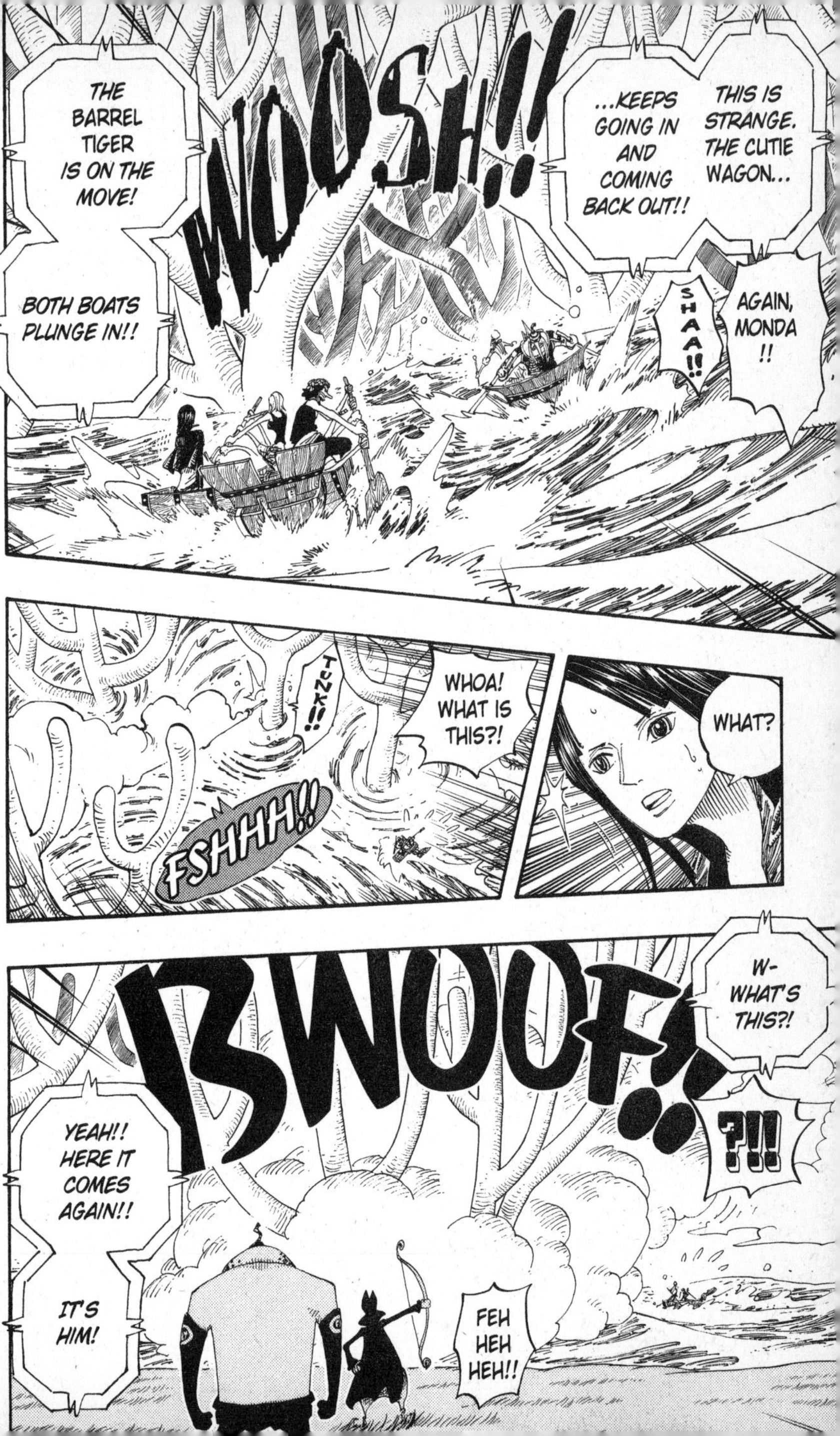
THIS IS STRANGE. THE CUTIE WAGON...
...KEEPS GOING IN AND COMING BACK OUT!!
WOOSH!!
THE BARREL TIGER IS ON THE MOVE!
AGAIN, MONDA!!
SHAAA!!
BOTH BOATS PLUNGE IN!!
WHAT?
WHOA! WHAT IS THIS?!
TUNK!!
FSHHH!!
W-WHAT'S THIS?!
?!!
BWOOF...
YEAH!! HERE IT COMES AGAIN!!
FEH HEH HEH!!
IT'S HIM!

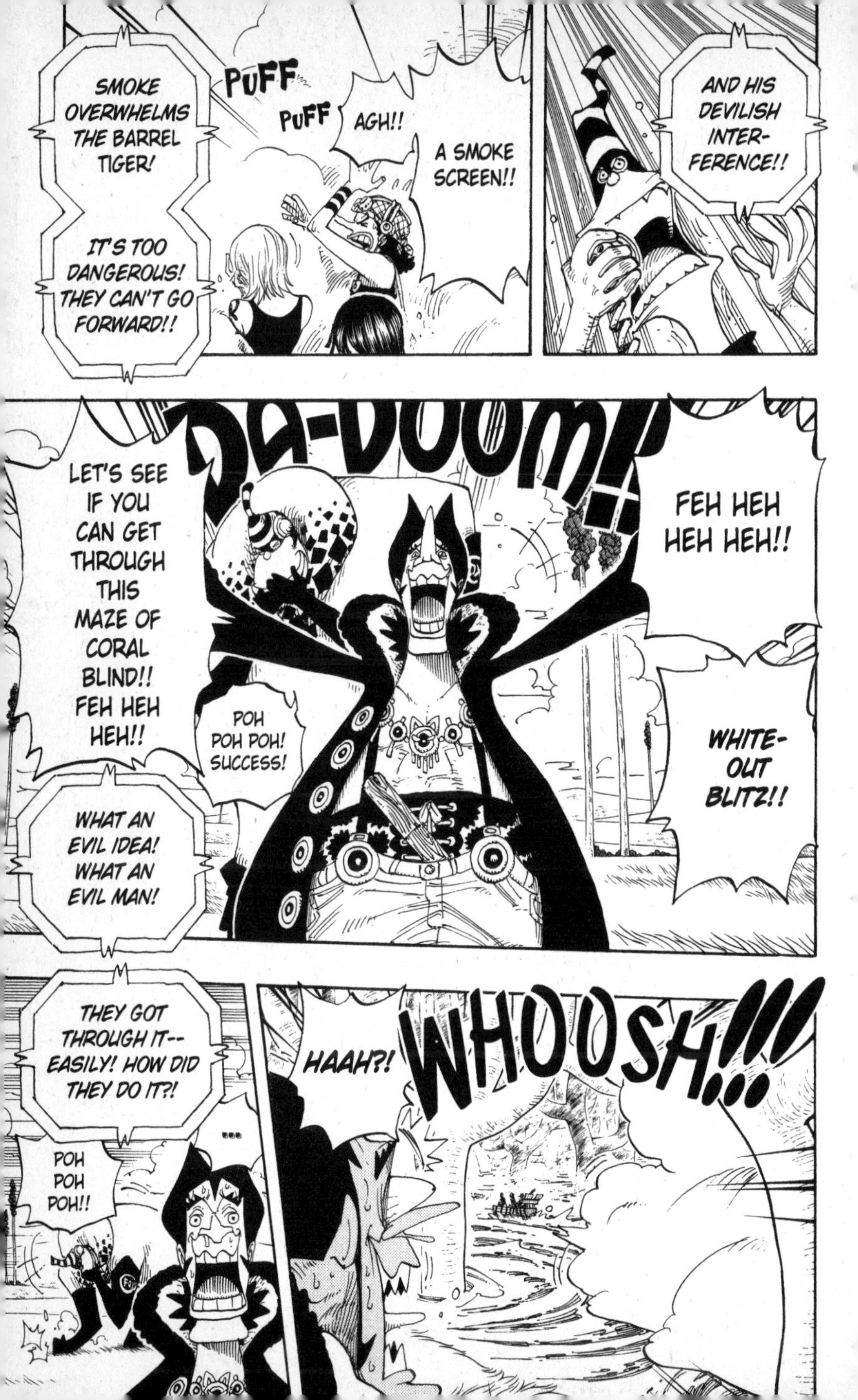
AND HIS DEVILISH INTER- FERENCE!!
AGH!!
A SMOKE SCREEN!!
PUFF
PUFF
SMOKE OVERWHELMS THE BARREL TIGER!
IT'S TOO DANGEROUS! THEY CAN'T GO FORWARD!!
DA-DOOM!!
FEH HEH HEH HEH!!
LET'S SEE IF YOU CAN GET THROUGH THIS MAZE OF CORAL BLIND!! FEH HEH HEH!!
WHITE-OUT BLITZ!!
POH POH POH! SUCCESS!
WHAT AN EVIL IDEA! WHAT AN EVIL MAN!
WHOOSH!!!
HAAH?!
THEY GOT THROUGH IT-- EASILY! HOW DID THEY DO IT?!
...
POH POH POH!!

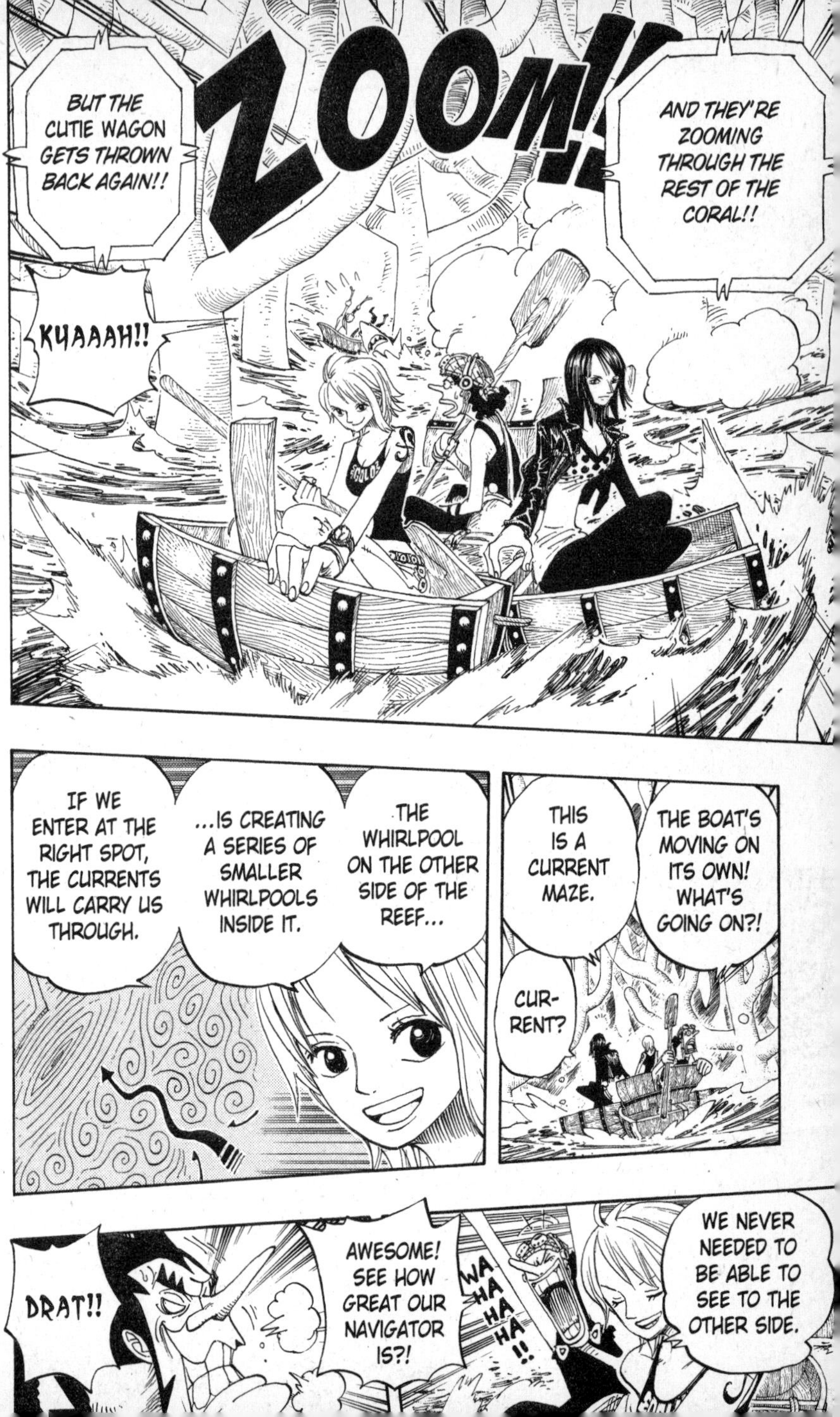
AND THEY'RE ZOOMING THROUGH THE REST OF THE CORAL!!
ZOOM!!
BUT THE CUTIE WAGON GETS THROWN BACK AGAIN!!
KYAAAH!!
THE BOAT'S MOVING ON ITS OWN! WHAT'S GOING ON?!
THIS IS A CURRENT MAZE.
CUR-RENT?
THE WHIRLPOOL ON THE OTHER SIDE OF THE REEF...
...IS CREATING A SERIES OF SMALLER WHIRLPOOLS INSIDE IT.
IF WE ENTER AT THE RIGHT SPOT, THE CURRENTS WILL CARRY US THROUGH.
WE NEVER NEEDED TO BE ABLE TO SEE TO THE OTHER SIDE.
WAHAHAHA!!
AWESOME! SEE HOW GREAT OUR NAVIGATOR IS?!
DRAT!!

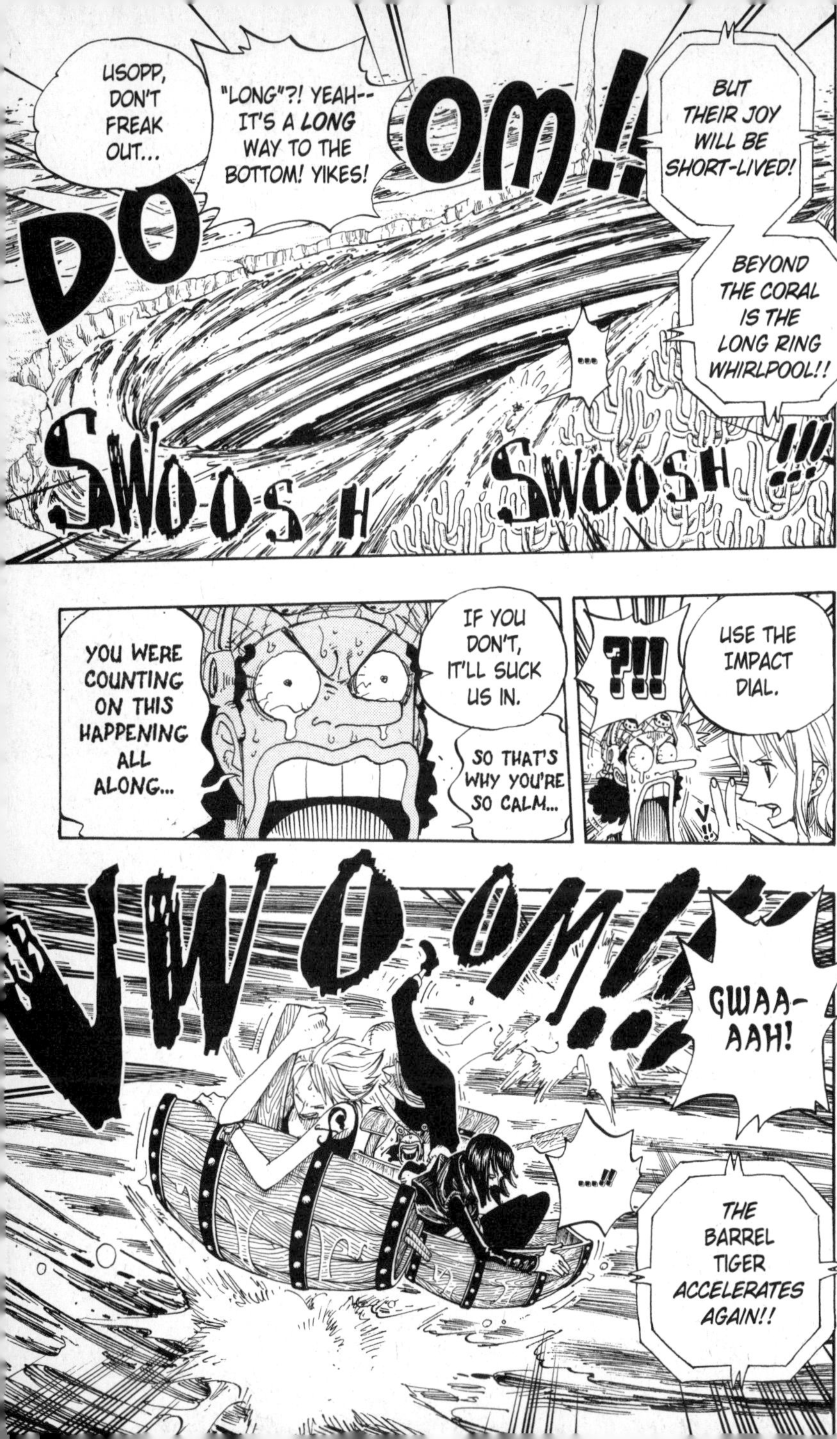
BUT THEIR JOY WILL BE SHORT-LIVED!
BEYOND THE CORAL IS THE LONG RING WHIRLPOOL!!
DOOM!!
...
"LONG"?! YEAH-- IT'S A LONG WAY TO THE BOTTOM! YIKES!
USOPP, DON'T FREAK OUT...
SWOOSH
SWOOSH!!
?!!
USE THE IMPACT DIAL.
IF YOU DON'T, IT'LL SUCK US IN.
SO THAT'S WHY YOU'RE SO CALM...
YOU WERE COUNTING ON THIS HAPPENING ALL ALONG...
VWOOM!!
GWAA-AAH!
...!!
THE BARREL TIGER ACCELERATES AGAIN!!

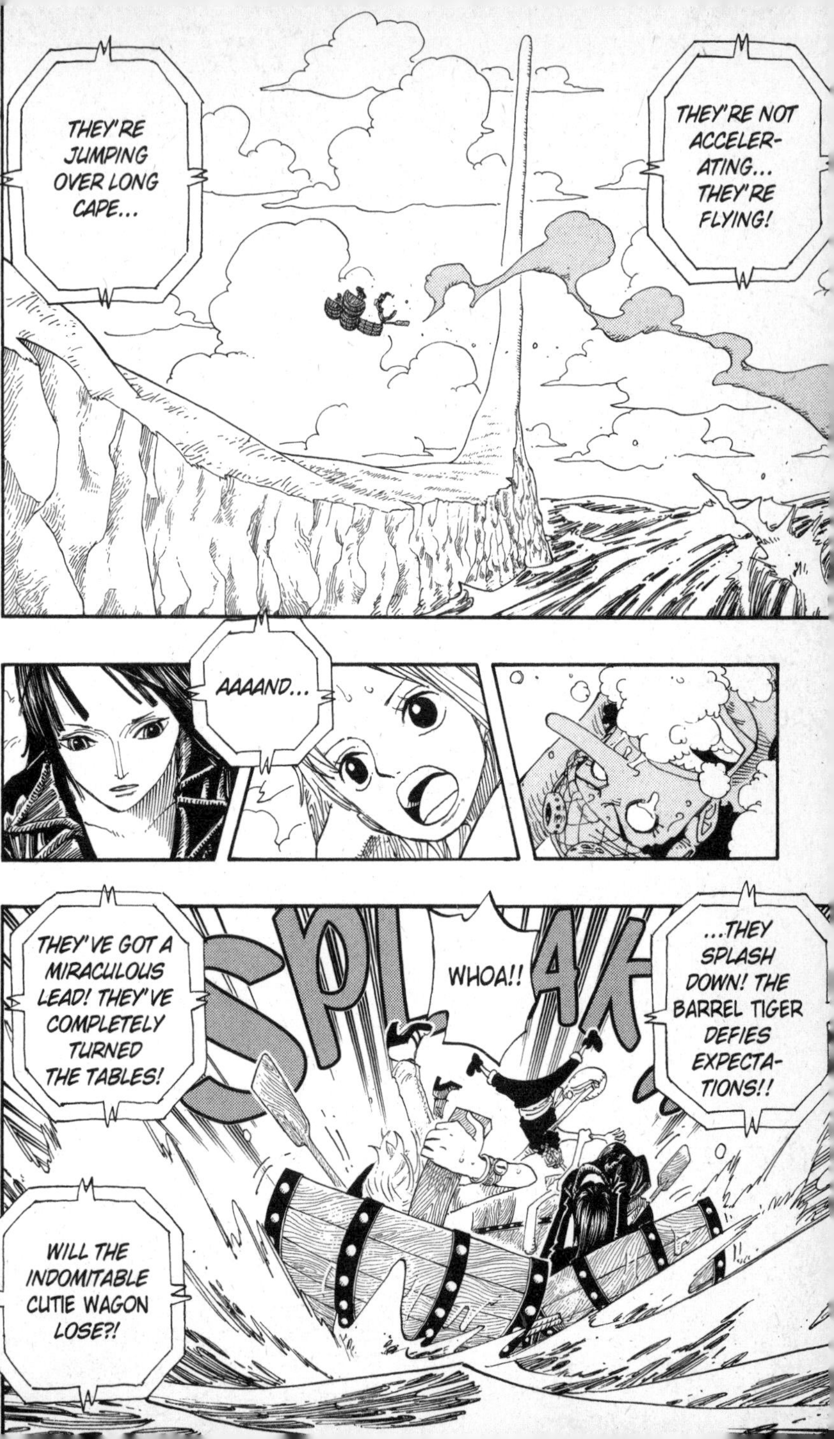
THEY'RE NOT ACCELER-ATING... THEY'RE FLYING!
THEY'RE JUMPING OVER LONG CAPE...
AAAAND...
...THEY SPLASH DOWN! THE BARREL TIGER DEFIES EXPECTA-TIONS!!
WHOA!!
SPLAK
THEY'VE GOT A MIRACULOUS LEAD! THEY'VE COMPLETELY TURNED THE TABLES!
WILL THE INDOMITABLE CUTIE WAGON LOSE?!

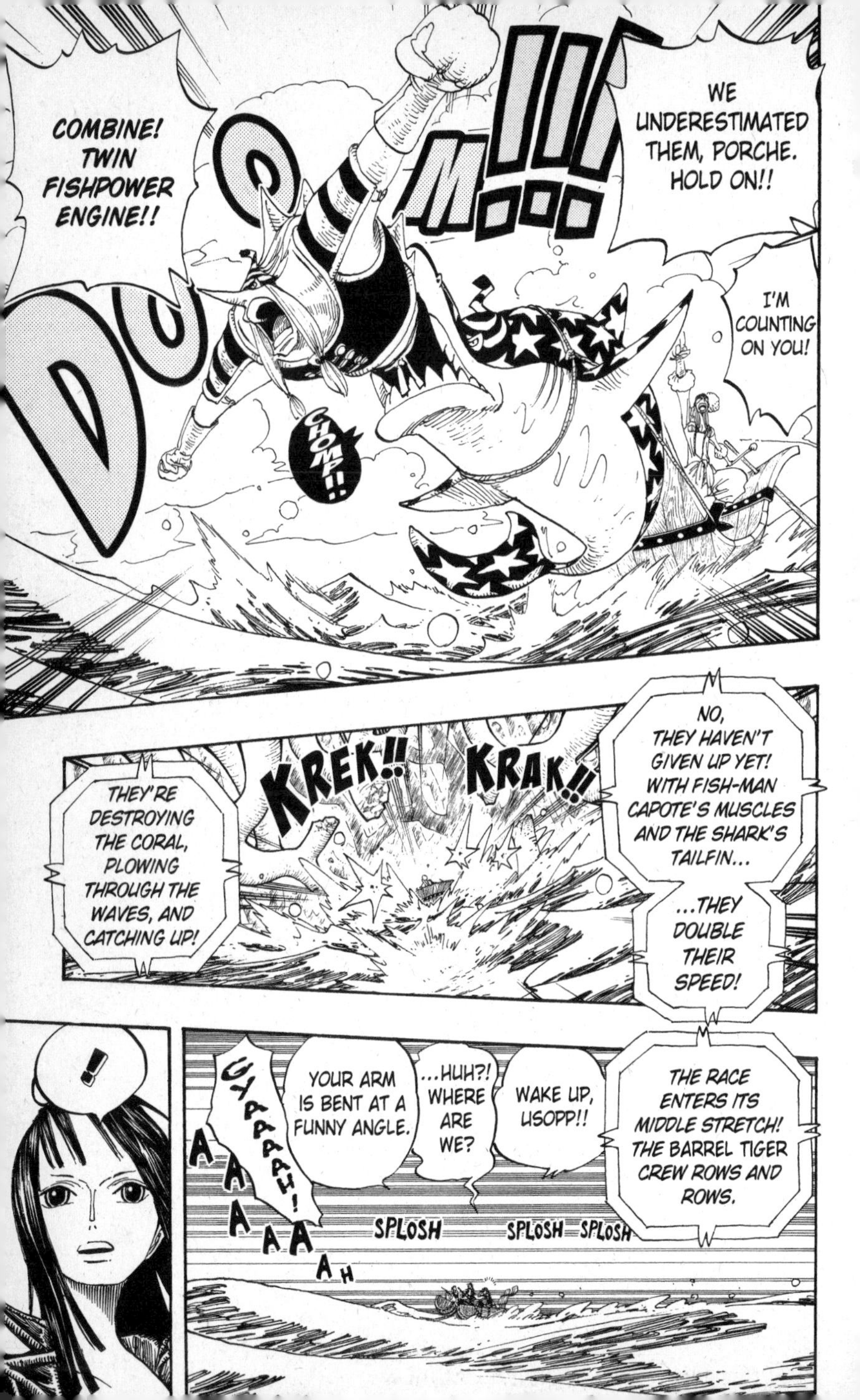

WE UNDERESTIMATED THEM, PORCHE. HOLD ON!!
I'M COUNTING ON YOU!
COMBINE! TWIN FISHPOWER ENGINE!!
DOOM!!!
CHOMP!!
NO, THEY HAVEN'T GIVEN UP YET! WITH FISH-MAN CAPOTE'S MUSCLES AND THE SHARK'S TAILFIN...
...THEY DOUBLE THEIR SPEED!
KRAK!!
KREK!!
THEY'RE DESTROYING THE CORAL, PLOWING THROUGH THE WAVES, AND CATCHING UP!
THE RACE ENTERS ITS MIDDLE STRETCH! THE BARREL TIGER CREW ROWS AND ROWS.
WAKE UP, USOPP!!
...HUH?! WHERE ARE WE?
YOUR ARM IS BENT AT A FUNNY ANGLE.
GYAAAAAH!!
AAAAAAAH
SPLOSH
SPLOSH
SPLOSH
!

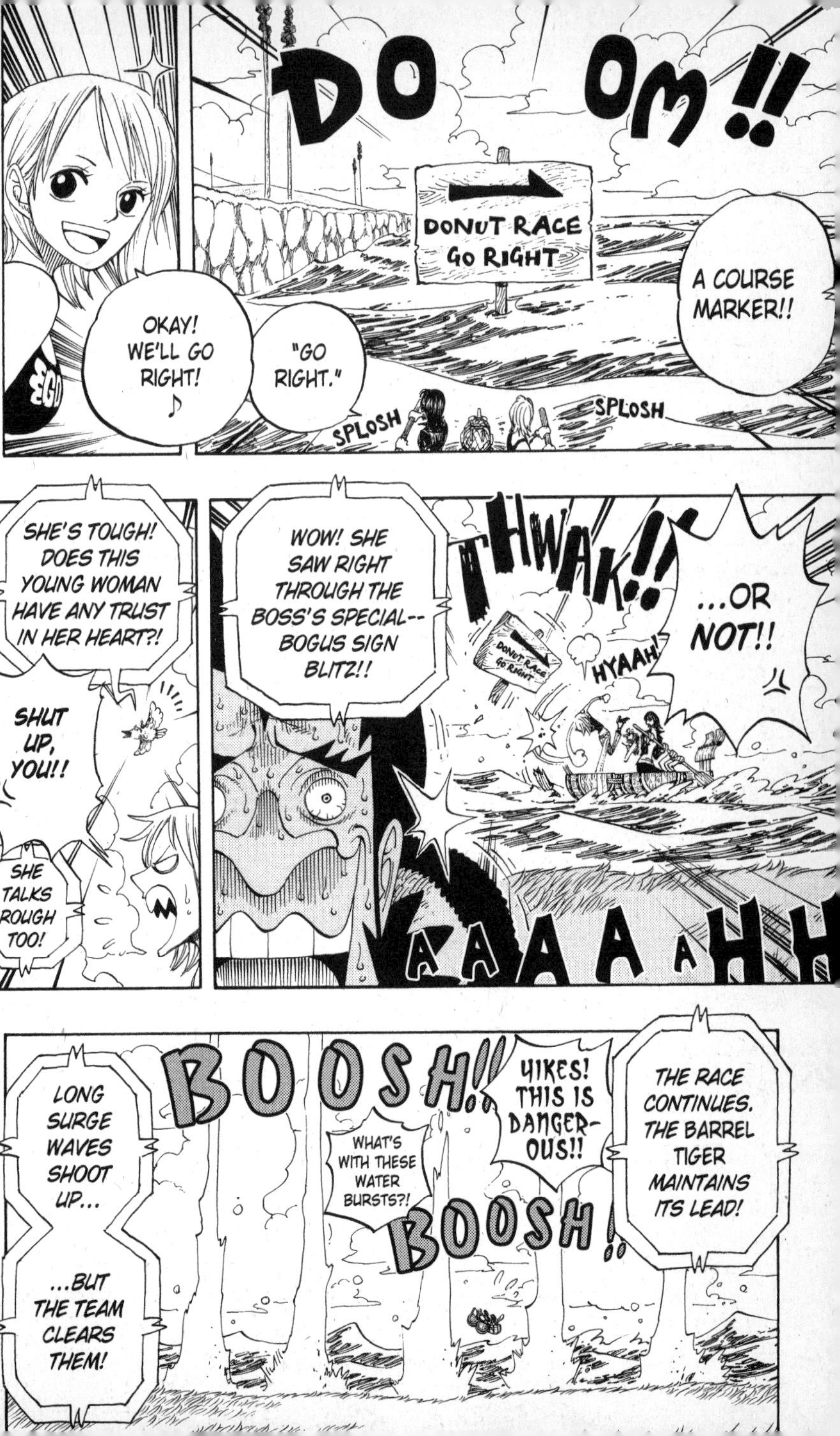
DOOM!!
DONUT RACE GO RIGHT
A COURSE MARKER!!
SPLOSH
SPLOSH
"GO RIGHT."
OKAY! WE'LL GO RIGHT! ♪
THWAK!!
...OR NOT!!
HYAAH
DONUT RACE GO RIGHT
WOW! SHE SAW RIGHT THROUGH THE BOSS'S SPECIAL-- BOGUS SIGN BLITZ!!
AAAAAHH
SHE'S TOUGH! DOES THIS YOUNG WOMAN HAVE ANY TRUST IN HER HEART?!
SHUT UP, YOU!!
SHE TALKS ROUGH TOO!
THE RACE CONTINUES. THE BARREL TIGER MAINTAINS ITS LEAD!
YIKES! THIS IS DANGER-OUS!!
BOOSH!!
WHAT'S WITH THESE WATER BURSTS?!
BOOSH!!
LONG SURGE WAVES SHOOT UP...
...BUT THE TEAM CLEARS THEM!

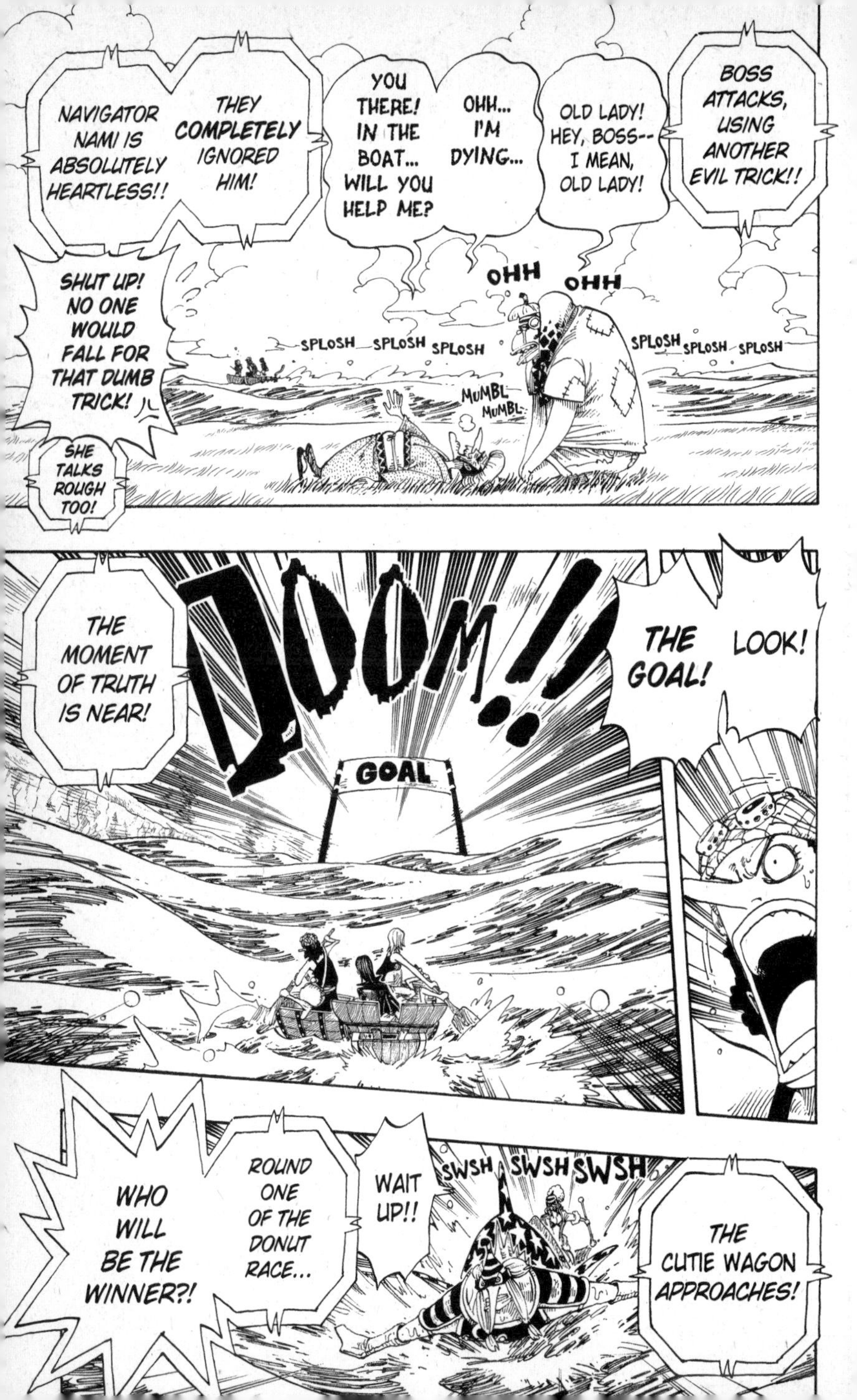
BOSS ATTACKS, USING ANOTHER EVIL TRICK!!
OLD LADY! HEY, BOSS-- I MEAN, OLD LADY!
OHH... I'M DYING...
YOU THERE! IN THE BOAT... WILL YOU HELP ME?
THEY COMPLETELY IGNORED HIM!
NAVIGATOR NAMI IS ABSOLUTELY HEARTLESS!!
OHH OHH
SPLOSH SPLOSH SPLOSH
SPLOSH SPLOSH SPLOSH
MUMBL MUMBL
SHUT UP! NO ONE WOULD FALL FOR THAT DUMB TRICK!
SHE TALKS ROUGH TOO!
LOOK!
THE GOAL!
DOOM!!
GOAL
THE MOMENT OF TRUTH IS NEAR!
THE CUTIE WAGON APPROACHES!
SWSH SWSH SWSH
WAIT UP!!
ROUND ONE OF THE DONUT RACE...
WHO WILL BE THE WINNER?!

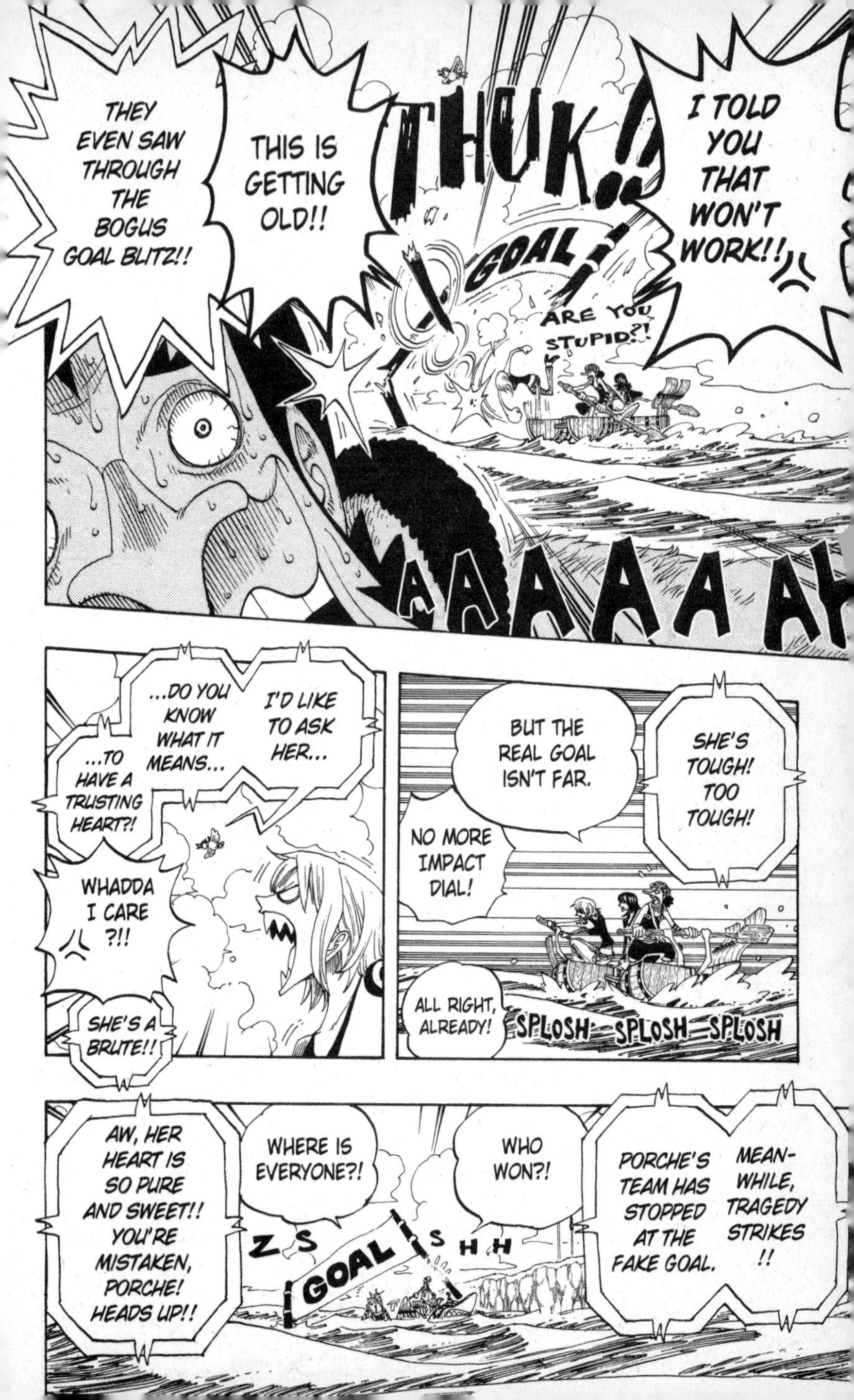
I TOLD YOU THAT WON'T WORK!!
ARE YOU STUPID?!
THUK!!
GOAL
THIS IS GETTING OLD!!
THEY EVEN SAW THROUGH THE BOGUS GOAL BLITZ!!
AAAAAAH
SHE'S TOUGH! TOO TOUGH!
BUT THE REAL GOAL ISN'T FAR.
NO MORE IMPACT DIAL!
ALL RIGHT, ALREADY!
SPLOSH SPLOSH SPLOSH
I'D LIKE TO ASK HER...
...DO YOU KNOW WHAT IT MEANS...
...TO HAVE A TRUSTING HEART?!
WHADDA I CARE?!!
SHE'S A BRUTE!!
MEANWHILE, TRAGEDY STRIKES!!
PORCHE'S TEAM HAS STOPPED AT THE FAKE GOAL.
WHO WON?!
WHERE IS EVERYONE?!
ZSHH
GOAL
AW, HER HEART IS SO PURE AND SWEET!! YOU'RE MISTAKEN, PORCHE! HEADS UP!!

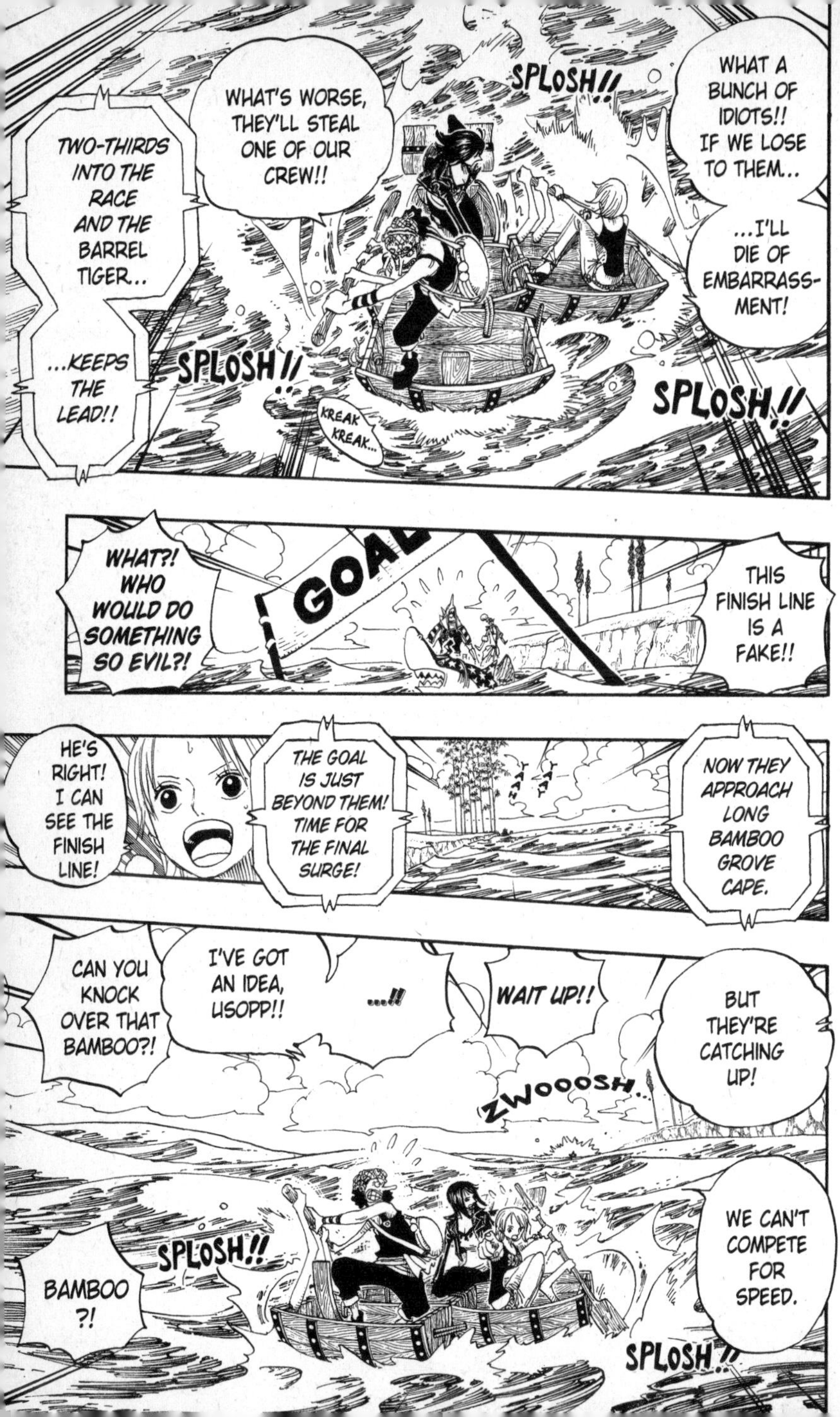
WHAT A BUNCH OF IDIOTS!! IF WE LOSE TO THEM...
...I'LL DIE OF EMBARRASS-MENT!
SPLOSH!!
WHAT'S WORSE, THEY'LL STEAL ONE OF OUR CREW!!
TWO-THIRDS INTO THE RACE AND THE BARREL TIGER...
...KEEPS THE LEAD!!
SPLOSH!!
KREAK KREAK...
SPLOSH!!
THIS FINISH LINE IS A FAKE!!
GOAL
WHAT?! WHO WOULD DO SOMETHING SO EVIL?!
NOW THEY APPROACH LONG BAMBOO GROVE CAPE.
THE GOAL IS JUST BEYOND THEM! TIME FOR THE FINAL SURGE!
HE'S RIGHT! I CAN SEE THE FINISH LINE!
BUT THEY'RE CATCHING UP!
WAIT UP!!
...!!
I'VE GOT AN IDEA, USOPP!!
CAN YOU KNOCK OVER THAT BAMBOO?!
ZWOOOSH...
WE CAN'T COMPETE FOR SPEED.
SPLOSH!!
SPLOSH!!
BAMBOO?!

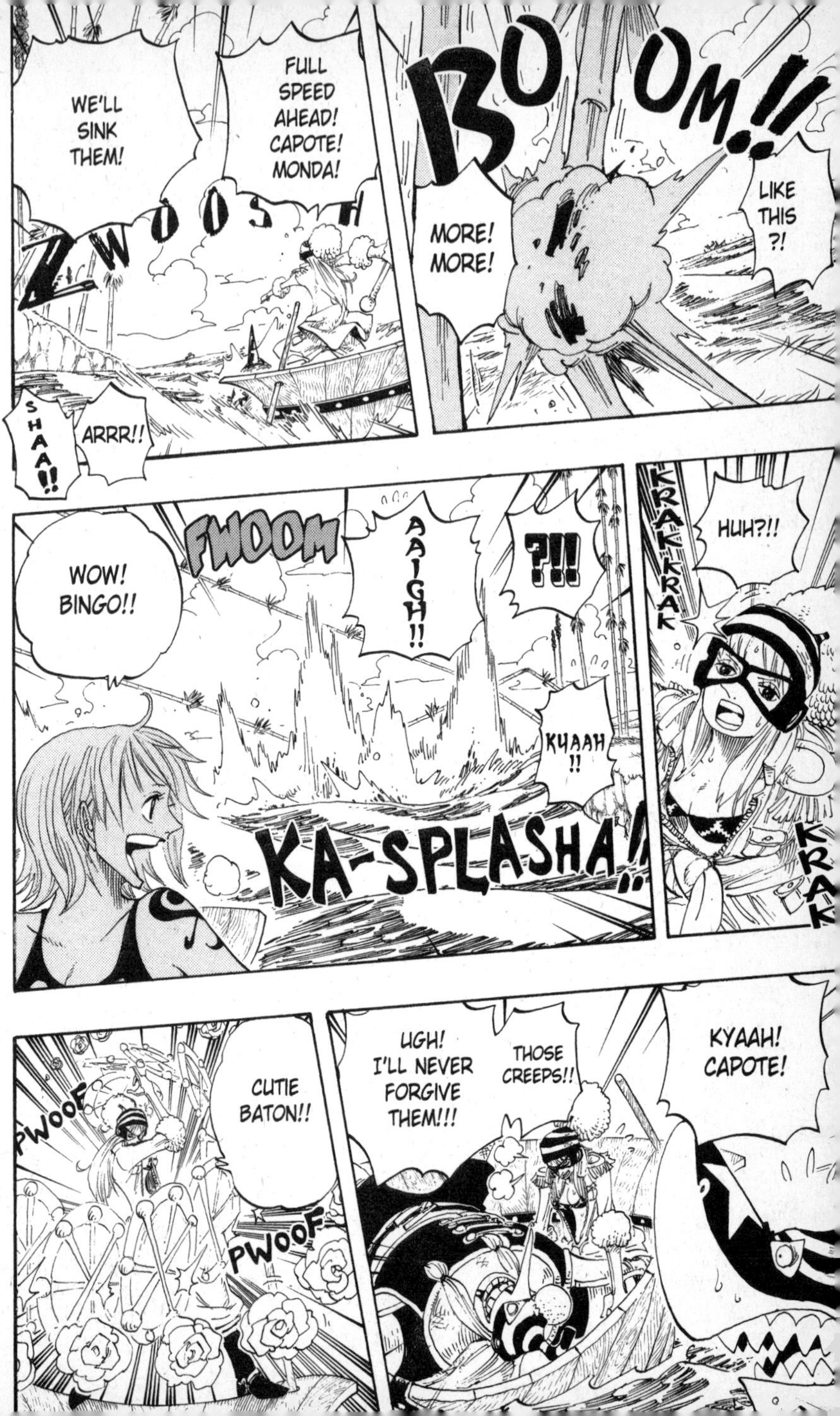
BOOM!!
LIKE THIS?!
MORE! MORE!
FULL SPEED AHEAD! CAPOTE! MONDA!
WE'LL SINK THEM!
ZWOOSH
ARRR!!
SHAAA!!
HUH?!!
KRAKKRAKKRAK
KRAKRAK
?!!
AAIGH!!
FWOOM
WOW! BINGO!!
KYAAH!!
KA-SPLASHA!!
KYAAH! CAPOTE!
THOSE CREEPS!!
UGH! I'LL NEVER FORGIVE THEM!!!
CUTIE BATON!!
PWOOF
PWOOF

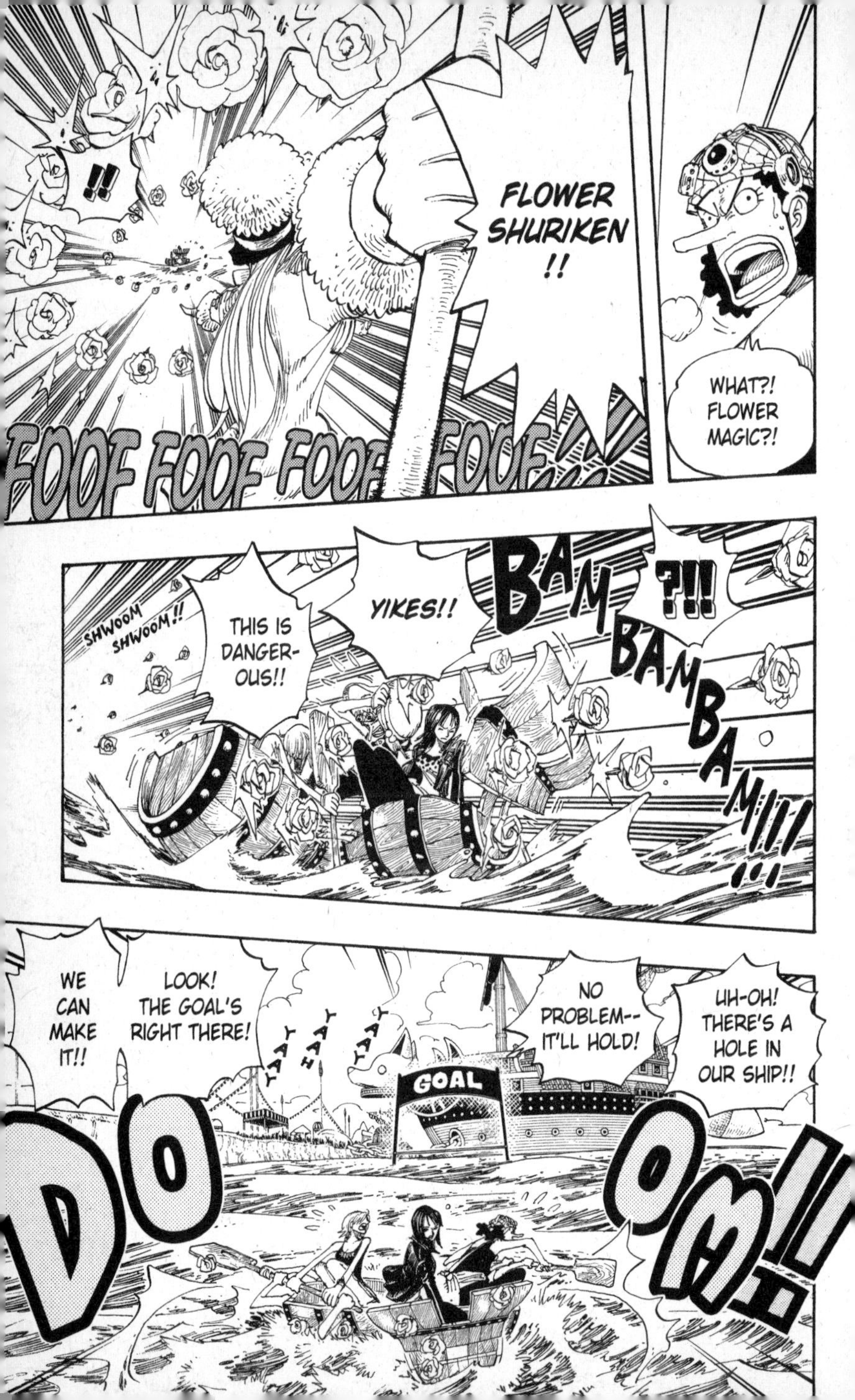

WHAT?! FLOWER MAGIC?!
FLOWER SHURIKEN!!
!!
FOOF FOOF FOOF FOOF
?!!
BAM BAMBABAM!!!
YIKES!!
THIS IS DANGER-OUS!!
SHWOOM SHWOOM!!
UH-OH! THERE'S A HOLE IN OUR SHIP!!
NO PROBLEM-- IT'LL HOLD!
YAAAY
GOAL
LOOK! THE GOAL'S RIGHT THERE!
WE CAN MAKE IT!!
DOOM!!

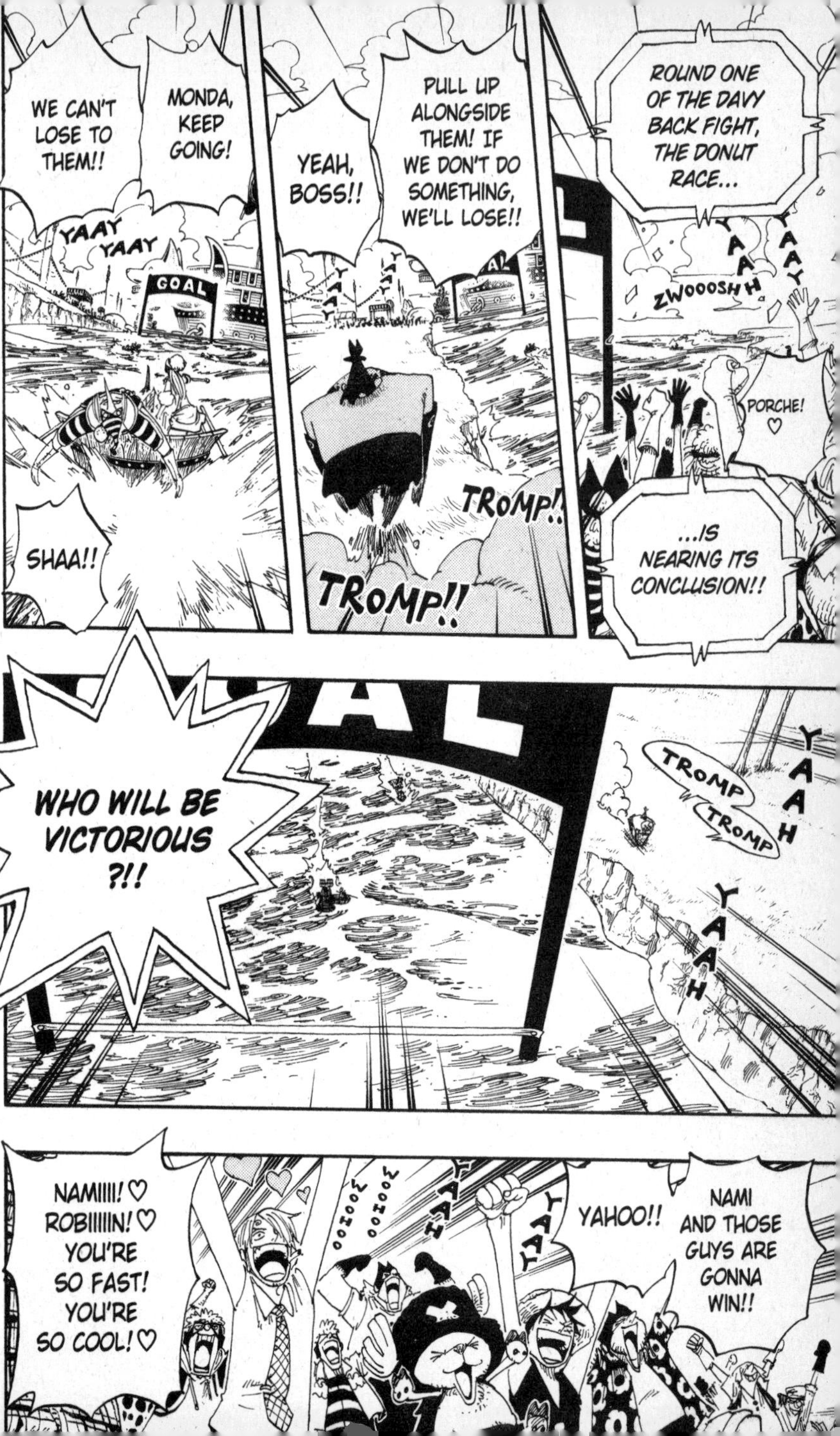
ROUND ONE OF THE DAVY BACK FIGHT, THE DONUT RACE...
YAAAH
YAAY
ZWOOOSH
PORCHE! ♡
...IS NEARING ITS CONCLUSION!!
PULL UP ALONGSIDE THEM! IF WE DON'T DO SOMETHING, WE'LL LOSE!!
YEAH, BOSS!!
YAAY
YAAY
TROMP!!
TROMP!!
MONDA, KEEP GOING!
WE CAN'T LOSE TO THEM!!
YAAY
YAAY
GOAL
SHAA!!
YAAAH
TROMP
TROMP
YAAAH
WHO WILL BE VICTORIOUS ?!!
NAMI AND THOSE GUYS ARE GONNA WIN!!
YAHOO!!
YAAY
YAAH
WOOHOO
WOOHOO
NAMIIII! ♡ ROBIIIIIN! ♡ YOU'RE SO FAST! YOU'RE SO COOL! ♡

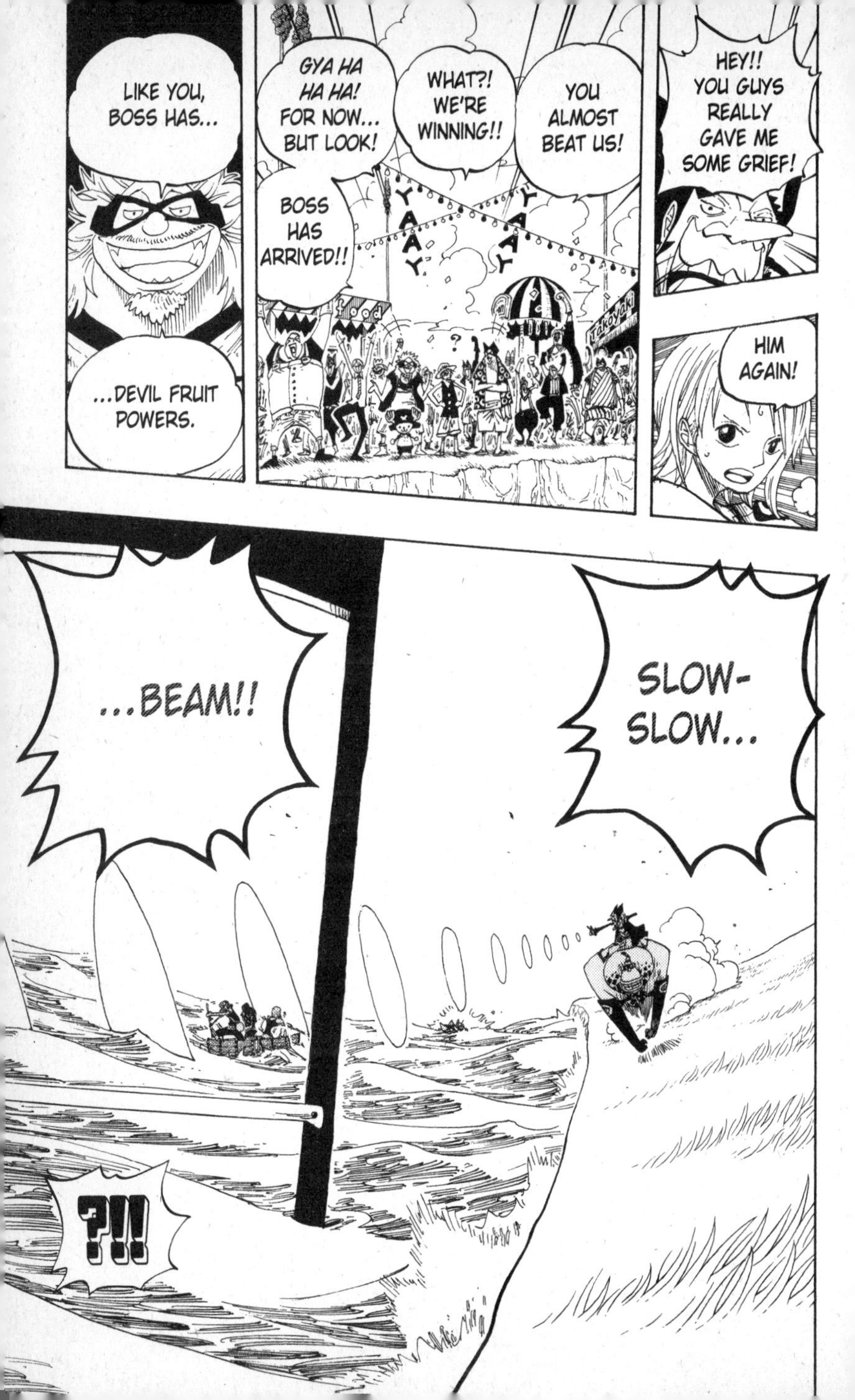
HEY!! YOU GUYS REALLY GAVE ME SOME GRIEF!
HIM AGAIN!
YOU ALMOST BEAT US!
WHAT?! WE'RE WINNING!!
GYA HA HA HA! FOR NOW... BUT LOOK!
BOSS HAS ARRIVED!!
YAAAY
YAAAY
Takoyaki
food
LIKE YOU, BOSS HAS...
...DEVIL FRUIT POWERS.
SLOW-SLOW...
...BEAM!!
?!!

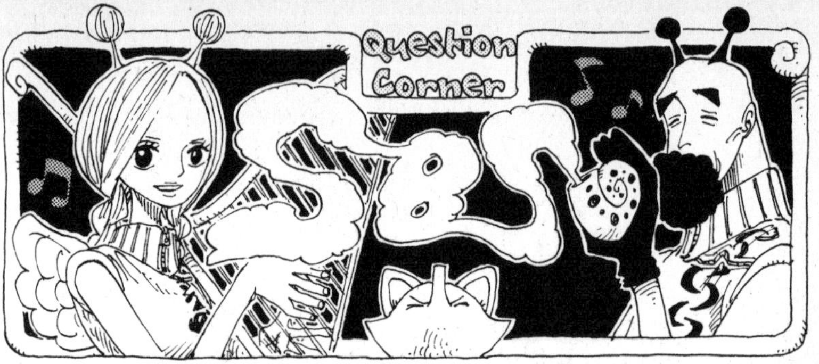
Question Corner
SBS

Q : I've got a question. If Wapol ate Luffy and Nami and Sanji and Zolo and Chopper and Usopp and Robin, and performed Miraculous Fusion like in volume 17, what would the result be?

--Kiyutarau(^_^;)

A :

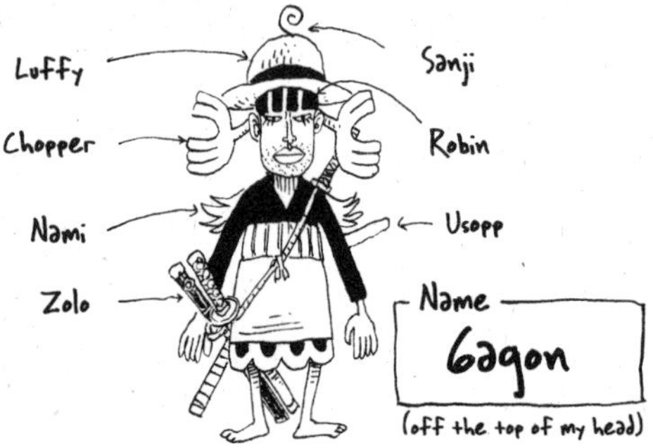
Luffy
Sanji
Chopper
Robin
Nami
Usopp
Zolo
Name
Gagon
(off the top of my head)

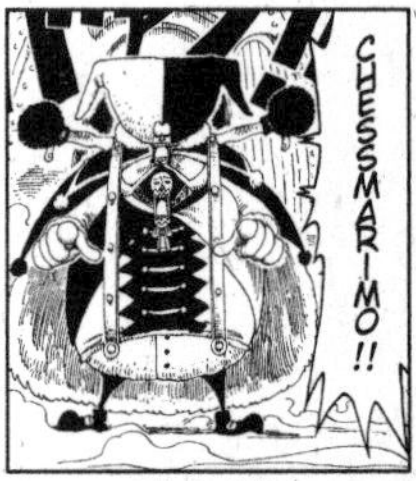
CHESSMARIMO!!
Vol. 17: MIRACULOUS FUSION

Q : Hello, Oda Sensei. I always enjoy reading your manga. I'll get right to my question. For the true identity of the "monster" in chapter 299 of volume 32, did you refer to the Brocken phenomenon often seen on the Brocken, the highest peak in Germany's Hartz Mountains? If you didn't, sorry. Please take care of your health and keep up the good work! ♡ --Akiu

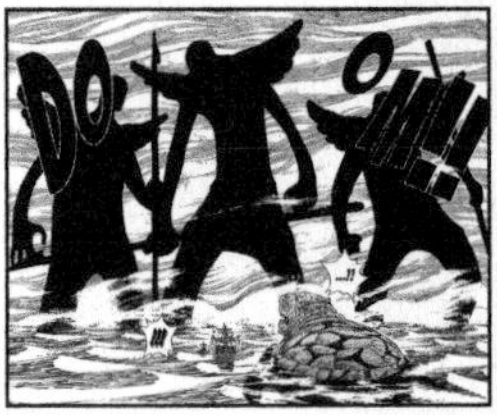
DO
OM!!

A : Yes, I did. Brocken phenomena are also known as Brocken spectres. The explanation for them is just like in the manga, but the same phenomenon also occurs in Japan. Apparently the rainbow ring that appears around the shadow's head is called a "goraigo" in Japanese, and a "glory" in English. I wish I could see it. It sounds amazing!

Chapter 309: GROGGY MONSTERS

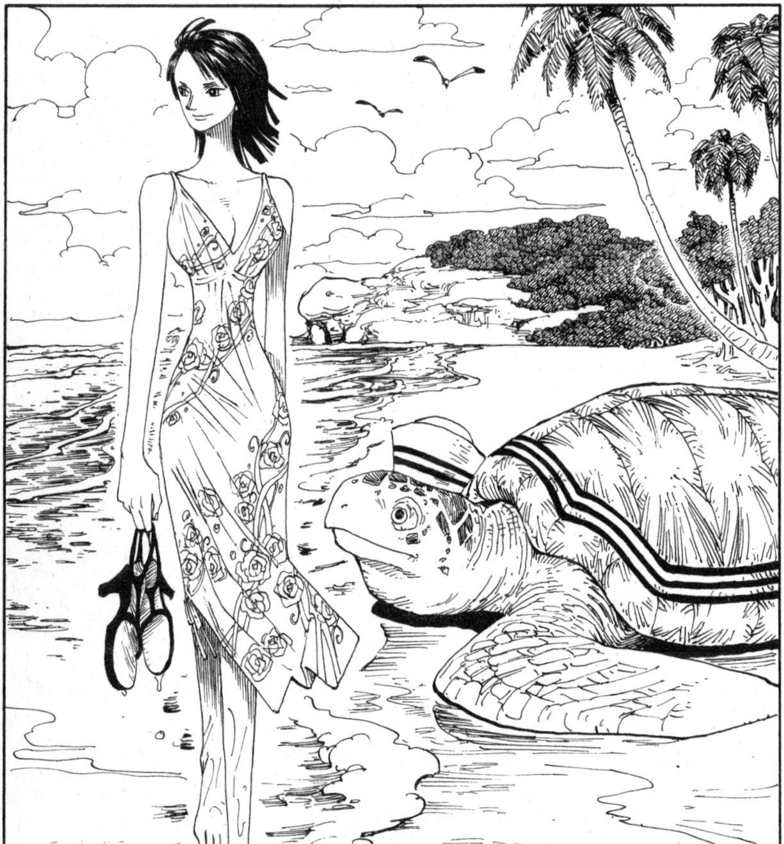

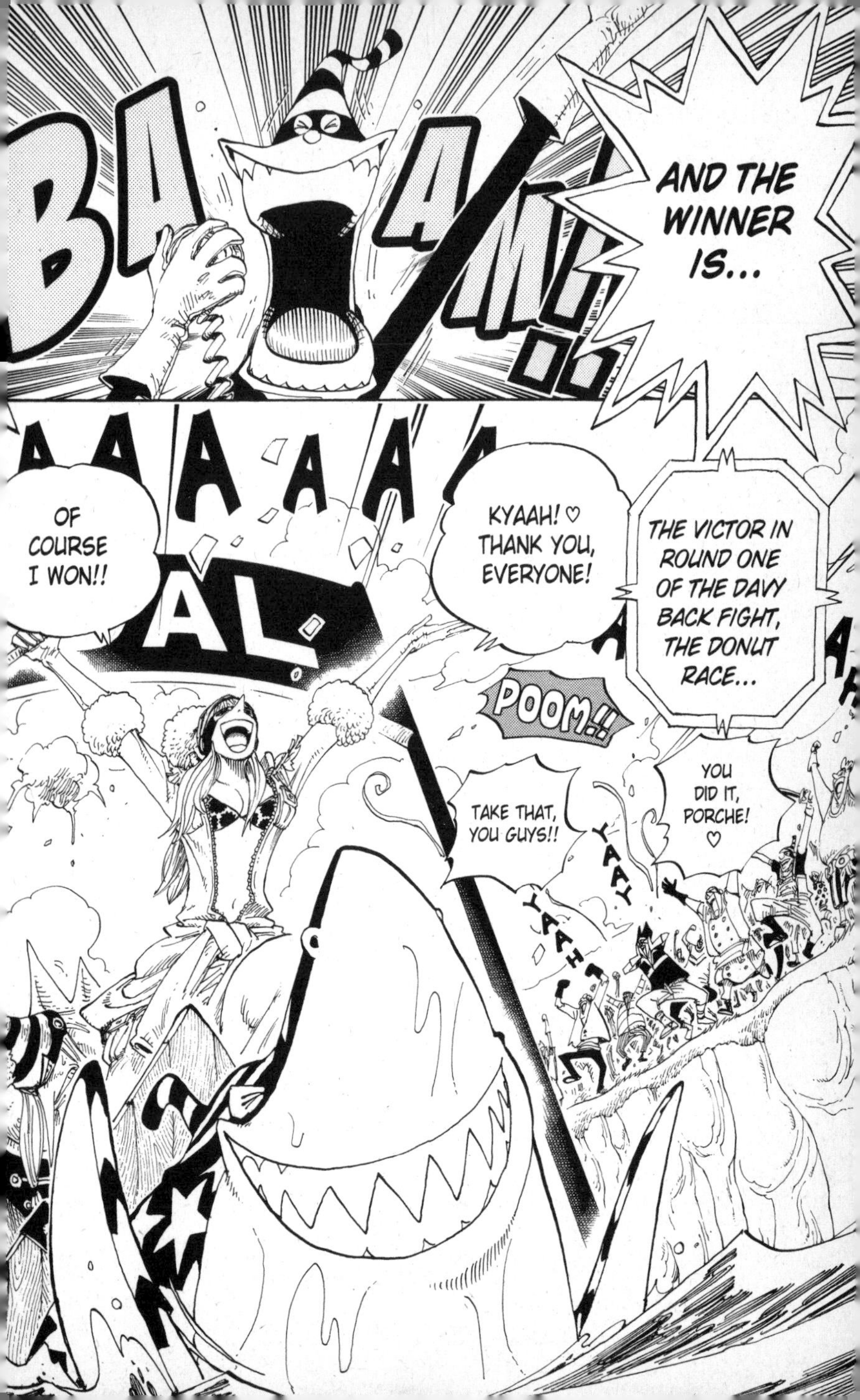
AND THE WINNER IS...
BAAM!!
THE VICTOR IN ROUND ONE OF THE DAVY BACK FIGHT, THE DONUT RACE...
POOM!!
KYAAH! ♡ THANK YOU, EVERYONE!
OF COURSE I WON!!
YOU DID IT, PORCHE! ♡
YAAAY
TAKE THAT, YOU GUYS!!
YAAAH

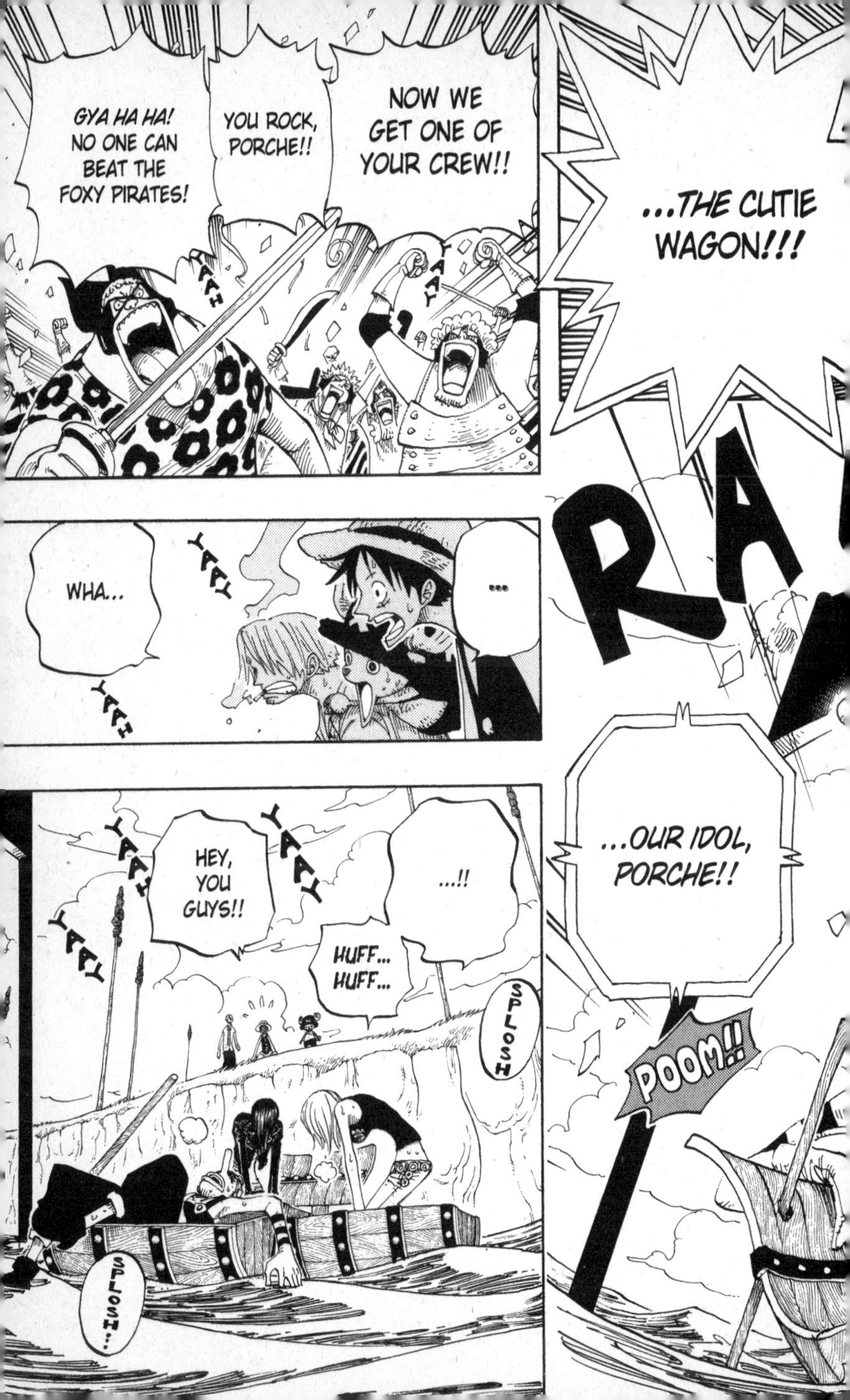
...THE CUTIE WAGON!!!
RA
...OUR IDOL, PORCHE!!
POOM!!
NOW WE GET ONE OF YOUR CREW!!
YAAY
YOU ROCK, PORCHE!!
YAAH
GYA HA HA! NO ONE CAN BEAT THE FOXY PIRATES!
...
YAAY
WHA...
YAAH
SPLOSH
...!!
YAAY
HUFF... HUFF...
HEY, YOU GUYS!!
YAAY
YAAY
SPLOSH...

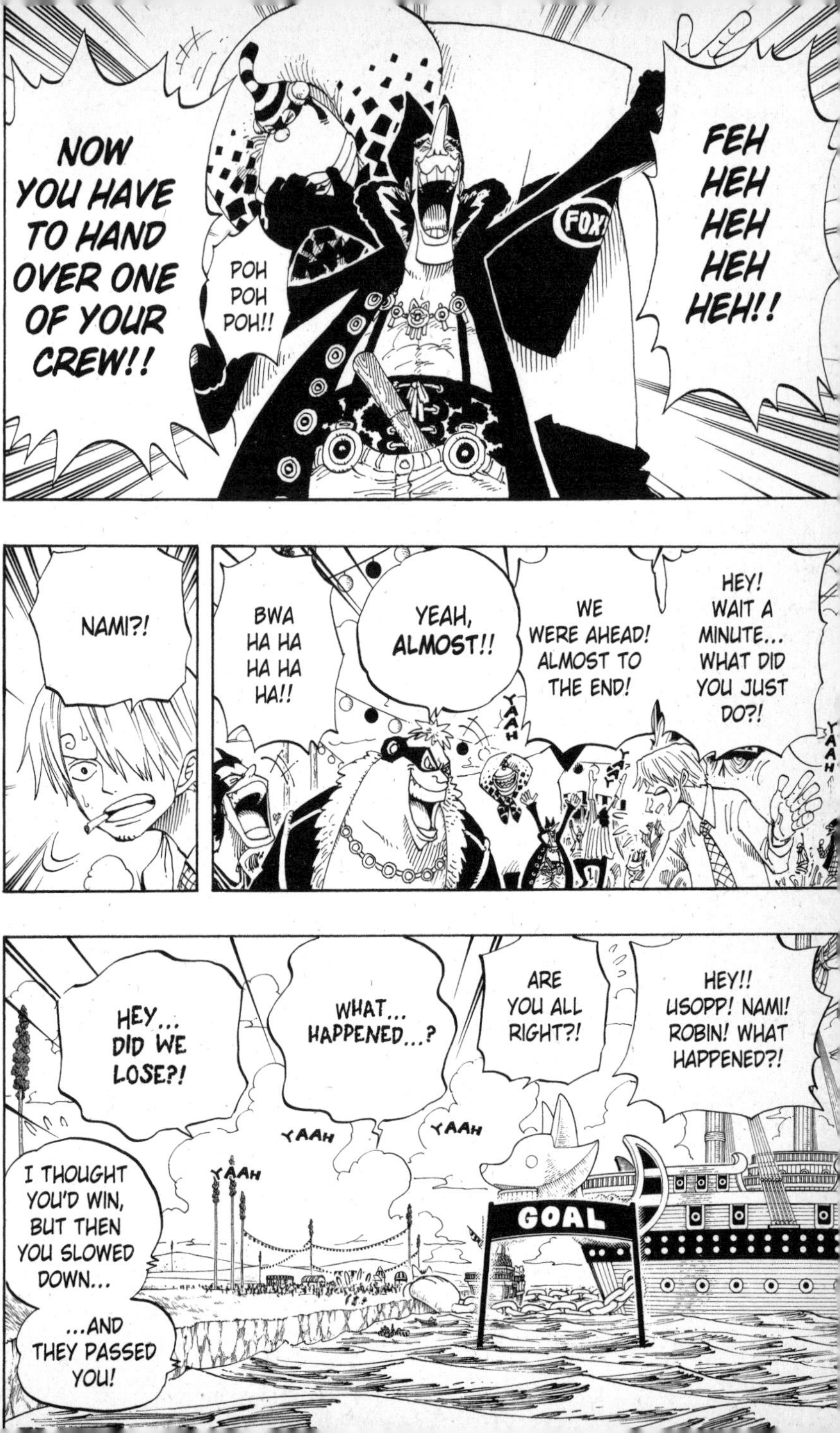
FEH HEH HEH HEH HEH!!
POH POH POH!!
NOW YOU HAVE TO HAND OVER ONE OF YOUR CREW!!
HEY! WAIT A MINUTE... WHAT DID YOU JUST DO?!
YAAH
WE WERE AHEAD! ALMOST TO THE END!
YEAH, ALMOST!!
YAAH
BWA HA HA HA HA HA!!
NAMI?!
HEY!! USOPP! NAMI! ROBIN! WHAT HAPPENED?!
ARE YOU ALL RIGHT?!
WHAT... HAPPENED...?
YAAH
HEY... DID WE LOSE?!
YAAH
GOAL
YAAH
I THOUGHT YOU'D WIN, BUT THEN YOU SLOWED DOWN...
...AND THEY PASSED YOU!

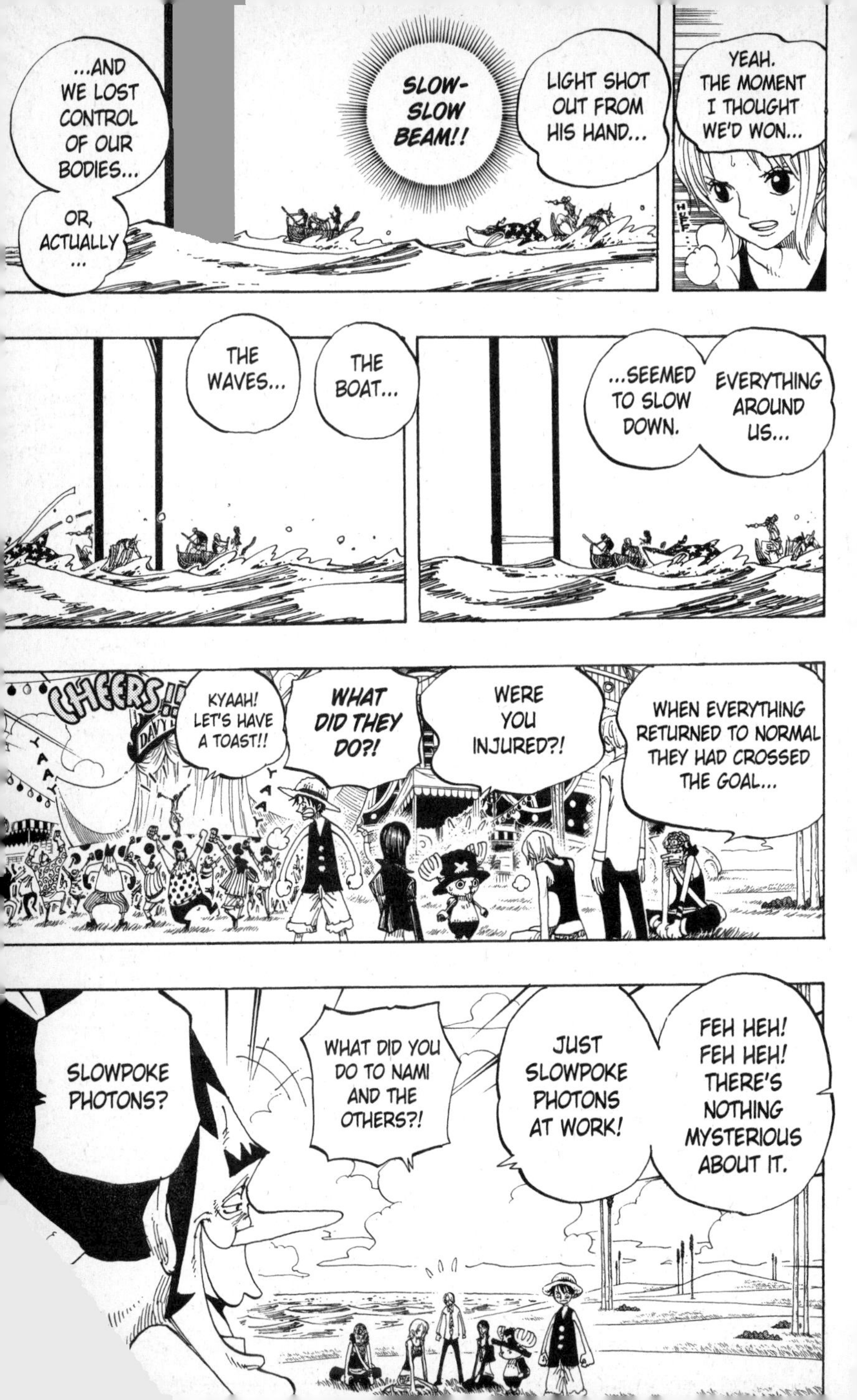
YEAH. THE MOMENT I THOUGHT WE'D WON...
LIGHT SHOT OUT FROM HIS HAND...
SLOW-SLOW BEAM!!
...AND WE LOST CONTROL OF OUR BODIES...
OR, ACTUALLY ...
EVERYTHING AROUND US...
...SEEMED TO SLOW DOWN.
THE BOAT...
THE WAVES...
WHEN EVERYTHING RETURNED TO NORMAL THEY HAD CROSSED THE GOAL...
WERE YOU INJURED?!
WHAT DID THEY DO?!
KYAAH! LET'S HAVE A TOAST!!
CHEERS!!
YAAY
YAAA
FEH HEH! FEH HEH! THERE'S NOTHING MYSTERIOUS ABOUT IT.
JUST SLOWPOKE PHOTONS AT WORK!
WHAT DID YOU DO TO NAMI AND THE OTHERS?!
SLOWPOKE PHOTONS?

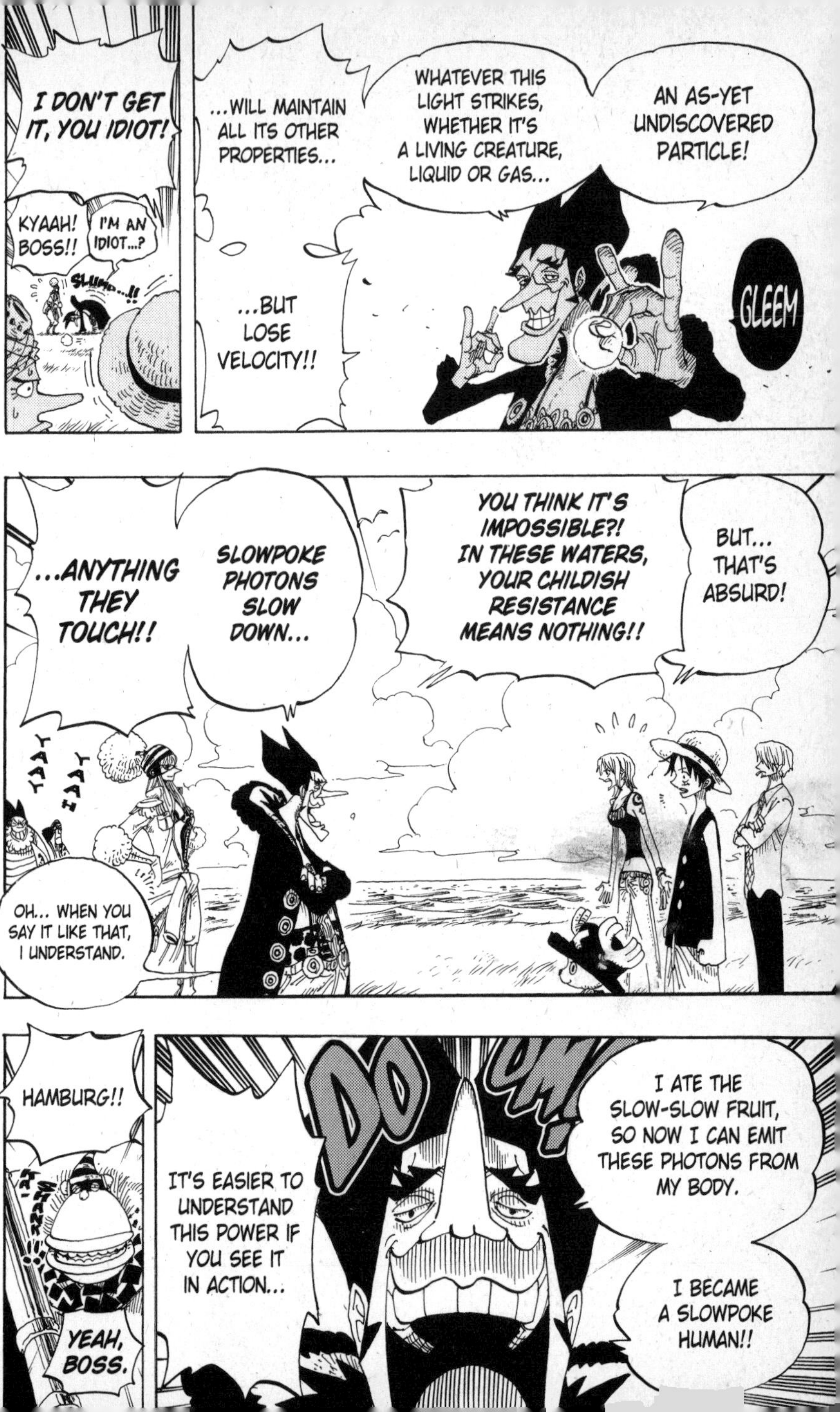
AN AS-YET UNDISCOVERED PARTICLE!
WHATEVER THIS LIGHT STRIKES, WHETHER IT'S A LIVING CREATURE, LIQUID OR GAS...
...WILL MAINTAIN ALL ITS OTHER PROPERTIES...
GLEEM
...BUT LOSE VELOCITY!!
I DON'T GET IT, YOU IDIOT!
I'M AN IDIOT...?
KYAAH! BOSS!!
BUT... THAT'S ABSURD!
YOU THINK IT'S IMPOSSIBLE?! IN THESE WATERS, YOUR CHILDISH RESISTANCE MEANS NOTHING!!
SLOWPOKE PHOTONS SLOW DOWN...
...ANYTHING THEY TOUCH!!
YAAY
YAAY
OH... WHEN YOU SAY IT LIKE THAT, I UNDERSTAND.
DOOM!
I ATE THE SLOW-SLOW FRUIT, SO NOW I CAN EMIT THESE PHOTONS FROM MY BODY.
IT'S EASIER TO UNDERSTAND THIS POWER IF YOU SEE IT IN ACTION...
I BECAME A SLOWPOKE HUMAN!!
HAMBURG!!
YEAH, BOSS.

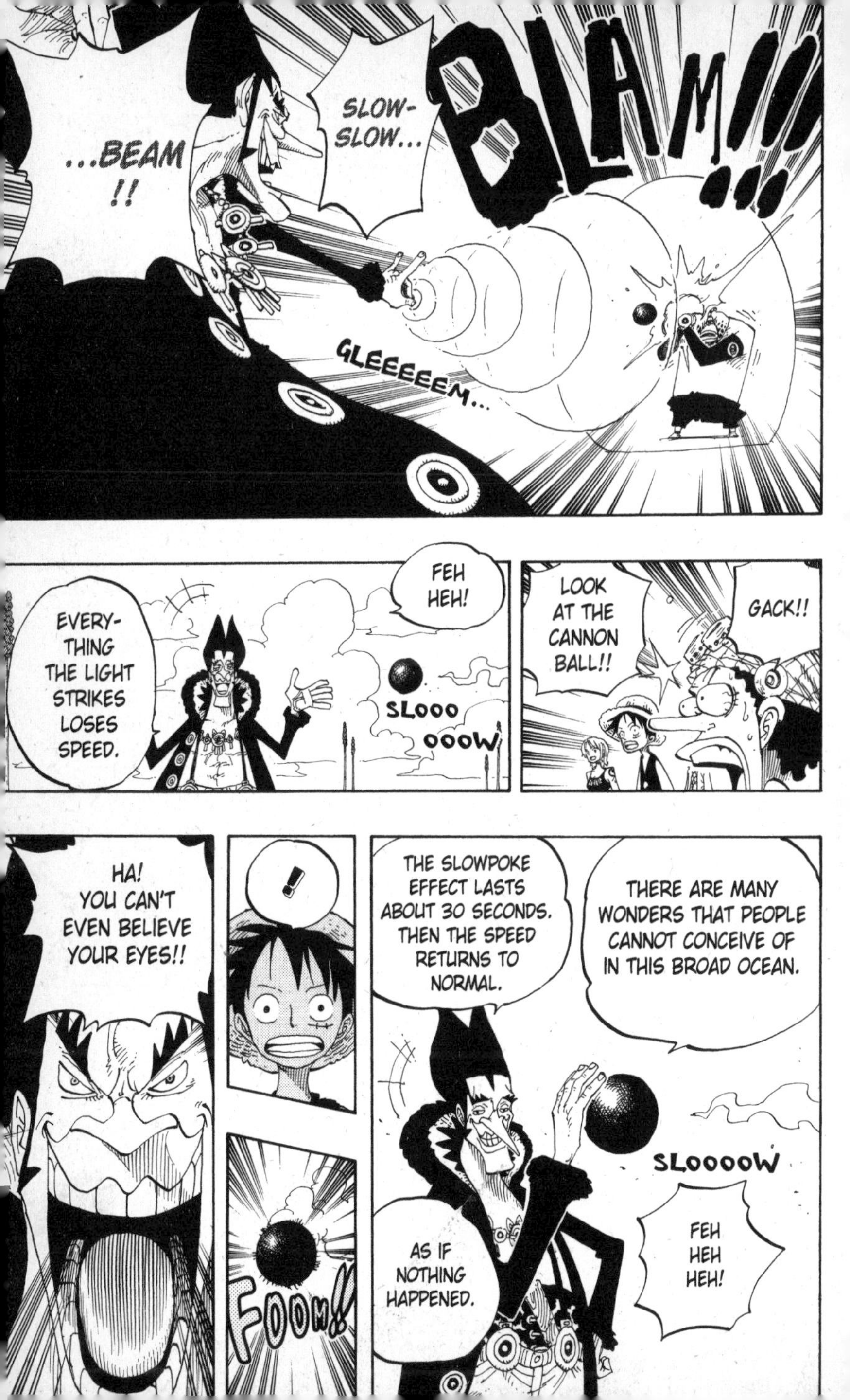
BLAM!!
SLOW-SLOW...
...BEAM !!
GLEEEEEEM...
GACK!!
LOOK AT THE CANNON BALL!!
FEH HEH!
SLOOO OOOW
EVERYTHING THE LIGHT STRIKES LOSES SPEED.
THERE ARE MANY WONDERS THAT PEOPLE CANNOT CONCEIVE OF IN THIS BROAD OCEAN.
THE SLOWPOKE EFFECT LASTS ABOUT 30 SECONDS. THEN THE SPEED RETURNS TO NORMAL.
SLOOOOW
FEH HEH HEH!
AS IF NOTHING HAPPENED.
!
FOOM!!
HA! YOU CAN'T EVEN BELIEVE YOUR EYES!!

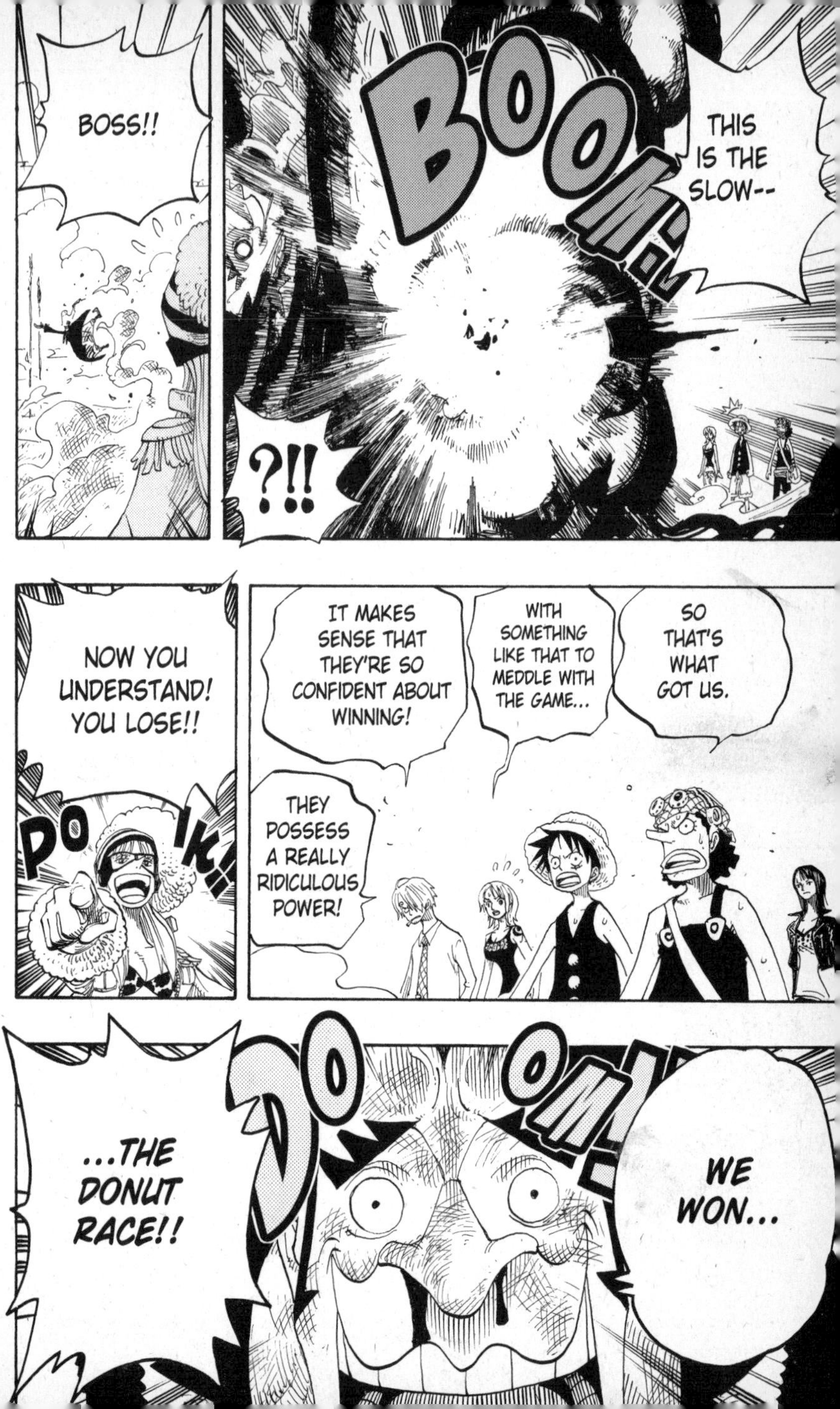
THIS IS THE SLOW--
BOOM
?!!
BOSS!!
SO THAT'S WHAT GOT US.
WITH SOMETHING LIKE THAT TO MEDDLE WITH THE GAME...
IT MAKES SENSE THAT THEY'RE SO CONFIDENT ABOUT WINNING!
THEY POSSESS A REALLY RIDICULOUS POWER!
NOW YOU UNDERSTAND! YOU LOSE!!
POIK!!
WE WON...
DOOM
...THE DONUT RACE!!

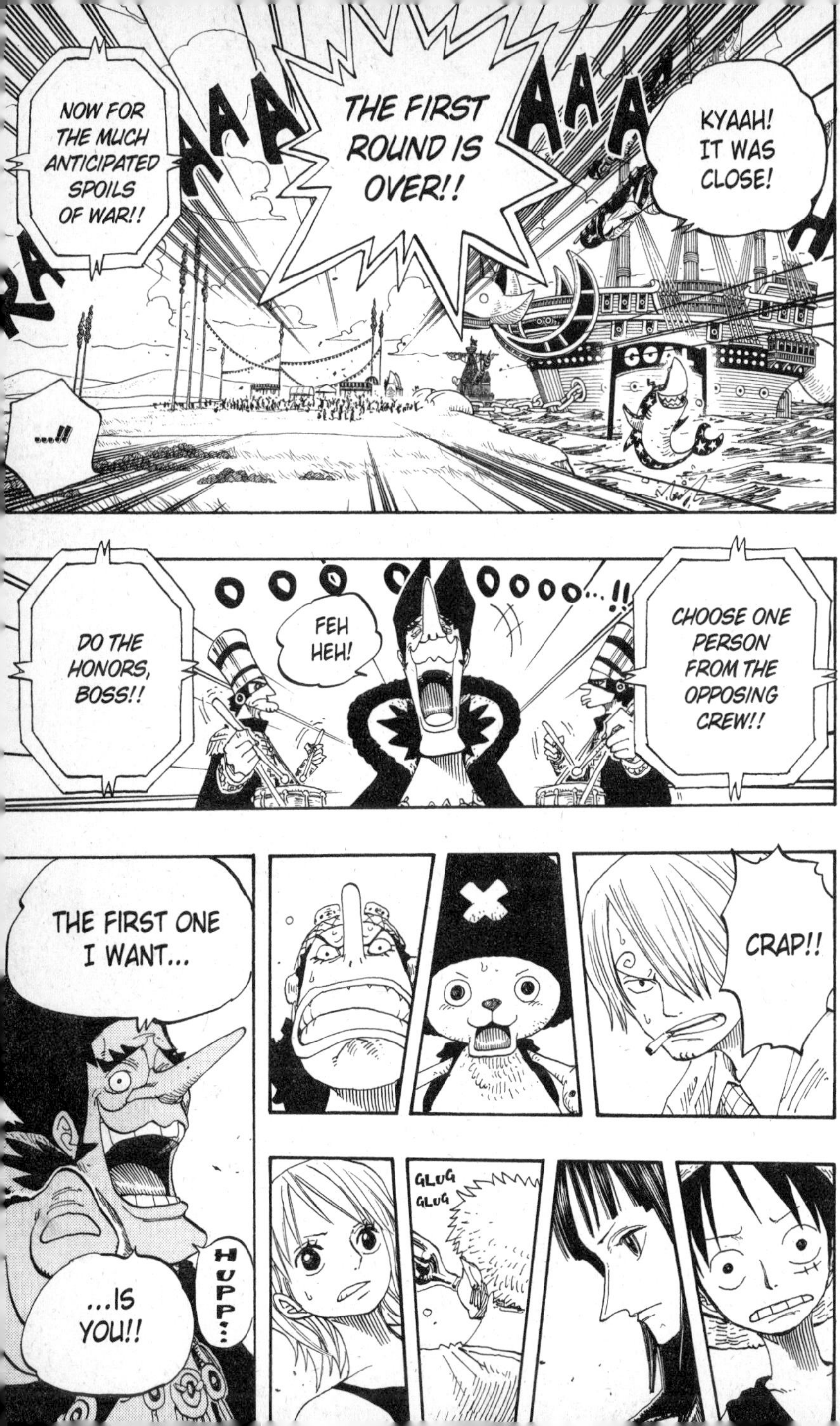
KYAAH! IT WAS CLOSE!
THE FIRST ROUND IS OVER!!
NOW FOR THE MUCH ANTICIPATED SPOILS OF WAR!!
...!!
CHOOSE ONE PERSON FROM THE OPPOSING CREW!!
OOOOOOOOO...!!
FEH HEH!
DO THE HONORS, BOSS!!
CRAP!!
GLUG GLUG
THE FIRST ONE I WANT...
...IS YOU!!
HUPP!..

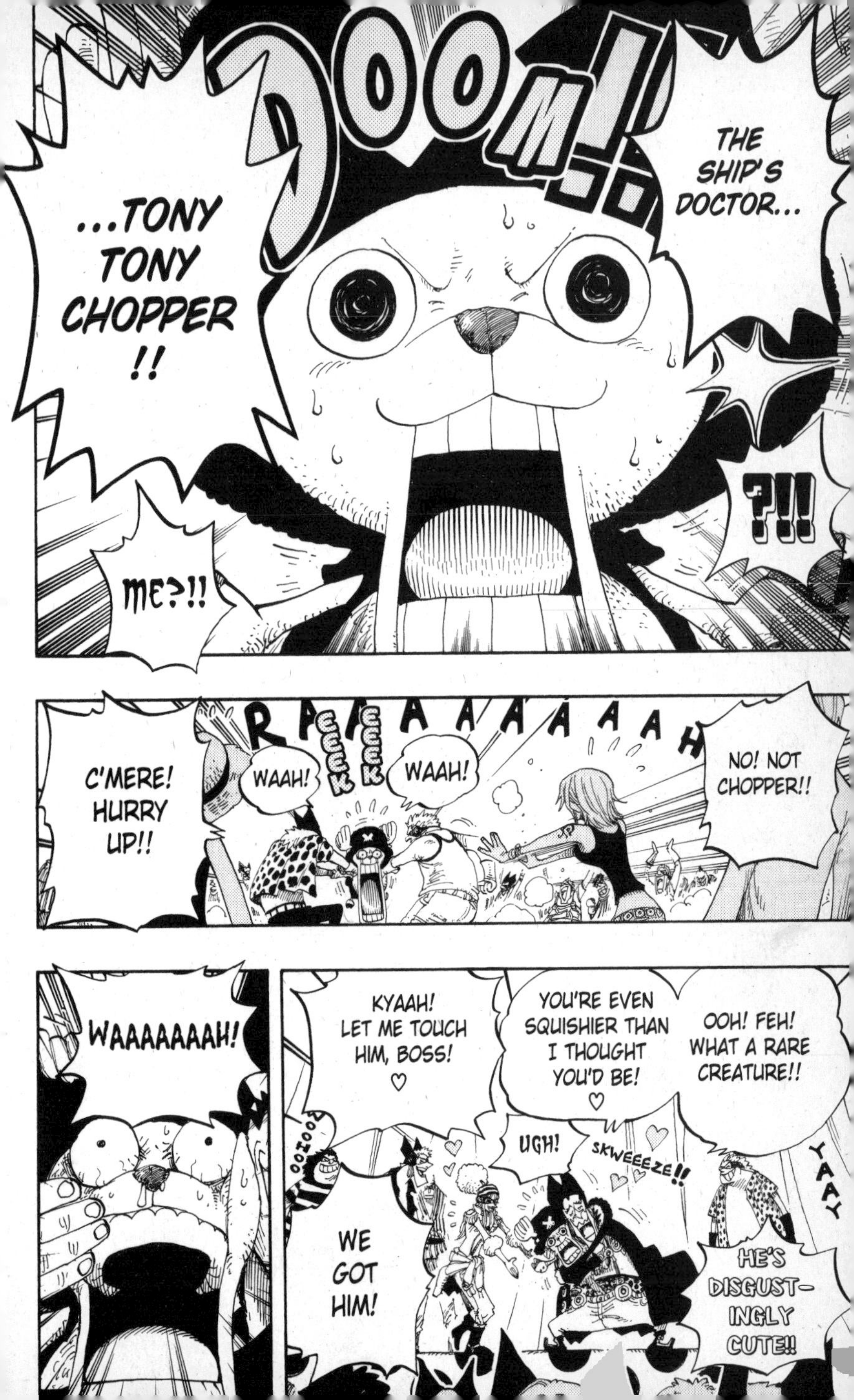
THE SHIP'S DOCTOR...
DOOM!
...TONY TONY CHOPPER!!
?!!
ME?!!
NO! NOT CHOPPER!!
RAAAAAAAAH
WAAH!
EEEK
EEEK
WAAH!
C'MERE! HURRY UP!!
OOH! FEH! WHAT A RARE CREATURE!!
YOU'RE EVEN SQUISHIER THAN I THOUGHT YOU'D BE! ♡
KYAAH! LET ME TOUCH HIM, BOSS! ♡
YAAY
SKWEEEZE!!
UGH!
HE'S DISGUST-INGLY CUTE!!
WE GOT HIM!
WAAAAAAAH!

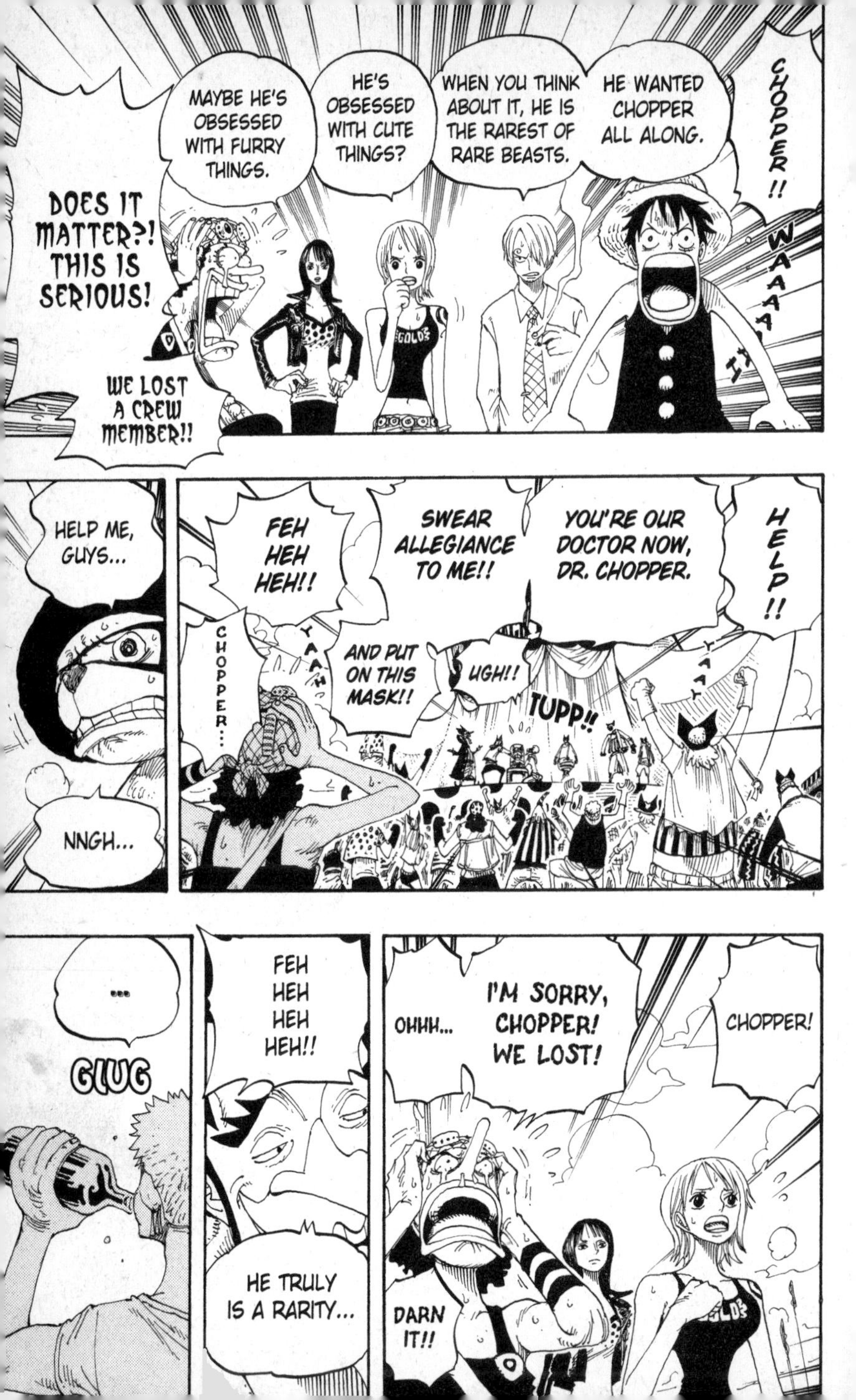
CHOPPER!!
HE WANTED CHOPPER ALL ALONG.
WHEN YOU THINK ABOUT IT, HE IS THE RAREST OF RARE BEASTS.
HE'S OBSESSED WITH CUTE THINGS?
MAYBE HE'S OBSESSED WITH FURRY THINGS.
WAAAA
DOES IT MATTER?! THIS IS SERIOUS!
WE LOST A CREW MEMBER!!
HELP!!
YOU'RE OUR DOCTOR NOW, DR. CHOPPER.
SWEAR ALLEGIANCE TO ME!!
FEH HEH HEH!!
YAAAY
UGH!!
AND PUT ON THIS MASK!!
TUPP!!
YAAH
CHOPPER...
HELP ME, GUYS...
NNGH...
CHOPPER!
I'M SORRY, CHOPPER! WE LOST!
OHHH...
DARN IT!!
FEH HEH HEH HEH!!
HE TRULY IS A RARITY...
...
GLUG

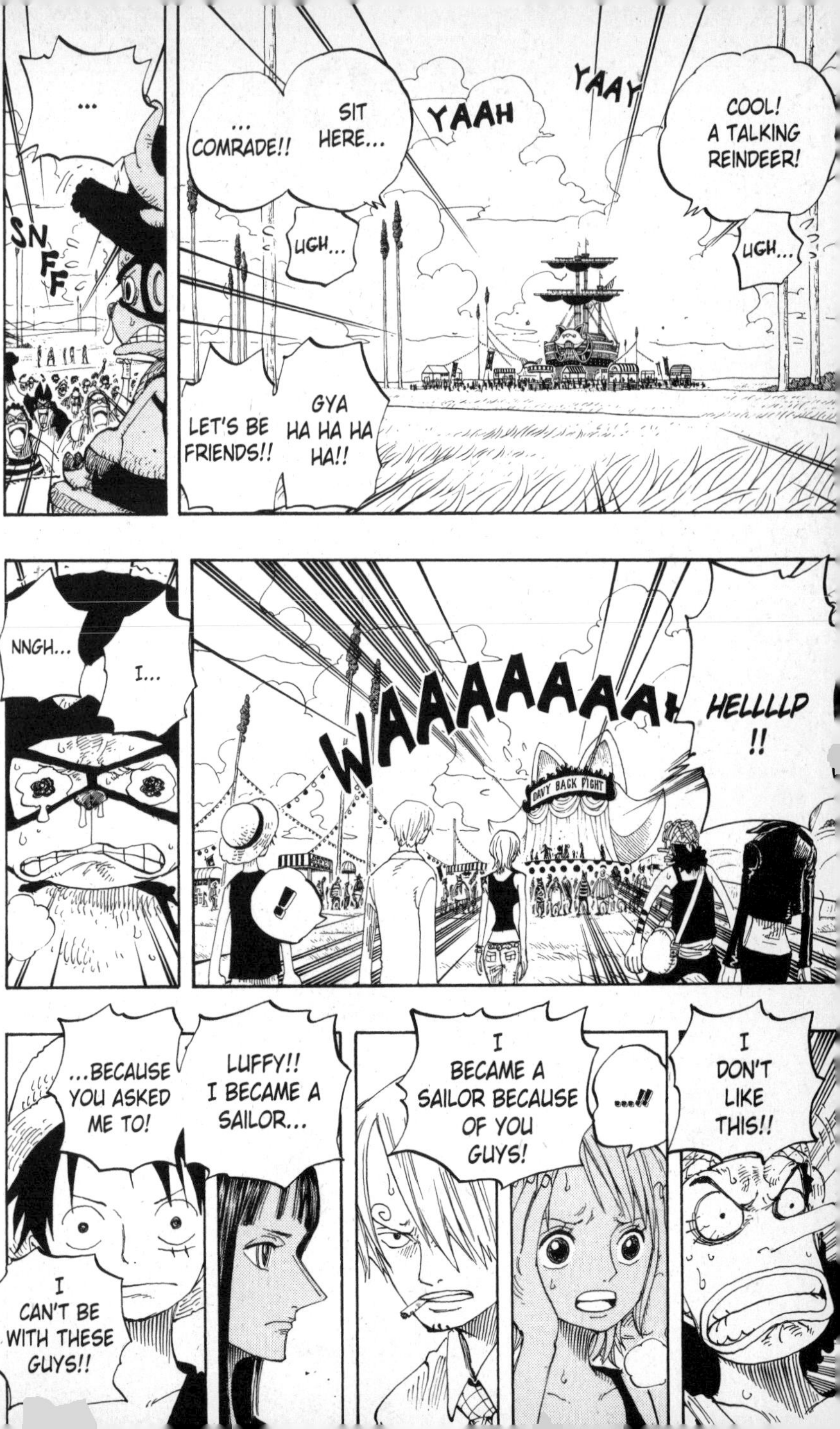
COOL! A TALKING REINDEER!
UGH...
YAAY
YAAH
SIT HERE...
... COMRADE!!
UGH...
GYA HA HA HA HA!!
LET'S BE FRIENDS!!
...
SNFF
HELLLLP !!
WAAAAAAA
!
I...
NNGH...
I DON'T LIKE THIS!!
...!!
I BECAME A SAILOR BECAUSE OF YOU GUYS!
LUFFY!! I BECAME A SAILOR...
...BECAUSE YOU ASKED ME TO!
I CAN'T BE WITH THESE GUYS!!

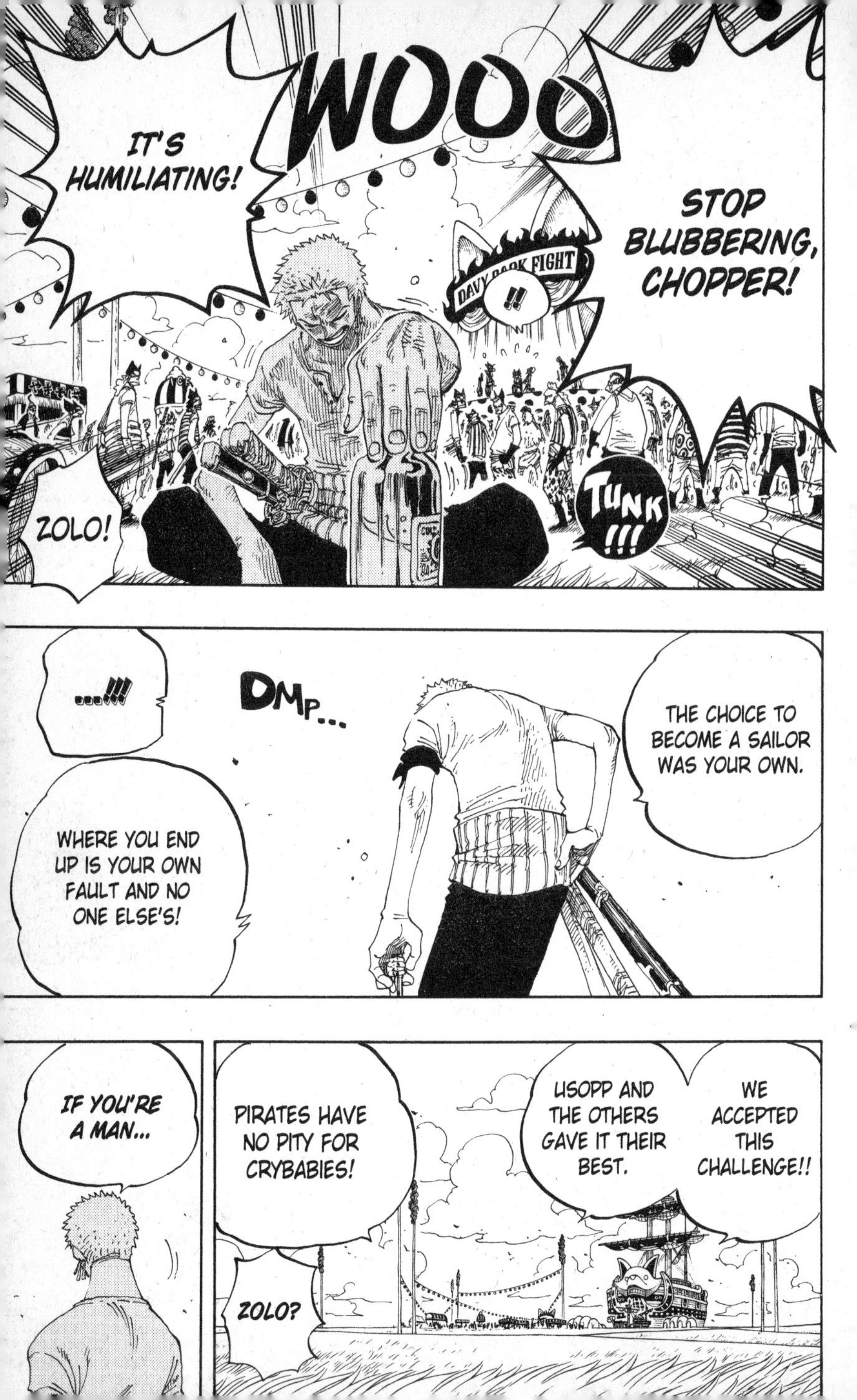
STOP BLUBBERING, CHOPPER!
WOOO
IT'S HUMILIATING!
DAVY BACK FIGHT
!!
TUNK!!!
ZOLO!
THE CHOICE TO BECOME A SAILOR WAS YOUR OWN.
DMP...
...!!!
WHERE YOU END UP IS YOUR OWN FAULT AND NO ONE ELSE'S!
WE ACCEPTED THIS CHALLENGE!!
USOPP AND THE OTHERS GAVE IT THEIR BEST.
PIRATES HAVE NO PITY FOR CRYBABIES!
ZOLO?
IF YOU'RE A MAN...

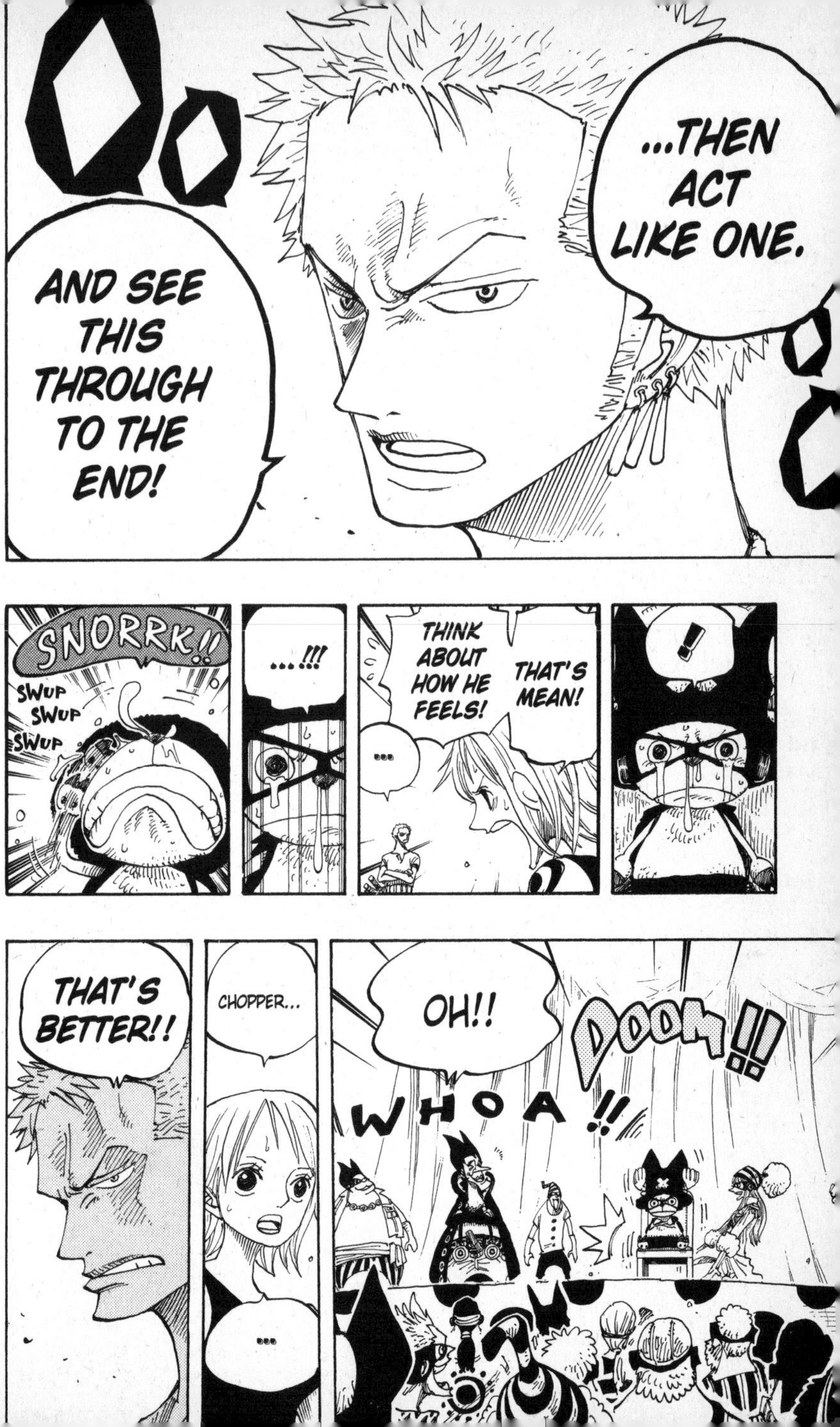
...THEN ACT LIKE ONE.
AND SEE THIS THROUGH TO THE END!
!
THAT'S MEAN!
THINK ABOUT HOW HE FEELS!
...
...!!!
SNORRK!!
SWUP SWUP SWUP
OH!!
DOOM!!
WHOA!!
CHOPPER...
...
THAT'S BETTER!!

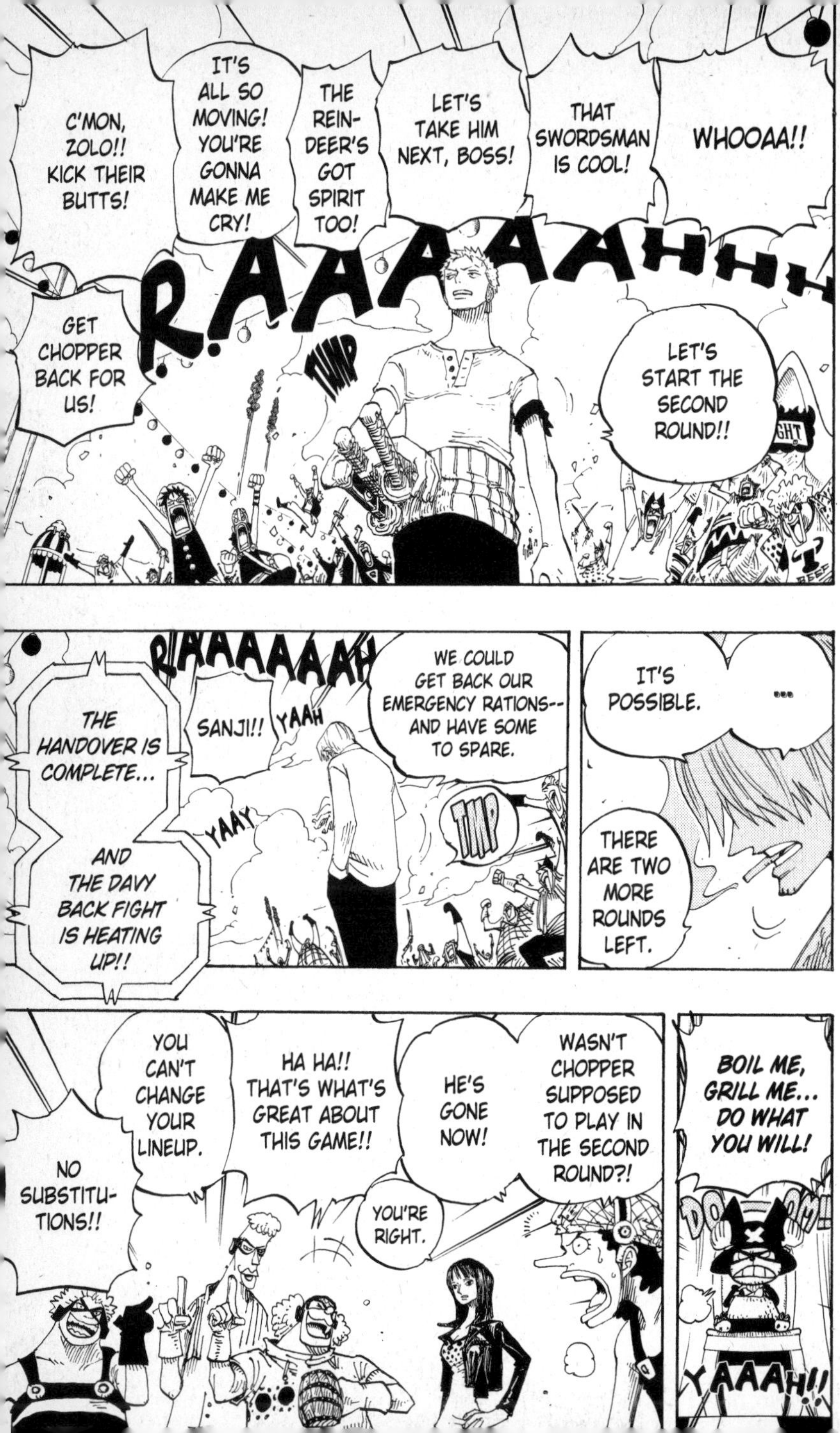
WHOOAA!!
THAT SWORDSMAN IS COOL!
LET'S TAKE HIM NEXT, BOSS!
THE REIN-DEER'S GOT SPIRIT TOO!
IT'S ALL SO MOVING! YOU'RE GONNA MAKE ME CRY!
C'MON, ZOLO!! KICK THEIR BUTTS!
RAAAAAHHHH
LET'S START THE SECOND ROUND!!
TMP
GET CHOPPER BACK FOR US!
...
IT'S POSSIBLE.
THERE ARE TWO MORE ROUNDS LEFT.
RAAAAAAH
WE COULD GET BACK OUR EMERGENCY RATIONS-- AND HAVE SOME TO SPARE.
SANJI!!
YAAH
THE HANDOVER IS COMPLETE...
TMP
YAAY
AND THE DAVY BACK FIGHT IS HEATING UP!!
BOIL ME, GRILL ME... DO WHAT YOU WILL!
YAAAH!!
WASN'T CHOPPER SUPPOSED TO PLAY IN THE SECOND ROUND?!
HE'S GONE NOW!
YOU'RE RIGHT.
HA HA!! THAT'S WHAT'S GREAT ABOUT THIS GAME!!
YOU CAN'T CHANGE YOUR LINEUP.
NO SUBSTITU-TIONS!!

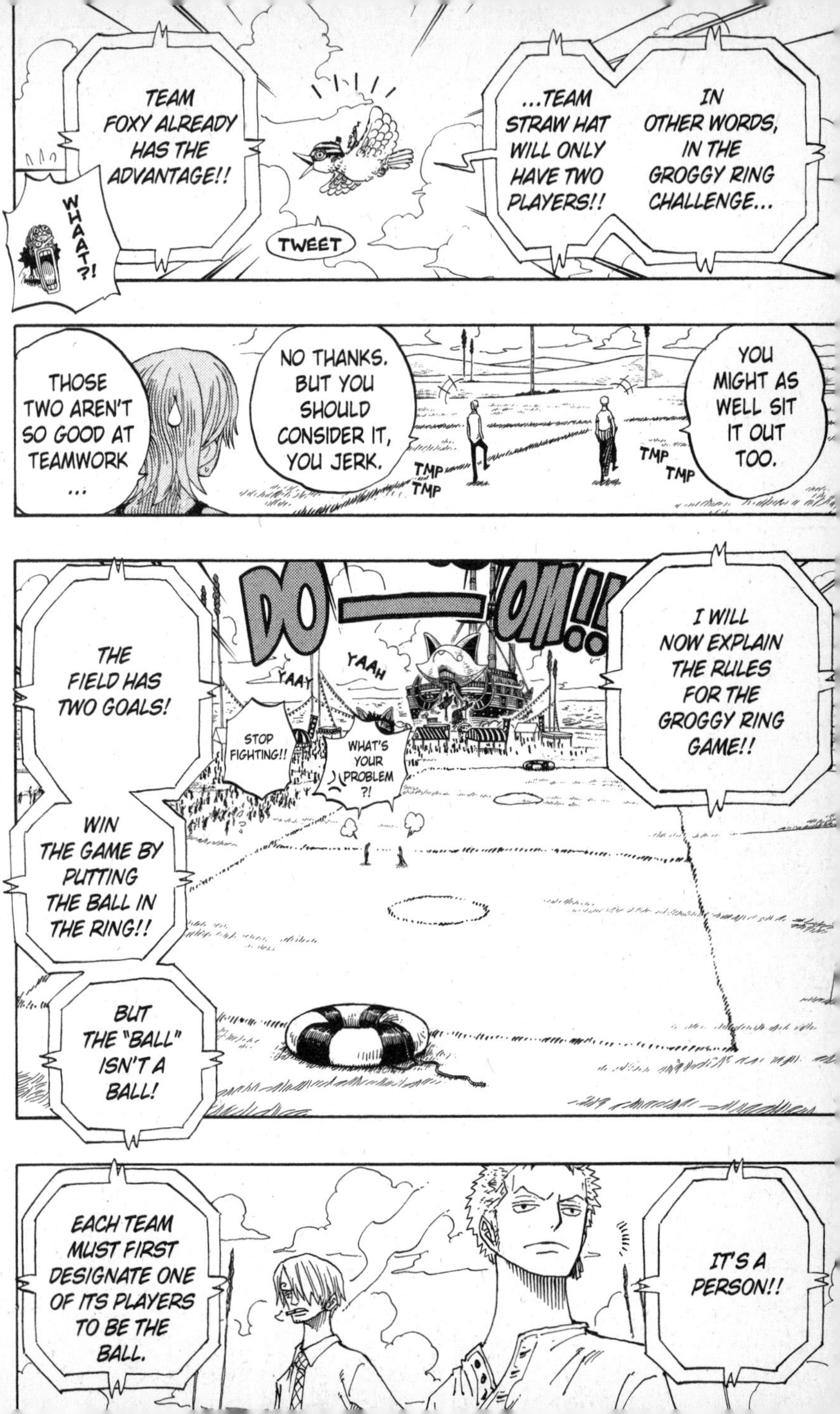
IN OTHER WORDS, IN THE GROGGY RING CHALLENGE...
...TEAM STRAW HAT WILL ONLY HAVE TWO PLAYERS!!
TWEET
TEAM FOXY ALREADY HAS THE ADVANTAGE!!
WHAAT?!
YOU MIGHT AS WELL SIT IT OUT TOO.
TMP TMP
NO THANKS. BUT YOU SHOULD CONSIDER IT, YOU JERK.
TMP TMP
THOSE TWO AREN'T SO GOOD AT TEAMWORK ...
I WILL NOW EXPLAIN THE RULES FOR THE GROGGY RING GAME!!
DO—OM!!
YAAH
YAAY
WHAT'S YOUR PROBLEM ?!
STOP FIGHTING!!
THE FIELD HAS TWO GOALS!
WIN THE GAME BY PUTTING THE BALL IN THE RING!!
BUT THE "BALL" ISN'T A BALL!
IT'S A PERSON!!
EACH TEAM MUST FIRST DESIGNATE ONE OF ITS PLAYERS TO BE THE BALL.

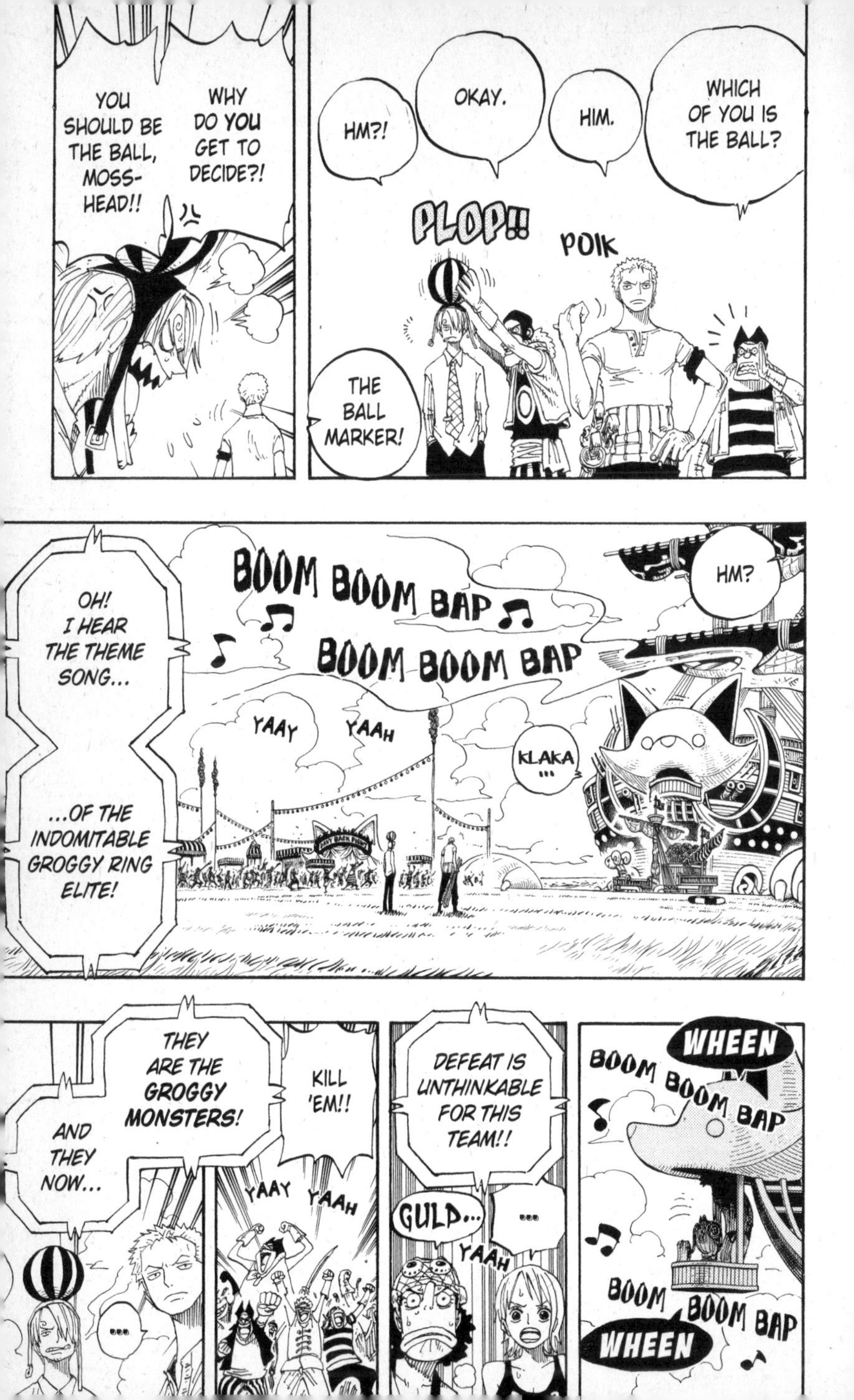
WHICH OF YOU IS THE BALL?
HIM.
OKAY.
HM?!
POIK
PLOP!!
THE BALL MARKER!
WHY DO YOU GET TO DECIDE?!
YOU SHOULD BE THE BALL, MOSS-HEAD!!
HM?
BOOM BOOM BAP
BOOM BOOM BAP
KLAKA ...
YAAH
YAAY
OH! I HEAR THE THEME SONG...
...OF THE INDOMITABLE GROGGY RING ELITE!
WHEEN
BOOM BOOM BAP
BOOM BOOM BAP
WHEEN
DEFEAT IS UNTHINKABLE FOR THIS TEAM!!
...
GULP...
YAAH
KILL 'EM!!
YAAH
YAAY
THEY ARE THE GROGGY MONSTERS!
AND THEY NOW...
...

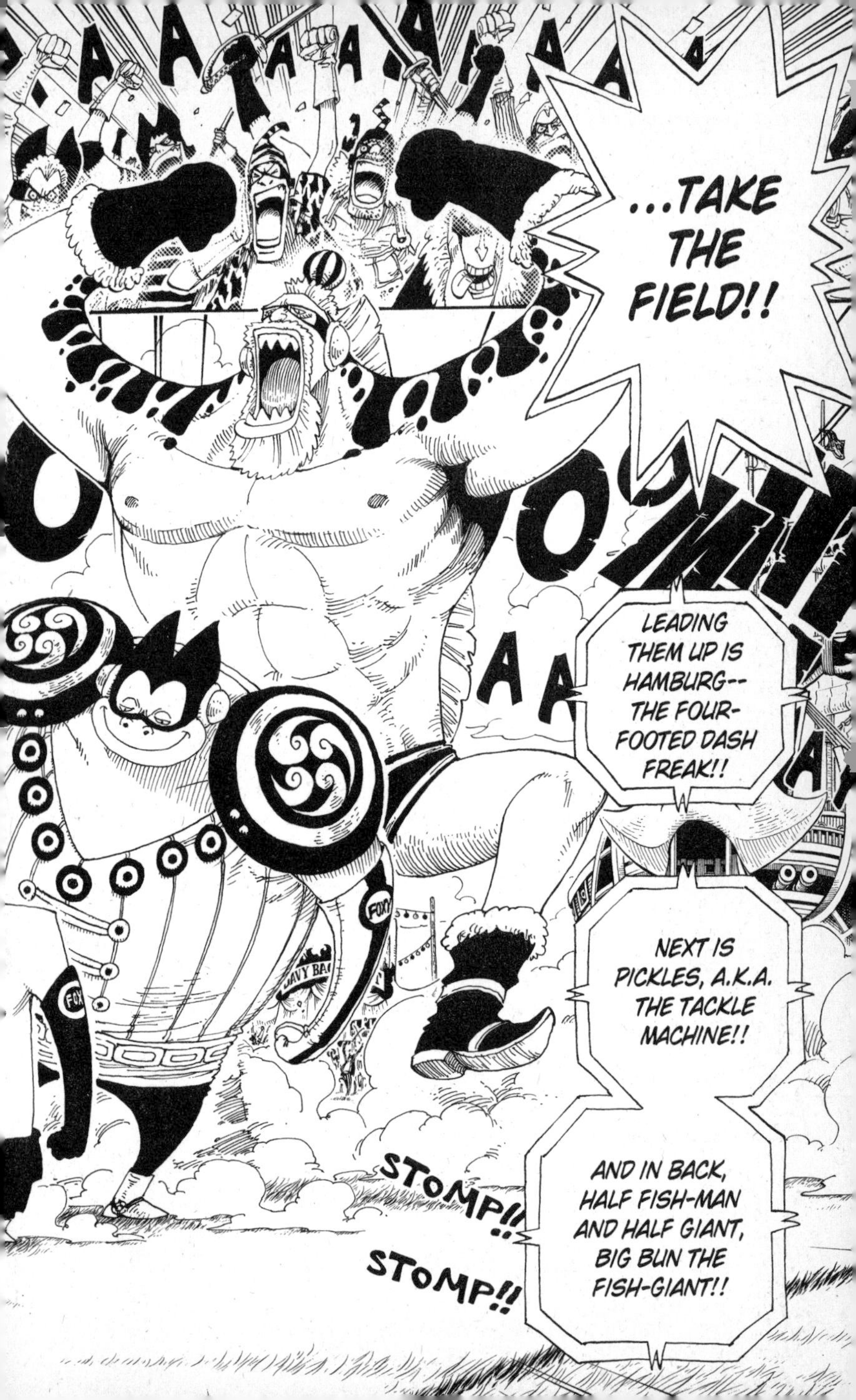
...TAKE THE FIELD!!
LEADING THEM UP IS HAMBURG-- THE FOUR-FOOTED DASH FREAK!!
NEXT IS PICKLES, A.K.A. THE TACKLE MACHINE!!
AND IN BACK, HALF FISH-MAN AND HALF GIANT, BIG BUN THE FISH-GIANT!!
STOMP!!
STOMP!!

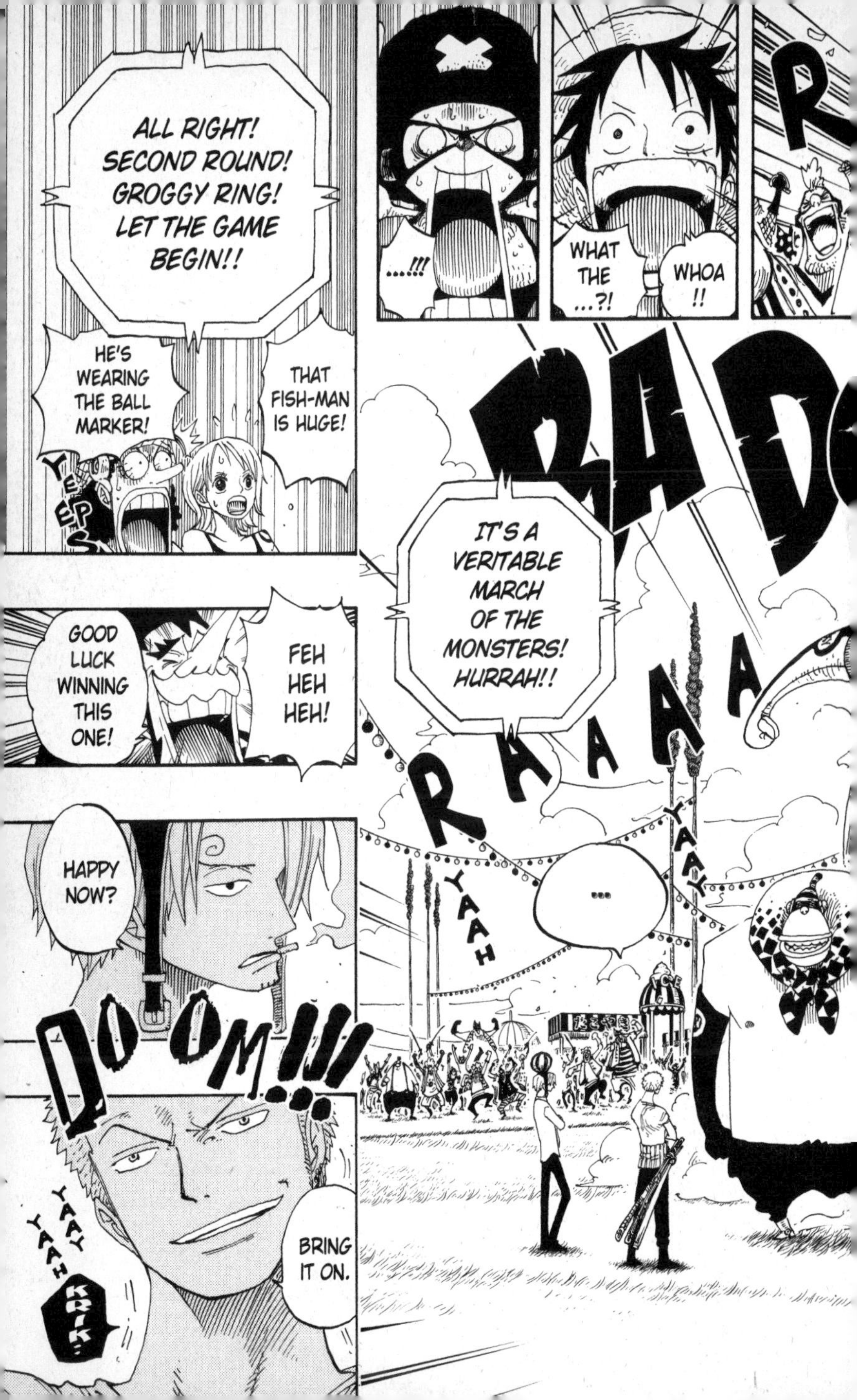
R
WHOA !!
WHAT THE ...?!
...!!!
RADO
IT'S A VERITABLE MARCH OF THE MONSTERS! HURRAH!!
RAAAAA
YAAAY
...
YAAH
ALL RIGHT! SECOND ROUND! GROGGY RING! LET THE GAME BEGIN!!
THAT FISH-MAN IS HUGE!
HE'S WEARING THE BALL MARKER!
YEEPS
FEH HEH HEH!
GOOD LUCK WINNING THIS ONE!
HAPPY NOW?
DOOM!!!
BRING IT ON.
YAAY
YAAH
KRIK

GROGGY RING!!

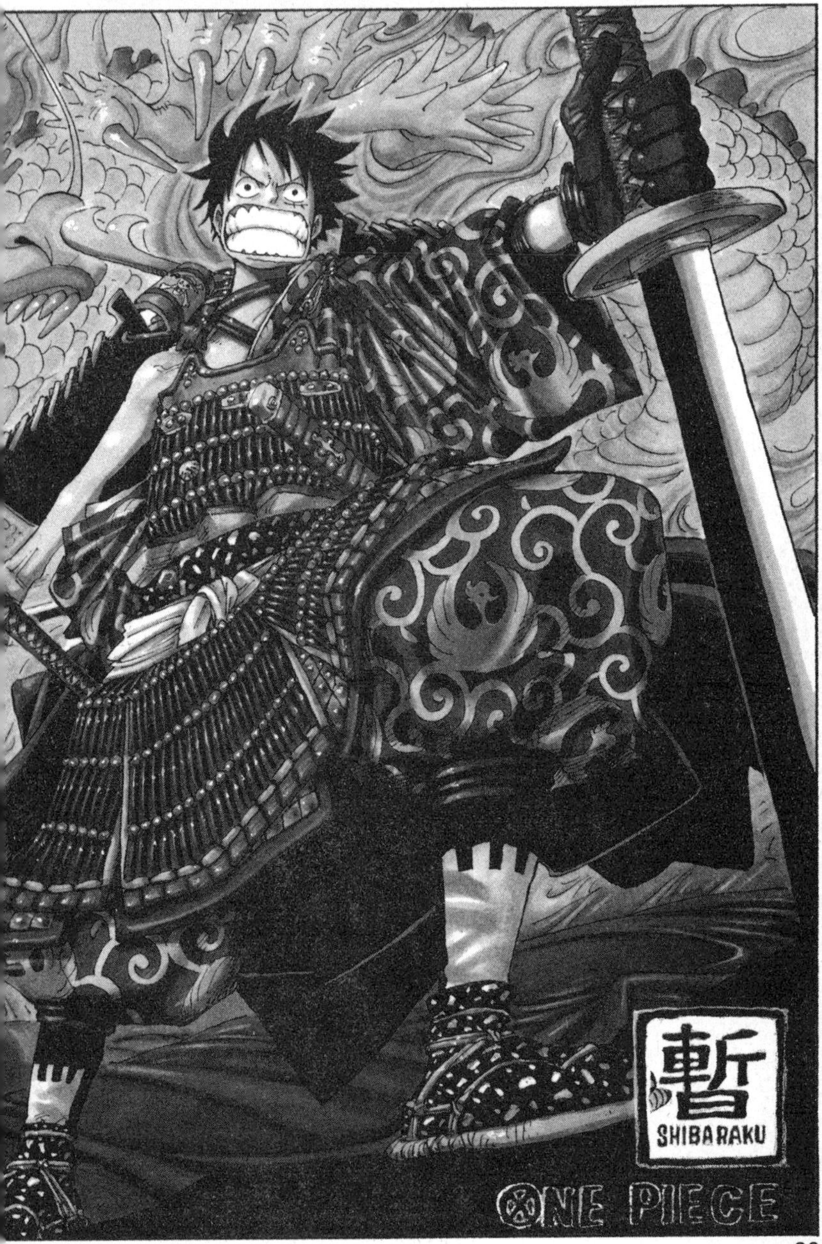
暫
SHIBARAKU
ONE PIECE

Chapter 310:

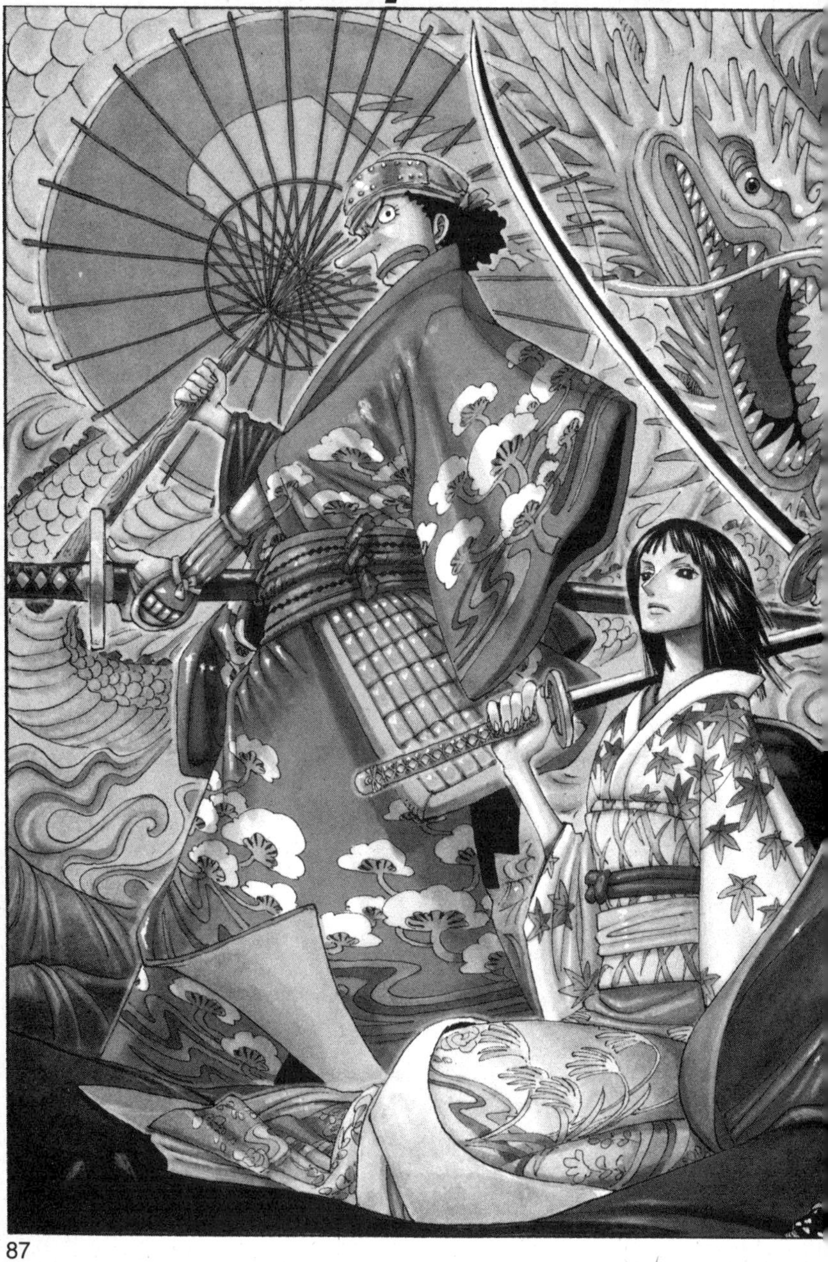

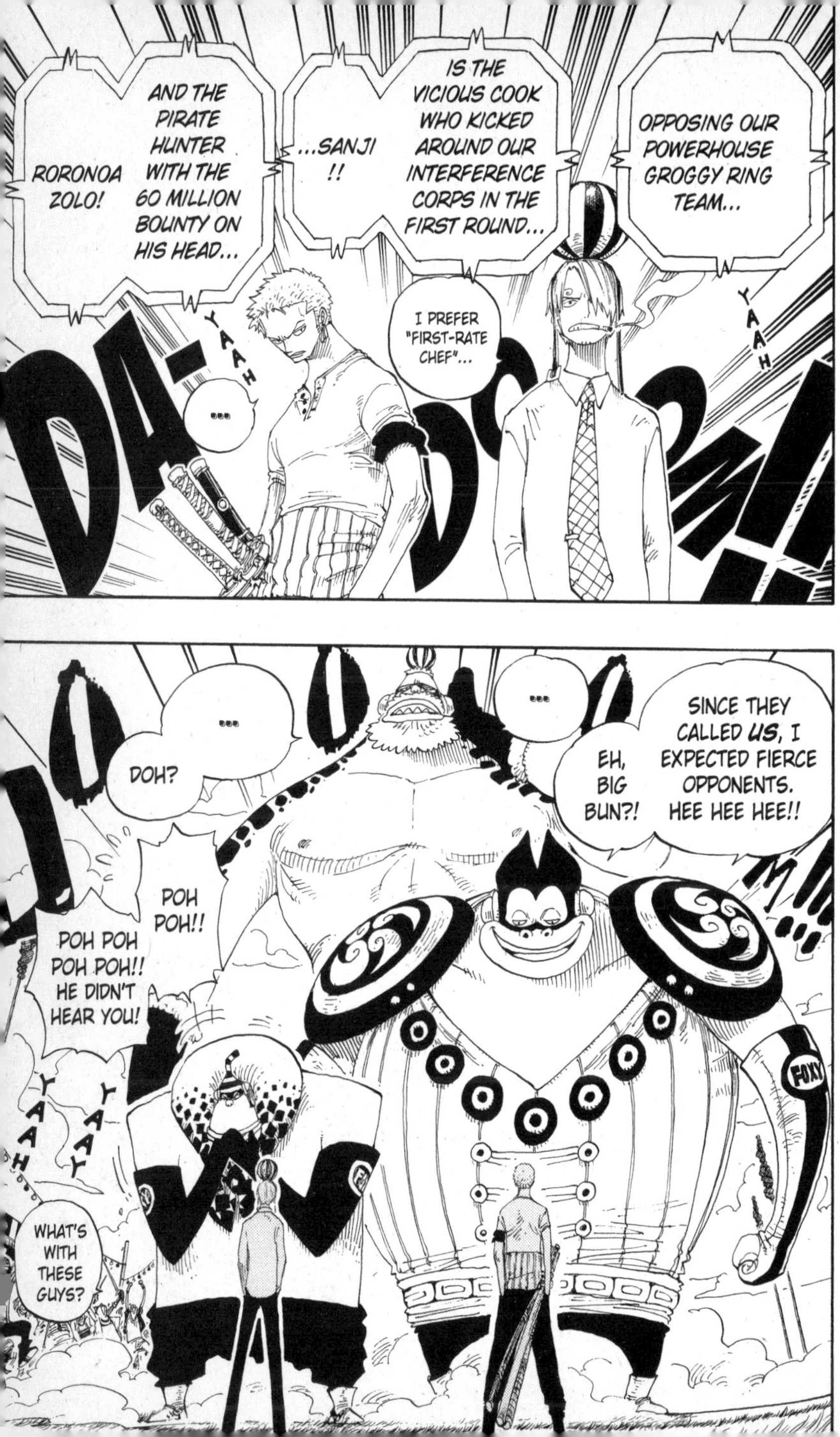
OPPOSING OUR POWERHOUSE GROGGY RING TEAM...
IS THE VICIOUS COOK WHO KICKED AROUND OUR INTERFERENCE CORPS IN THE FIRST ROUND...
...SANJI !!
AND THE PIRATE HUNTER WITH THE 60 MILLION BOUNTY ON HIS HEAD...
RORONOA ZOLO!
YAAH
I PREFER "FIRST-RATE CHEF"...
YAAH
...
DA-DOOM!!
SINCE THEY CALLED US, I EXPECTED FIERCE OPPONENTS. HEE HEE HEE!!
EH, BIG BUN?!
...
...
DOH?
POH POH!!
POH POH POH POH!! HE DIDN'T HEAR YOU!
FOXY
YAAY
YAAAH
WHAT'S WITH THESE GUYS?

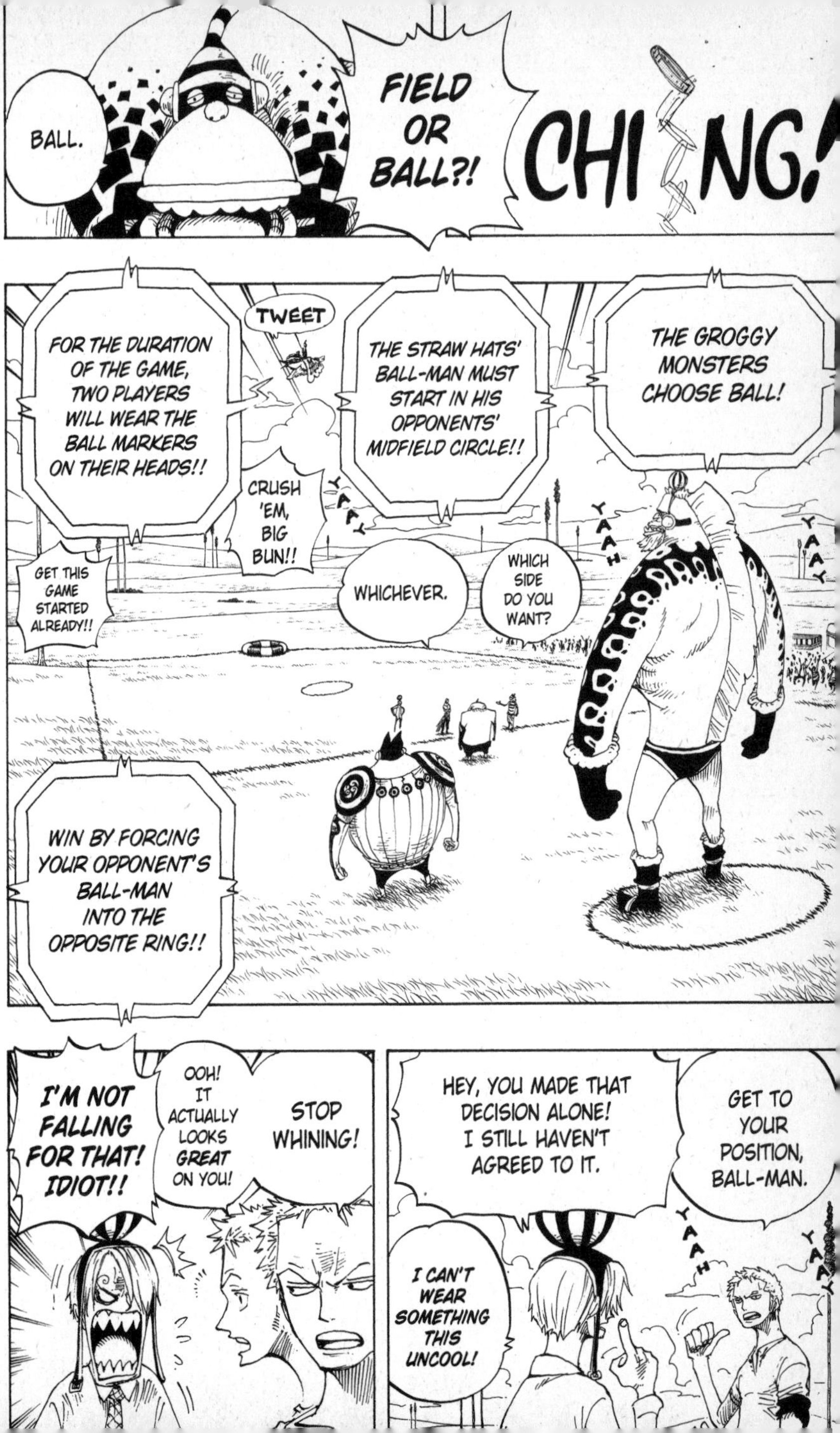
CHI NG!
FIELD OR BALL?!
BALL.
THE GROGGY MONSTERS CHOOSE BALL!
THE STRAW HATS' BALL-MAN MUST START IN HIS OPPONENTS' MIDFIELD CIRCLE!!
TWEET
FOR THE DURATION OF THE GAME, TWO PLAYERS WILL WEAR THE BALL MARKERS ON THEIR HEADS!!
YAAY
YAAH
WHICH SIDE DO YOU WANT?
WHICHEVER.
YAAY
CRUSH 'EM, BIG BUN!!
GET THIS GAME STARTED ALREADY!!
WIN BY FORCING YOUR OPPONENT'S BALL-MAN INTO THE OPPOSITE RING!!
GET TO YOUR POSITION, BALL-MAN.
HEY, YOU MADE THAT DECISION ALONE! I STILL HAVEN'T AGREED TO IT.
YAAY
YAAH
I CAN'T WEAR SOMETHING THIS UNCOOL!
STOP WHINING!
OOH! IT ACTUALLY LOOKS GREAT ON YOU!
I'M NOT FALLING FOR THAT! IDIOT!!

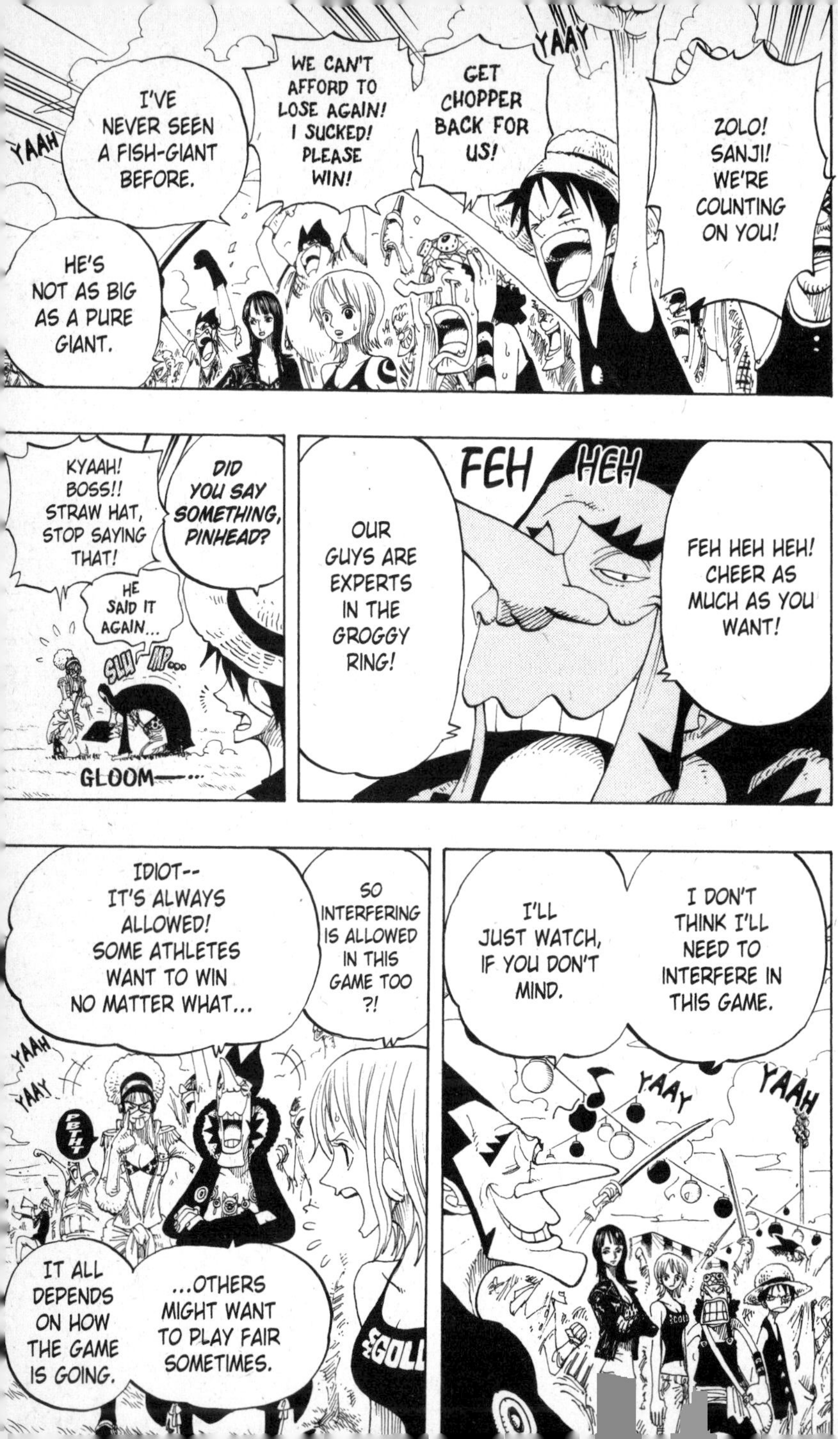
ZOLO! SANJI! WE'RE COUNTING ON YOU!
YAAY
GET CHOPPER BACK FOR US!
WE CAN'T AFFORD TO LOSE AGAIN! I SUCKED! PLEASE WIN!
I'VE NEVER SEEN A FISH-GIANT BEFORE.
YAAH
HE'S NOT AS BIG AS A PURE GIANT.
FEH HEH
FEH HEH HEH! CHEER AS MUCH AS YOU WANT!
OUR GUYS ARE EXPERTS IN THE GROGGY RING!
DID YOU SAY SOMETHING, PINHEAD?
KYAAH! BOSS!! STRAW HAT, STOP SAYING THAT!
HE SAID IT AGAIN...
SLUMP...
GLOOM—...
I DON'T THINK I'LL NEED TO INTERFERE IN THIS GAME.
I'LL JUST WATCH, IF YOU DON'T MIND.
YAAH
YAAY
SO INTERFERING IS ALLOWED IN THIS GAME TOO ?!
IDIOT-- IT'S ALWAYS ALLOWED! SOME ATHLETES WANT TO WIN NO MATTER WHAT...
...OTHERS MIGHT WANT TO PLAY FAIR SOMETIMES.
IT ALL DEPENDS ON HOW THE GAME IS GOING.
YAAH
YAAY
PBTHT

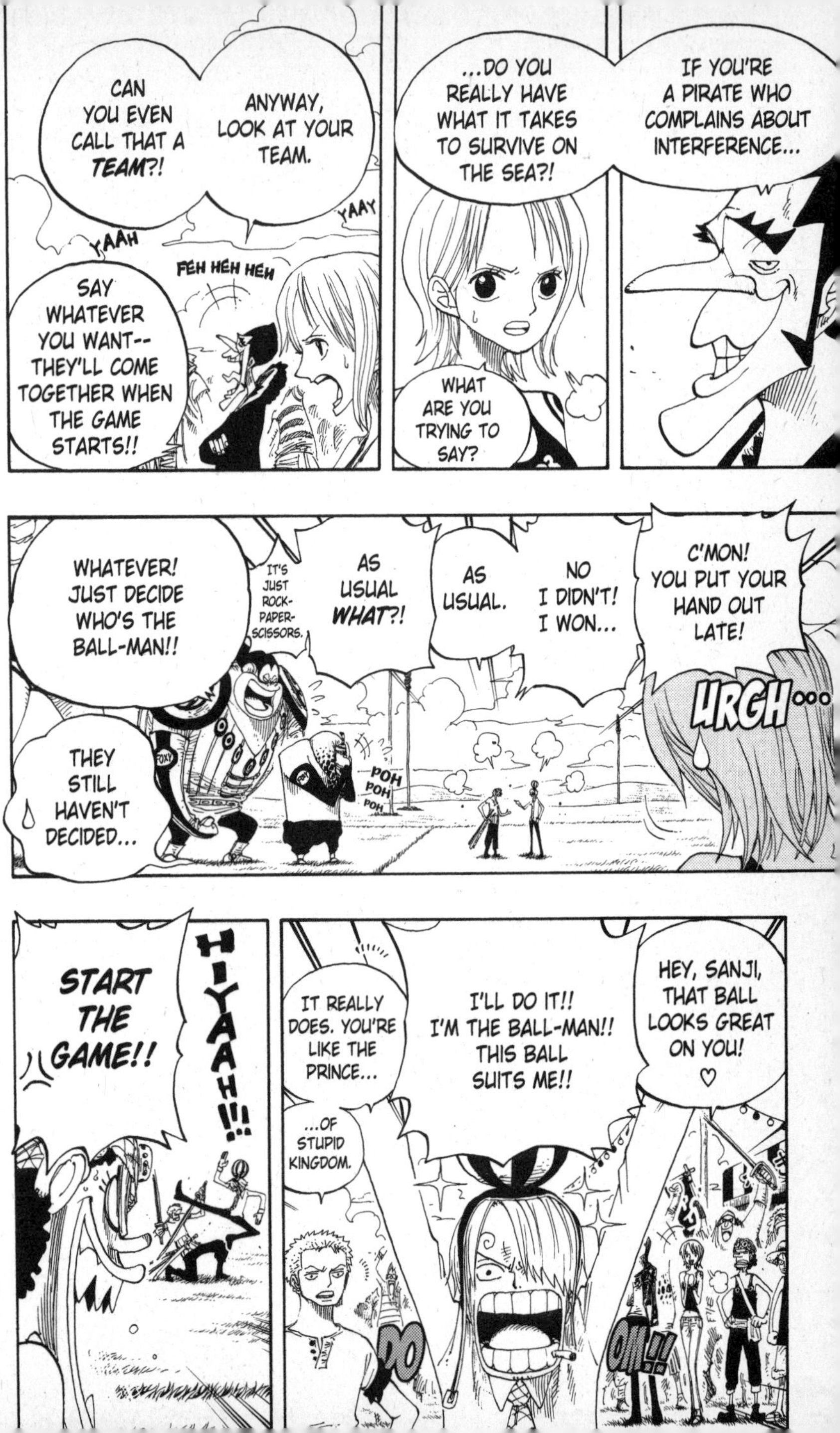
IF YOU'RE A PIRATE WHO COMPLAINS ABOUT INTERFERENCE...
...DO YOU REALLY HAVE WHAT IT TAKES TO SURVIVE ON THE SEA?!
WHAT ARE YOU TRYING TO SAY?
ANYWAY, LOOK AT YOUR TEAM.
CAN YOU EVEN CALL THAT A TEAM?!
YAAY
YAAH
FEH HEH HEH
SAY WHATEVER YOU WANT-- THEY'LL COME TOGETHER WHEN THE GAME STARTS!!
C'MON! YOU PUT YOUR HAND OUT LATE!
URGH...
NO I DIDN'T! I WON...
AS USUAL.
AS USUAL WHAT?!
IT'S JUST ROCK-PAPER-SCISSORS.
WHATEVER! JUST DECIDE WHO'S THE BALL-MAN!!
POH POH POH
THEY STILL HAVEN'T DECIDED...
HEY, SANJI, THAT BALL LOOKS GREAT ON YOU! ♡
I'LL DO IT!! I'M THE BALL-MAN!! THIS BALL SUITS ME!!
IT REALLY DOES. YOU'RE LIKE THE PRINCE...
...OF STUPID KINGDOM.
DOOM!!
HIYAAAH!!!
START THE GAME!!

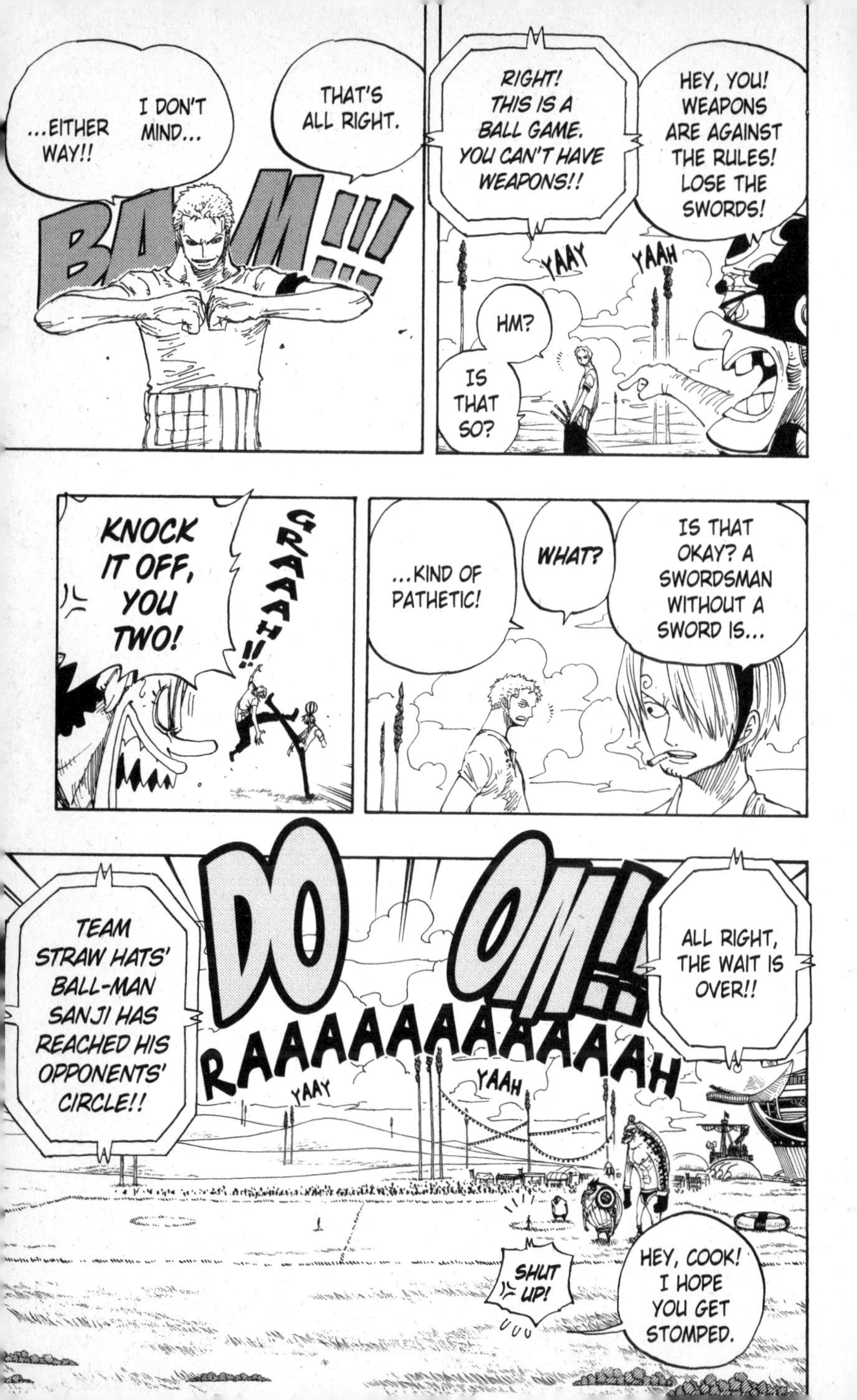
HEY, YOU! WEAPONS ARE AGAINST THE RULES! LOSE THE SWORDS!
RIGHT! THIS IS A BALL GAME. YOU CAN'T HAVE WEAPONS!!
YAAH
YAAY
HM?
IS THAT SO?
THAT'S ALL RIGHT.
I DON'T MIND...
...EITHER WAY!!
BAM!!!
IS THAT OKAY? A SWORDSMAN WITHOUT A SWORD IS...
WHAT?
...KIND OF PATHETIC!
KNOCK IT OFF, YOU TWO!
GRAAAAH!!
ALL RIGHT, THE WAIT IS OVER!!
DOOM!!
TEAM STRAW HATS' BALL-MAN SANJI HAS REACHED HIS OPPONENTS' CIRCLE!!
RAAAAAAAAAAAH
YAAH
YAAY
HEY, COOK! I HOPE YOU GET STOMPED.
SHUT UP!

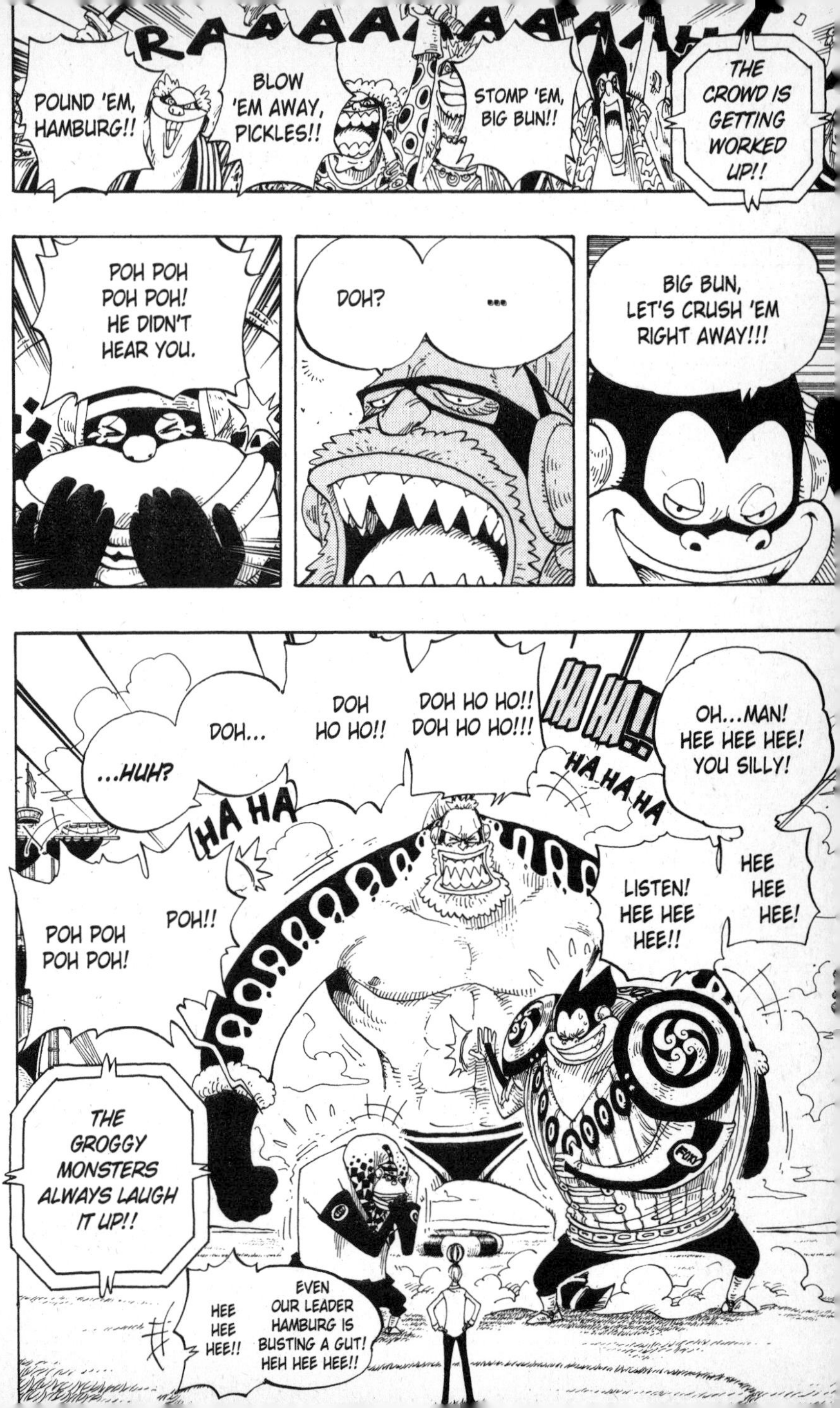
THE CROWD IS GETTING WORKED UP!!
STOMP 'EM, BIG BUN!!
BLOW 'EM AWAY, PICKLES!!
POUND 'EM, HAMBURG!!
BIG BUN, LET'S CRUSH 'EM RIGHT AWAY!!!
...
DOH?
POH POH POH POH! HE DIDN'T HEAR YOU.
OH...MAN! HEE HEE HEE! YOU SILLY!
HA HA!!
HA HA HA HA
DOH HO HO!! DOH HO HO!!!
DOH HO HO!!
DOH...
...HUH?
HA HA
HEE HEE HEE!
LISTEN! HEE HEE HEE!!
POH!!
POH POH POH POH!
THE GROGGY MONSTERS ALWAYS LAUGH IT UP!!
EVEN OUR LEADER HAMBURG IS BUSTING A GUT! HEH HEE HEE!!
HEE HEE HEE!!

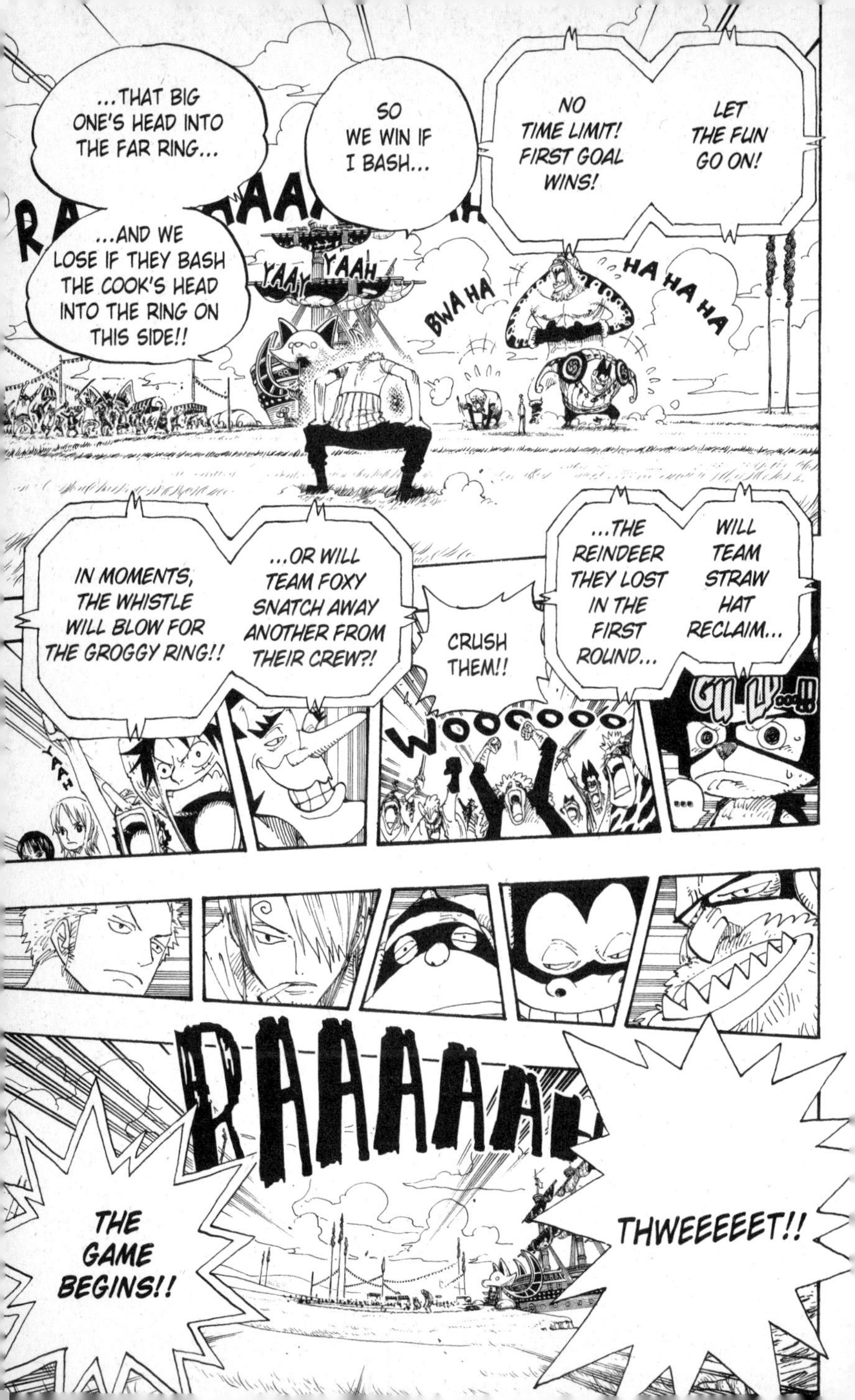
LET THE FUN GO ON!
NO TIME LIMIT! FIRST GOAL WINS!
HA HA HA HA
BWA HA
YAAAH
SO WE WIN IF I BASH...
...THAT BIG ONE'S HEAD INTO THE FAR RING...
...AND WE LOSE IF THEY BASH THE COOK'S HEAD INTO THE RING ON THIS SIDE!!
WILL TEAM STRAW HAT RECLAIM...
...THE REINDEER THEY LOST IN THE FIRST ROUND...
CRUSH THEM!!
...OR WILL TEAM FOXY SNATCH AWAY ANOTHER FROM THEIR CREW?!
IN MOMENTS, THE WHISTLE WILL BLOW FOR THE GROGGY RING!!
...
WOOOOOO
YAAH
THWEEEEET!!
RAAAAA
THE GAME BEGINS!!

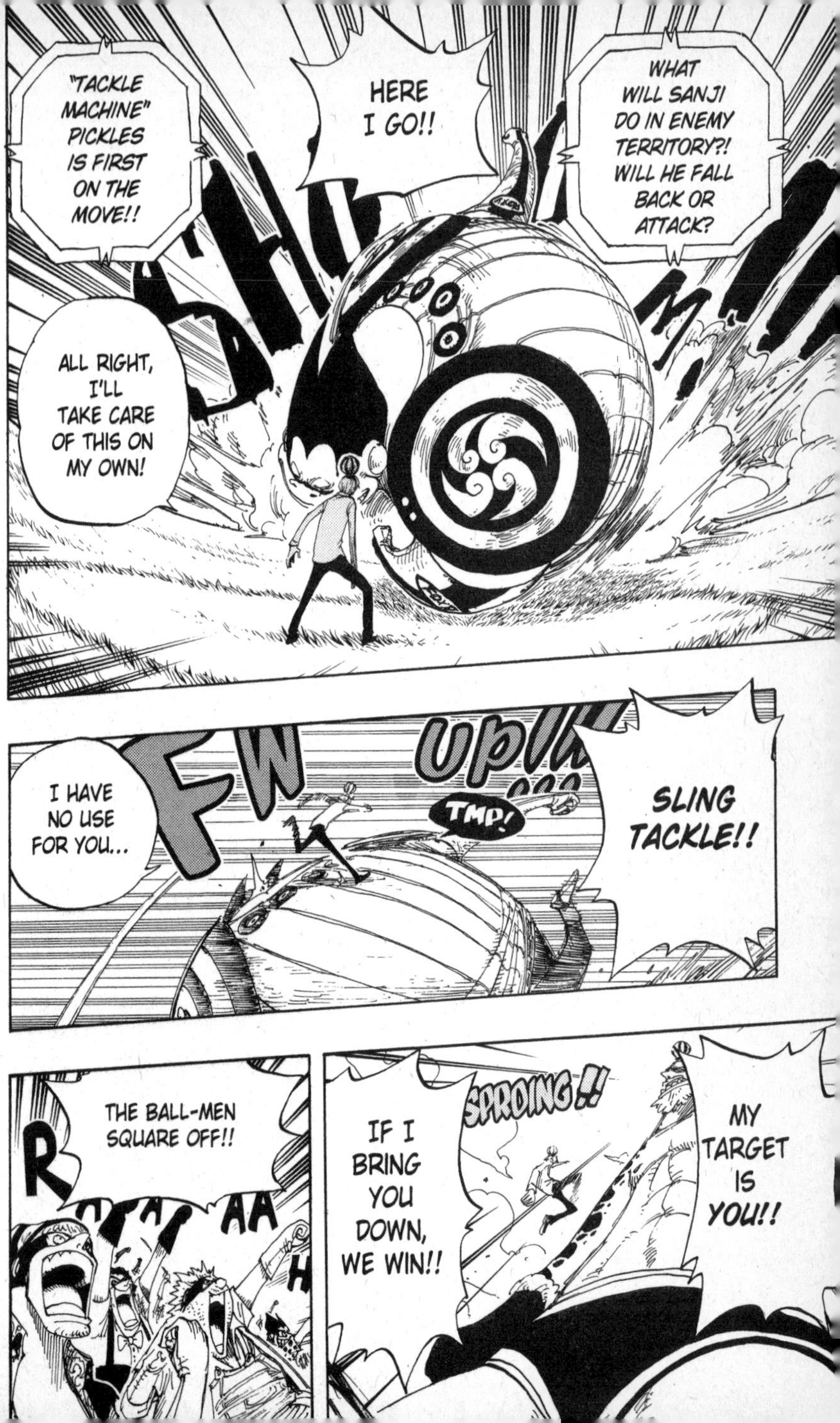
WHAT WILL SANJI DO IN ENEMY TERRITORY?! WILL HE FALL BACK OR ATTACK?
HERE I GO!!
"TACKLE MACHINE" PICKLES IS FIRST ON THE MOVE!!
ALL RIGHT, I'LL TAKE CARE OF THIS ON MY OWN!
SLING TACKLE!!
TMP!
I HAVE NO USE FOR YOU...
MY TARGET IS YOU!!
SPROING!!
IF I BRING YOU DOWN, WE WIN!!
THE BALL-MEN SQUARE OFF!!

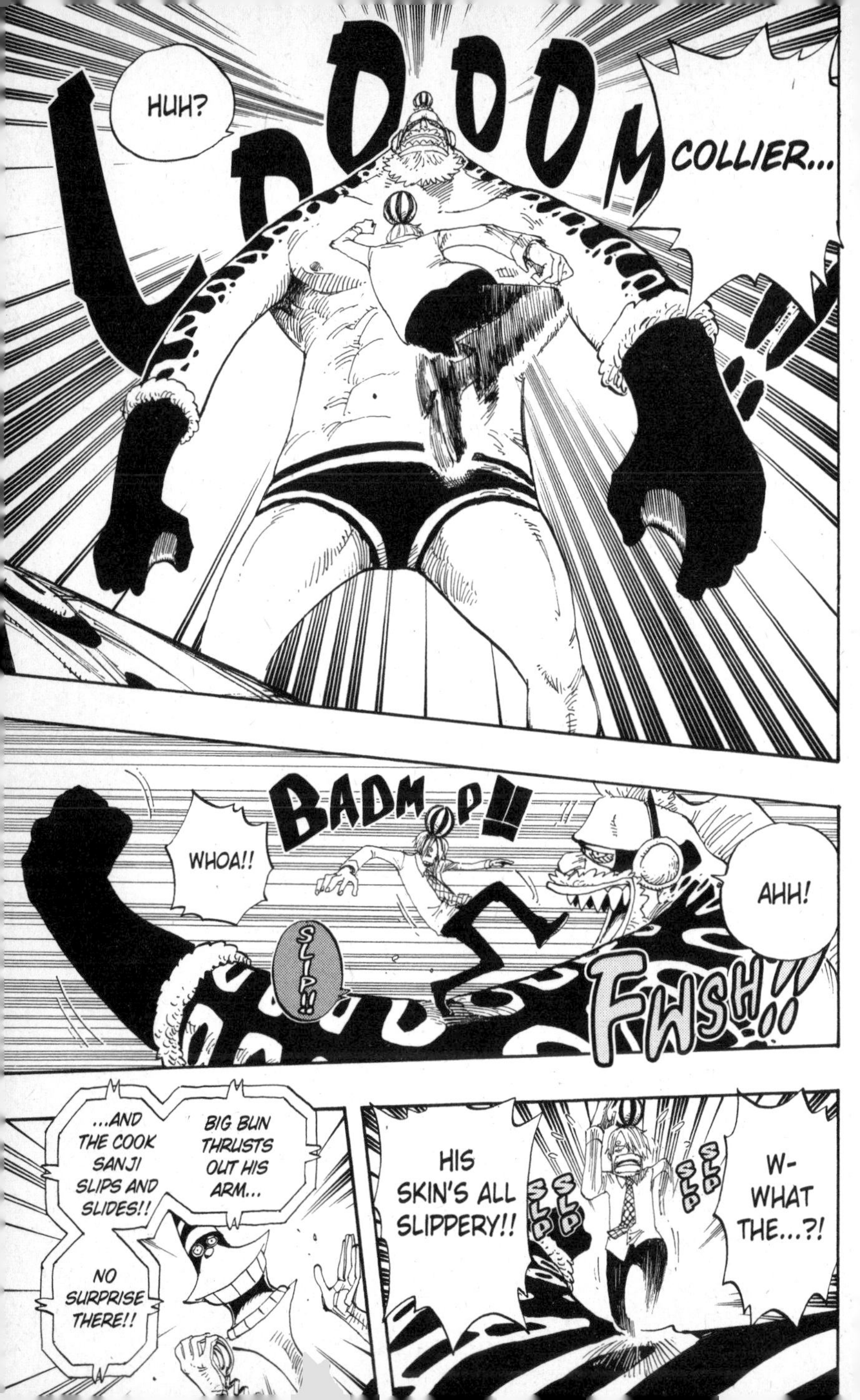

COLLIER...
HUH?
DOOOM
AHH!
FWSH!!
BADMP!!
WHOA!!
SLIP!!
W- WHAT THE...?!
SLP SLP
SLP SLP
HIS SKIN'S ALL SLIPPERY!!
BIG BUN THRUSTS OUT HIS ARM...
...AND THE COOK SANJI SLIPS AND SLIDES!!
NO SURPRISE THERE!!

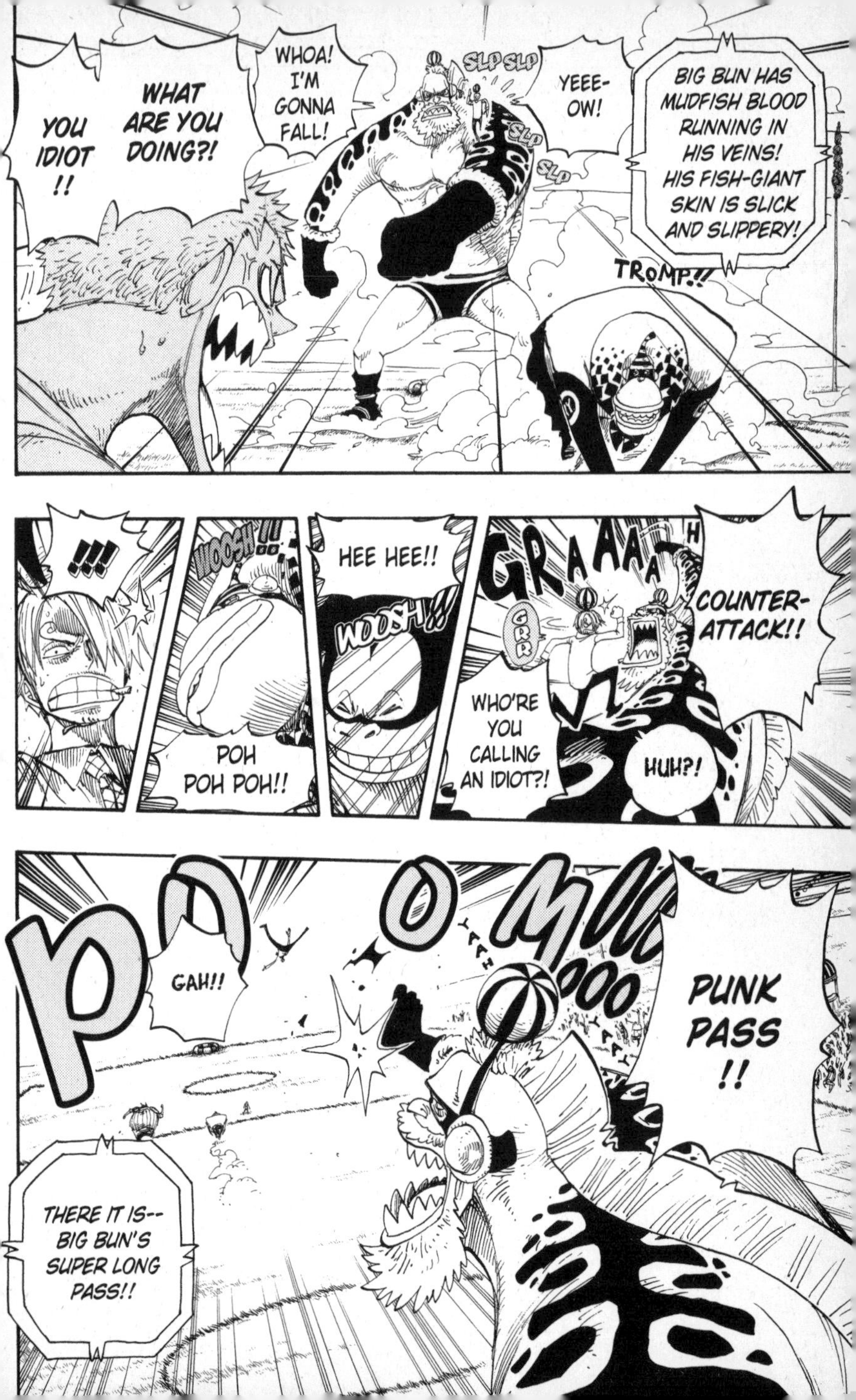

BIG BUN HAS MUDFISH BLOOD RUNNING IN HIS VEINS! HIS FISH-GIANT SKIN IS SLICK AND SLIPPERY!!
YEEE-OW!
SLP SLP
WHOA! I'M GONNA FALL!
SLP
SLP
WHAT ARE YOU DOING?!
YOU IDIOT !!
TROMP!!
COUNTER-ATTACK!!
GRAAAAH
GRR
HUH?!
WHO'RE YOU CALLING AN IDIOT?!
HEE HEE!!
WOOSH!!
WOOSH!!
POH POH POH!!
!!!
PUNK PASS !!
YAAAY
GAH!!
THERE IT IS-- BIG BUN'S SUPER LONG PASS!!

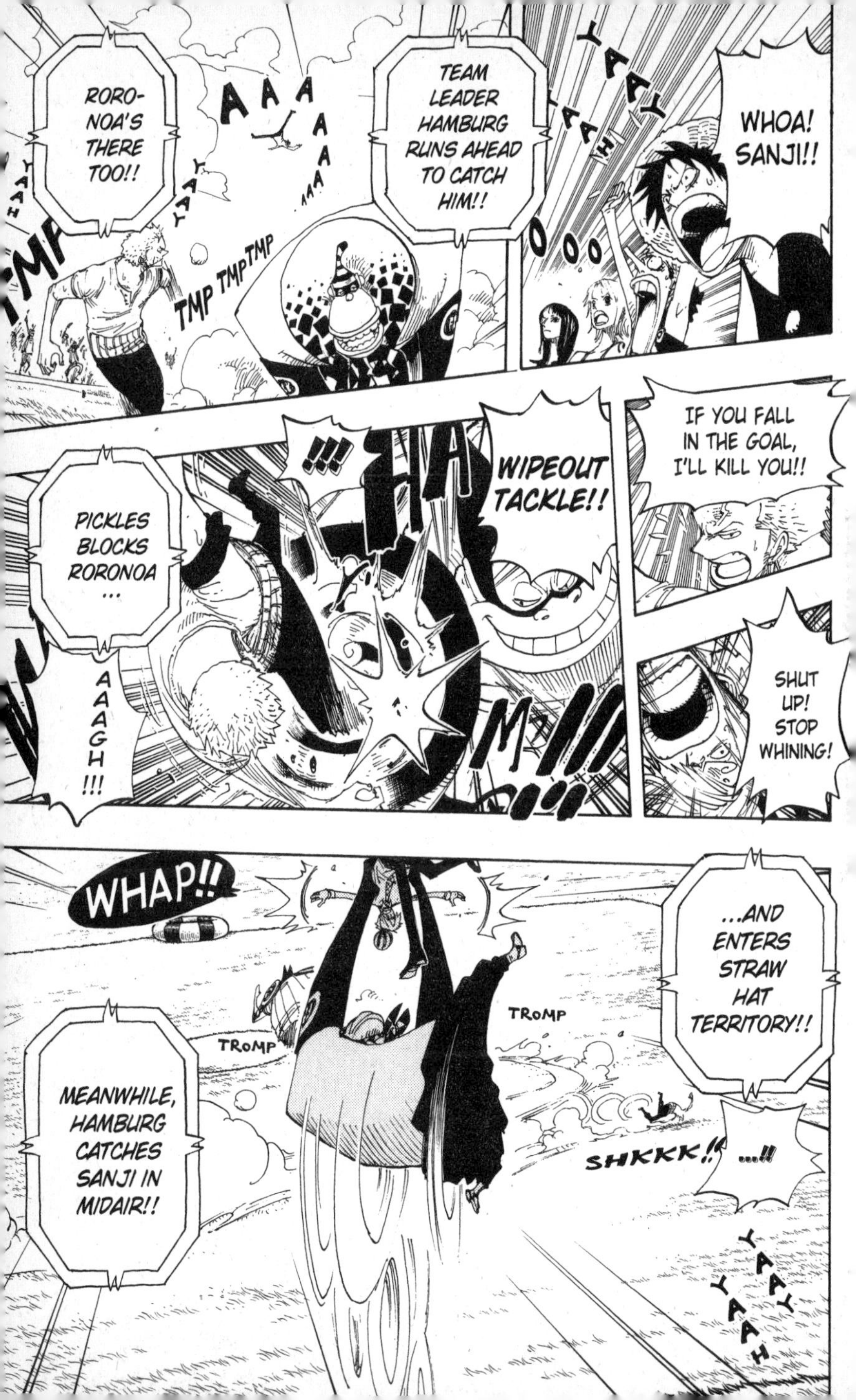
YAAAY
YAAAH
WHOA! SANJI!!
OOO
TEAM LEADER HAMBURG RUNS AHEAD TO CATCH HIM!!
AAAAAAAA
TMP TMP TMP
RORONOA'S THERE TOO!!
YAAAY
YAAAH
TMP
IF YOU FALL IN THE GOAL, I'LL KILL YOU!!
SHUT UP! STOP WHINING!
WIPEOUT TACKLE!!
!!!
HA
PICKLES BLOCKS RORONOA ...
AAAAGH!!!
...AND ENTERS STRAW HAT TERRITORY!!
...!!
SHKKK!!
YAAAY
YAAAH
TROMP
TROMP
WHAP!!
MEANWHILE, HAMBURG CATCHES SANJI IN MIDAIR!!

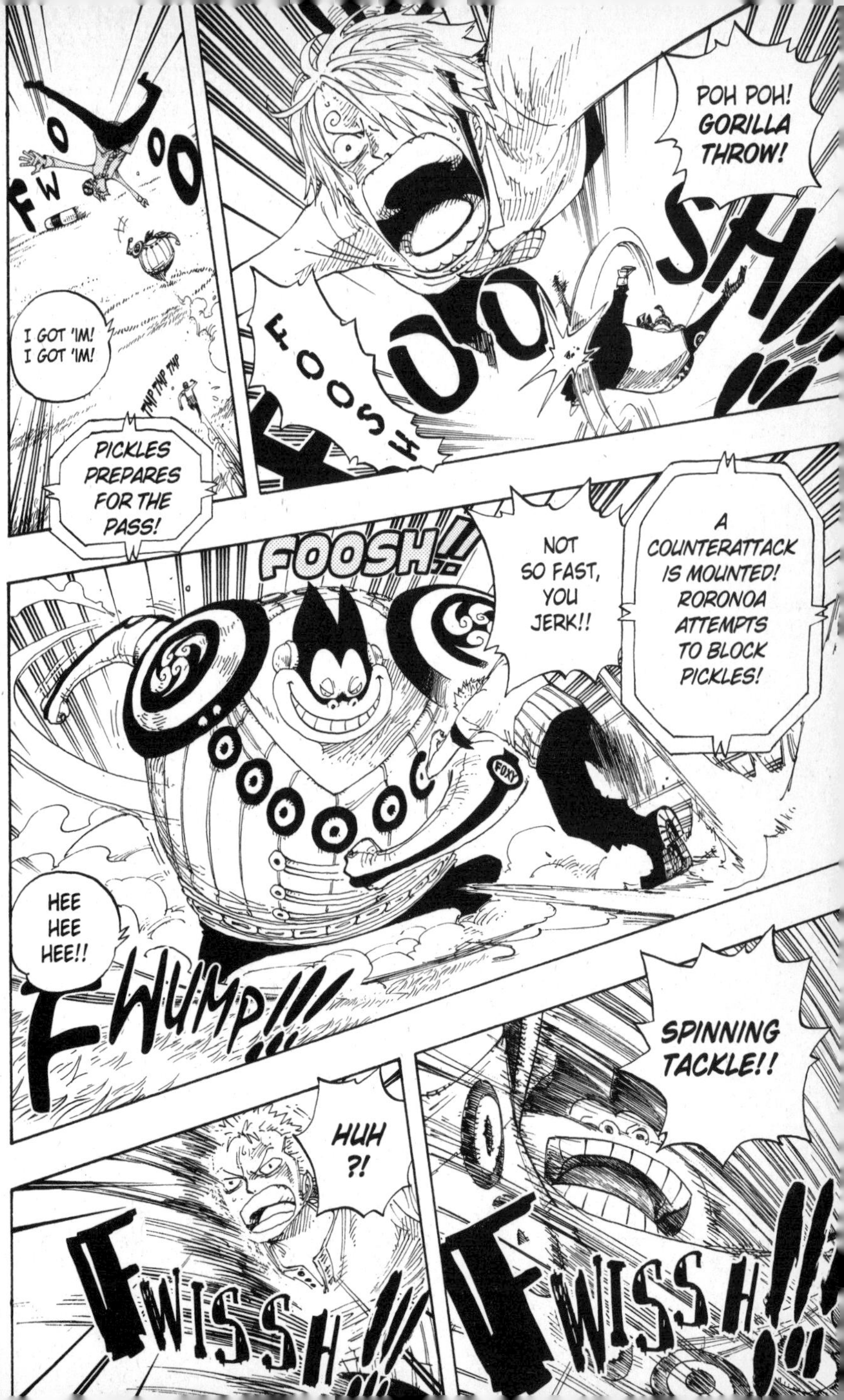
POH POH! GORILLA THROW!
FOOSH
FWOOO
I GOT 'IM! I GOT 'IM!
TMP TMP TMP
PICKLES PREPARES FOR THE PASS!
A COUNTERATTACK IS MOUNTED! RORONOA ATTEMPTS TO BLOCK PICKLES!
NOT SO FAST, YOU JERK!!
FOOSH!!
HEE HEE HEE!!
FWUMP!!!
SPINNING TACKLE!!
FWISSH!!
HUH ?!
FWISSH!!

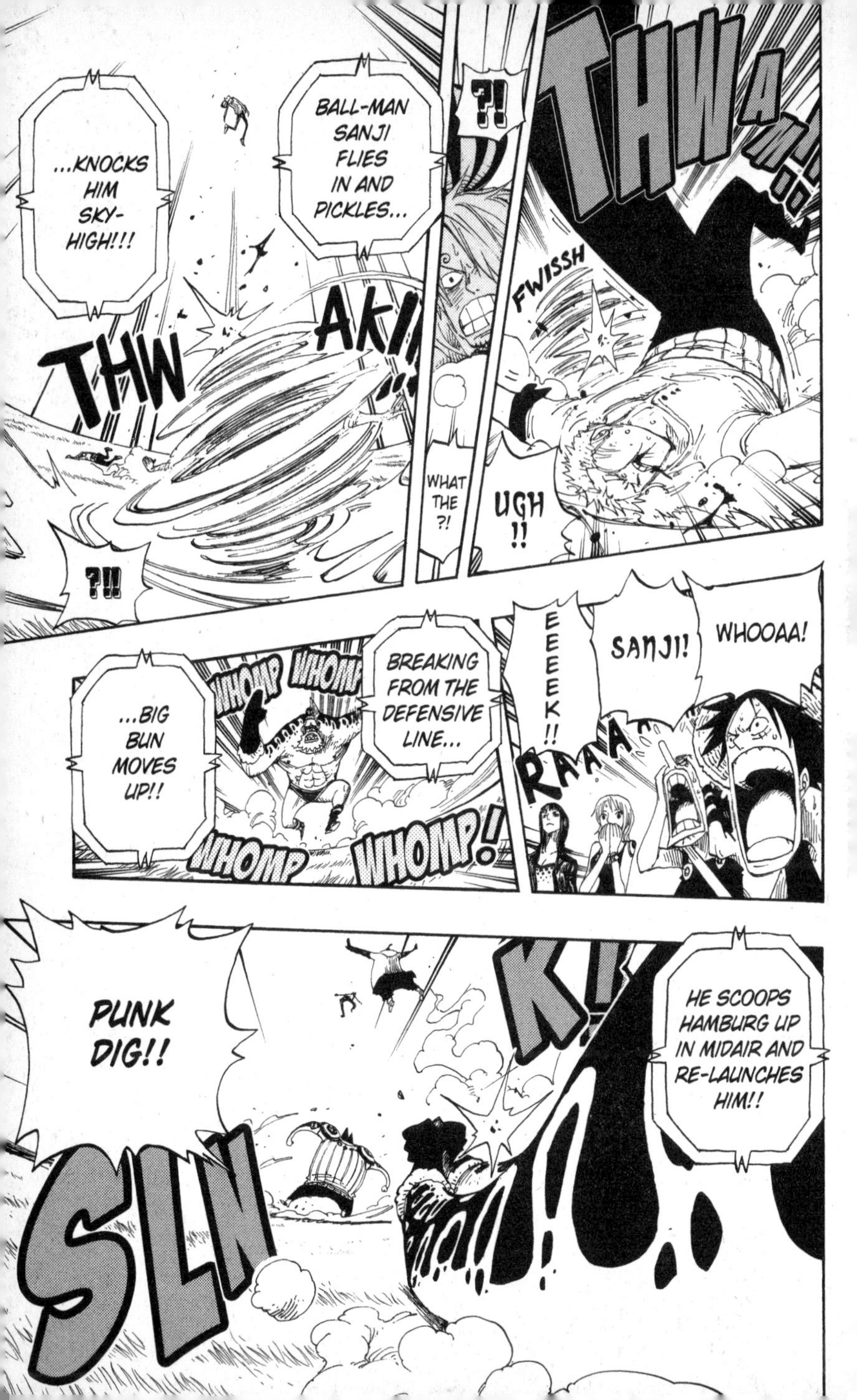
THWAM!!
?!
FWISSH
WHAT THE ?!
UGH !!
BALL-MAN SANJI FLIES IN AND PICKLES...
...KNOCKS HIM SKY-HIGH!!!
THW
AKI
?!!
WHOOAA!
SANJI!
EEEEEK!!
RAAA
BREAKING FROM THE DEFENSIVE LINE...
...BIG BUN MOVES UP!!
WHOMP WHOMP
WHOMP
WHOMP!
HE SCOOPS HAMBURG UP IN MIDAIR AND RE-LAUNCHES HIM!!
K!
PUNK DIG!!
SLN

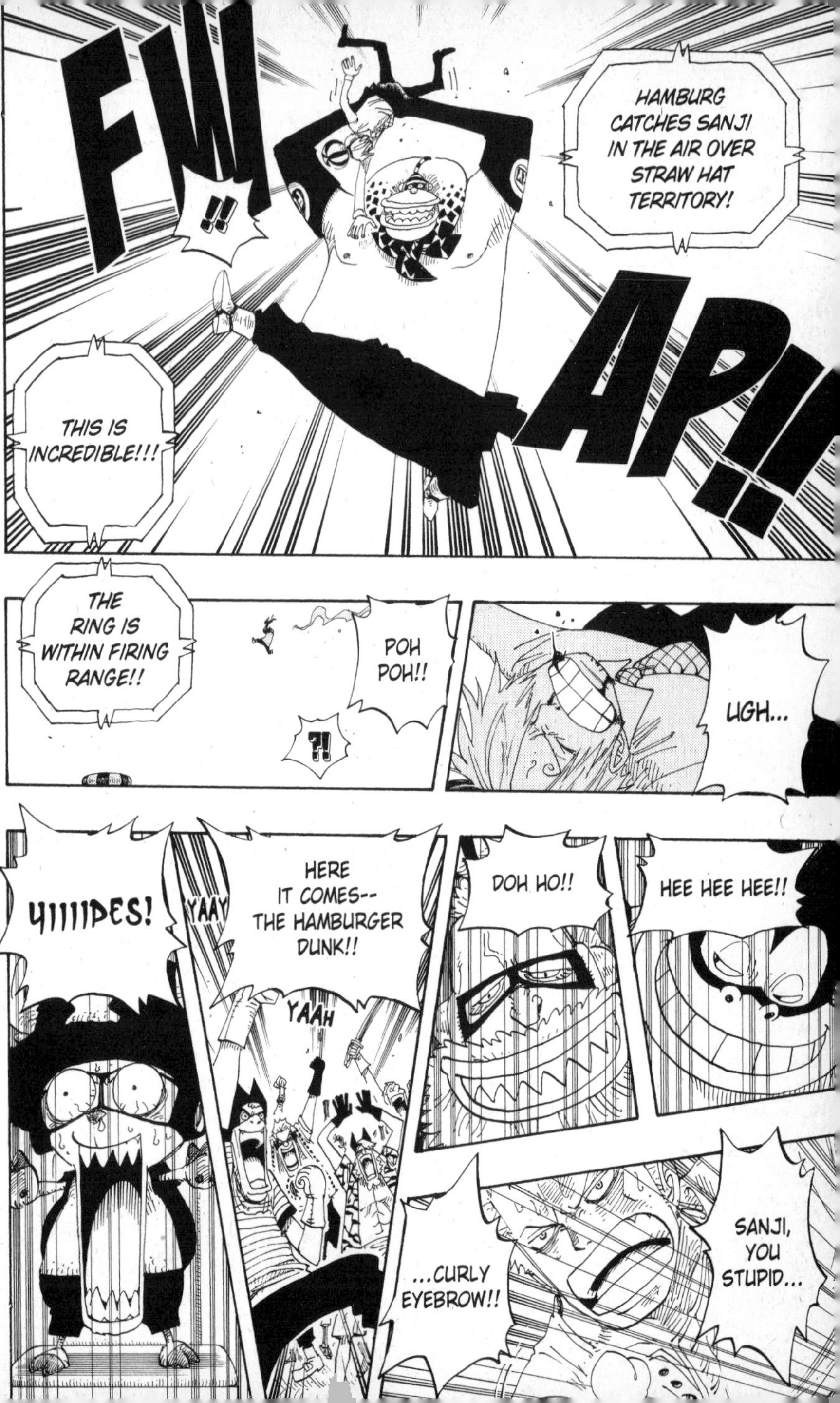

HAMBURG CATCHES SANJI IN THE AIR OVER STRAW HAT TERRITORY!
FWAP!!
!!
THIS IS INCREDIBLE!!!
UGH...
POH POH!!
THE RING IS WITHIN FIRING RANGE!!
?!
HEE HEE HEE!!
DOH HO!!
SANJI, YOU STUPID...
...CURLY EYEBROW!!
HERE IT COMES-- THE HAMBURGER DUNK!!
YAAY
YAAH
YIIIIIPES!

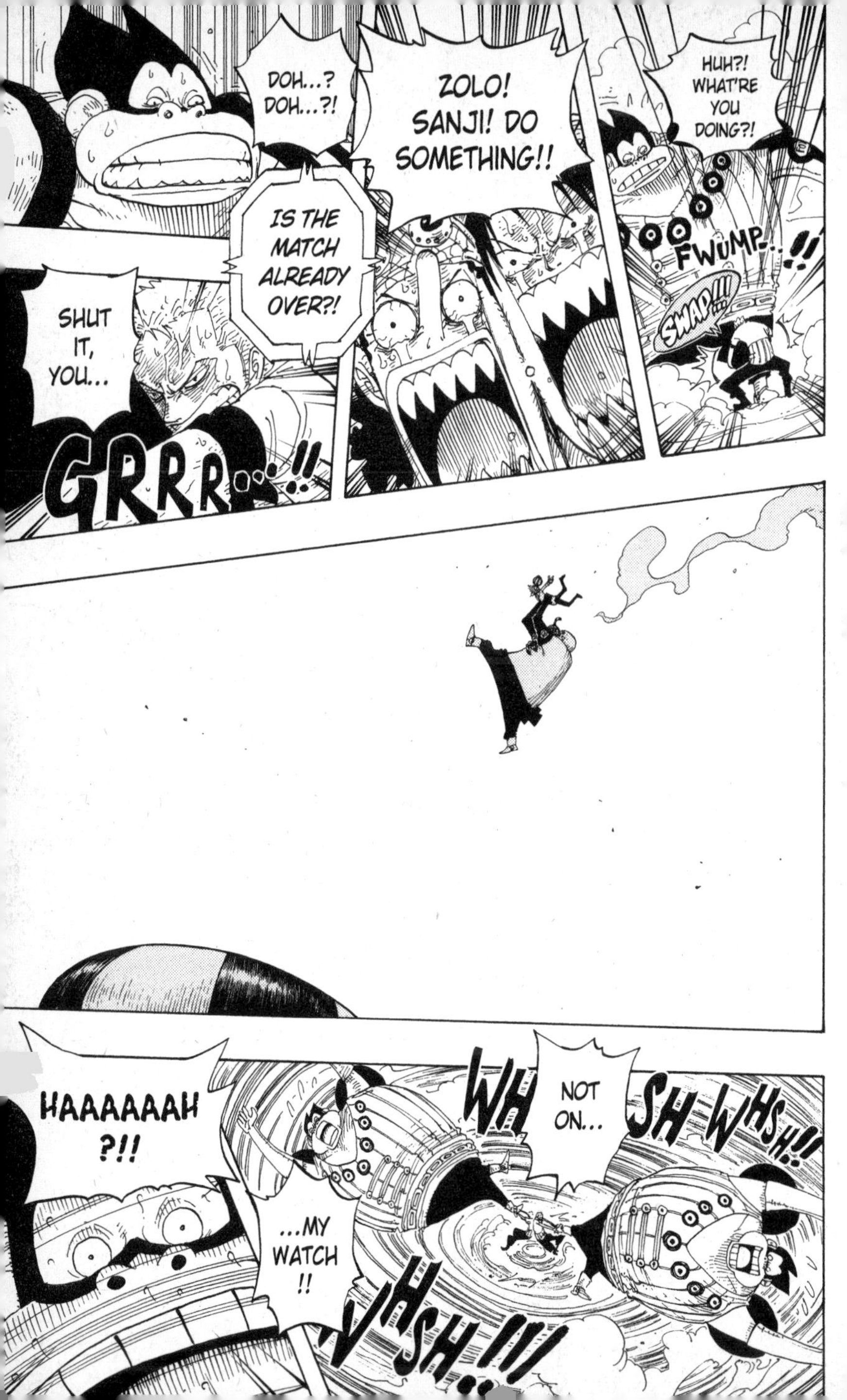
HUH?! WHAT'RE YOU DOING?!
FWUMP...!!
SWAP!!!
ZOLO! SANJI! DO SOMETHING!!
IS THE MATCH ALREADY OVER?!
DOH...? DOH...?!
SHUT IT, YOU...
GRRR...!!
WHSH WHSH!!
NOT ON...
...MY WATCH!!
HAAAAAH?!!
WHSH!!!

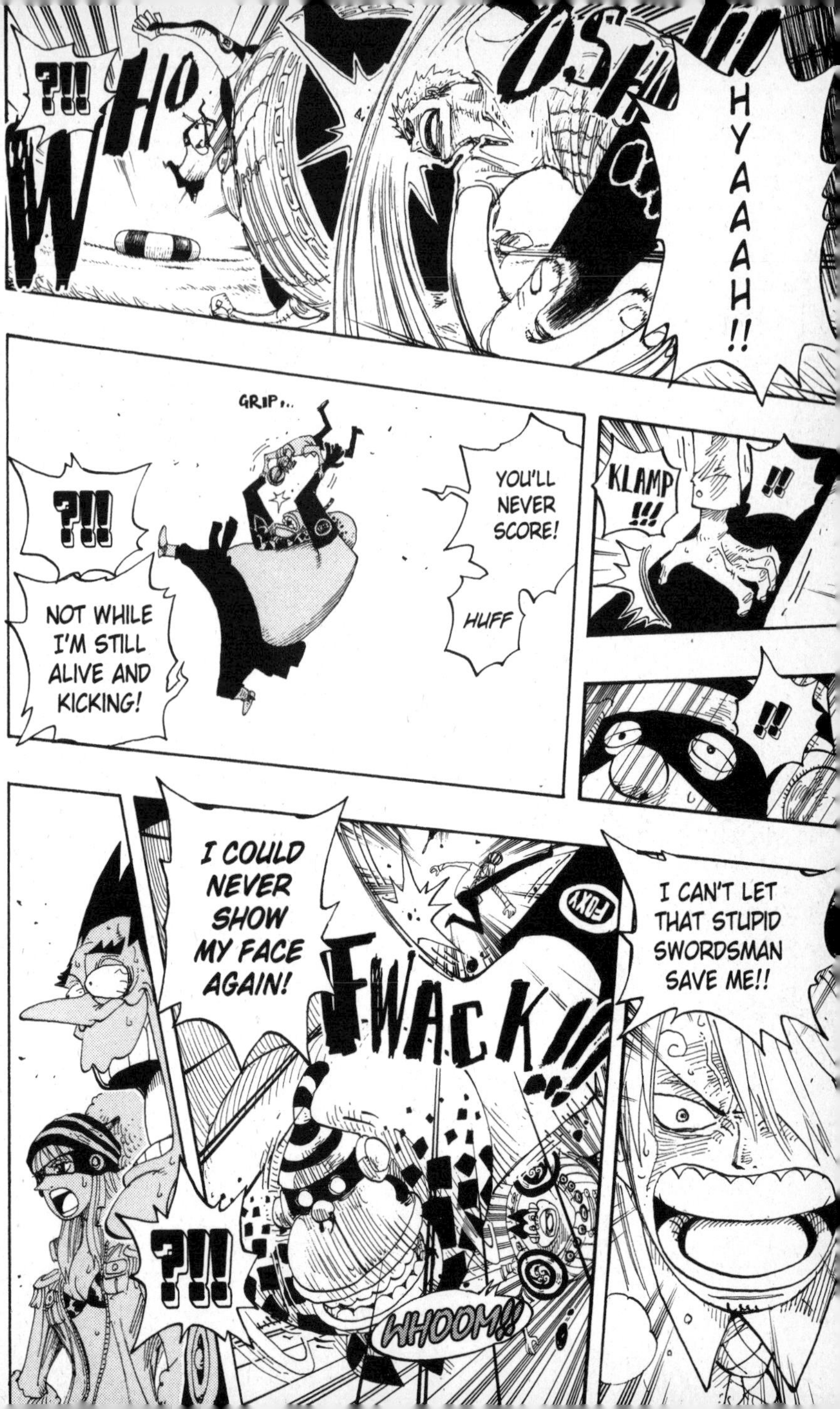
HYAAAAH!!
WHOOSH
?!!
!!
KLAMP!!!
!!
YOU'LL NEVER SCORE!
HUFF
GRIP...
?!!
NOT WHILE I'M STILL ALIVE AND KICKING!
I CAN'T LET THAT STUPID SWORDSMAN SAVE ME!!
FOXY
FWACK!!
I COULD NEVER SHOW MY FACE AGAIN!
?!!
WHOOM!!

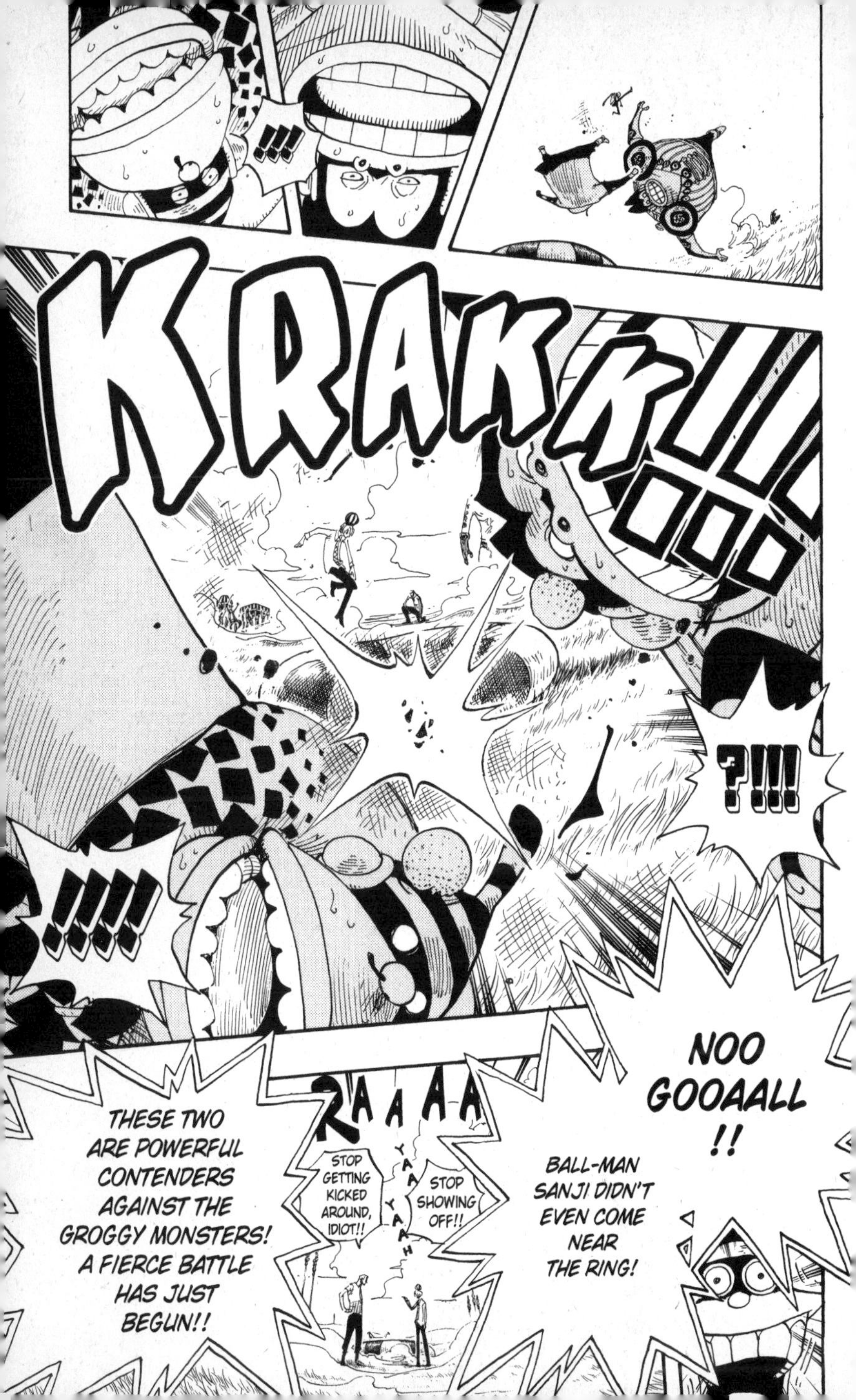
!!!
KRAKK!!...
?!!!
?!!!!
NOO GOOAALL!!
BALL-MAN SANJI DIDN'T EVEN COME NEAR THE RING!
RAAAA
YAAAAH
STOP SHOWING OFF!!
STOP GETTING KICKED AROUND, IDIOT!!
THESE TWO ARE POWERFUL CONTENDERS AGAINST THE GROGGY MONSTERS! A FIERCE BATTLE HAS JUST BEGUN!!

Chapter 311:
ROUGH GAME

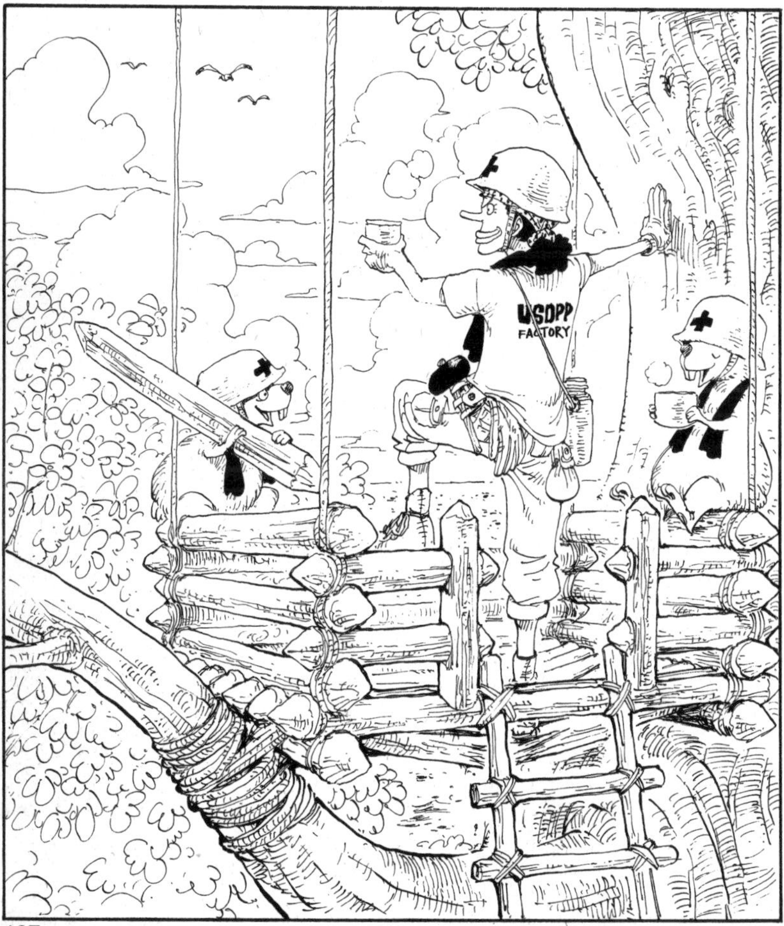
USOPP
FACTORY

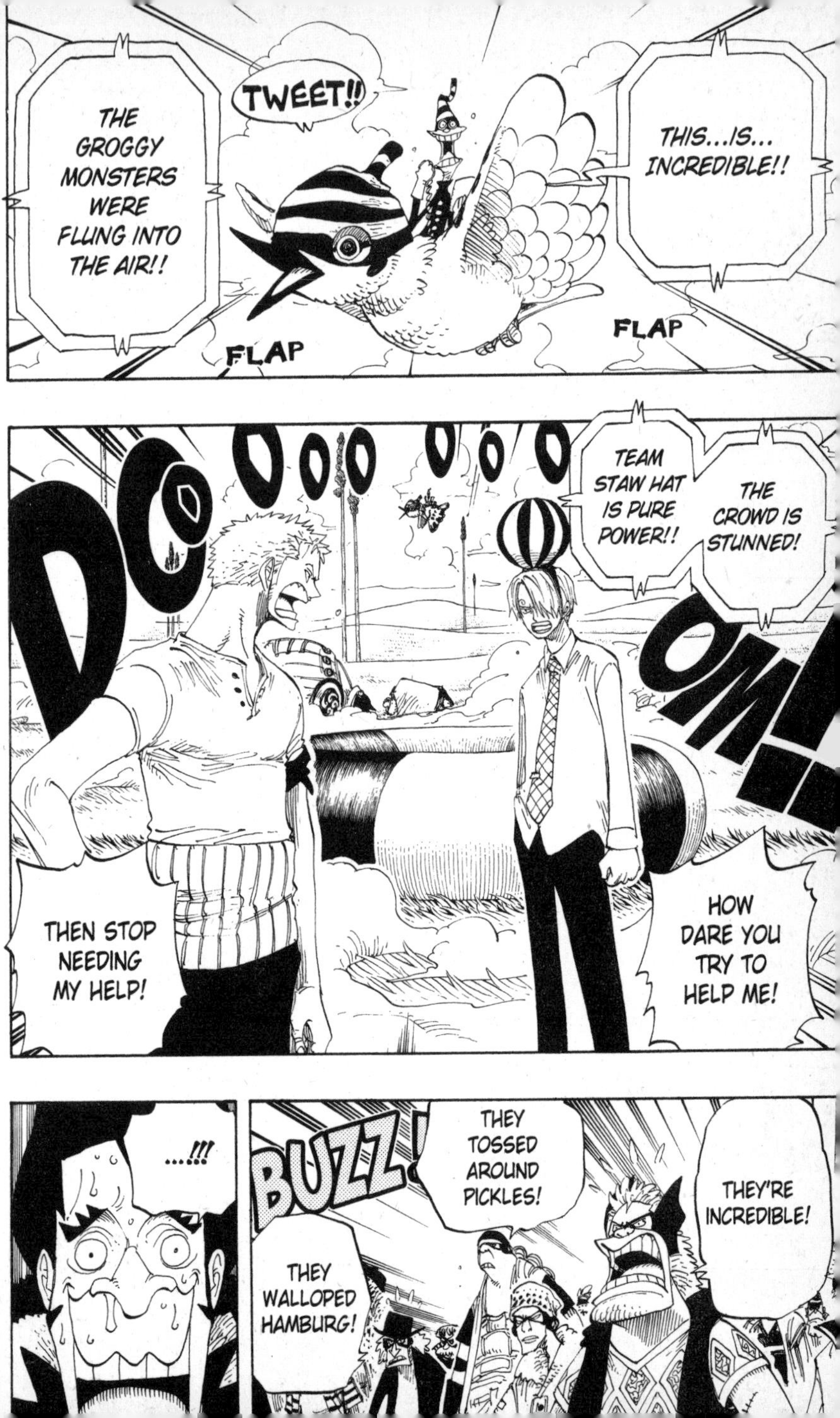
THIS...IS... INCREDIBLE!!
TWEET!!
THE GROGGY MONSTERS WERE FLUNG INTO THE AIR!!
FLAP
FLAP
THE CROWD IS STUNNED!
TEAM STAW HAT IS PURE POWER!!
DOOOOOOOOM!!
HOW DARE YOU TRY TO HELP ME!
THEN STOP NEEDING MY HELP!
THEY'RE INCREDIBLE!
THEY TOSSED AROUND PICKLES!
BUZZ!
THEY WALLOPED HAMBURG!
...!!!

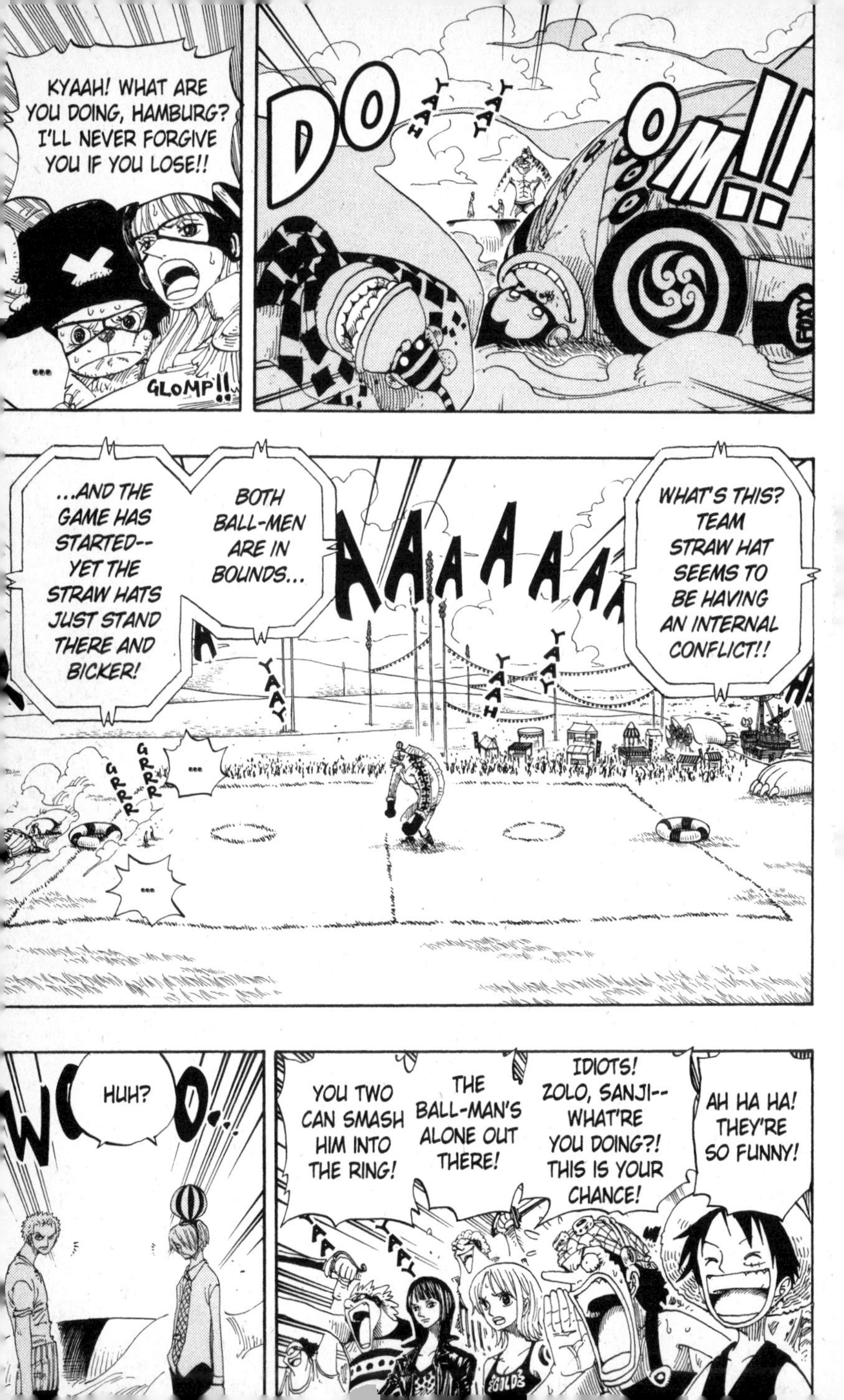
DOOOOM!!
YAAAY
YAAAH
KYAAH! WHAT ARE YOU DOING, HAMBURG? I'LL NEVER FORGIVE YOU IF YOU LOSE!!
GLOMP!!
...
WHAT'S THIS? TEAM STRAW HAT SEEMS TO BE HAVING AN INTERNAL CONFLICT!!
BOTH BALL-MEN ARE IN BOUNDS...
...AND THE GAME HAS STARTED-- YET THE STRAW HATS JUST STAND THERE AND BICKER!
AAAAAA
YAAAH
YAAAY
GRRR
GRRR
...
...
AH HA HA! THEY'RE SO FUNNY!
IDIOTS! ZOLO, SANJI-- WHAT'RE YOU DOING?! THIS IS YOUR CHANCE!
THE BALL-MAN'S ALONE OUT THERE!
YOU TWO CAN SMASH HIM INTO THE RING!
YAAY
YAAY
HUH?

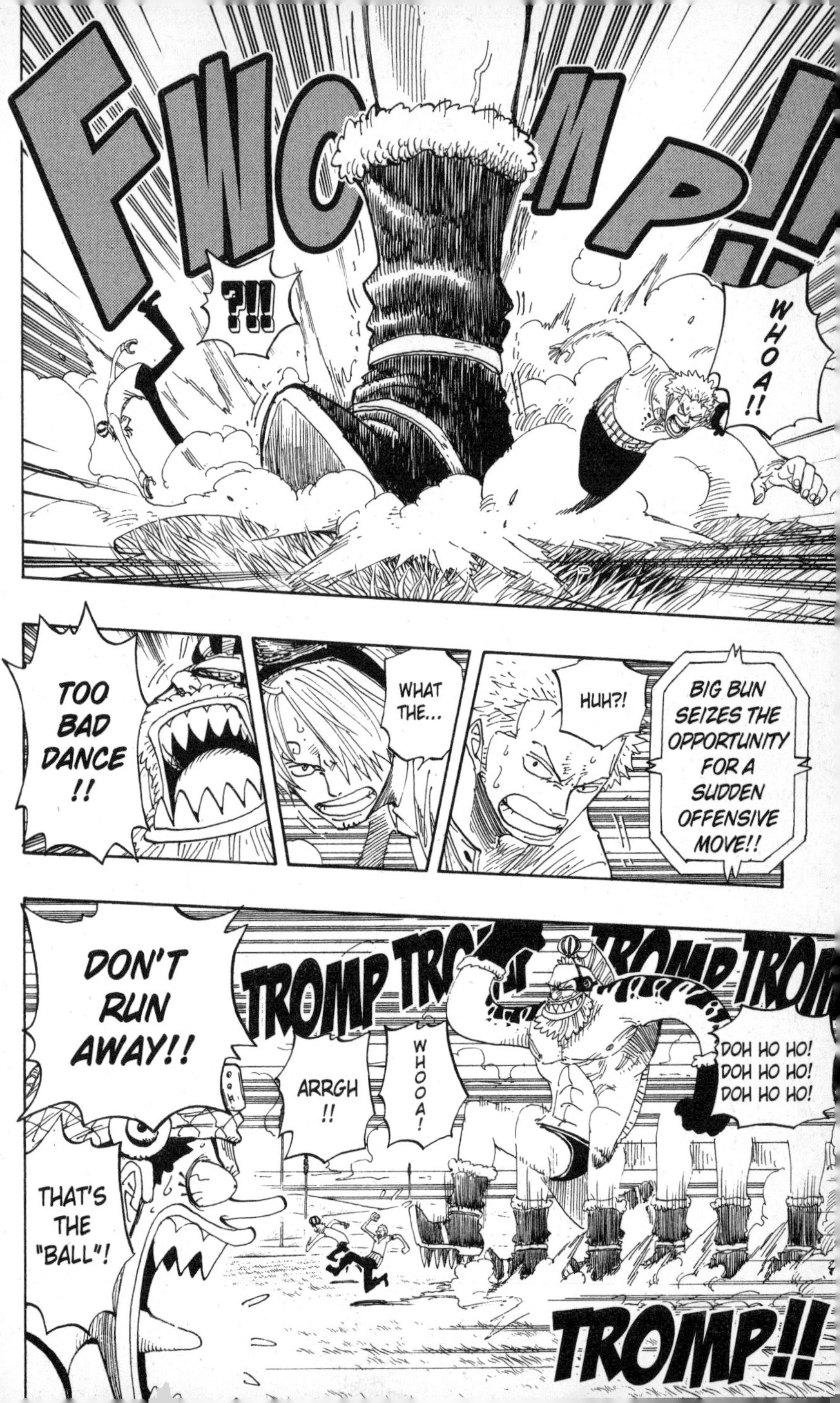
FWOMP!!
WHOA!!
?!!
BIG BUN SEIZES THE OPPORTUNITY FOR A SUDDEN OFFENSIVE MOVE!!
HUH?!
WHAT THE...
TOO BAD DANCE!!
TROMP TROMP TROMP TROMP
DOH HO HO! DOH HO HO! DOH HO HO!
WHOOA!
ARRGH!!
DON'T RUN AWAY!!
TROMP!!
THAT'S THE "BALL"!

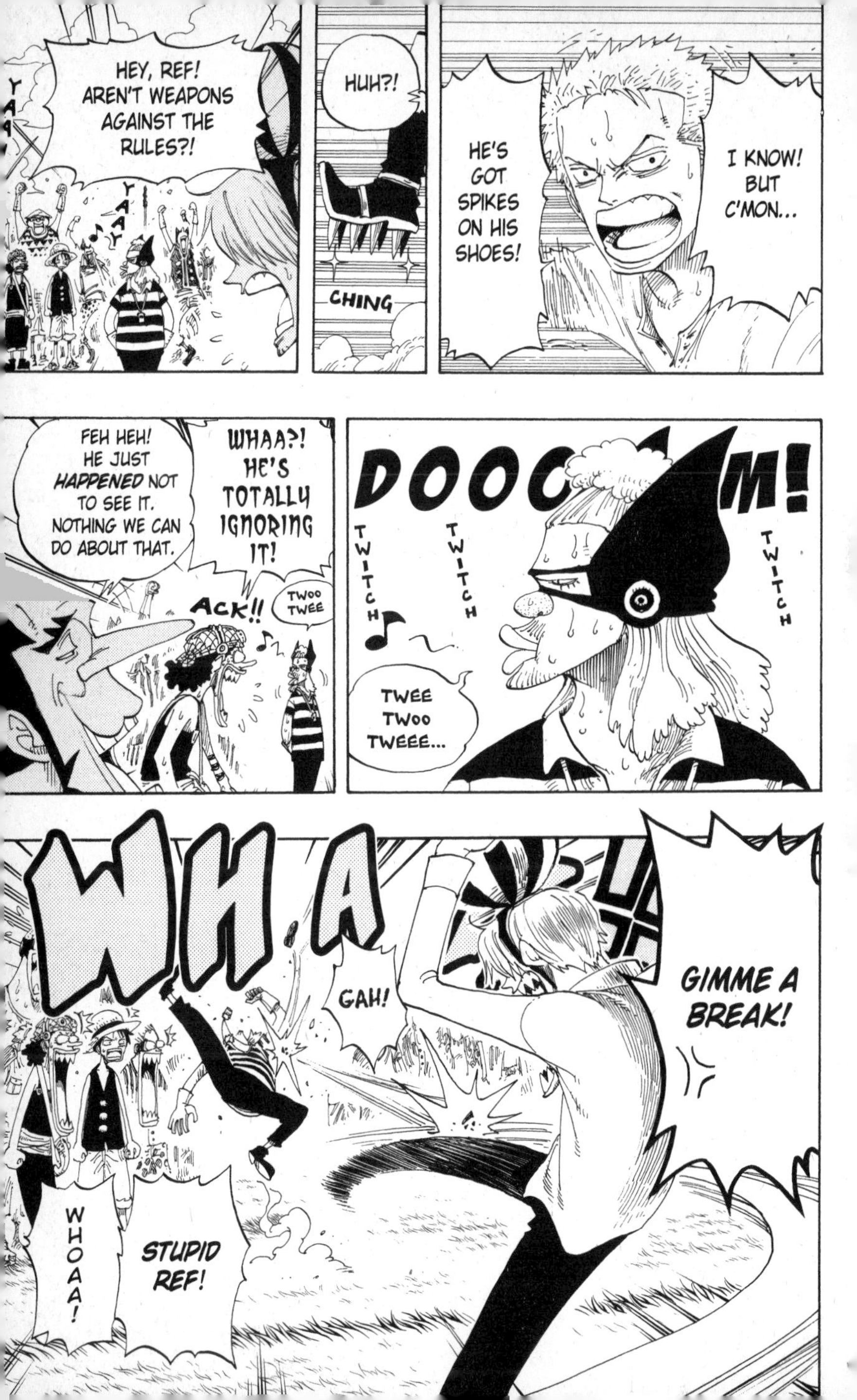
I KNOW! BUT C'MON...
HE'S GOT SPIKES ON HIS SHOES!
HUH?!
CHING
HEY, REF! AREN'T WEAPONS AGAINST THE RULES?!
YAY
YAAY
DOOO M!
TWITCH
TWITCH
TWITCH
TWEE TWOO TWEEE...
WHAA?! HE'S TOTALLY IGNORING IT!
FEH HEH! HE JUST *HAPPENED* NOT TO SEE IT. NOTHING WE CAN DO ABOUT THAT.
ACK!!
TWOO TWEE
GIMME A BREAK!
WH A
GAH!
STUPID REF!
WHOAA!

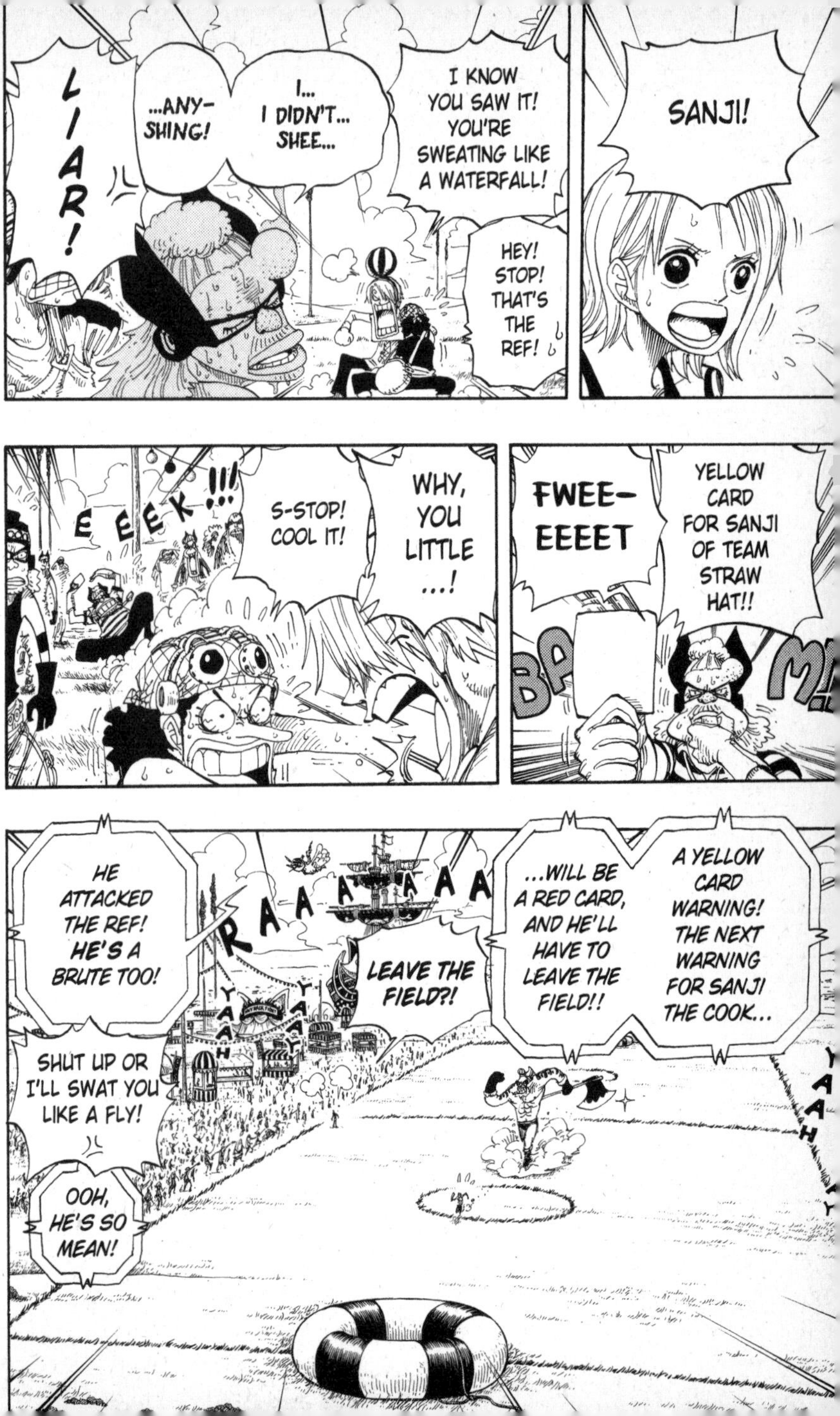
SANJI!
I KNOW YOU SAW IT! YOU'RE SWEATING LIKE A WATERFALL!
HEY! STOP! THAT'S THE REF!
I... I DIDN'T... SHEE...
...ANY-SHING!
LIAR!
YELLOW CARD FOR SANJI OF TEAM STRAW HAT!!
FWEE-EEEET
WHY, YOU LITTLE ...!
S-STOP! COOL IT!
EEEK!!!
A YELLOW CARD WARNING! THE NEXT WARNING FOR SANJI THE COOK...
...WILL BE A RED CARD, AND HE'LL HAVE TO LEAVE THE FIELD!!
YAAAH
LEAVE THE FIELD?!
RAAAAAAA
YAAAH
YAAAH
HE ATTACKED THE REF! HE'S A BRUTE TOO!
SHUT UP OR I'LL SWAT YOU LIKE A FLY!
OOH, HE'S SO MEAN!

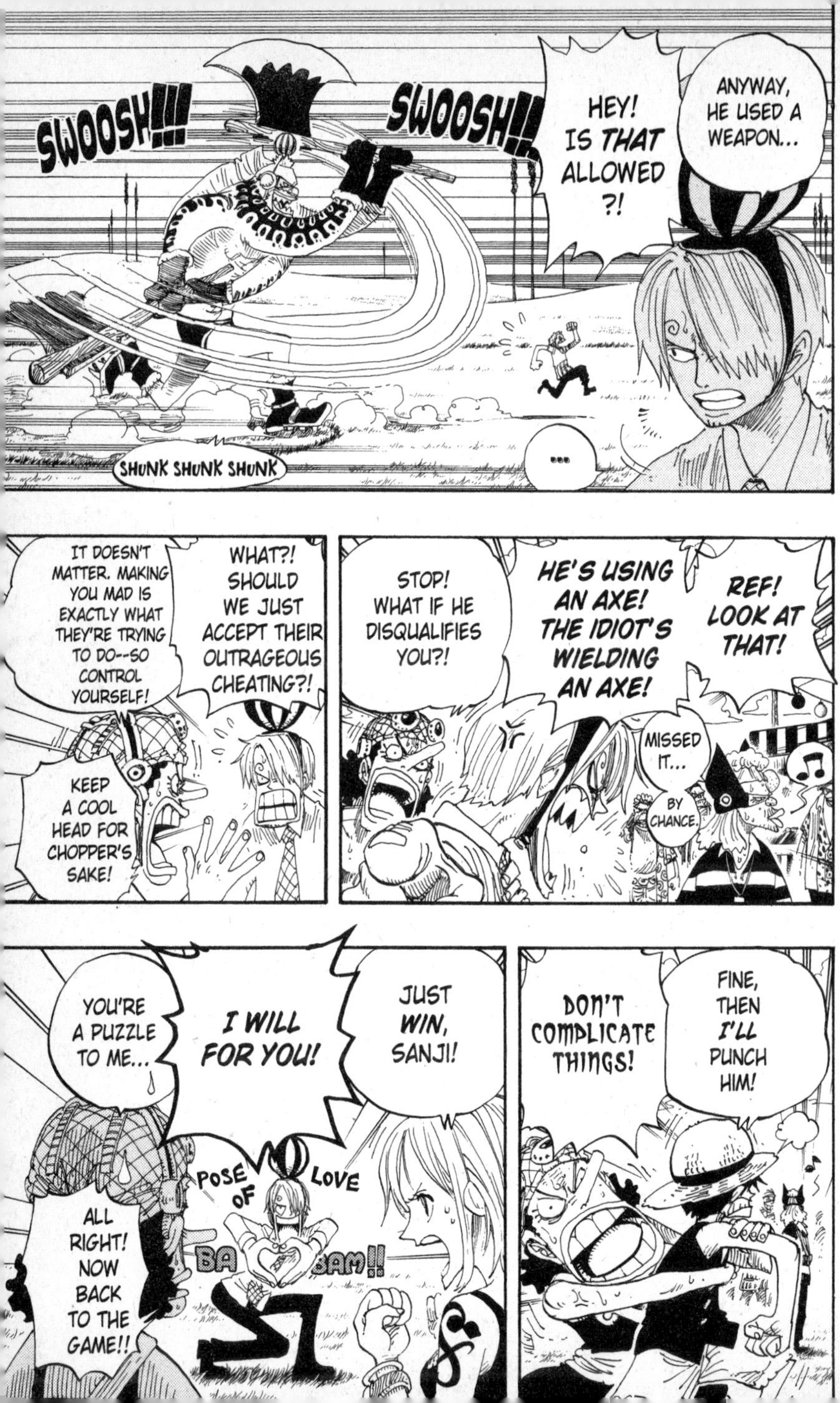
ANYWAY, HE USED A WEAPON...
HEY! IS THAT ALLOWED?!
SWOOSH!!
SWOOSH!!!
...
SHUNK SHUNK SHUNK
REF! LOOK AT THAT!
HE'S USING AN AXE! THE IDIOT'S WIELDING AN AXE!
STOP! WHAT IF HE DISQUALIFIES YOU?!
MISSED IT...
BY CHANCE.
WHAT?! SHOULD WE JUST ACCEPT THEIR OUTRAGEOUS CHEATING?!
IT DOESN'T MATTER. MAKING YOU MAD IS EXACTLY WHAT THEY'RE TRYING TO DO--SO CONTROL YOURSELF!
KEEP A COOL HEAD FOR CHOPPER'S SAKE!
FINE, THEN I'LL PUNCH HIM!
DON'T COMPLICATE THINGS!
JUST WIN, SANJI!
I WILL FOR YOU!
YOU'RE A PUZZLE TO ME...
POSE OF LOVE
BA BAM!!
ALL RIGHT! NOW BACK TO THE GAME!!

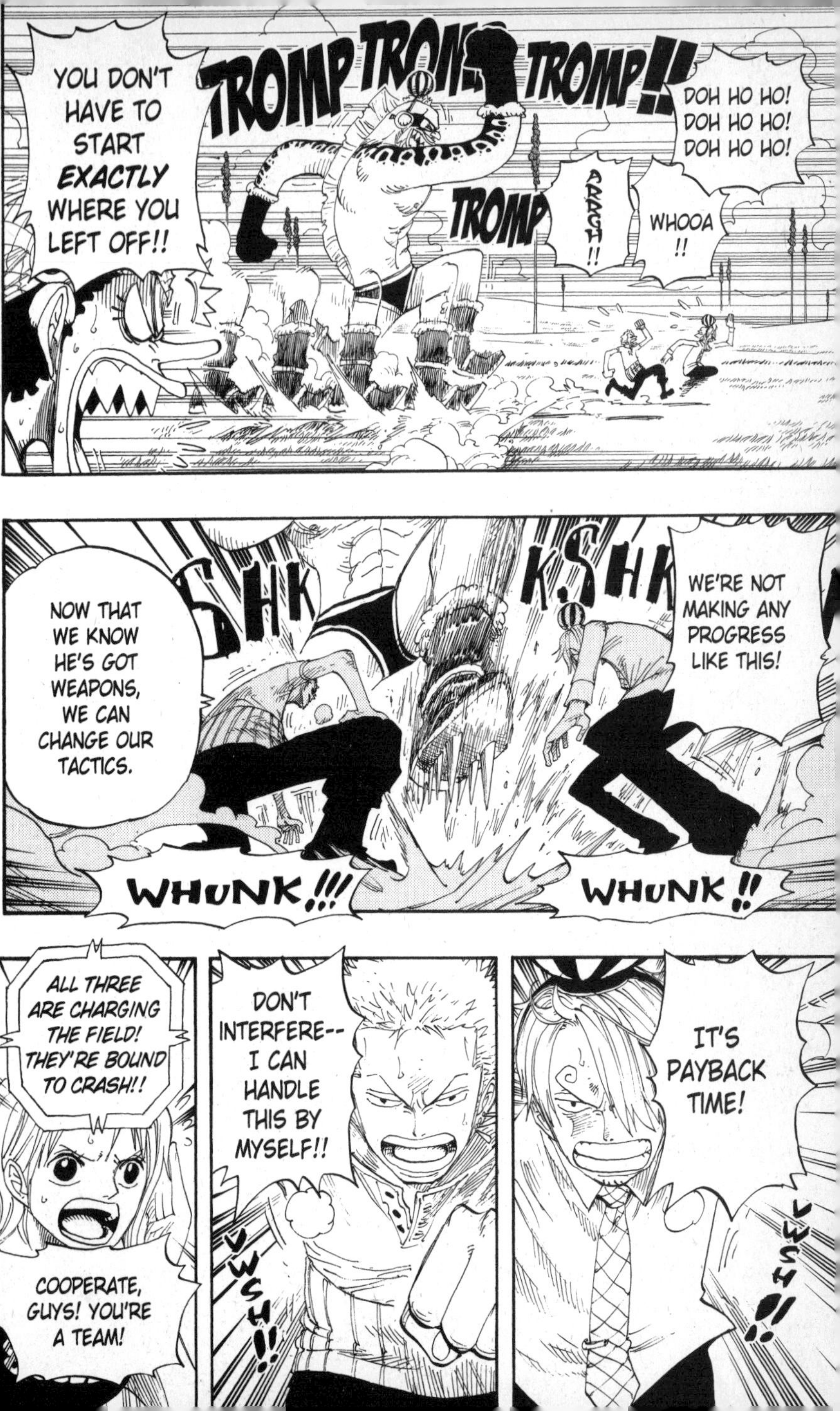
DOH HO HO! DOH HO HO! DOH HO HO!
TROMP!!
WHOOA !!
ARRGH!!
TROMP
TROMP
YOU DON'T HAVE TO START *EXACTLY* WHERE YOU LEFT OFF!!
WE'RE NOT MAKING ANY PROGRESS LIKE THIS!
KSHK
SHK
NOW THAT WE KNOW HE'S GOT WEAPONS, WE CAN CHANGE OUR TACTICS.
WHUNK!!
WHUNK!!!
IT'S PAYBACK TIME!
VWSH!!
DON'T INTERFERE-- I CAN HANDLE THIS BY MYSELF!!
VWSH!!
ALL THREE ARE CHARGING THE FIELD! THEY'RE BOUND TO CRASH!!
COOPERATE, GUYS! YOU'RE A TEAM!

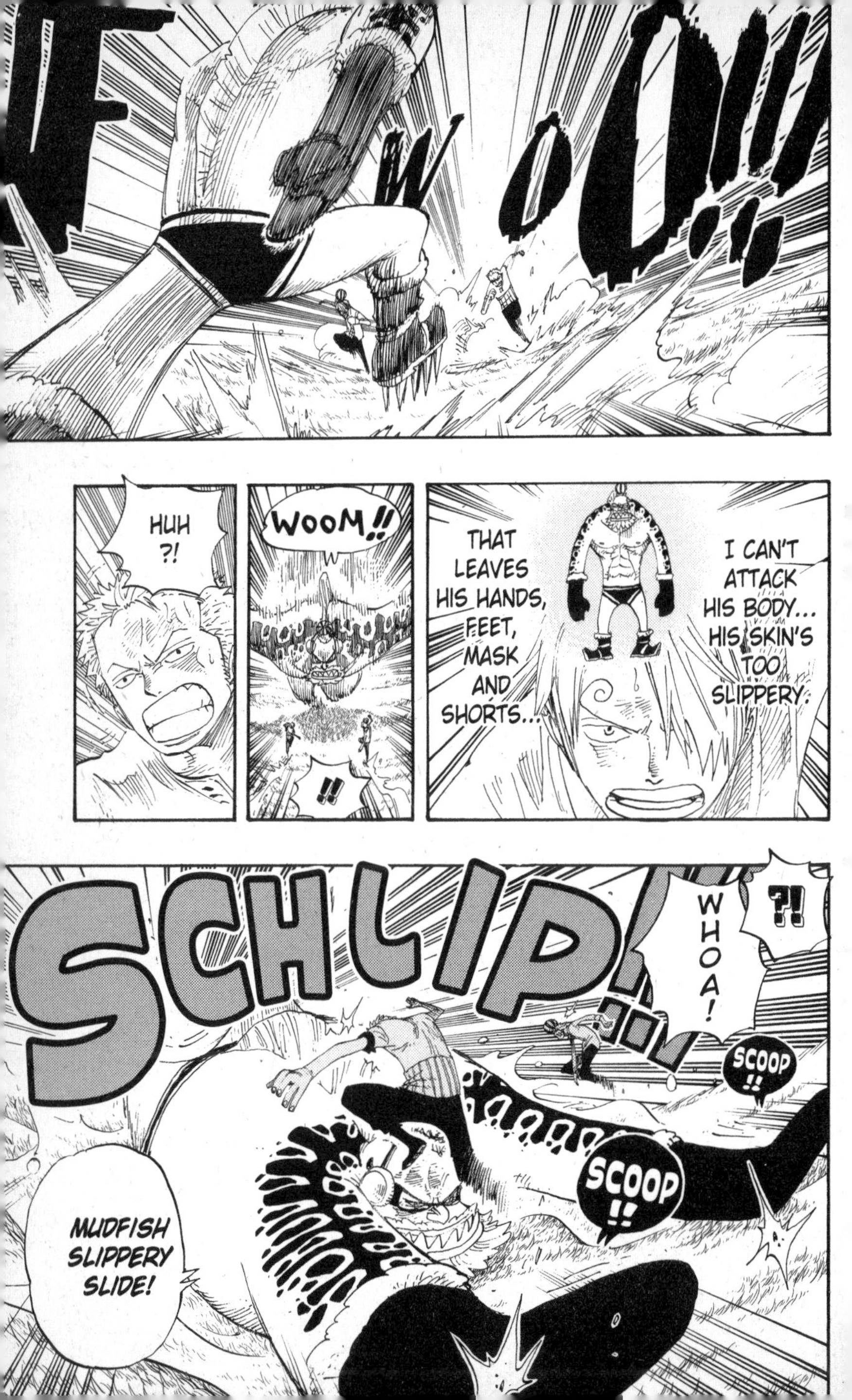
FWOOD!!
I CAN'T ATTACK HIS BODY... HIS SKIN'S TOO SLIPPERY.
THAT LEAVES HIS HANDS, FEET, MASK AND SHORTS...
WOOM!!
!!
HUH ?!
?!
WHOA!
SCHLIP!!
SCOOP!!
SCOOP!!
MUDFISH SLIPPERY SLIDE!

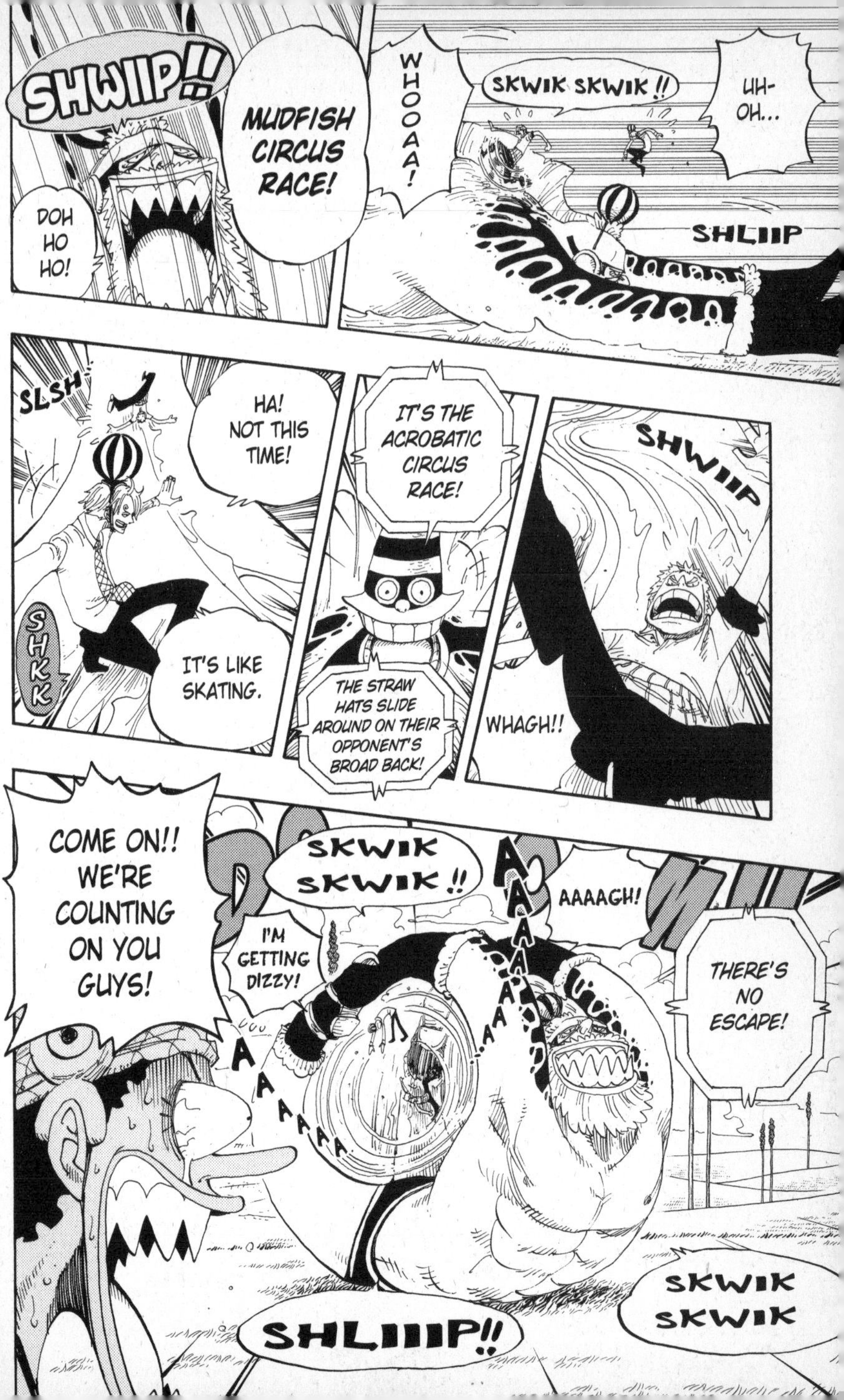
UH-OH...
SKWIK SKWIK !!
WHOOAA!
SHLIIP
SHWIIP!!
MUDFISH CIRCUS RACE!
DOH HO HO!
SHWIIP
WHAGH!!
IT'S THE ACROBATIC CIRCUS RACE!
THE STRAW HATS SLIDE AROUND ON THEIR OPPONENT'S BROAD BACK!
HA! NOT THIS TIME!
SLSH
IT'S LIKE SKATING.
SHKK
THERE'S NO ESCAPE!
AAAAGH!
SKWIK SKWIK !!
I'M GETTING DIZZY!
COME ON!! WE'RE COUNTING ON YOU GUYS!
SKWIK SKWIK
SHLIIIP!!

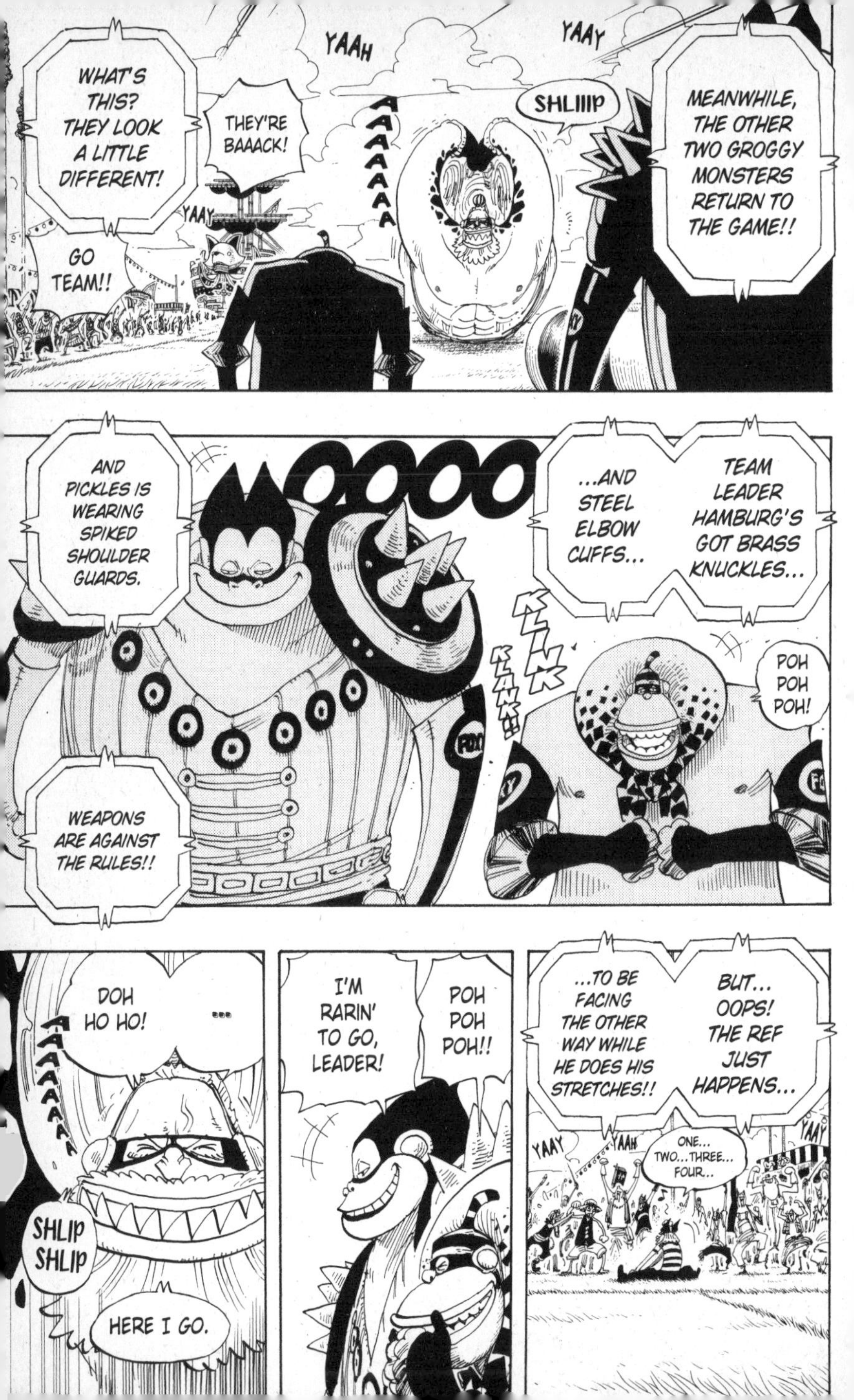

MEANWHILE, THE OTHER TWO GROGGY MONSTERS RETURN TO THE GAME!!
YAAY
SHLIIIP
AAAAAAA
YAAH
THEY'RE BAAACK!
WHAT'S THIS? THEY LOOK A LITTLE DIFFERENT!
YAAY
GO TEAM!!
TEAM LEADER HAMBURG'S GOT BRASS KNUCKLES...
...AND STEEL ELBOW CUFFS...
POH POH POH!
KLINK
KLANK!!
AND PICKLES IS WEARING SPIKED SHOULDER GUARDS.
WEAPONS ARE AGAINST THE RULES!!
BUT... OOPS! THE REF JUST HAPPENS...
...TO BE FACING THE OTHER WAY WHILE HE DOES HIS STRETCHES!!
YAAY
ONE... TWO...THREE... FOUR...
YAAH
YAAY
POH POH POH!!
I'M RARIN' TO GO, LEADER!
...
DOH HO HO!
AAAAAAA
SHLIP SHLIP
HERE I GO.

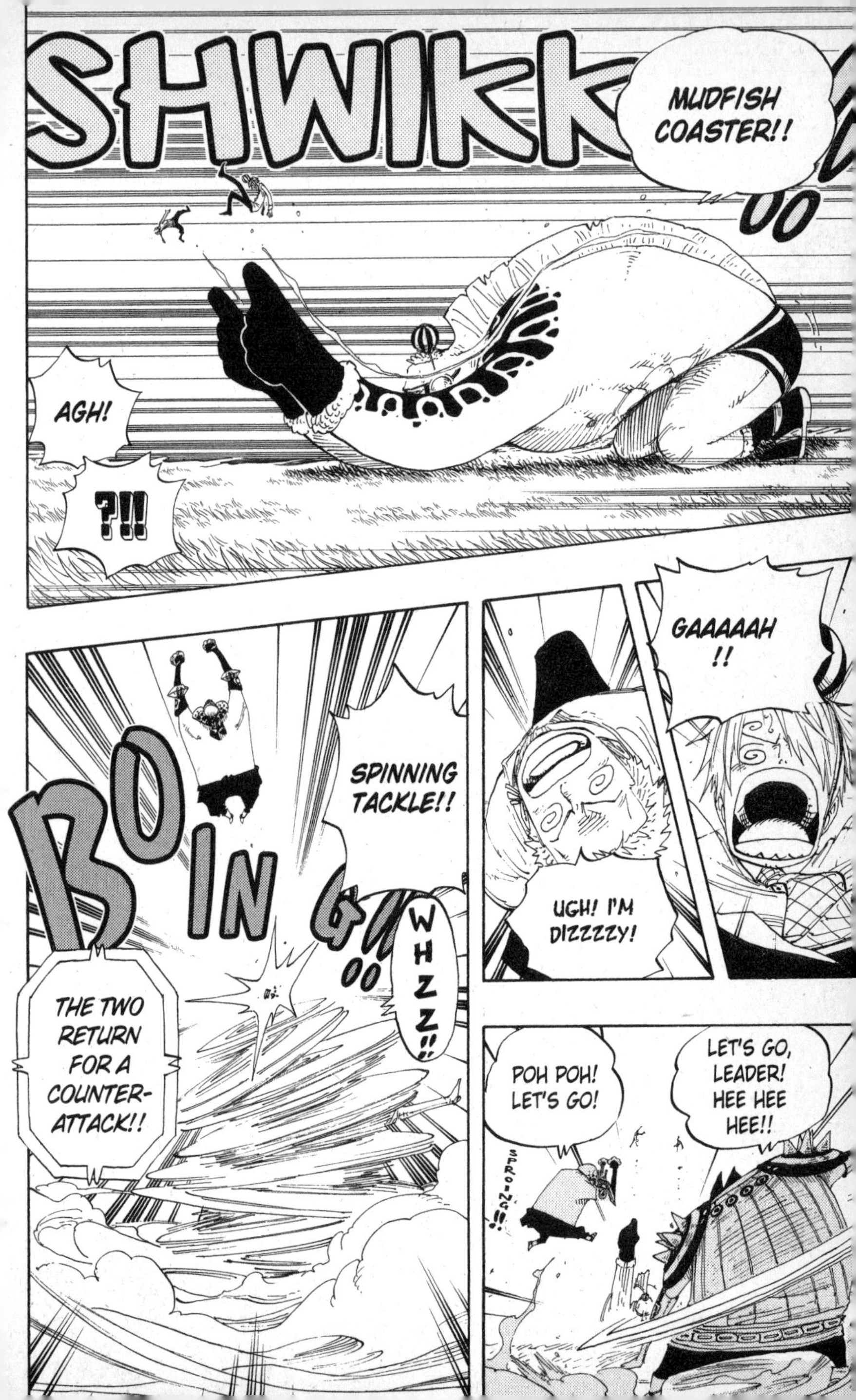
SHWIKK
MUDFISH COASTER!!
OO
AGH!
?!!
GAAAAAH!!
UGH! I'M DIZZZZY!
LET'S GO, LEADER! HEE HEE HEE!!
POH POH! LET'S GO!
SPROING!!
SPINNING TACKLE!!
BOING
WHZZZ!!
OO
THE TWO RETURN FOR A COUNTER-ATTACK!!

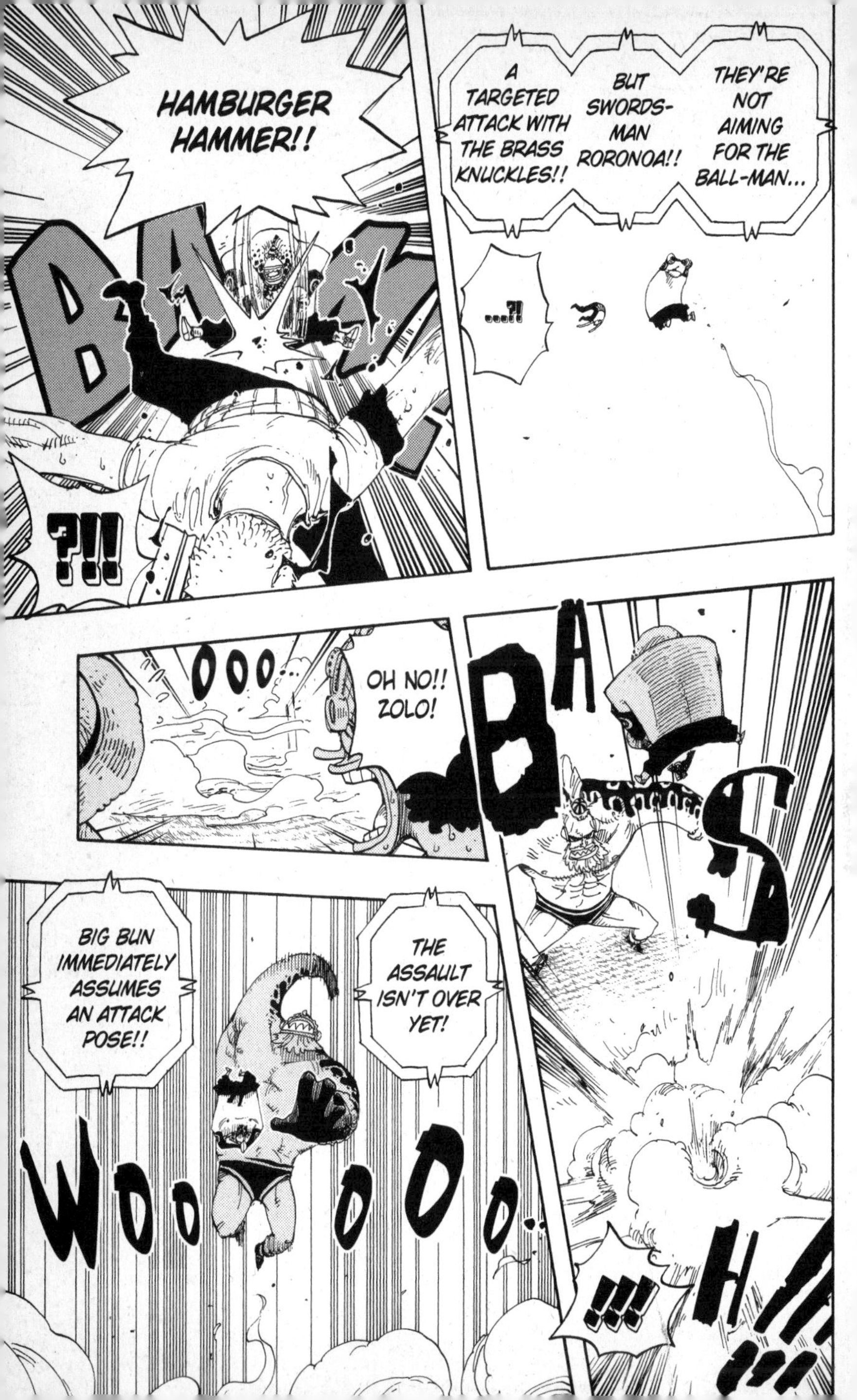
THEY'RE NOT AIMING FOR THE BALL-MAN... BUT SWORDSMAN RORONOA!! A TARGETED ATTACK WITH THE BRASS KNUCKLES!!
...?!
HAMBURGER HAMMER!!
BAM
?!!
BAS
H!!
!!!
OH NO!! ZOLO!
OOO...
THE ASSAULT ISN'T OVER YET!
BIG BUN IMMEDIATELY ASSUMES AN ATTACK POSE!!
WOOOOOO..

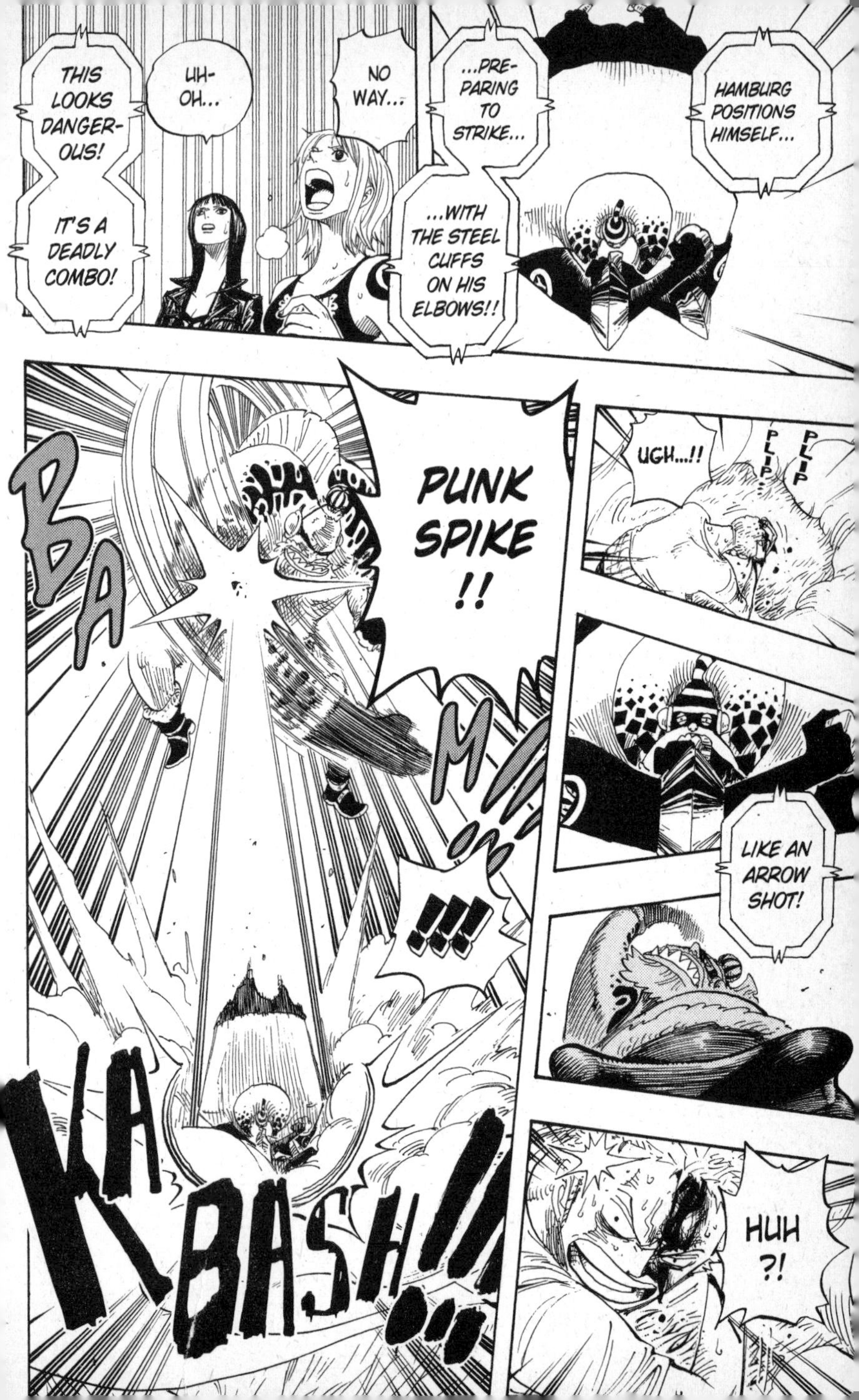
HAMBURG POSITIONS HIMSELF...
...PRE-PARING TO STRIKE...
...WITH THE STEEL CUFFS ON HIS ELBOWS!!
NO WAY...
UH-OH...
THIS LOOKS DANGER-OUS!
IT'S A DEADLY COMBO!
PLIP PLIP
UGH...!!
LIKE AN ARROW SHOT!
HUH ?!
PUNK SPIKE !!
BAM!!!
KA BASH!!...

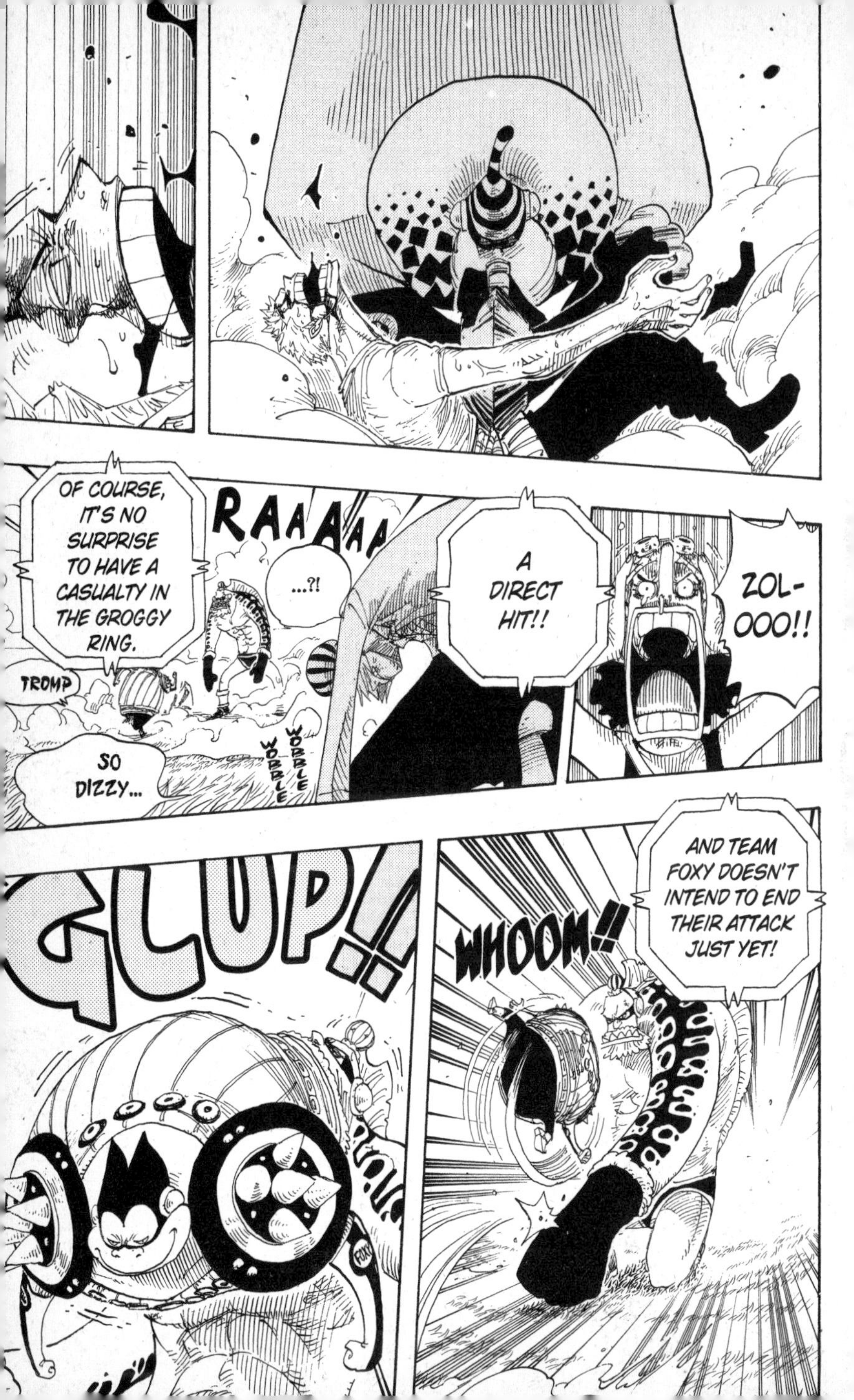
ZOL-OOO!!
A DIRECT HIT!!
RAAAAA
...?!
OF COURSE, IT'S NO SURPRISE TO HAVE A CASUALTY IN THE GROGGY RING.
WOBBLE WOBBLE
TROMP
SO DIZZY...
AND TEAM FOXY DOESN'T INTEND TO END THEIR ATTACK JUST YET!
WHOOM!!
GLUP!!

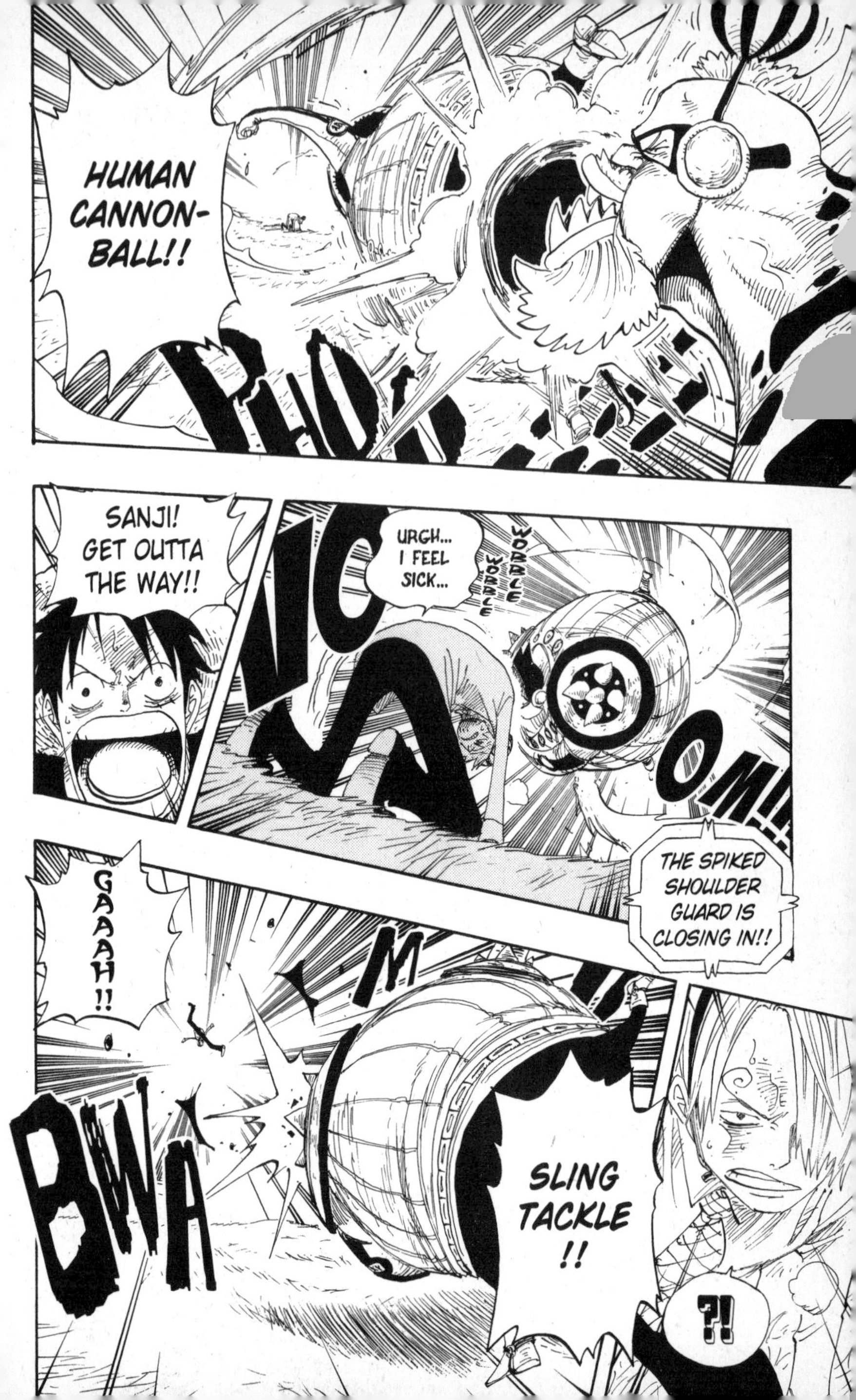
HUMAN CANNON-BALL!!
URGH... I FEEL SICK...
WOBBLE WOBBLE
SANJI! GET OUTTA THE WAY!!
THE SPIKED SHOULDER GUARD IS CLOSING IN!!
?!
SLING TACKLE!!
GAAAAH!!

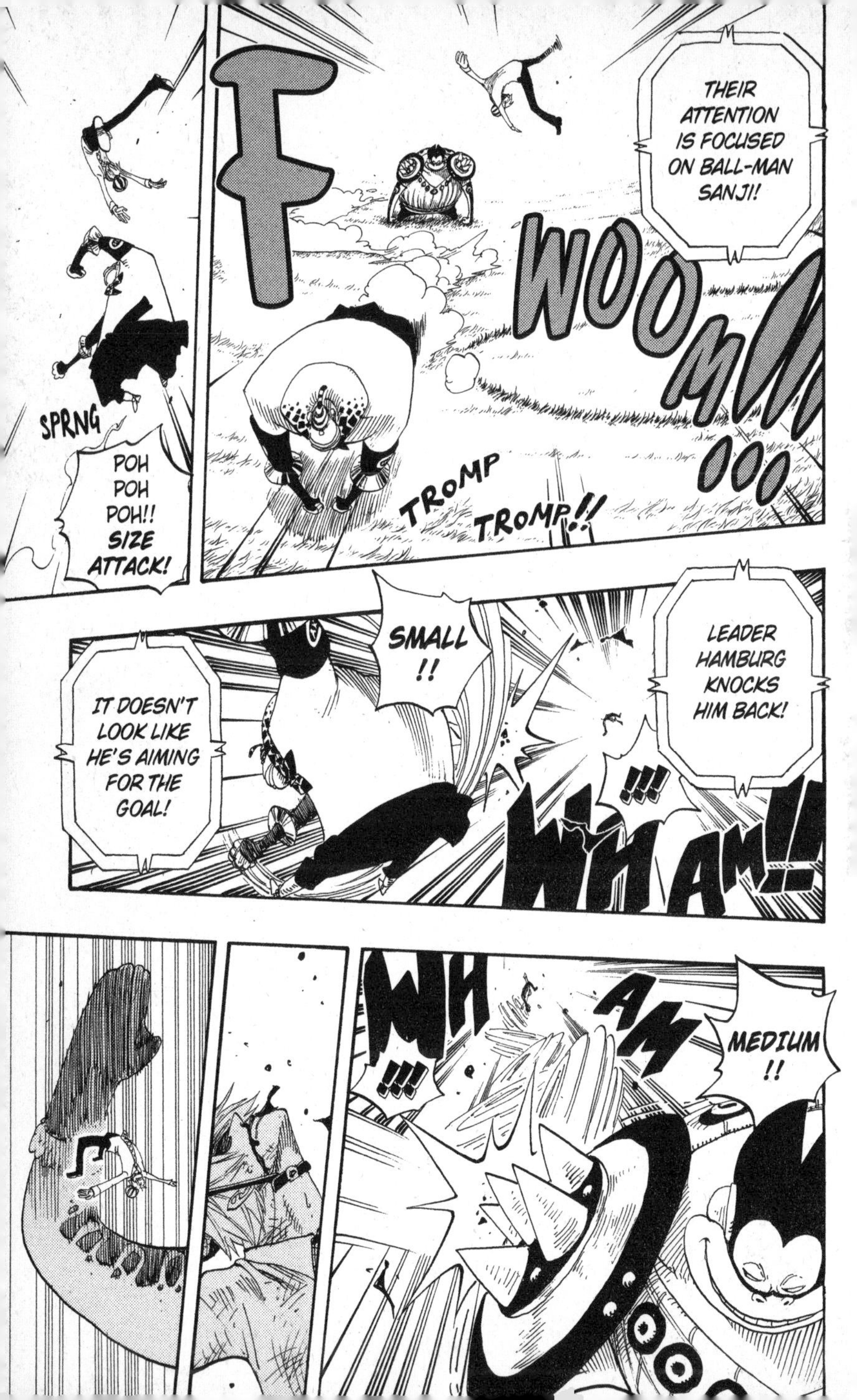
THEIR ATTENTION IS FOCUSED ON BALL-MAN SANJI!
F
WOOMMM...
TROMP TROMP!!
SPRNG
POH POH POH!! SIZE ATTACK!
LEADER HAMBURG KNOCKS HIM BACK!
SMALL!!
!!!
WHAM!!
IT DOESN'T LOOK LIKE HE'S AIMING FOR THE GOAL!
MEDIUM!!
WHAM
!!!

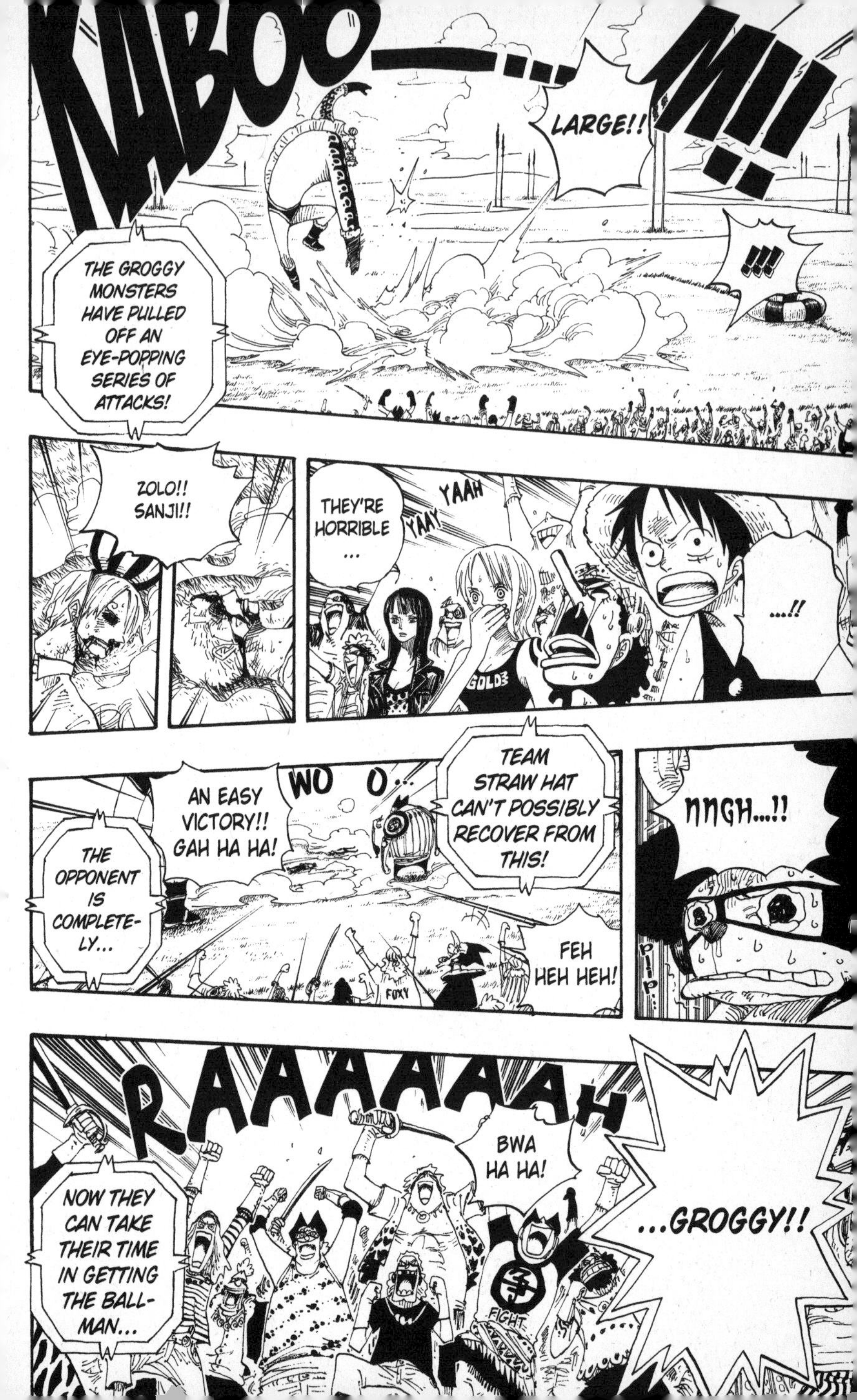
KABOO—...M!!
LARGE!!
!!!
THE GROGGY MONSTERS HAVE PULLED OFF AN EYE-POPPING SERIES OF ATTACKS!
...!!
YAAH
YAAY
THEY'RE HORRIBLE ...
ZOLO!! SANJI!!
NNGH...!!
plip...
TEAM STRAW HAT CAN'T POSSIBLY RECOVER FROM THIS!
WO O...
AN EASY VICTORY!! GAH HA HA!
THE OPPONENT IS COMPLETE-LY...
FEH HEH HEH!
...GROGGY!!
BWA HA HA!
RAAAAAAH
NOW THEY CAN TAKE THEIR TIME IN GETTING THE BALL-MAN...

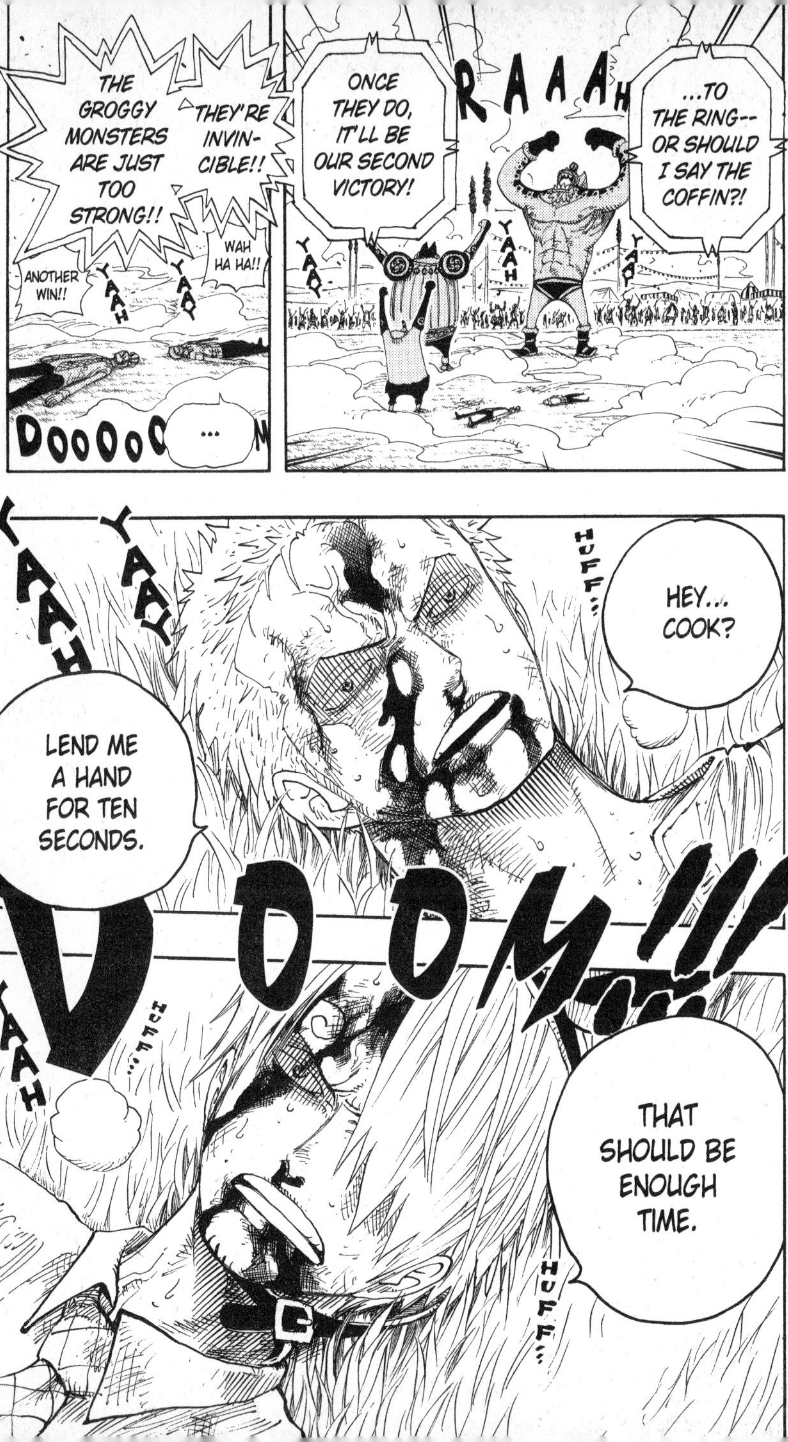
...TO THE RING-- OR SHOULD I SAY THE COFFIN?!
RAAAH
ONCE THEY DO, IT'LL BE OUR SECOND VICTORY!
YAAY
YAAH
YAAY
THE GROGGY MONSTERS ARE JUST TOO STRONG!!
THEY'RE INVIN-CIBLE!!
WAH HA HA!!
YAAY
YAAH
ANOTHER WIN!!
DOOOOO
...
N
YAAAY
YAAAH
HUFF...
HEY... COOK?
LEND ME A HAND FOR TEN SECONDS.
DOOM!!!
YAAAH
HUFF...
THAT SHOULD BE ENOUGH TIME.
HUFF...

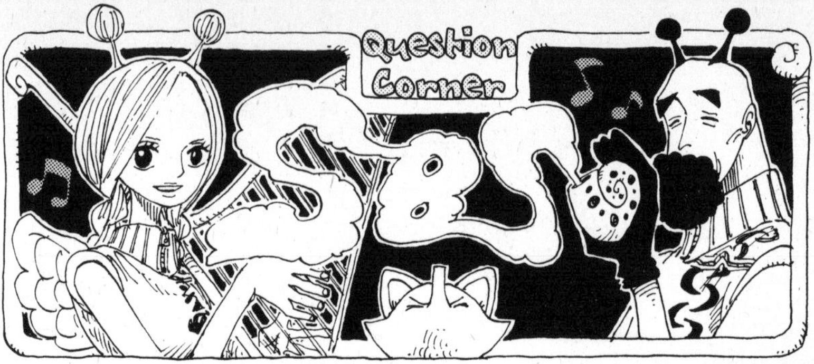
Question Corner
SBS

Q : Hello, Oda Sensei. Let me get right to my question. In vol. 28, Luffy sang songs entitled “Song of the South Island” and “Song of the North Island.” Are there songs for the east and west? Please×99 tell me. --Yuzo Kawaguchi

A : Let's have Luffy sing them himself! Take it away, Luffy!

Luffy: Oh, you wanna hear me sing? All right!

"Laaa la-la-la-laaa ♪
Morning comes early on East Island
Everyone is lively but stupid ♪
Nights are late on West Island
Everyone is cheery but stupid ♪
AAAH AAH I just yawned ♪
Everyone smiles but they're stupid" ♪

A : Hmm, that song made me feel like I should stop taking life so seriously. Okay, now for the next question.

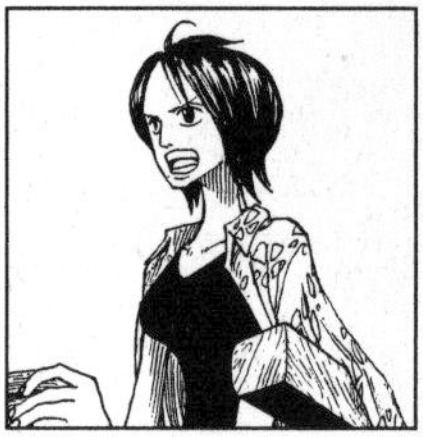

Q : Hello, Odacchi! We want to know our idol Tashigi's birthday. How about October 6. Since that can be read in Japanese to sound like the word “Clumsy”? Okay, that should be fine! How incredibly awesome--Chief Petty Officer Tashigi's birthday is October 6!

IT'S SETTLED!!

If anyone doesn't like that, say it to my face! Graah! (Oh, sorry! Seriously, I like Tashigi a lot. Please decide on her birthday!) --Spicy☆Taro

A : October 6, it is.

Chapter 312:
GOAL!!

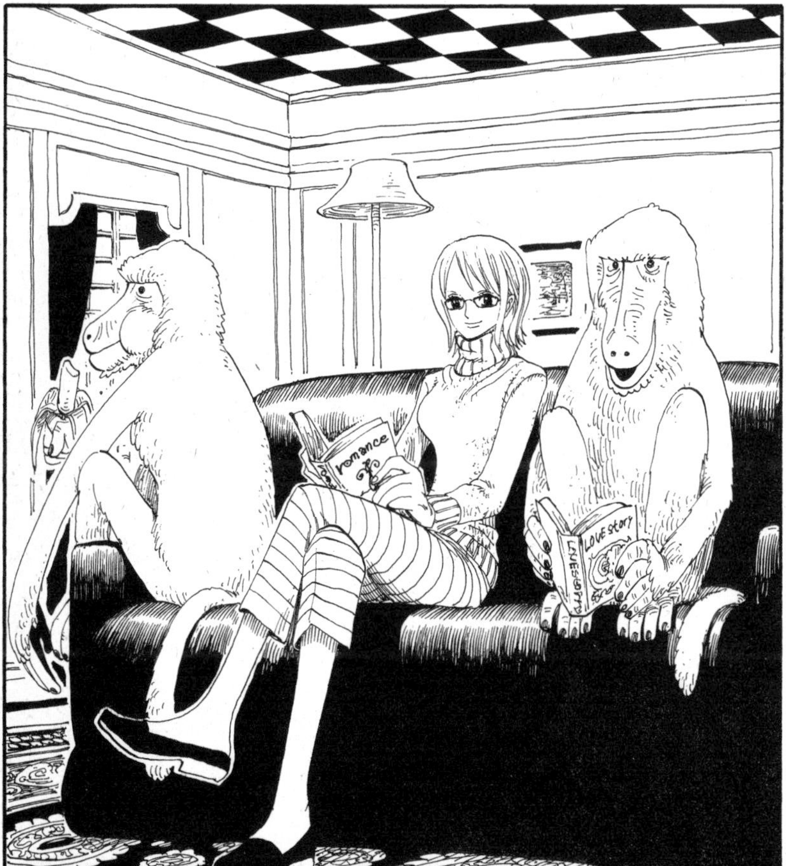
romance
LOVE story
LOVE story

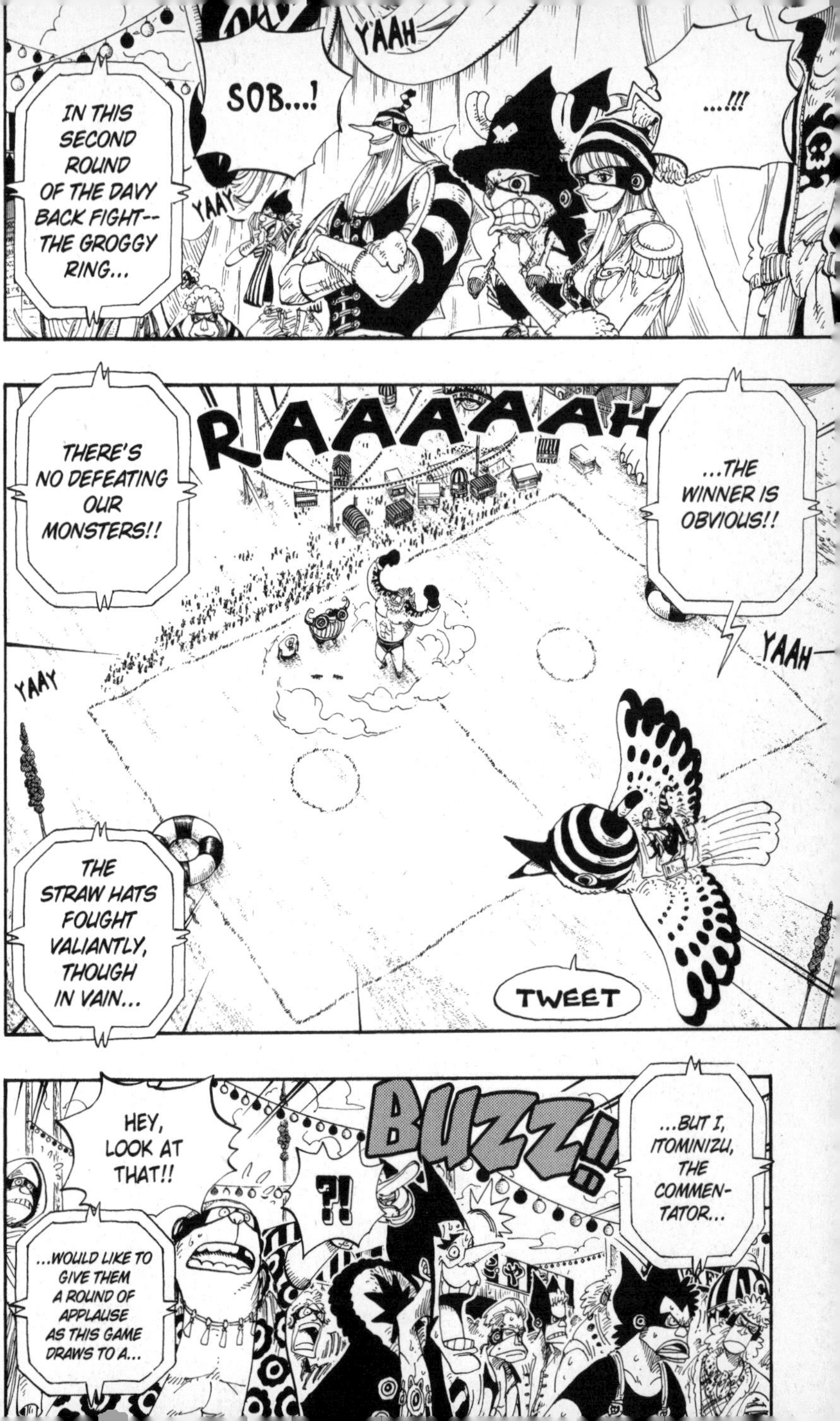
...!!!
YAAH
SOB...!
IN THIS SECOND ROUND OF THE DAVY BACK FIGHT-- THE GROGGY RING...
YAAY
...THE WINNER IS OBVIOUS!!
RAAAAAAH
THERE'S NO DEFEATING OUR MONSTERS!!
YAAH
YAAY
THE STRAW HATS FOUGHT VALIANTLY, THOUGH IN VAIN...
TWEET
...BUT I, ITOMINIZU, THE COMMEN-TATOR...
BUZZ!!
?!
HEY, LOOK AT THAT!!
...WOULD LIKE TO GIVE THEM A ROUND OF APPLAUSE AS THIS GAME DRAWS TO A...

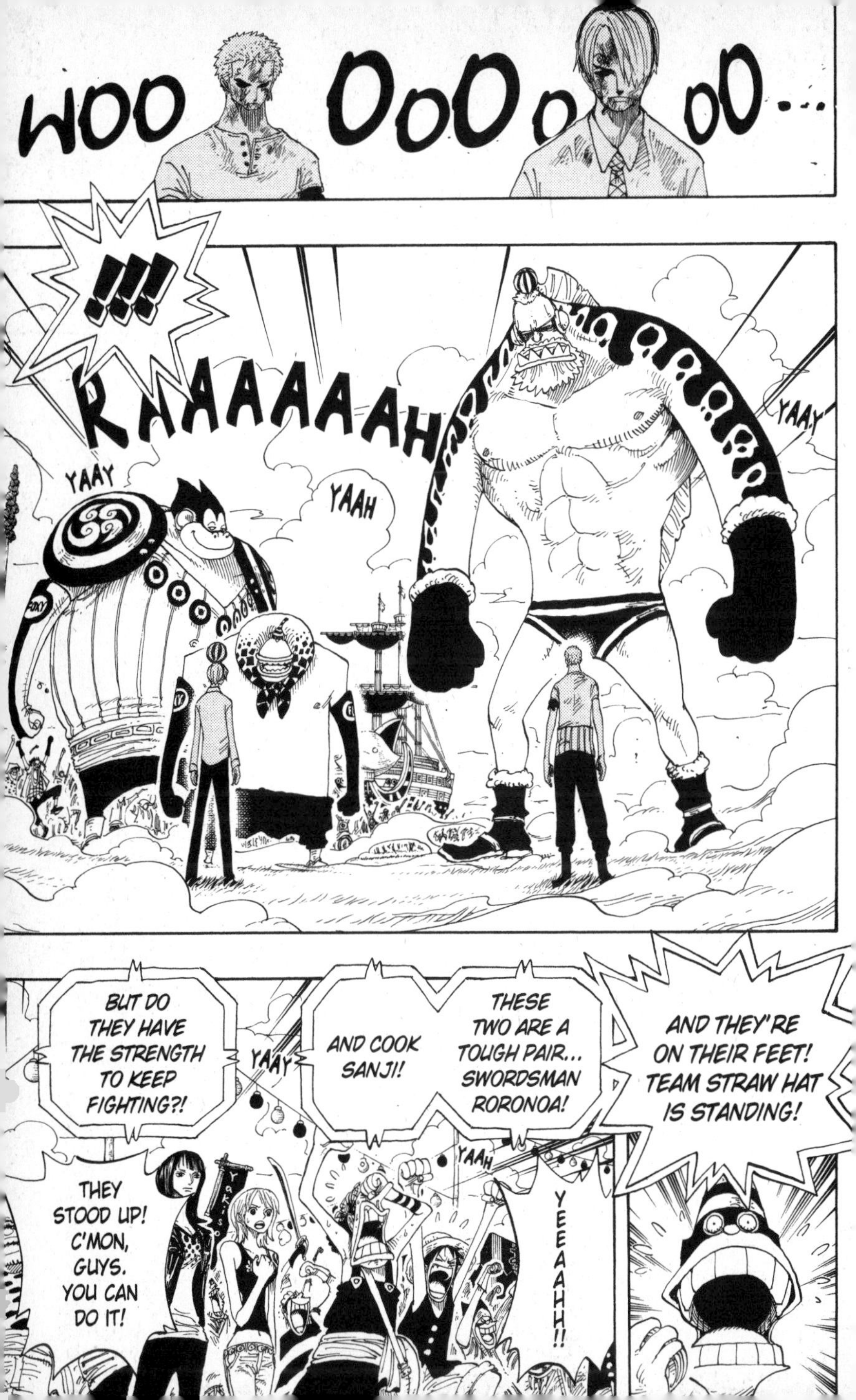
WOO OoOo o oO...
!!!
RAAAAAAAH
YAAY
YAAH
YAAY
AND THEY'RE ON THEIR FEET! TEAM STRAW HAT IS STANDING!
THESE TWO ARE A TOUGH PAIR... SWORDSMAN RORONOA!
AND COOK SANJI!
YAAY
BUT DO THEY HAVE THE STRENGTH TO KEEP FIGHTING?!
YAAH
YEEAAHH!!
THEY STOOD UP! C'MON, GUYS. YOU CAN DO IT!

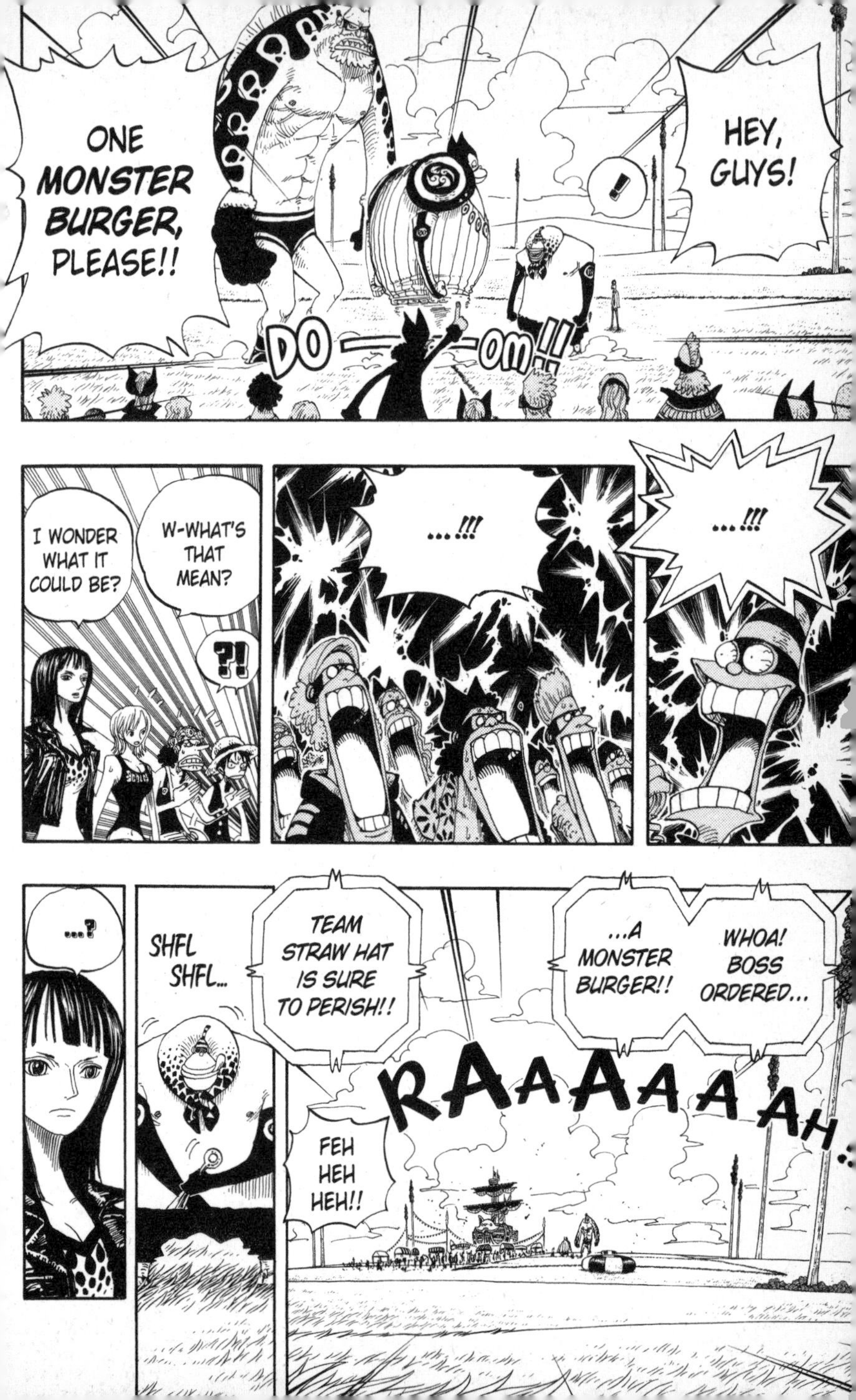
HEY, GUYS!
!
ONE MONSTER BURGER, PLEASE!!
DO—OM!!
...!!!
...!!!
W-WHAT'S THAT MEAN?
I WONDER WHAT IT COULD BE?
?!
WHOA! BOSS ORDERED...
...A MONSTER BURGER!!
TEAM STRAW HAT IS SURE TO PERISH!!
RAAAAAAAH..
FEH HEH HEH!!
SHFL SHFL...
...?

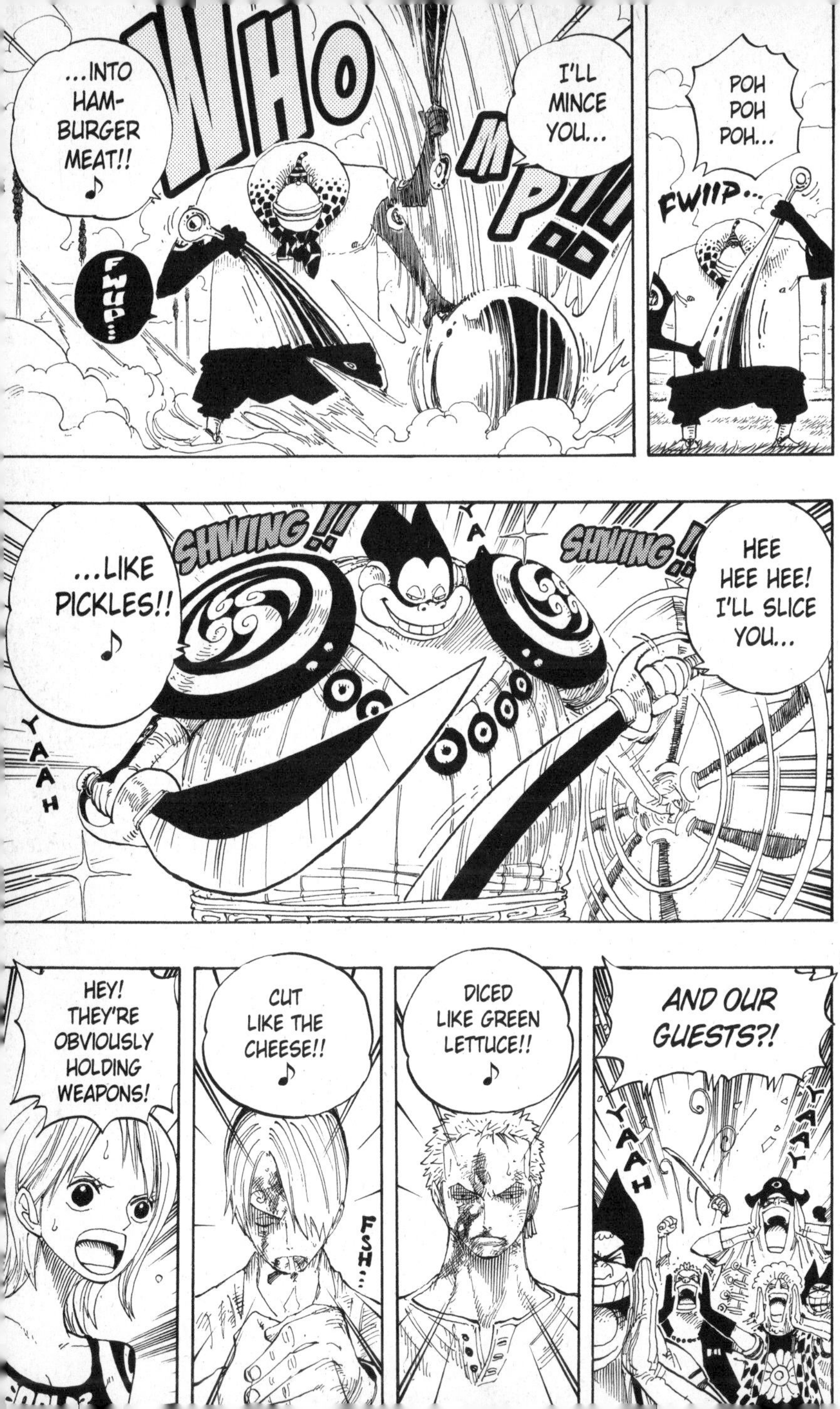

POH POH POH...
FWIIP...
I'LL MINCE YOU...
WHOMP
...INTO HAM-BURGER MEAT!! ♪
FWUP...
HEE HEE HEE! I'LL SLICE YOU...
SHWING!!
SHWING!!
...LIKE PICKLES!! ♪
YAAH
AND OUR GUESTS?!
YAAAY
YAAAH
DICED LIKE GREEN LETTUCE!! ♪
CUT LIKE THE CHEESE!! ♪
FSH...
HEY! THEY'RE OBVIOUSLY HOLDING WEAPONS!

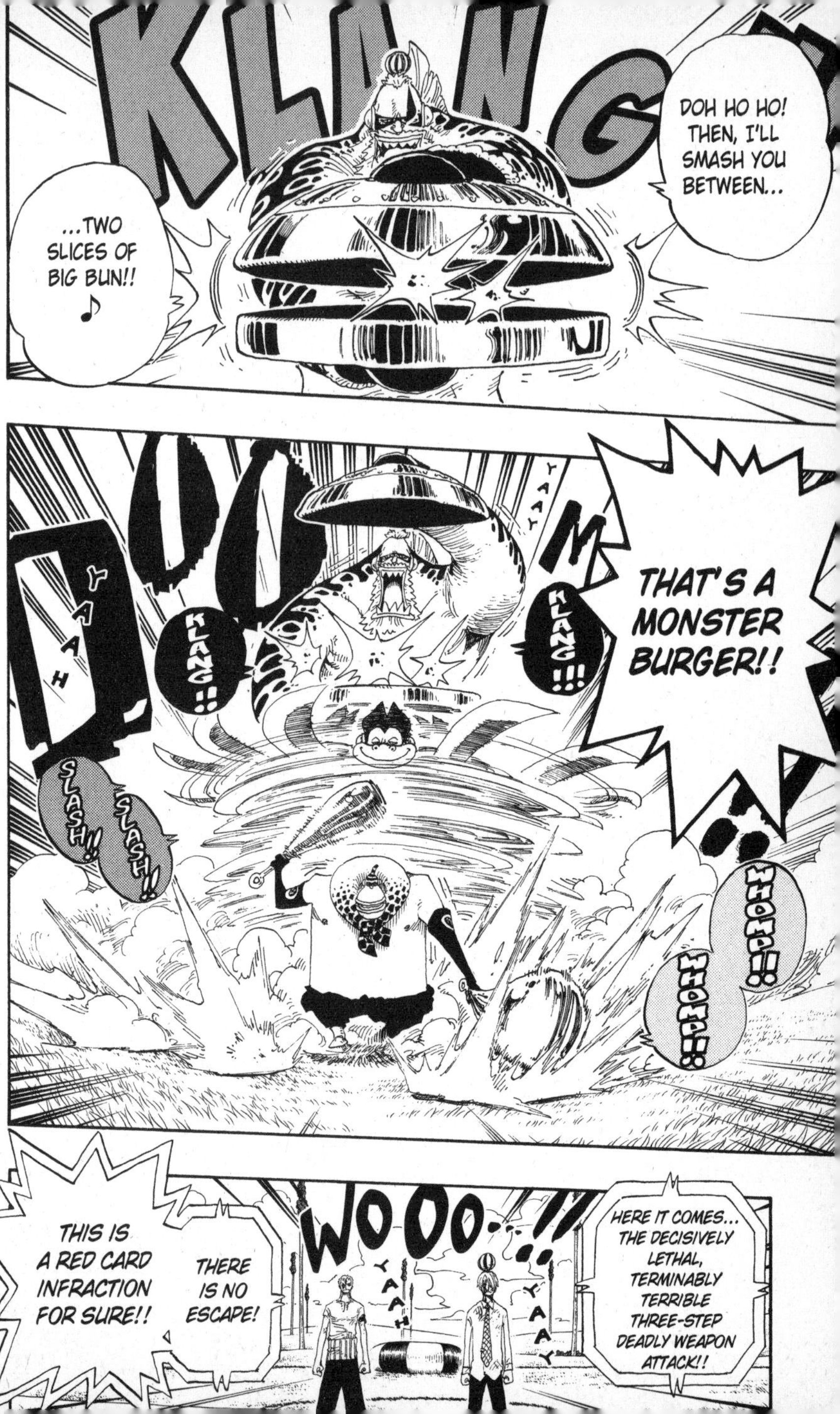
KLANG
DOH HO HO! THEN, I'LL SMASH YOU BETWEEN...
...TWO SLICES OF BIG BUN!! ♪
YAAAY
THAT'S A MONSTER BURGER!!
KLANG!!!
DOOM
KLANG!!
YAAH
SLASH!!
SLASH!!
WHOMP!!
WHOMP!!
HERE IT COMES... THE DECISIVELY LETHAL, TERMINABLY TERRIBLE THREE-STEP DEADLY WEAPON ATTACK!!
YAAAY
WOOO..!!
YAAH
THERE IS NO ESCAPE!
THIS IS A RED CARD INFRACTION FOR SURE!!

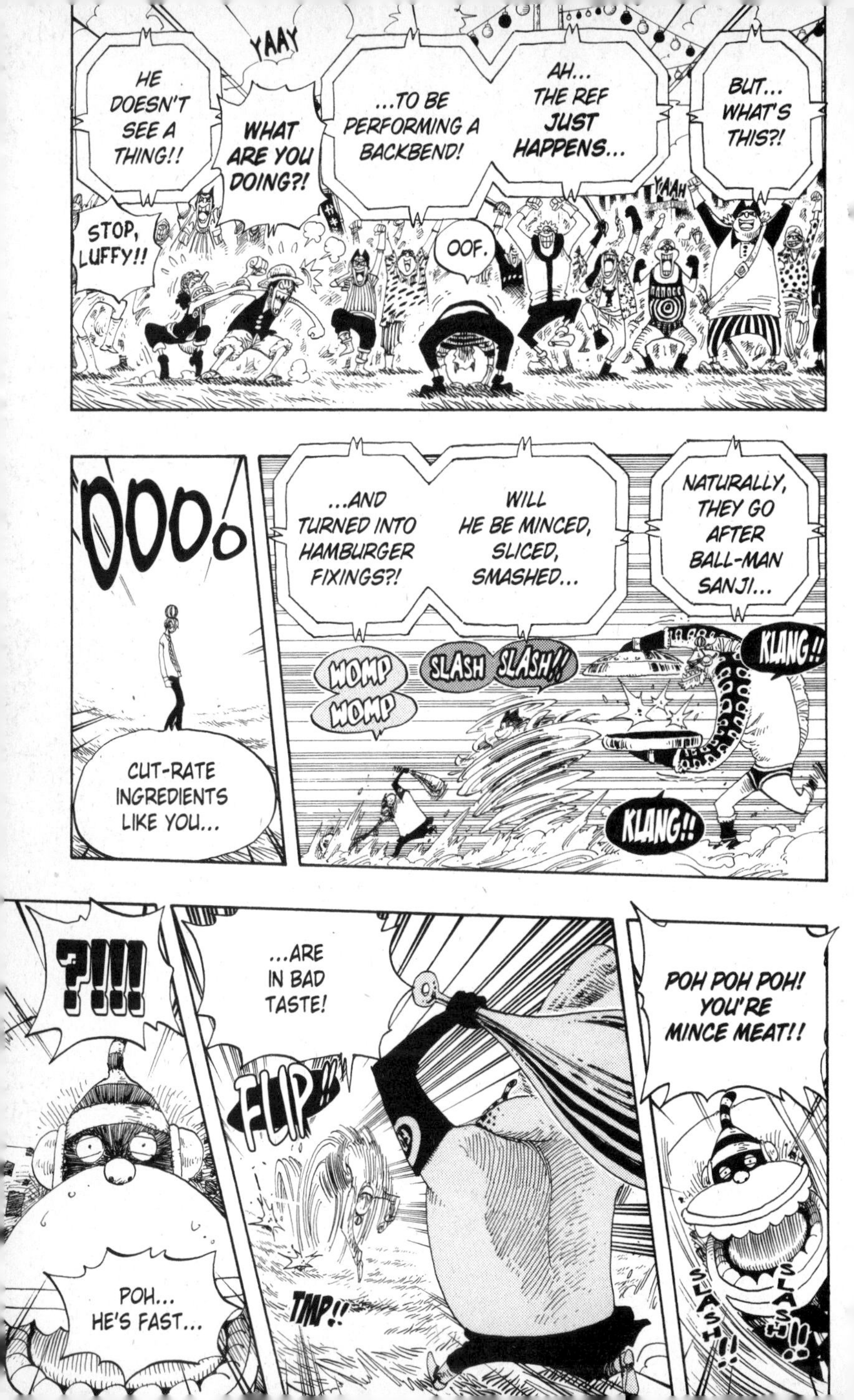
BUT... WHAT'S THIS?!
YAAH
AH... THE REF JUST HAPPENS...
...TO BE PERFORMING A BACKBEND!
OOF.
YAAY
WHAT ARE YOU DOING?!
HE DOESN'T SEE A THING!!
STOP, LUFFY!!
NATURALLY, THEY GO AFTER BALL-MAN SANJI...
WILL HE BE MINCED, SLICED, SMASHED...
...AND TURNED INTO HAMBURGER FIXINGS?!
KLANG!!
SLASH SLASH!!
WOMP WOMP
KLANG!!
OOOo
CUT-RATE INGREDIENTS LIKE YOU...
POH POH POH! YOU'RE MINCE MEAT!!
SLASH!!
SLASH!!
...ARE IN BAD TASTE!
FLIP!!
TMP!!
?!!!
POH... HE'S FAST...

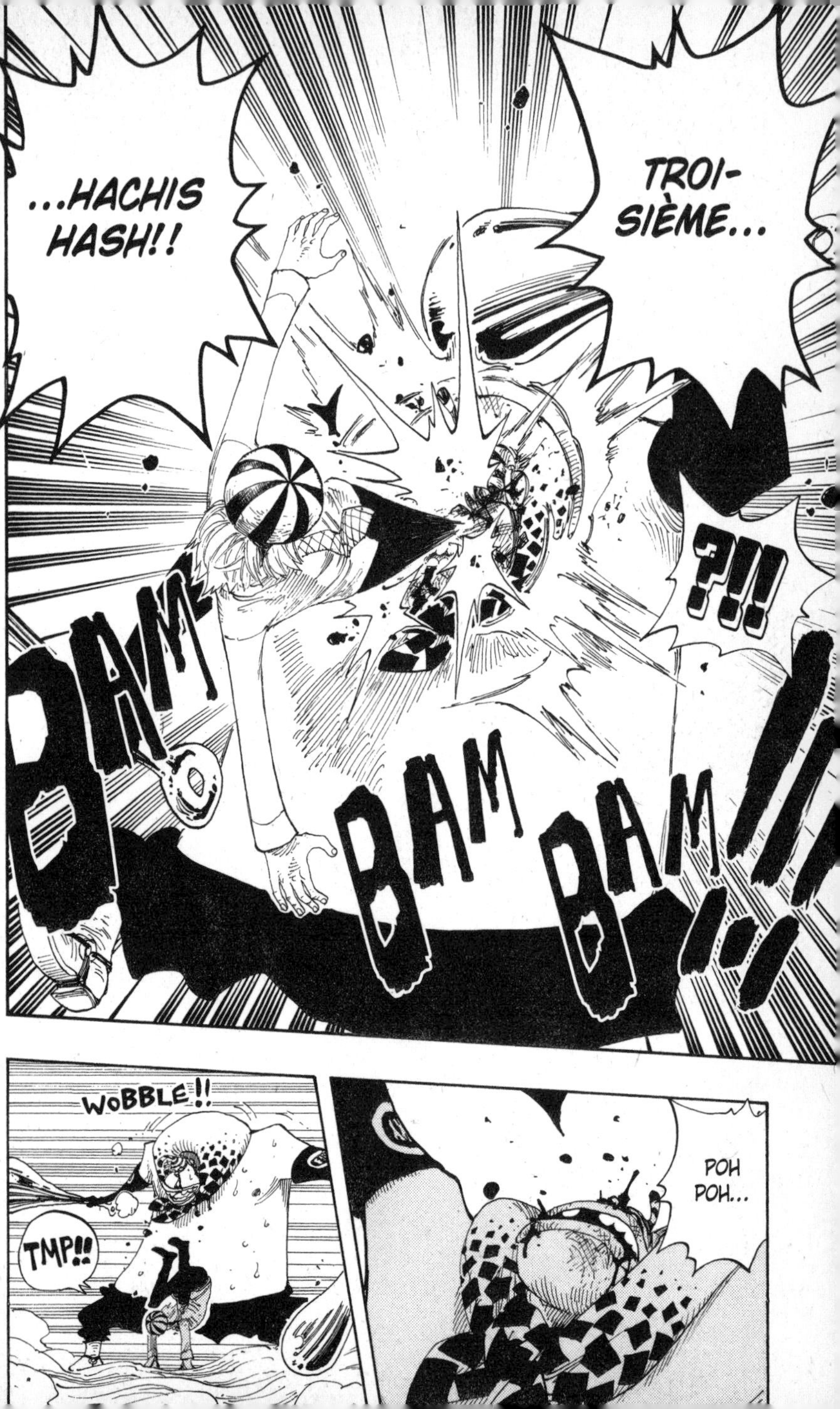
TROI-SIÈME...
...HACHIS HASH!!
?!!
BAM BAM BAM!!!
POH POH...
WOBBLE!!
TMP!!

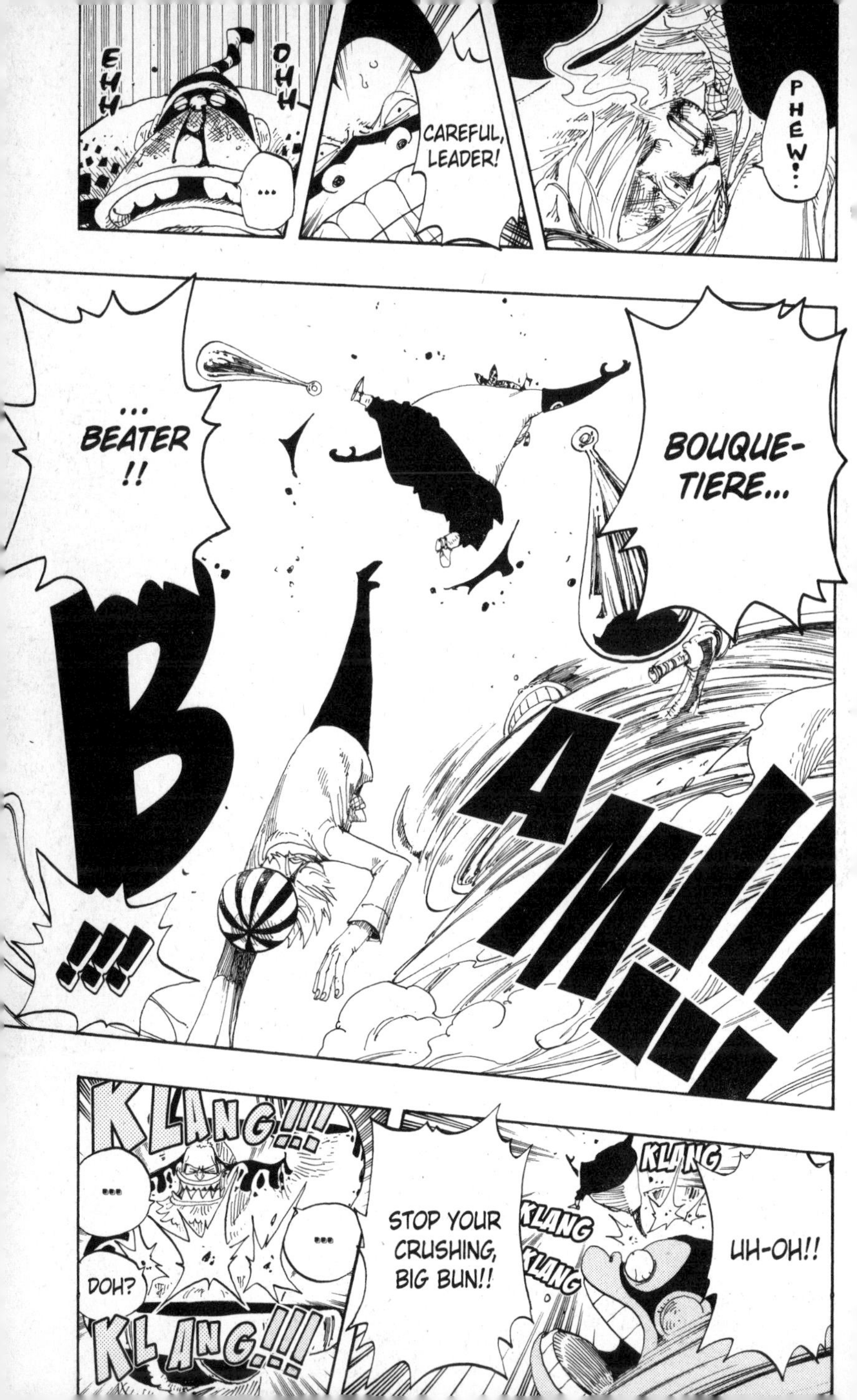

PHEW...
CAREFUL, LEADER!
OHHH
EHHH
...
BOUQUETIERE...
...BEATER!!
BAM!!!
KLANG
KLANG
KLANG
UH-OH!!
STOP YOUR CRUSHING, BIG BUN!!
KLANG!!!
...
...
DOH?
KLANG!!!

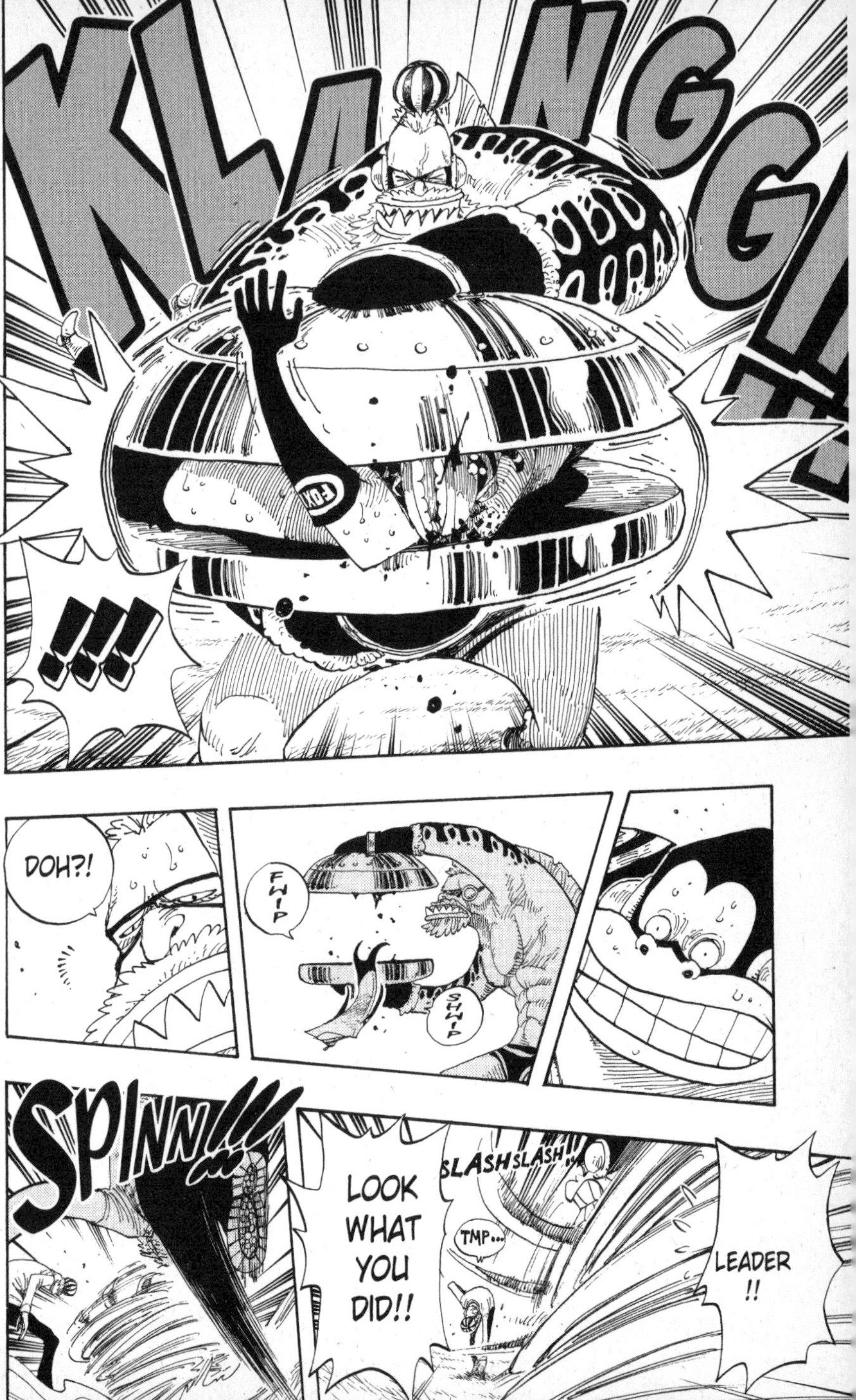
KLANGG!!
!!!
SHWIP
FWIP
DOH?!
LEADER !!
SLASH SLASH
TMP...
LOOK WHAT YOU DID!!
SPINN!!!

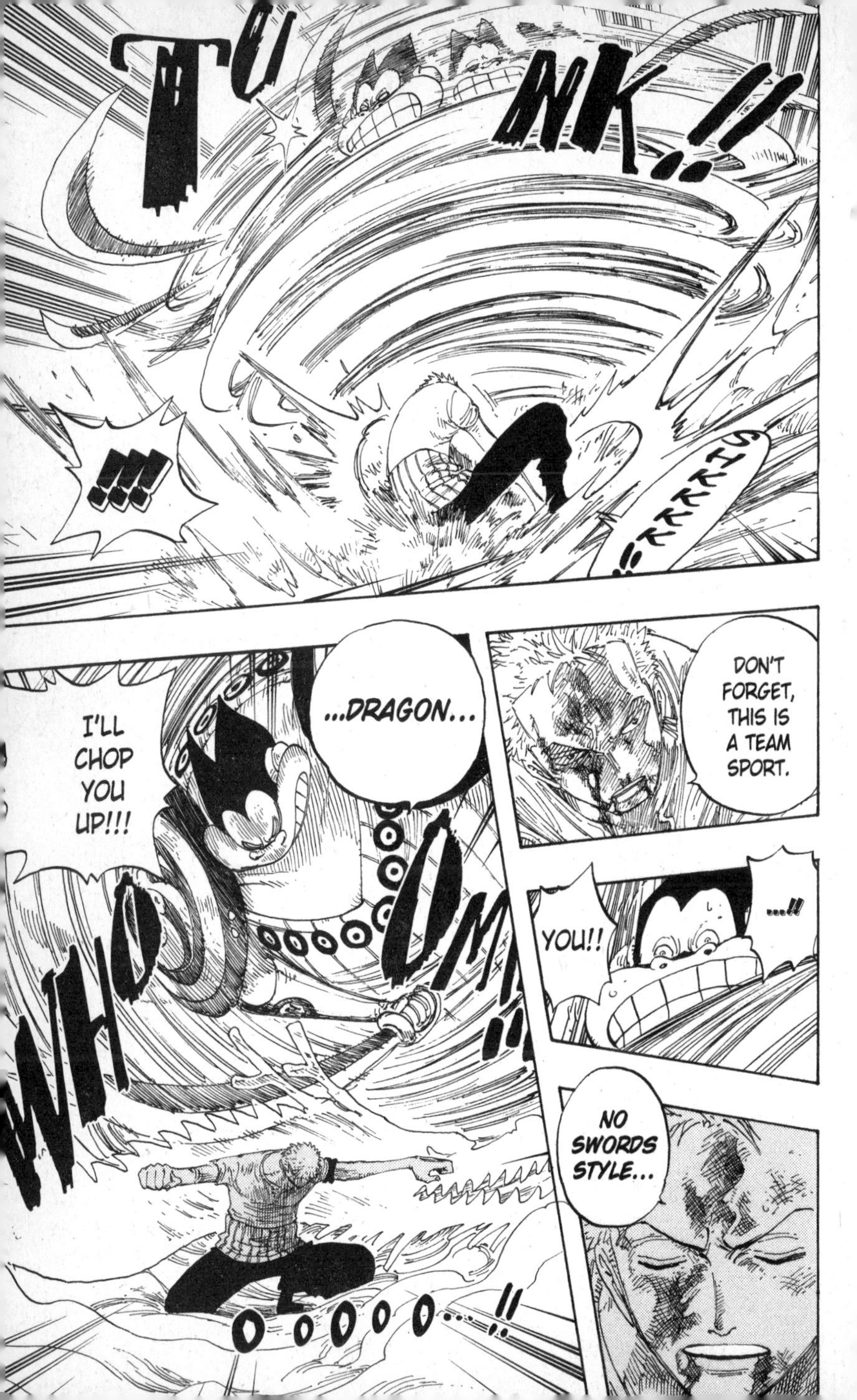

TUNK!!
!!!
SHKKKKK!!
DON'T FORGET, THIS IS A TEAM SPORT.
...!!
YOU!!
NO SWORDS STYLE...
...DRAGON...
I'LL CHOP YOU UP!!!
WHOOOM!!
OOOOO...!!

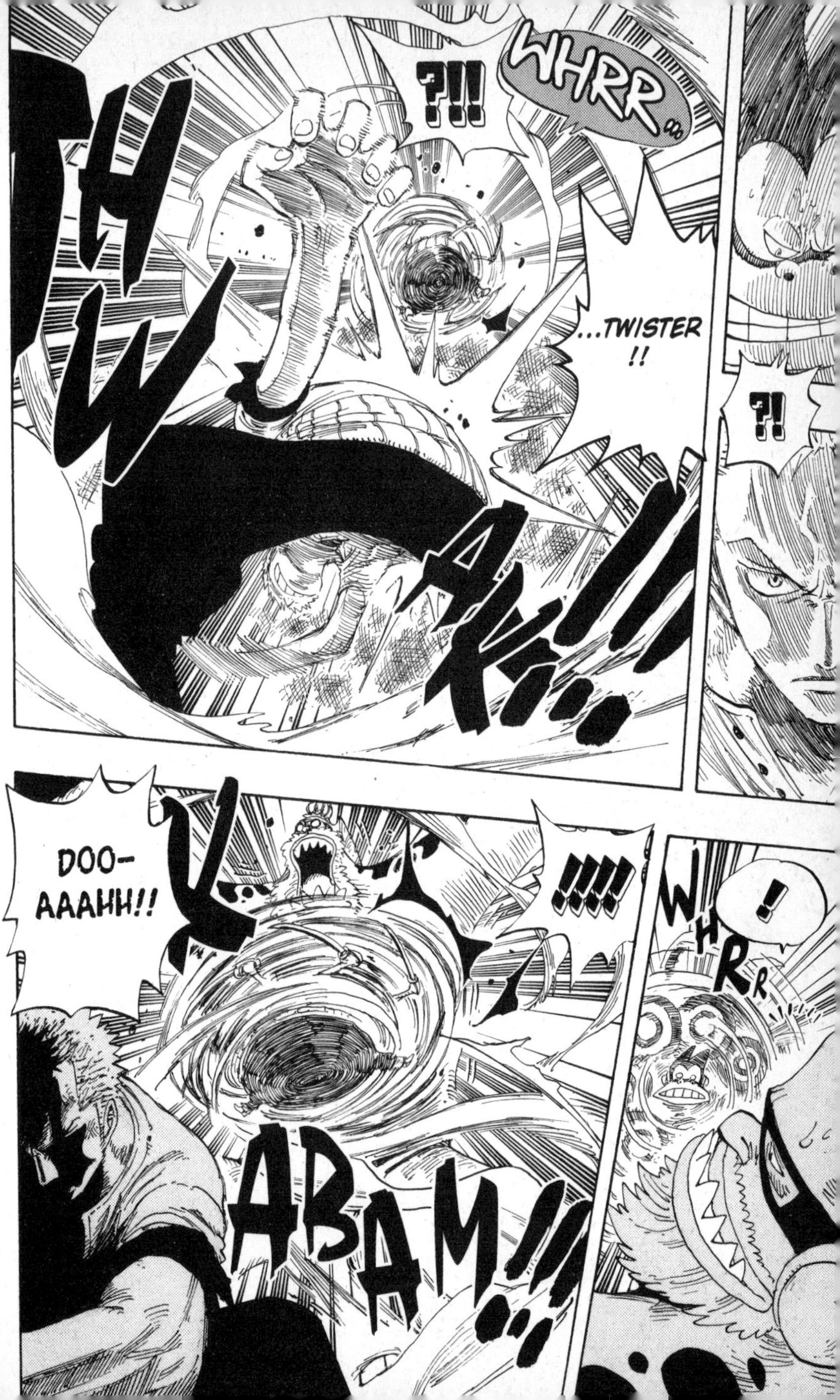

?!
WHRR...
?!!
...TWISTER !!
THWAK!!
WHRR
!
!!!!
DOO-AAAHH!!
KABAM!!

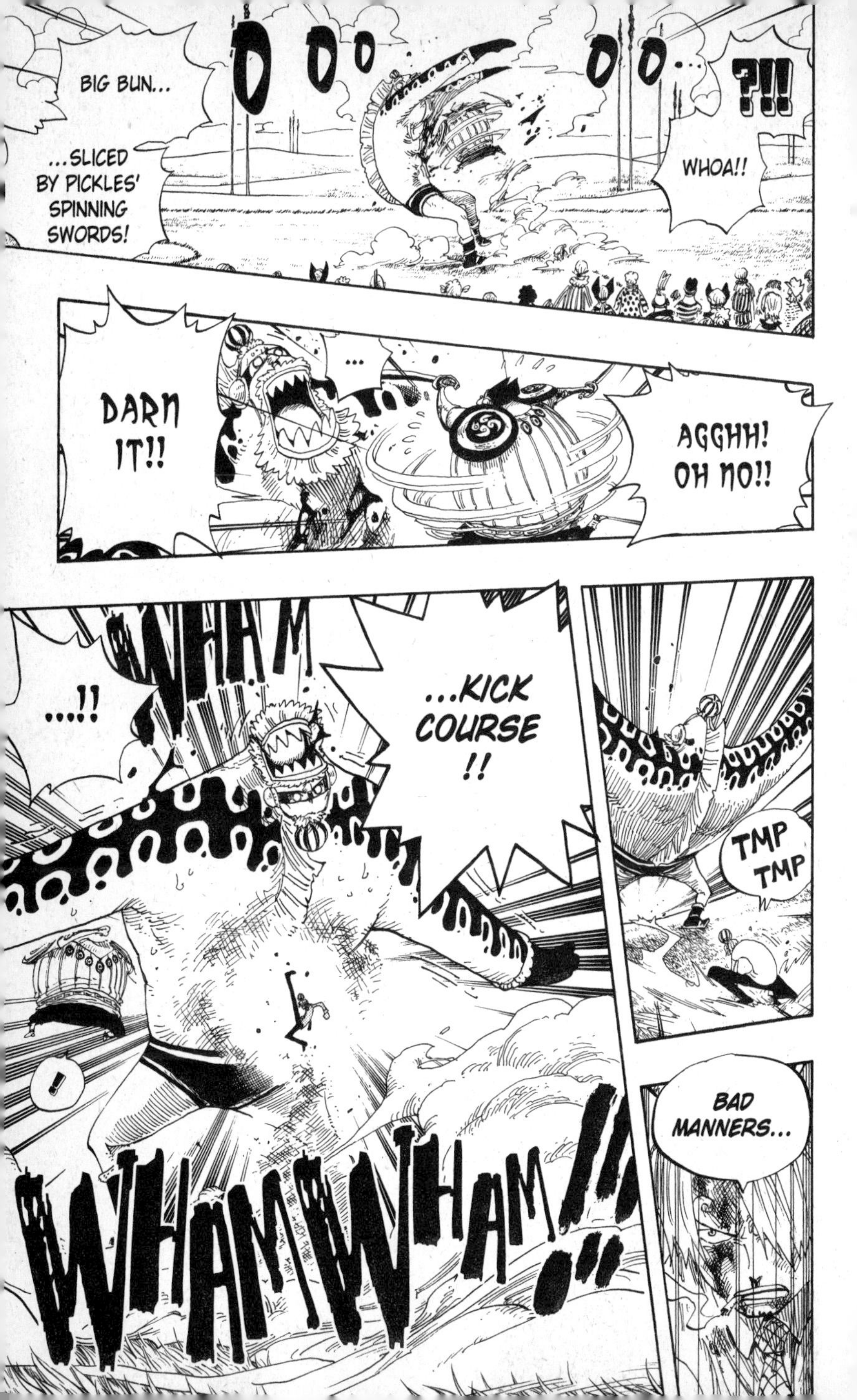
?!!
O O...
WHOA!!
O O O
BIG BUN...
...SLICED BY PICKLES' SPINNING SWORDS!
AGGHH! OH NO!!
...
DARN IT!!
TMP TMP
BAD MANNERS...
...KICK COURSE !!
WHAM
...!!
!
WHAM WHAM!!

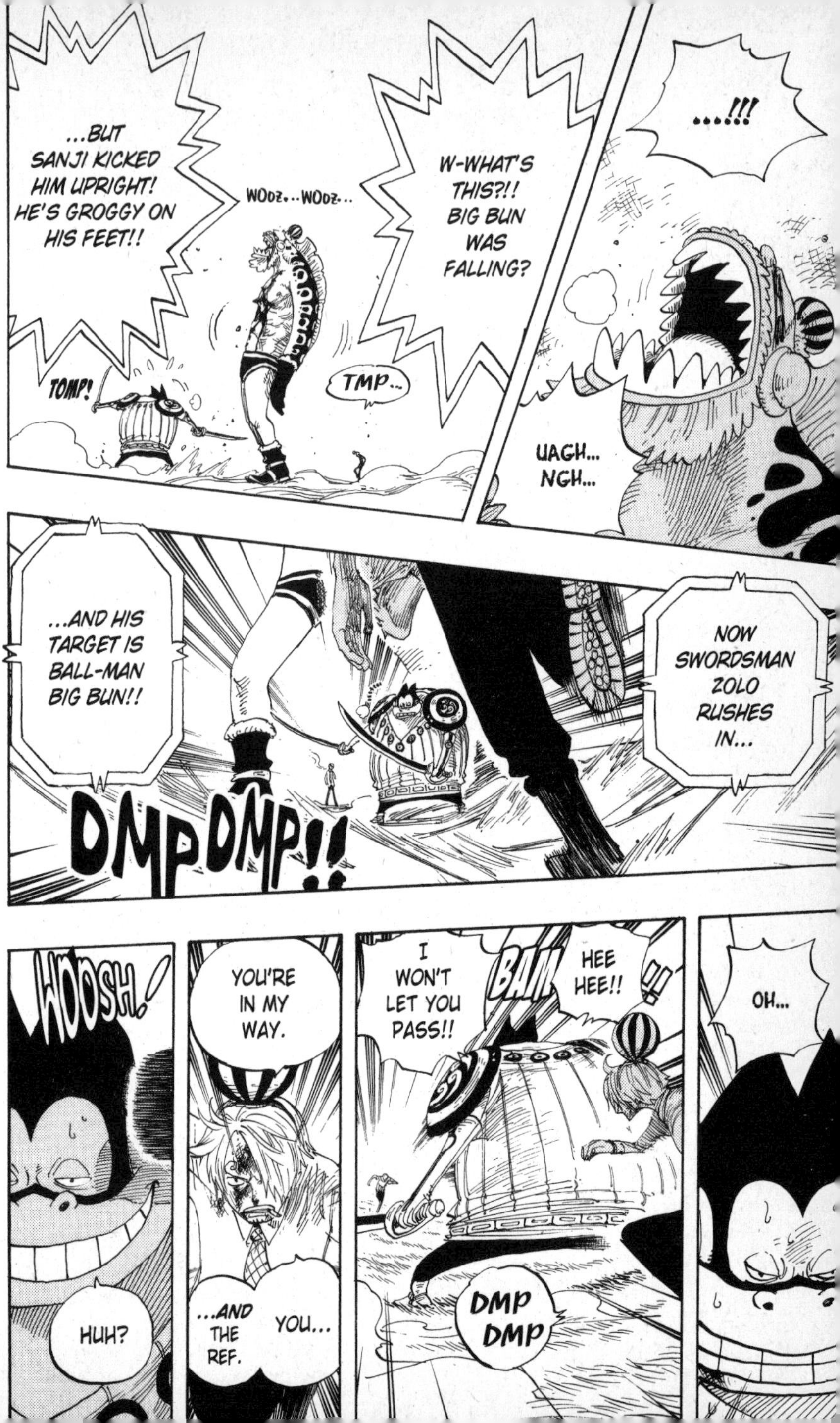

...!!!
UAGH... NGH...
W-WHAT'S THIS?!! BIG BUN WAS FALLING?
WOOZ...WOOZ...
...BUT SANJI KICKED HIM UPRIGHT! HE'S GROGGY ON HIS FEET!!
TMP...
TOMP!
NOW SWORDSMAN ZOLO RUSHES IN...
...AND HIS TARGET IS BALL-MAN BIG BUN!!
DMP DMP!!
OH...
HEE HEE!!
BAM!!
I WON'T LET YOU PASS!!
DMP DMP
YOU'RE IN MY WAY.
YOU...
...AND THE REF.
WOOSH!
HUH?

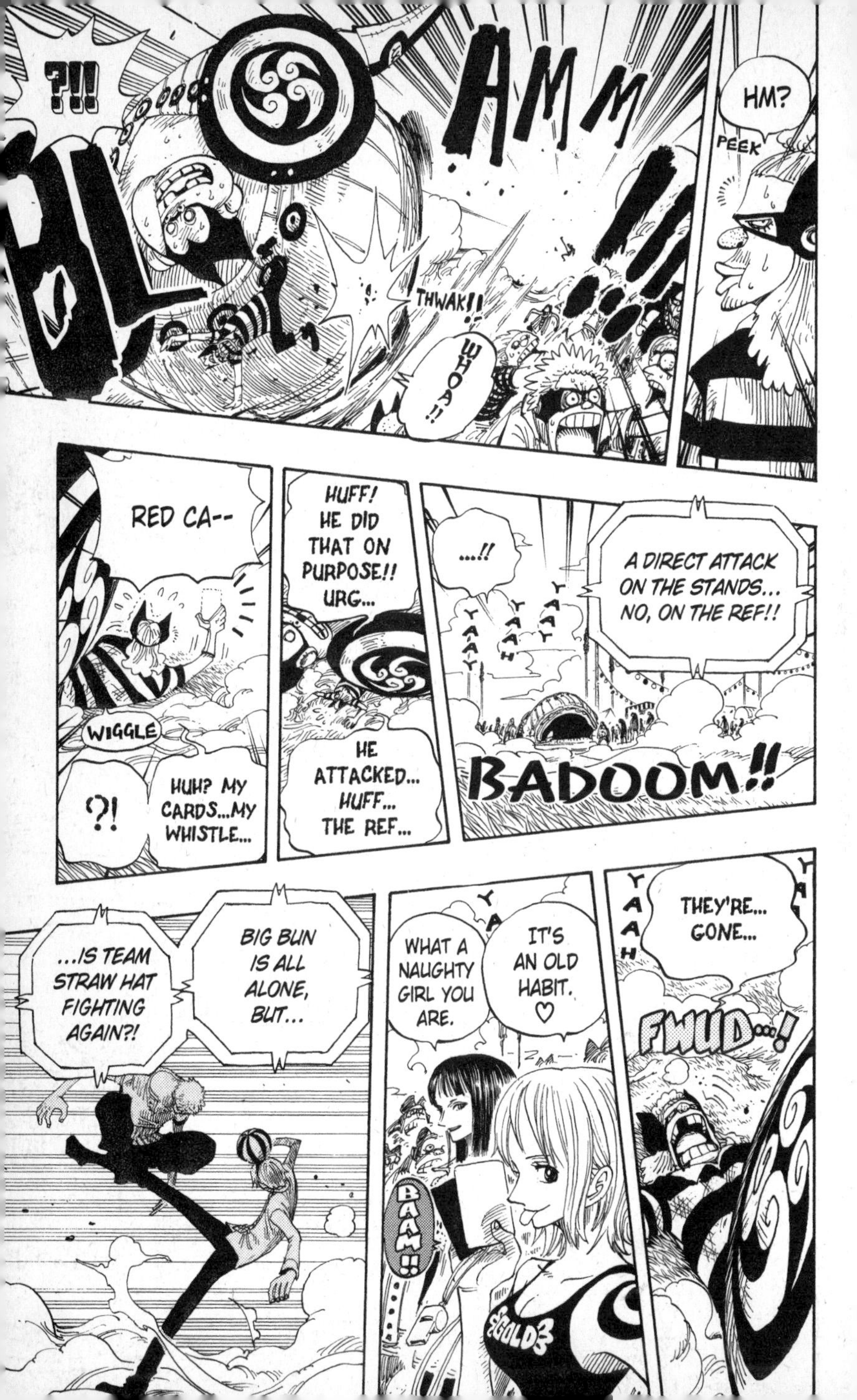

HM?
PEEK
BLAMM!!
?!!
THWAK!!
WHOA!!
...!!
A DIRECT ATTACK ON THE STANDS... NO, ON THE REF!!
YAAAY
YAAAH
YAAAY
BADOOM!!
HUFF! HE DID THAT ON PURPOSE!! URG...
HE ATTACKED... HUFF... THE REF...
RED CA--
WIGGLE
HUH? MY CARDS...MY WHISTLE...
?!
THEY'RE... GONE...
YAAAH
FWUD...!
YAA
IT'S AN OLD HABIT. ♡
WHAT A NAUGHTY GIRL YOU ARE.
BAAM!!
GOLD
BIG BUN IS ALL ALONE, BUT...
...IS TEAM STRAW HAT FIGHTING AGAIN?!

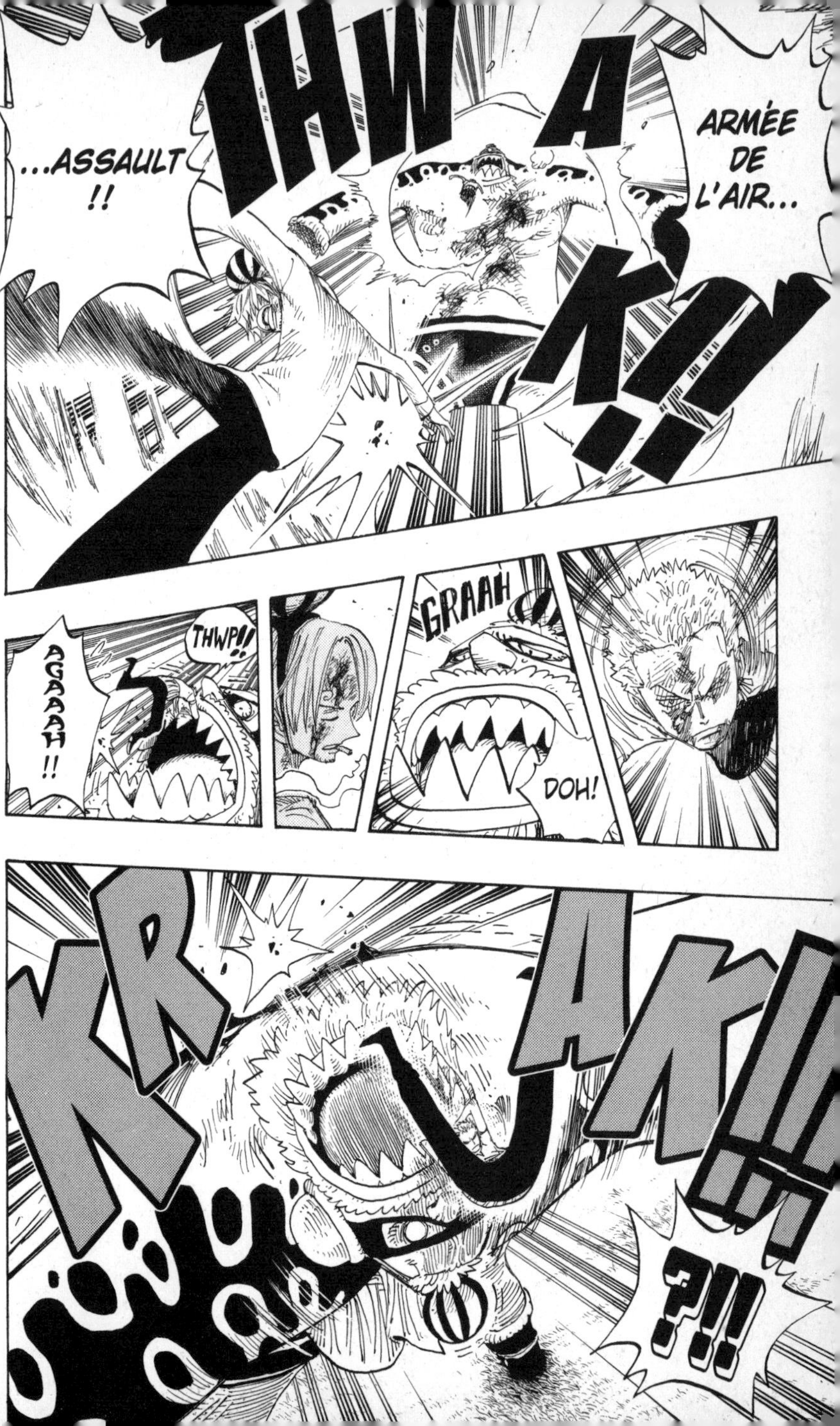
ARMÉE DE L'AIR...
THWAKK!!
...ASSAULT !!
GRAAH
DOH!
THWP!!
AGAAAAH!!
KRAK!!!
?!!

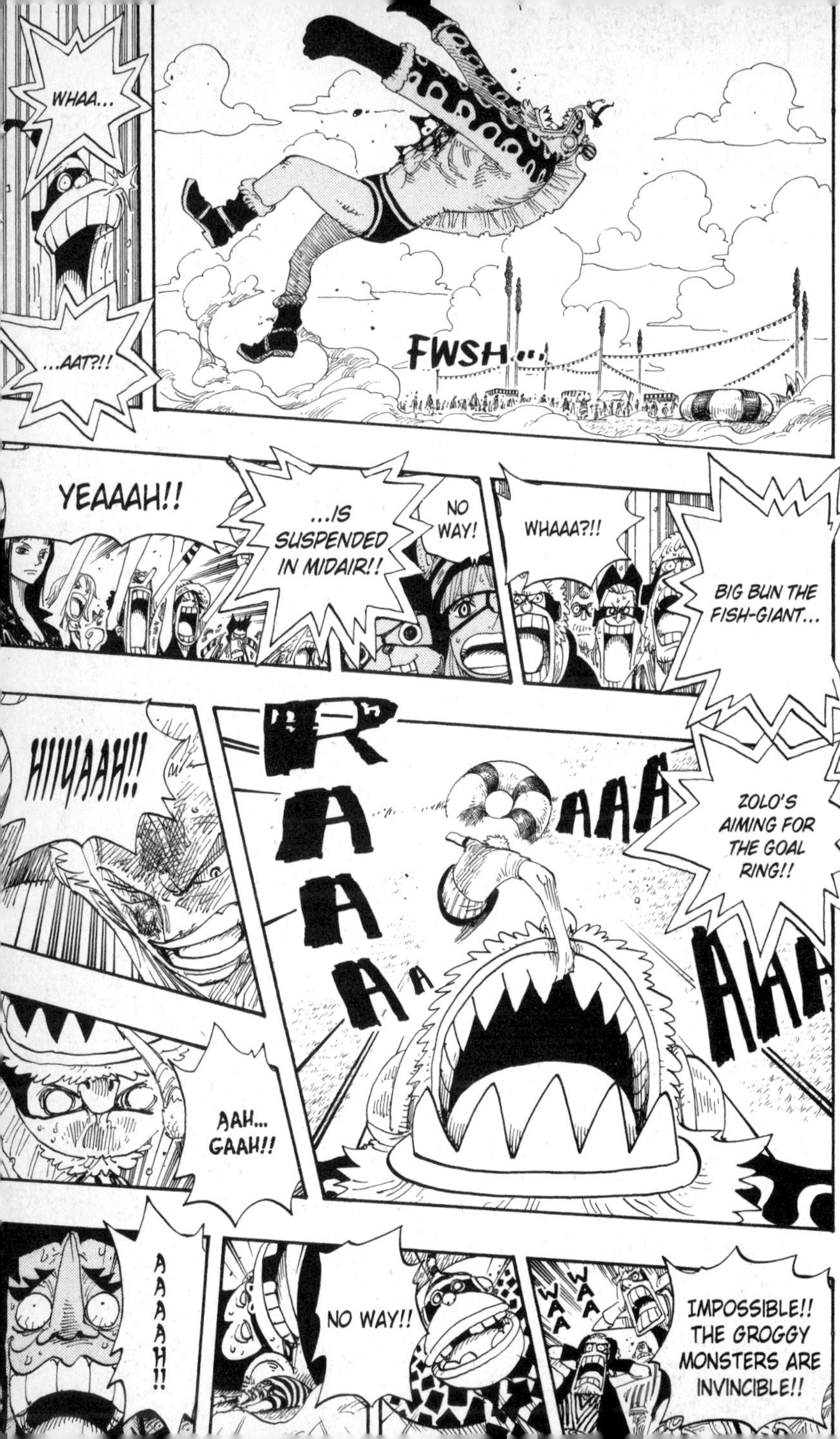
FWSH...
WHAA...
...AAT?!!
BIG BUN THE FISH-GIANT...
WHAAA?!!
NO WAY!
...IS SUSPENDED IN MIDAIR!!
YEAAAH!!
ZOLO'S AIMING FOR THE GOAL RING!!
RAAAAAAAAAAA
HIIYAAH!!
AAH... GAAH!!
IMPOSSIBLE!! THE GROGGY MONSTERS ARE INVINCIBLE!!
WAA WAA WAA WAA
NO WAY!!
AAAAAH!!

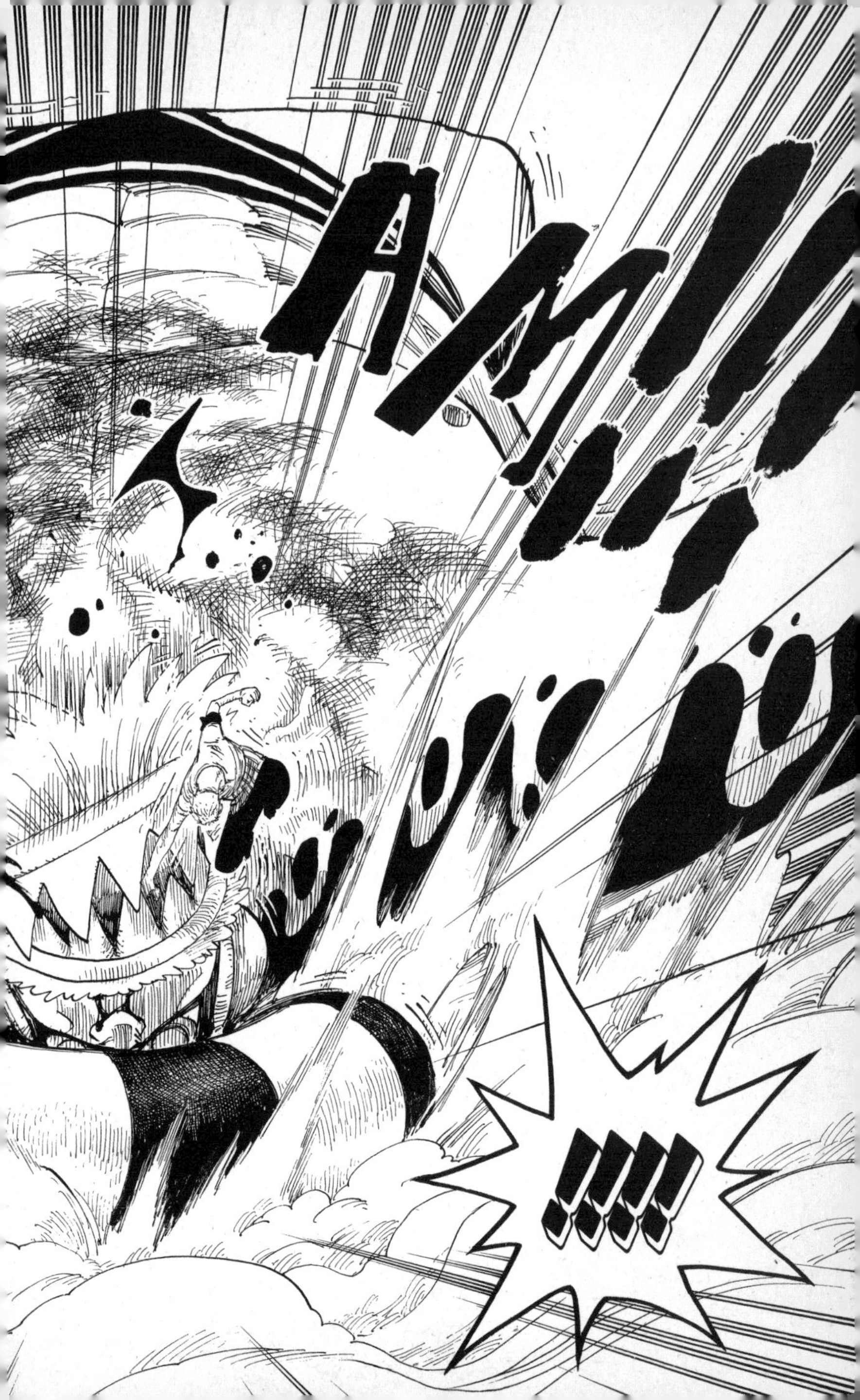
!!!!

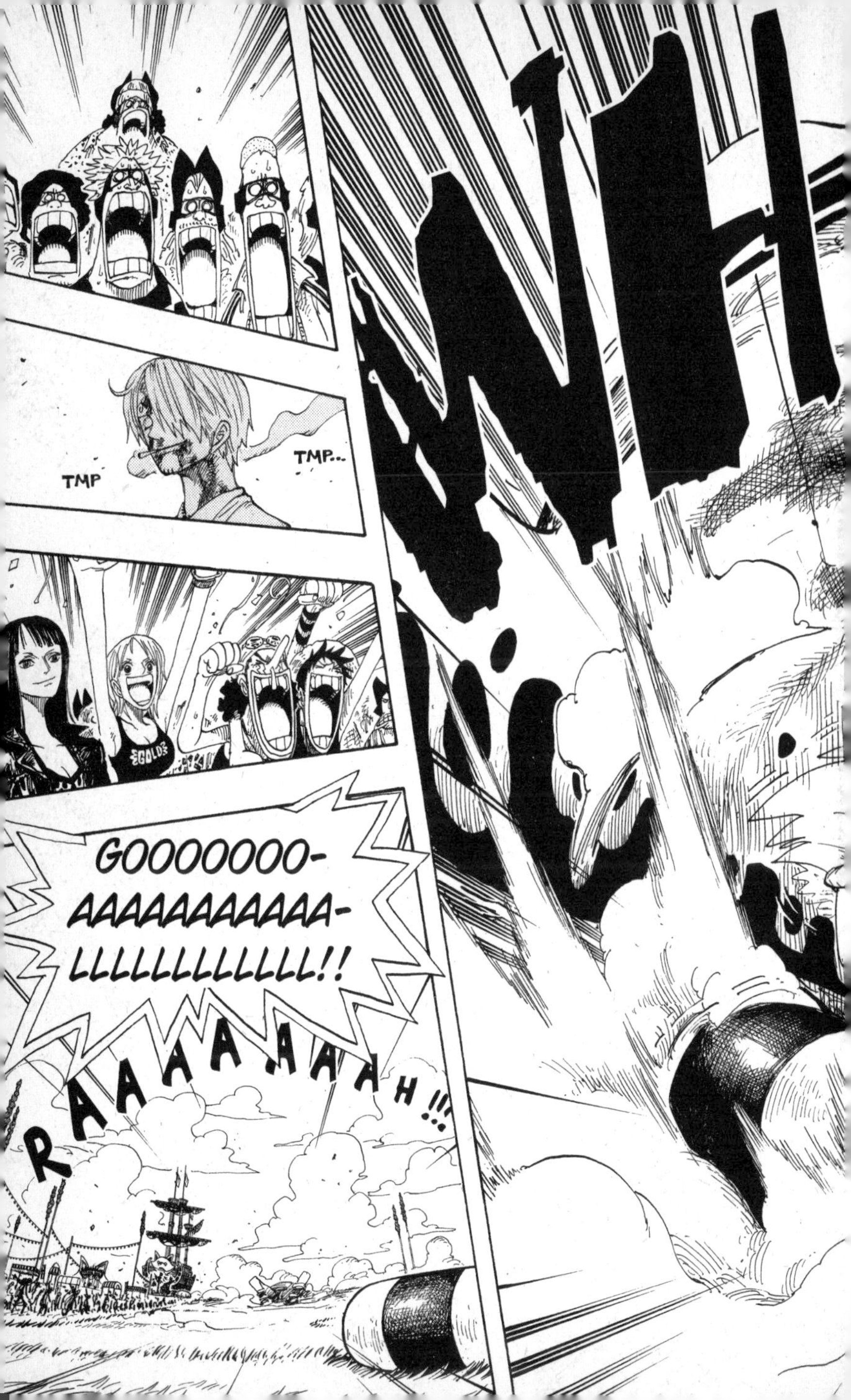
TMP...
TMP
GOOOOOOO-AAAAAAAAAAA-LLLLLLLLLLLL!!
RAAAAAAAH!!!

ONE PIECE Storyboard Preview!! #21

FROM PAGES 63-64 OF VOLUME 32. --ED

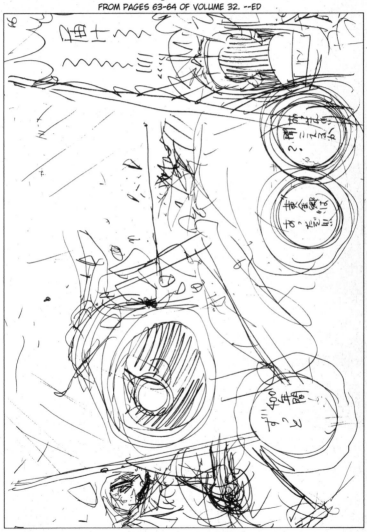

Chapter 313: MAIN EVENT

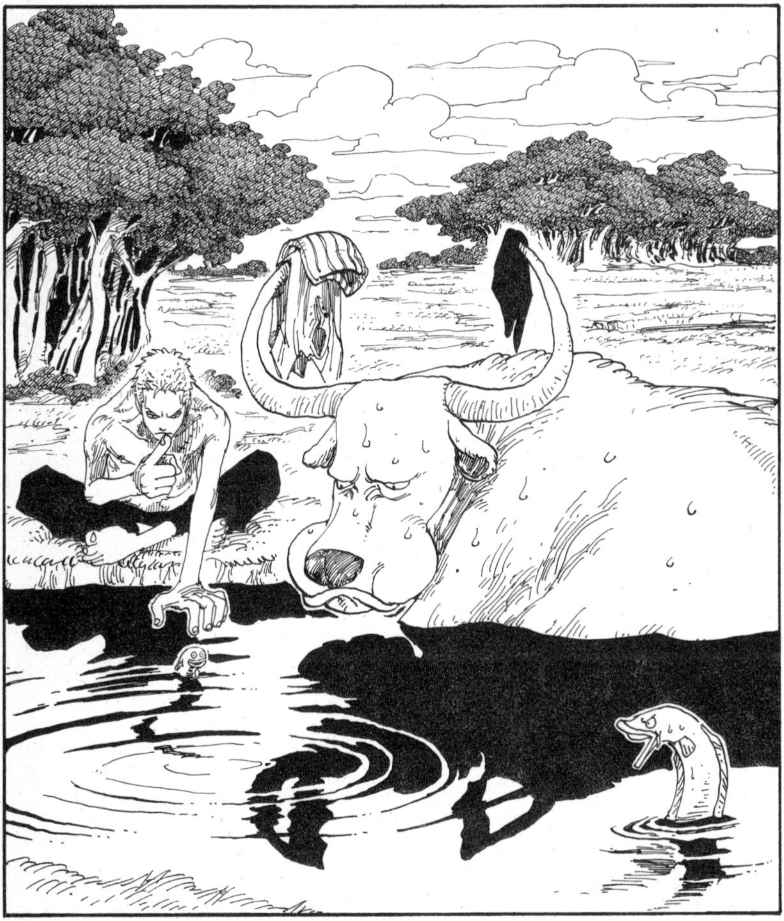

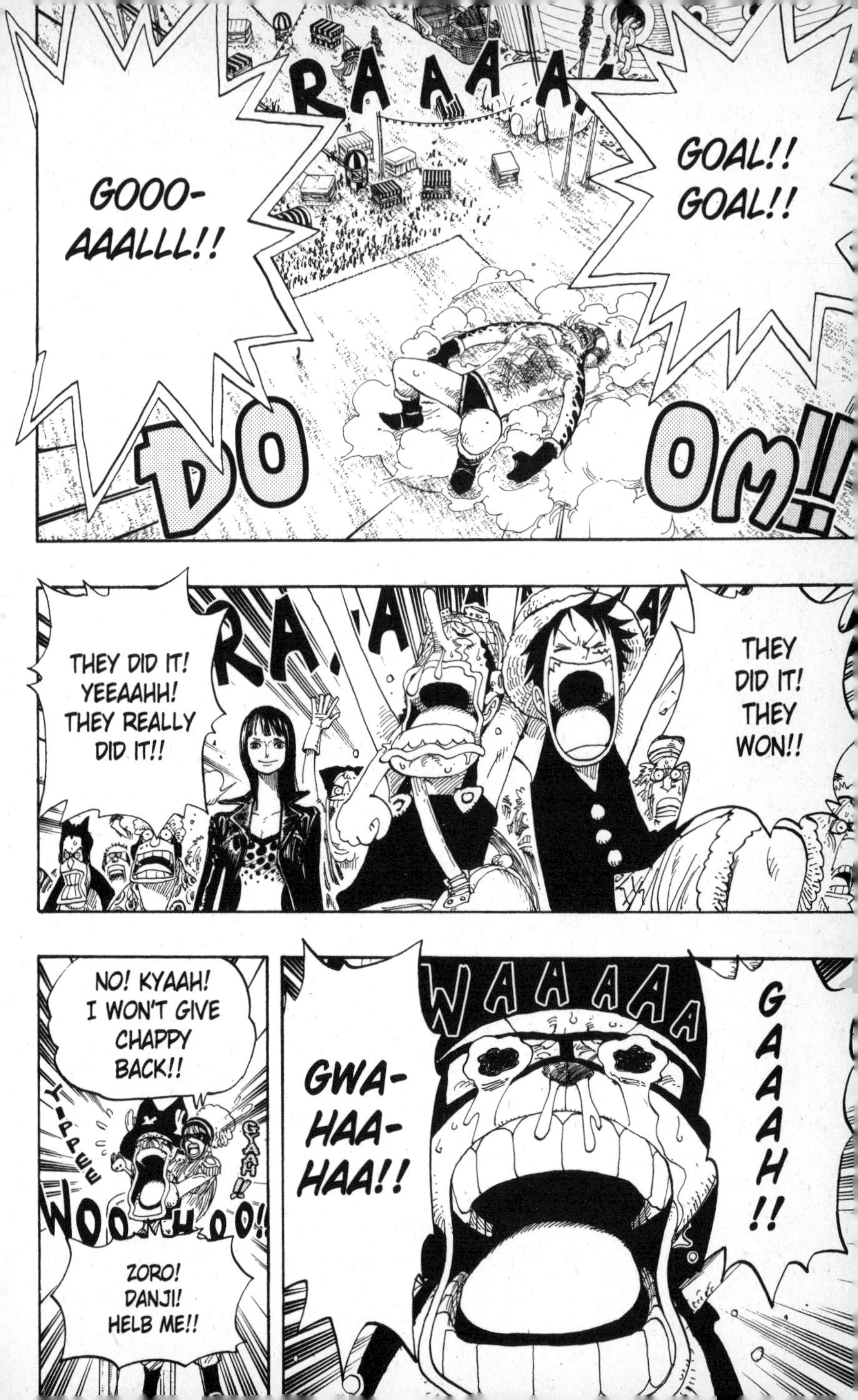
RAAAA
GOAL!! GOAL!!
GOOO-AAALLL!!
DO OM!!
THEY DID IT! THEY WON!!
RA A A
THEY DID IT! YEEAAHH! THEY REALLY DID IT!!
WAAAAA
GAAAAH!!
GWA-HAA-HAA!!
NO! KYAAH! I WON'T GIVE CHAPPY BACK!!
YIPPEE
GAAH!!
WOO-HOO!!
ZORO! DANJI! HELB ME!!

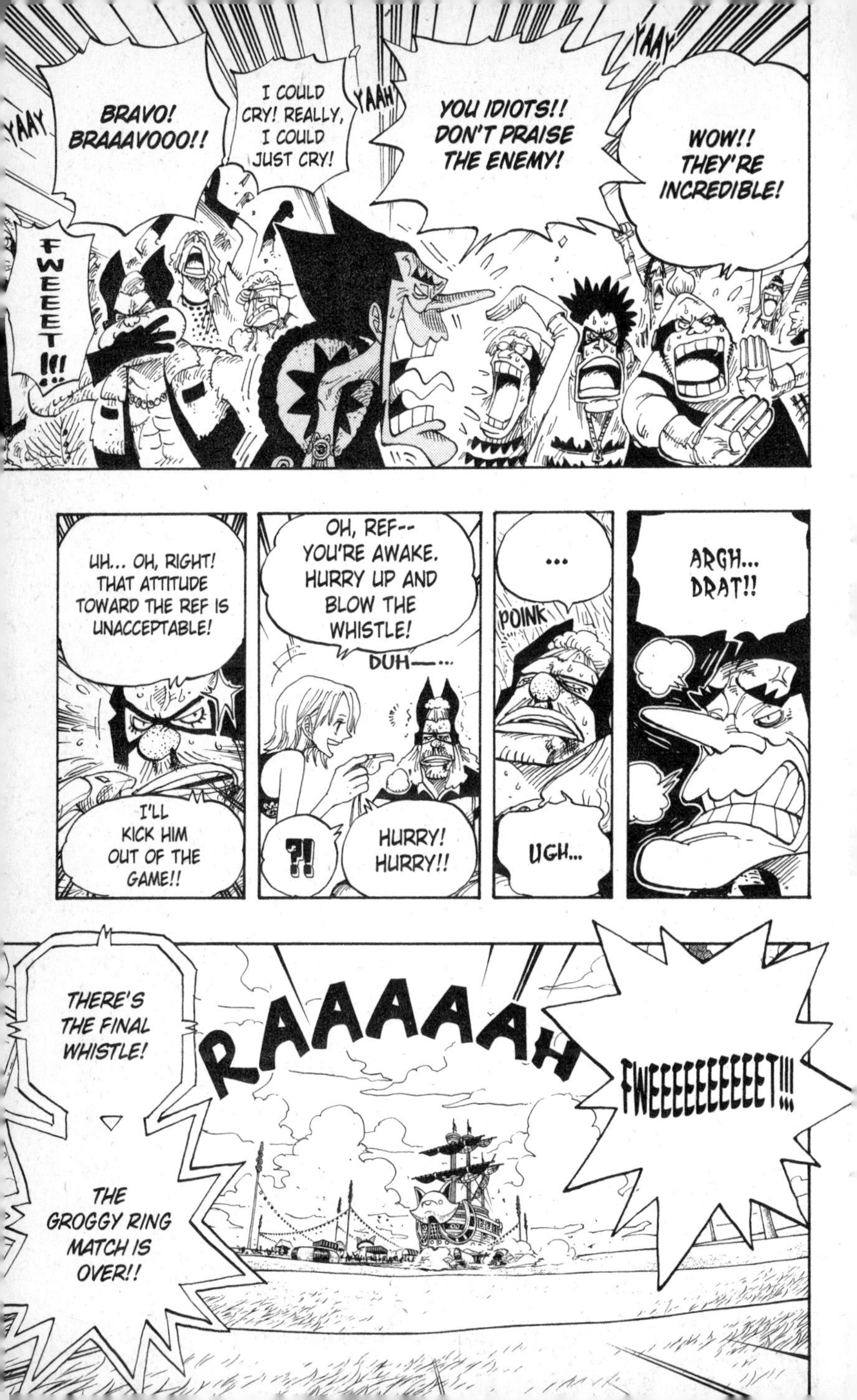
YAAY
WOW!! THEY'RE INCREDIBLE!
YOU IDIOTS!! DON'T PRAISE THE ENEMY!
YAAH
I COULD CRY! REALLY, I COULD JUST CRY!
BRAVO! BRAAAVOOO!!
YAAY
FWEEEET!!!
ARGH... DRAT!!
...
POINK
UGH...
OH, REF-- YOU'RE AWAKE. HURRY UP AND BLOW THE WHISTLE!
DUH---...
HURRY! HURRY!!
?!
UH... OH, RIGHT! THAT ATTITUDE TOWARD THE REF IS UNACCEPTABLE!
I'LL KICK HIM OUT OF THE GAME!!
FWEEEEEEEEEET!!!
RAAAAAH
THERE'S THE FINAL WHISTLE!
THE GROGGY RING MATCH IS OVER!!

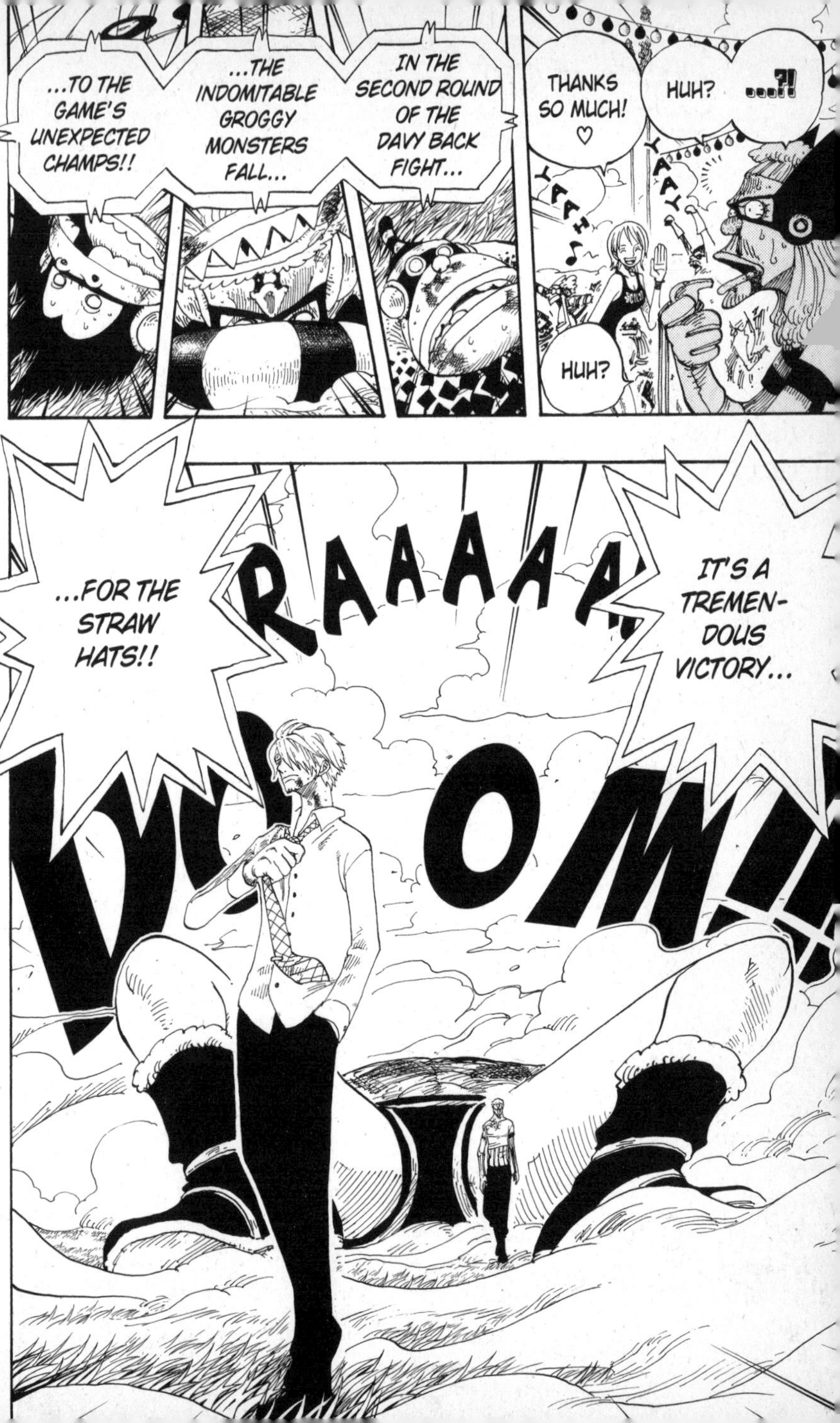
...?!
HUH?
THANKS SO MUCH! ♡
YAAAY
YAAH ♪
HUH?
IN THE SECOND ROUND OF THE DAVY BACK FIGHT...
...THE INDOMITABLE GROGGY MONSTERS FALL...
...TO THE GAME'S UNEXPECTED CHAMPS!!
IT'S A TREMENDOUS VICTORY...
RAAAAA
...FOR THE STRAW HATS!!
VOOM!!

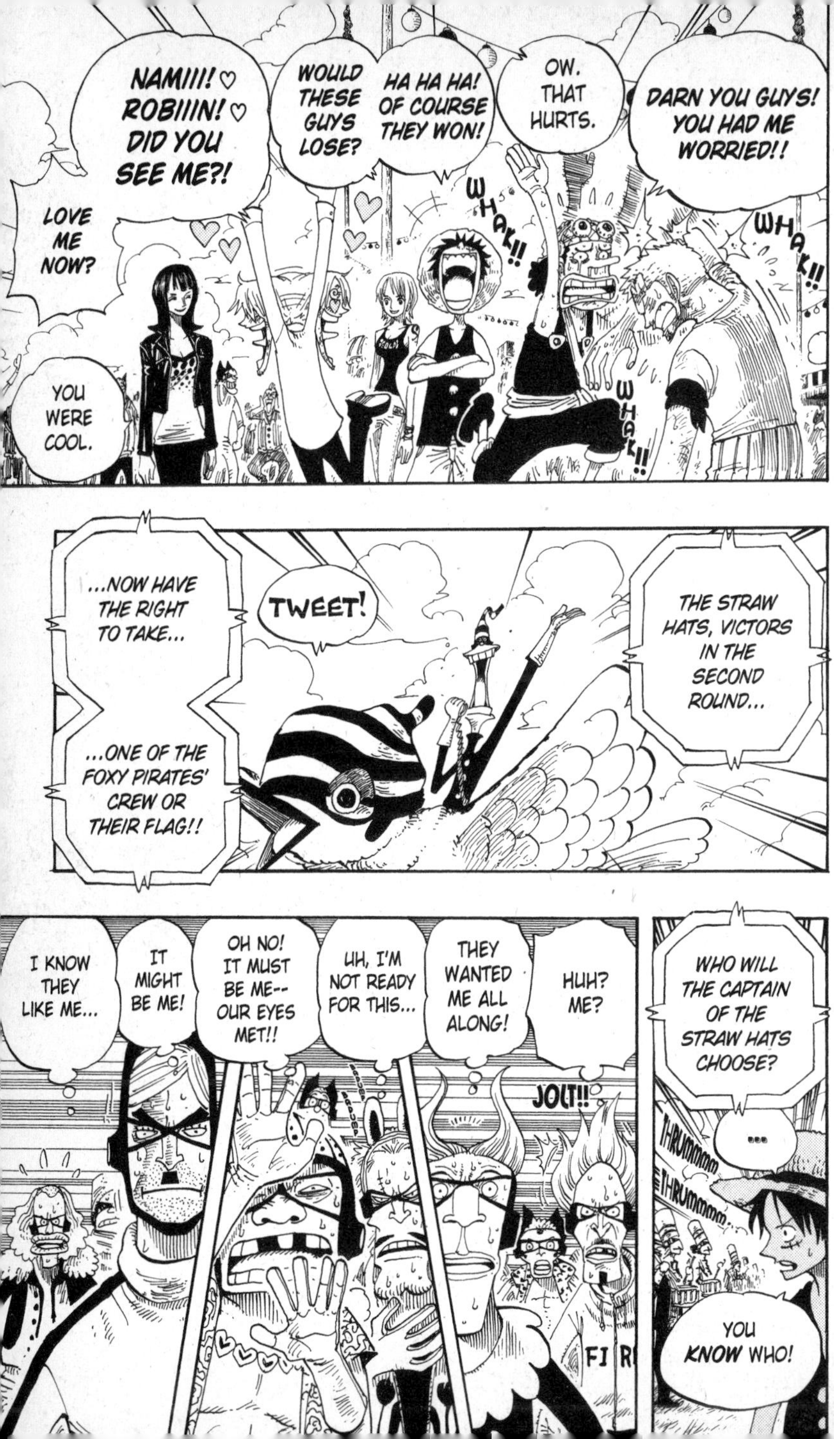
DARN YOU GUYS! YOU HAD ME WORRIED!!
WHAK!!
OW. THAT HURTS.
WHAK!!
HA HA HA! OF COURSE THEY WON!
WOULD THESE GUYS LOSE?
NAMIIII! ♡ ROBIIIN! ♡ DID YOU SEE ME?!
LOVE ME NOW?
YOU WERE COOL.
WHAK!!
THE STRAW HATS, VICTORS IN THE SECOND ROUND...
TWEET!
...NOW HAVE THE RIGHT TO TAKE...
...ONE OF THE FOXY PIRATES' CREW OR THEIR FLAG!!
WHO WILL THE CAPTAIN OF THE STRAW HATS CHOOSE?
...
THRUMMMM
THRUMMMM
YOU KNOW WHO!
HUH? ME?
JOLT!!
THEY WANTED ME ALL ALONG!
UH, I'M NOT READY FOR THIS...
OH NO! IT MUST BE ME-- OUR EYES MET!!
IT MIGHT BE ME!
I KNOW THEY LIKE ME...

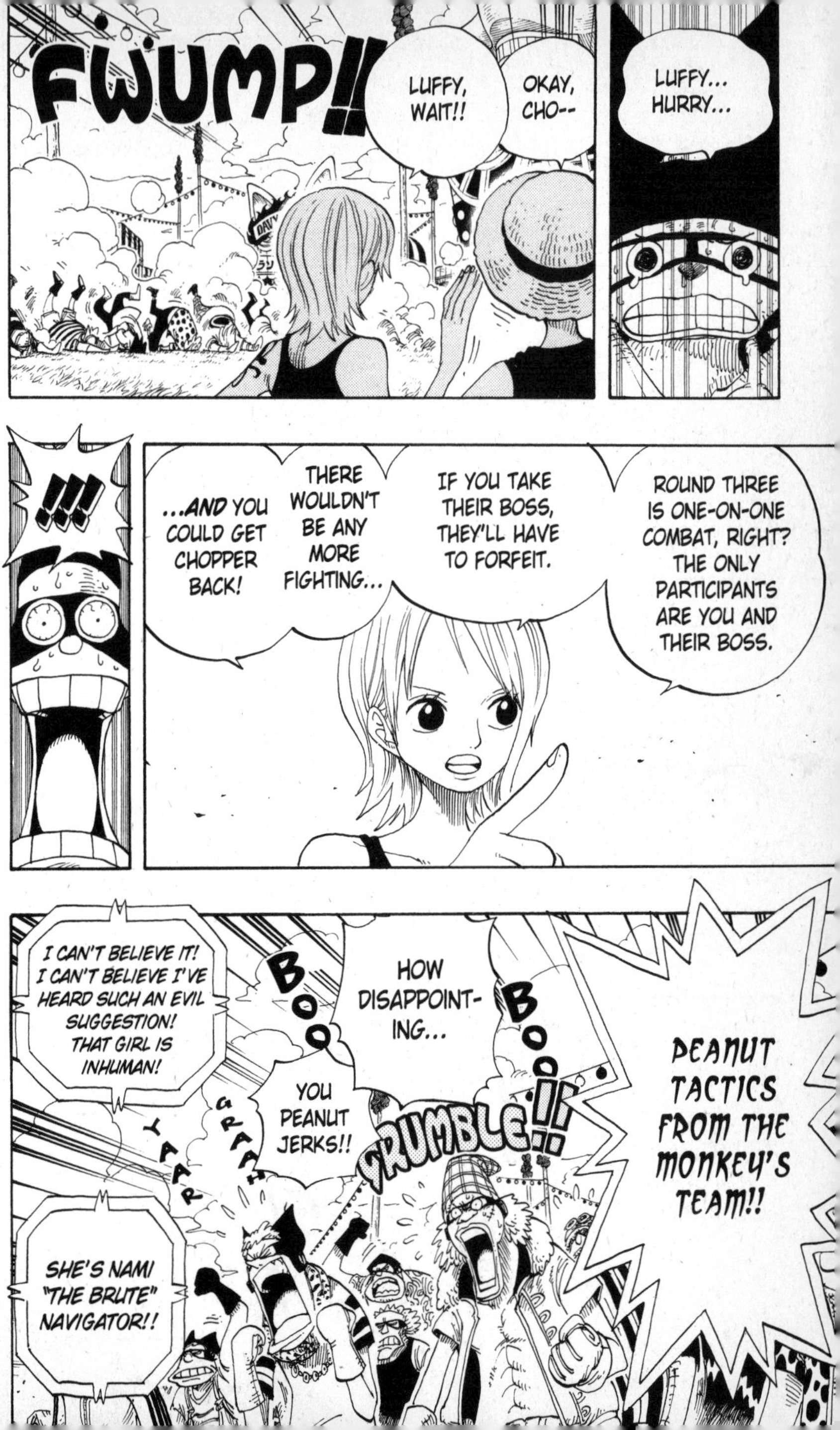
LUFFY... HURRY...
OKAY, CHO--
LUFFY, WAIT!!
FWUMP!!
ROUND THREE IS ONE-ON-ONE COMBAT, RIGHT? THE ONLY PARTICIPANTS ARE YOU AND THEIR BOSS.
IF YOU TAKE THEIR BOSS, THEY'LL HAVE TO FORFEIT.
THERE WOULDN'T BE ANY MORE FIGHTING...
...AND YOU COULD GET CHOPPER BACK!
!!!
PEANUT TACTICS FROM THE MONKEY'S TEAM!!
BOOO!!
HOW DISAPPOINT-ING...
BOOO
YOU PEANUT JERKS!!
GRUMBLE!!
GRAAAH
YAAAR
I CAN'T BELIEVE IT! I CAN'T BELIEVE I'VE HEARD SUCH AN EVIL SUGGESTION! THAT GIRL IS INHUMAN!
SHE'S NAMI "THE BRUTE" NAVIGATOR!!

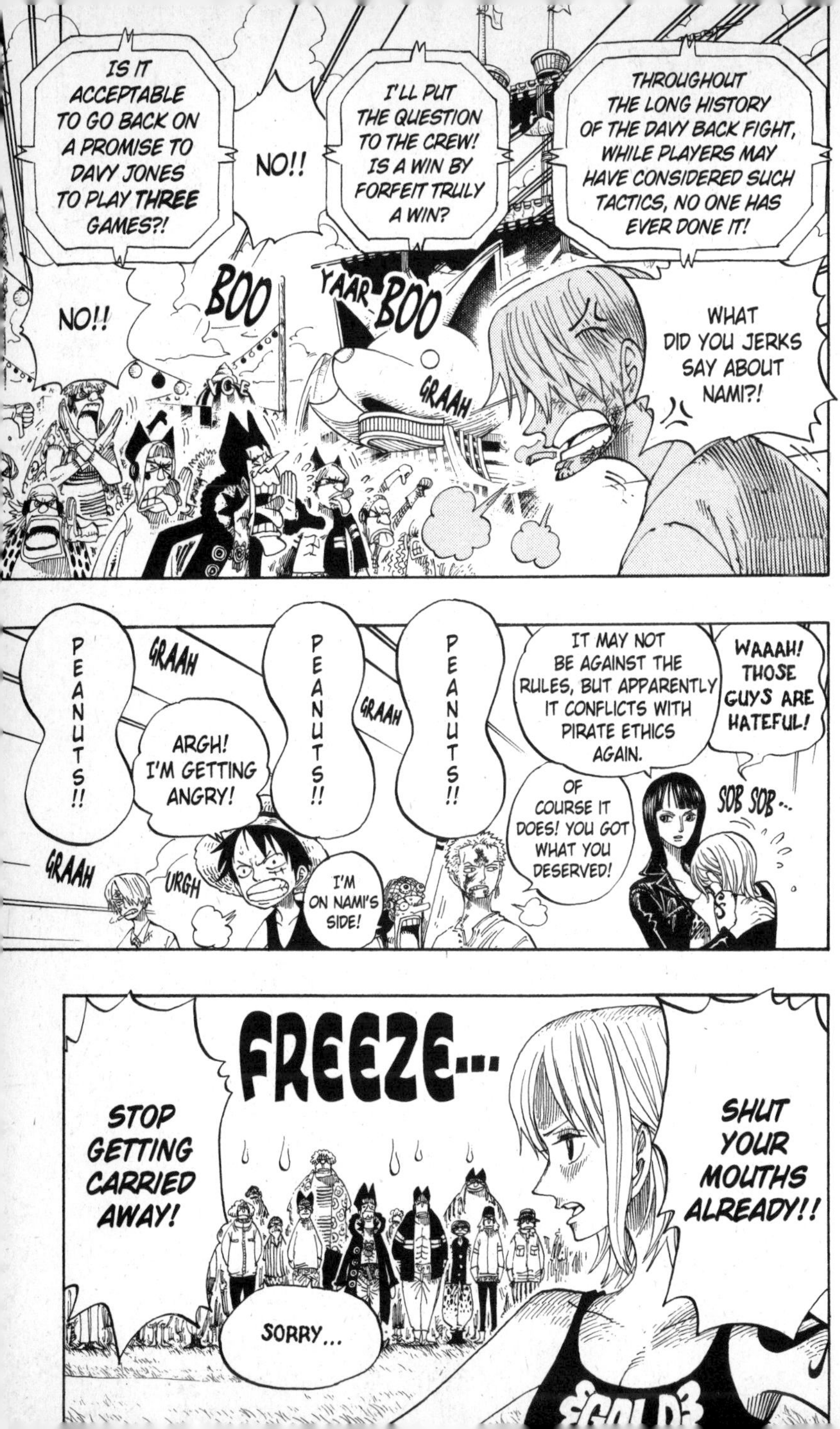
THROUGHOUT THE LONG HISTORY OF THE DAVY BACK FIGHT, WHILE PLAYERS MAY HAVE CONSIDERED SUCH TACTICS, NO ONE HAS EVER DONE IT!
I'LL PUT THE QUESTION TO THE CREW! IS A WIN BY FORFEIT TRULY A WIN?
NO!!
IS IT ACCEPTABLE TO GO BACK ON A PROMISE TO DAVY JONES TO PLAY THREE GAMES?!
WHAT DID YOU JERKS SAY ABOUT NAMI?!
GRAAH
BOO
YAAR
BOO
NO!!
WAAAH! THOSE GUYS ARE HATEFUL!
SOB SOB...
IT MAY NOT BE AGAINST THE RULES, BUT APPARENTLY IT CONFLICTS WITH PIRATE ETHICS AGAIN.
OF COURSE IT DOES! YOU GOT WHAT YOU DESERVED!
PEANUTS!!
I'M ON NAMI'S SIDE!
GRAAH
PEANUTS!!
ARGH! I'M GETTING ANGRY!
GRAAH
PEANUTS!!
URGH
GRAAH
SHUT YOUR MOUTHS ALREADY!!
FREEZE...
STOP GETTING CARRIED AWAY!
SORRY...

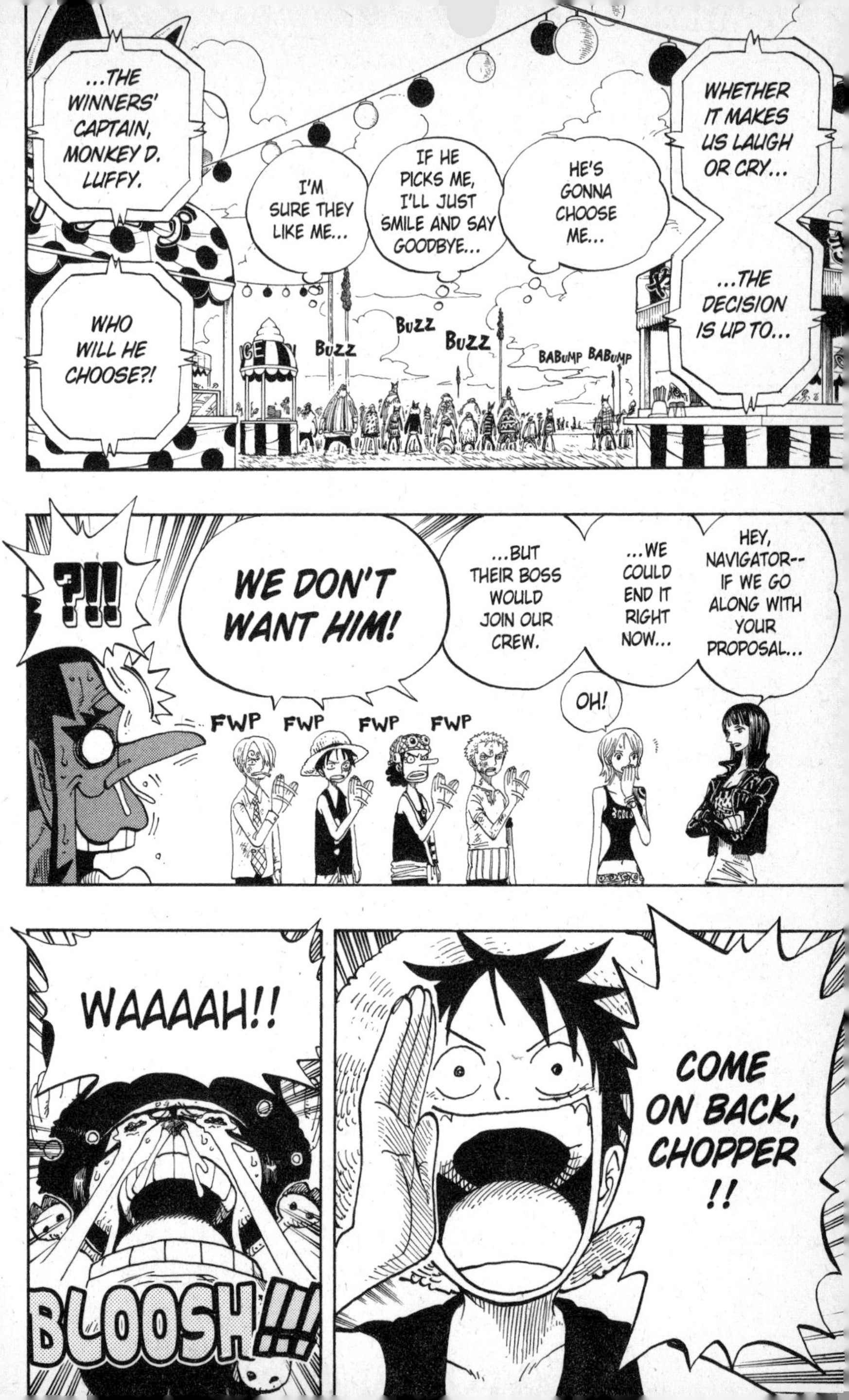
WHETHER IT MAKES US LAUGH OR CRY...
...THE DECISION IS UP TO...
HE'S GONNA CHOOSE ME...
IF HE PICKS ME, I'LL JUST SMILE AND SAY GOODBYE...
I'M SURE THEY LIKE ME...
...THE WINNERS' CAPTAIN, MONKEY D. LUFFY.
BABUMP BABUMP
BUZZ
BUZZ
BUZZ
WHO WILL HE CHOOSE?!
HEY, NAVIGATOR-- IF WE GO ALONG WITH YOUR PROPOSAL...
...WE COULD END IT RIGHT NOW...
...BUT THEIR BOSS WOULD JOIN OUR CREW.
OH!
WE DON'T WANT HIM!
FWP FWP FWP FWP
?!!
COME ON BACK, CHOPPER!!
WAAAAH!!
BLOOSH!!!

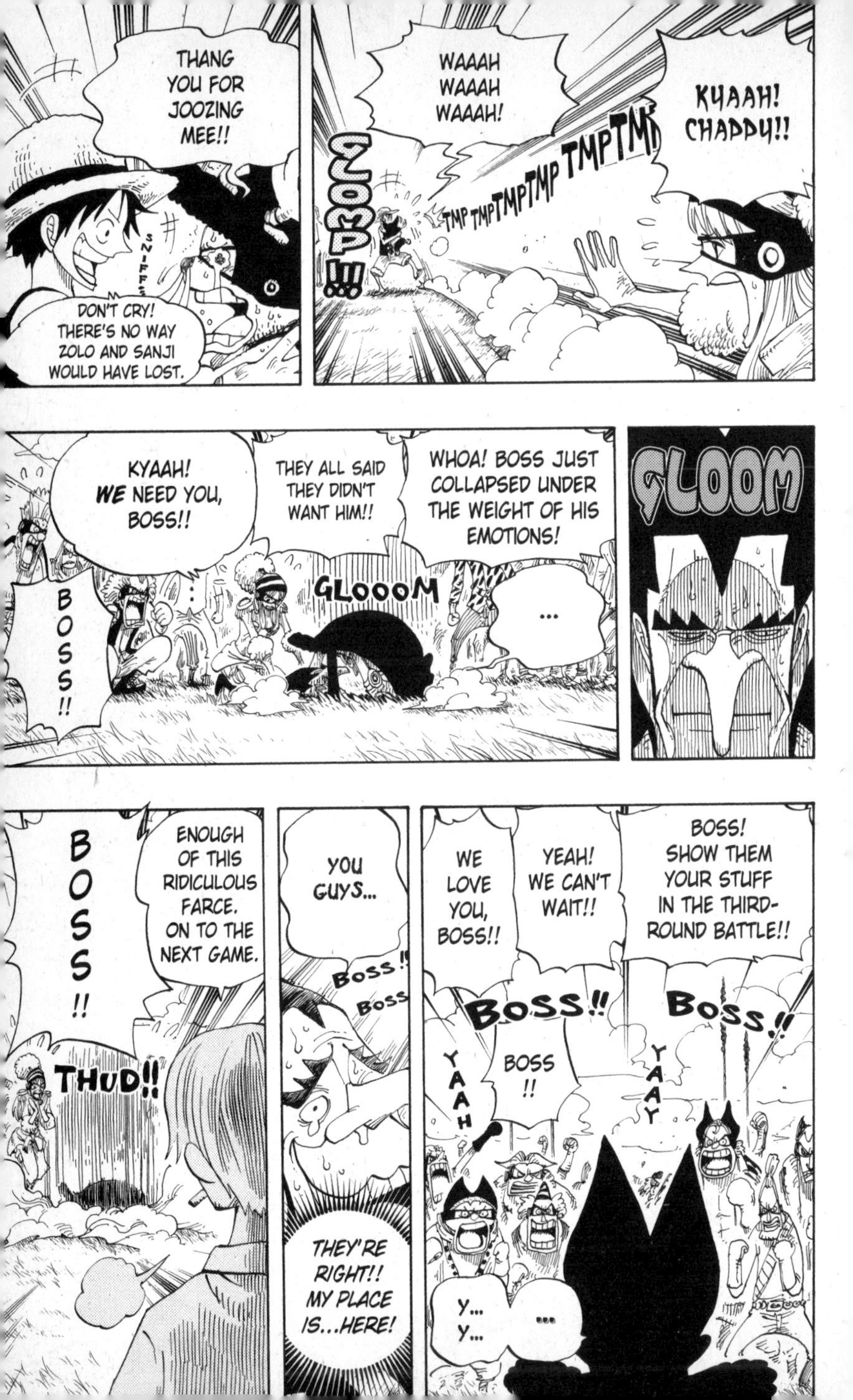
KYAAH! CHAPPY!!
TMP TMP TMPTMP TMPTMP TMPTMP
WAAAH WAAAH WAAAH!
GLOMP!!!
THANG YOU FOR JOOZING MEE!!
SNIFF
DON'T CRY! THERE'S NO WAY ZOLO AND SANJI WOULD HAVE LOST.
GLOOM
WHOA! BOSS JUST COLLAPSED UNDER THE WEIGHT OF HIS EMOTIONS!
...
THEY ALL SAID THEY DIDN'T WANT HIM!!
GLOOOM
KYAAH! WE NEED YOU, BOSS!!
BOSS!!
BOSS! SHOW THEM YOUR STUFF IN THE THIRD-ROUND BATTLE!!
YEAH! WE CAN'T WAIT!!
WE LOVE YOU, BOSS!!
BOSS!!
BOSS!!
YAAY
BOSS !!
YAAH
...
Y... Y...
YOU GUYS...
BOSS!!
BOSS
THEY'RE RIGHT!! MY PLACE IS...HERE!
ENOUGH OF THIS RIDICULOUS FARCE. ON TO THE NEXT GAME.
BOSS !!
THUD!!

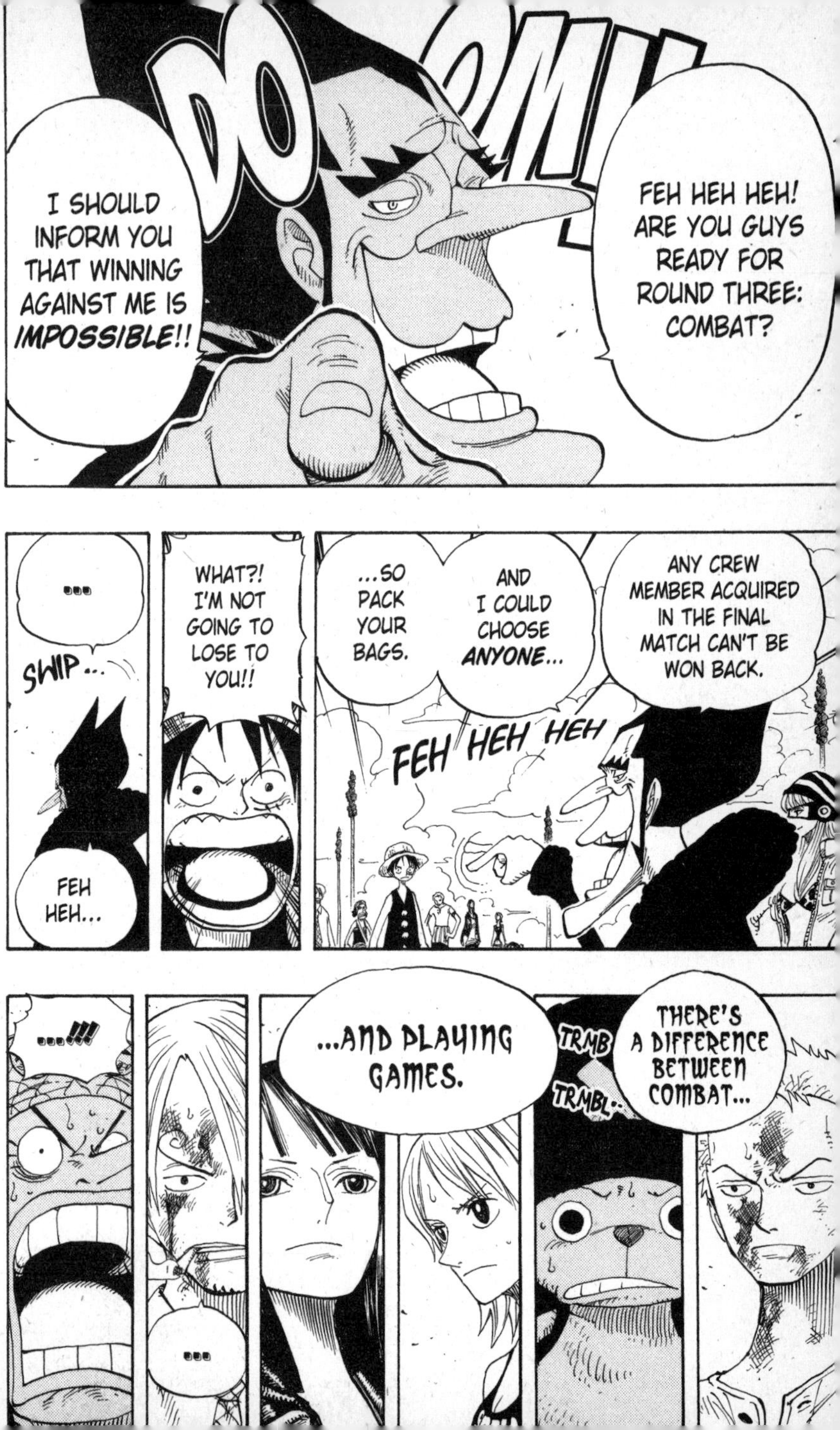
FEH HEH HEH! ARE YOU GUYS READY FOR ROUND THREE: COMBAT?
DO OM!
I SHOULD INFORM YOU THAT WINNING AGAINST ME IS IMPOSSIBLE!!
ANY CREW MEMBER ACQUIRED IN THE FINAL MATCH CAN'T BE WON BACK.
AND I COULD CHOOSE ANYONE...
...SO PACK YOUR BAGS.
FEH HEH HEH
WHAT?! I'M NOT GOING TO LOSE TO YOU!!
...
SWIP...
FEH HEH...
THERE'S A DIFFERENCE BETWEEN COMBAT...
TRMB
TRMBL...
...AND PLAYING GAMES.
...
...!!!

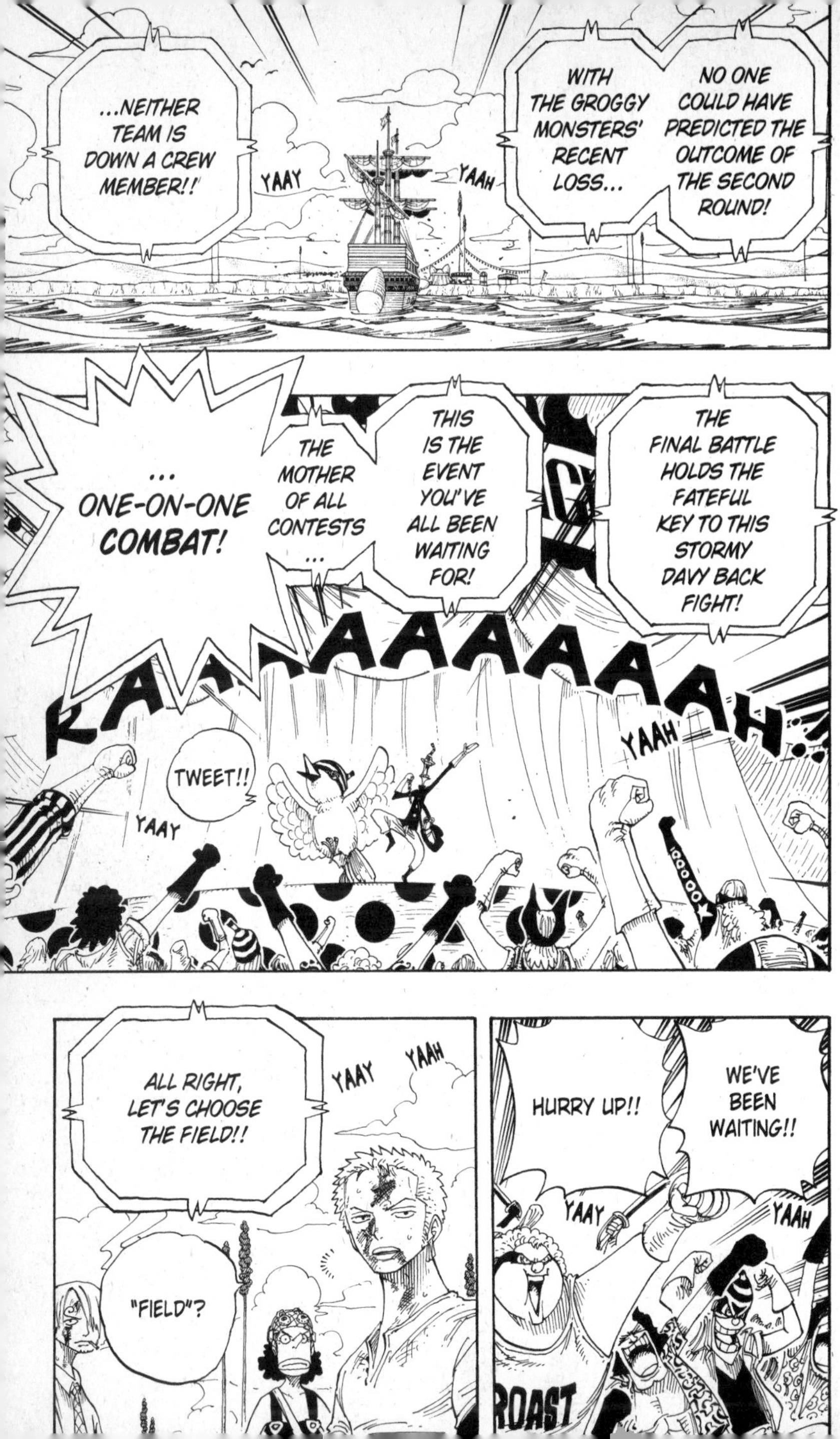
NO ONE COULD HAVE PREDICTED THE OUTCOME OF THE SECOND ROUND!
WITH THE GROGGY MONSTERS' RECENT LOSS...
YAAH
YAAY
...NEITHER TEAM IS DOWN A CREW MEMBER!!
THE FINAL BATTLE HOLDS THE FATEFUL KEY TO THIS STORMY DAVY BACK FIGHT!
THIS IS THE EVENT YOU'VE ALL BEEN WAITING FOR!
THE MOTHER OF ALL CONTESTS...
... ONE-ON-ONE COMBAT!
RAAAAAAAAAH!!
YAAH
TWEET!!
YAAY
WE'VE BEEN WAITING!!
HURRY UP!!
YAAH
YAAY
ROAST
YAAH
YAAY
ALL RIGHT, LET'S CHOOSE THE FIELD!!
"FIELD"?

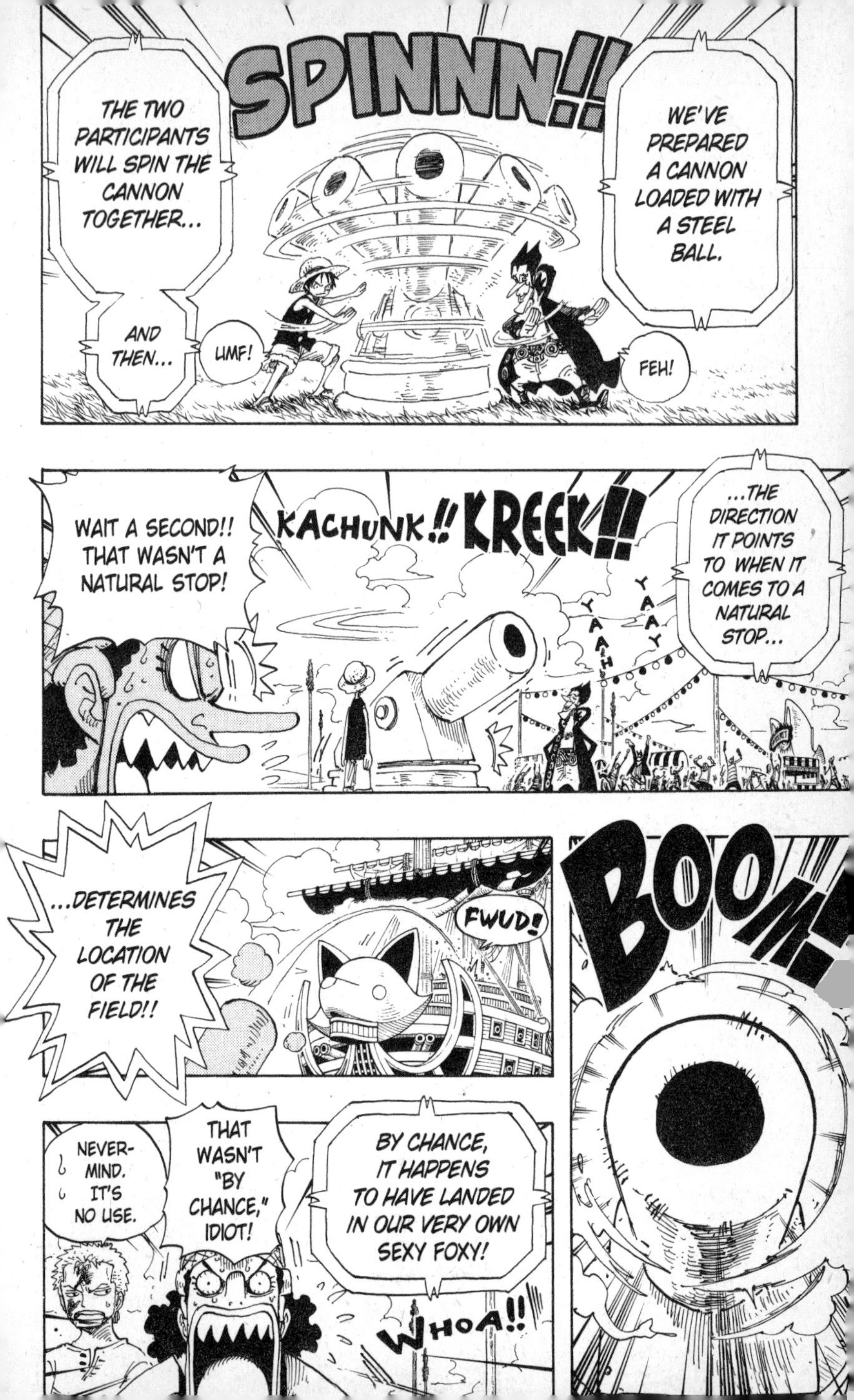
WE'VE PREPARED A CANNON LOADED WITH A STEEL BALL.
SPINNN!!
THE TWO PARTICIPANTS WILL SPIN THE CANNON TOGETHER...
AND THEN...
FEH!
UMF!
...THE DIRECTION IT POINTS TO WHEN IT COMES TO A NATURAL STOP...
YAAAY
YAAAH
KREEK!!
KACHUNK!!
WAIT A SECOND!! THAT WASN'T A NATURAL STOP!
BOOM
...DETERMINES THE LOCATION OF THE FIELD!!
FWUD!
BY CHANCE, IT HAPPENS TO HAVE LANDED IN OUR VERY OWN SEXY FOXY!
WHOA!!
THAT WASN'T "BY CHANCE," IDIOT!
NEVER-MIND. IT'S NO USE.

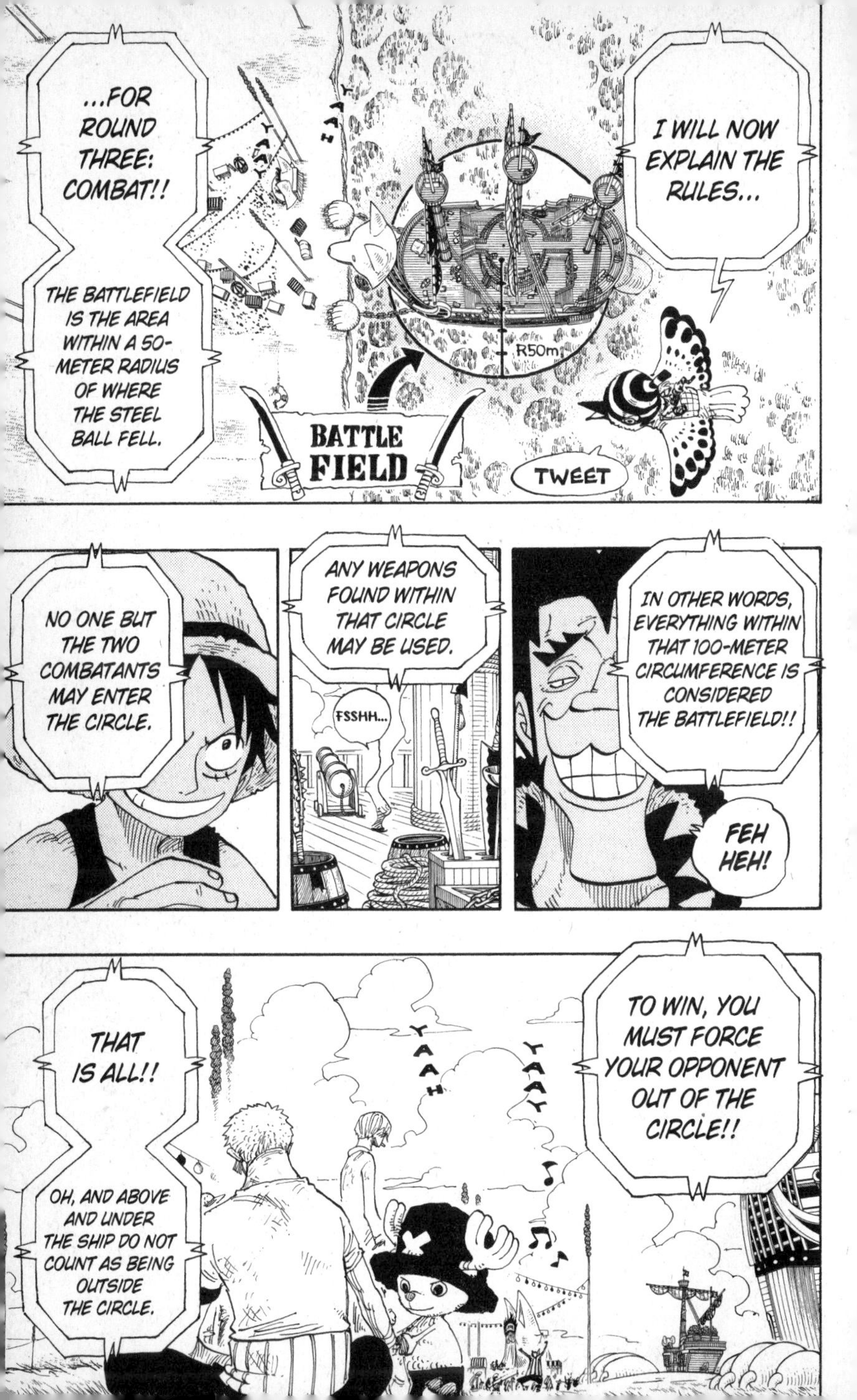
I WILL NOW EXPLAIN THE RULES...
...FOR ROUND THREE: COMBAT!!
THE BATTLEFIELD IS THE AREA WITHIN A 50-METER RADIUS OF WHERE THE STEEL BALL FELL.
R50m
BATTLE FIELD
TWEET
IN OTHER WORDS, EVERYTHING WITHIN THAT 100-METER CIRCUMFERENCE IS CONSIDERED THE BATTLEFIELD!!
FEH HEH!
ANY WEAPONS FOUND WITHIN THAT CIRCLE MAY BE USED.
FSSHH...
NO ONE BUT THE TWO COMBATANTS MAY ENTER THE CIRCLE.
TO WIN, YOU MUST FORCE YOUR OPPONENT OUT OF THE CIRCLE!!
YAAY
YAAH
THAT IS ALL!!
OH, AND ABOVE AND UNDER THE SHIP DO NOT COUNT AS BEING OUTSIDE THE CIRCLE.

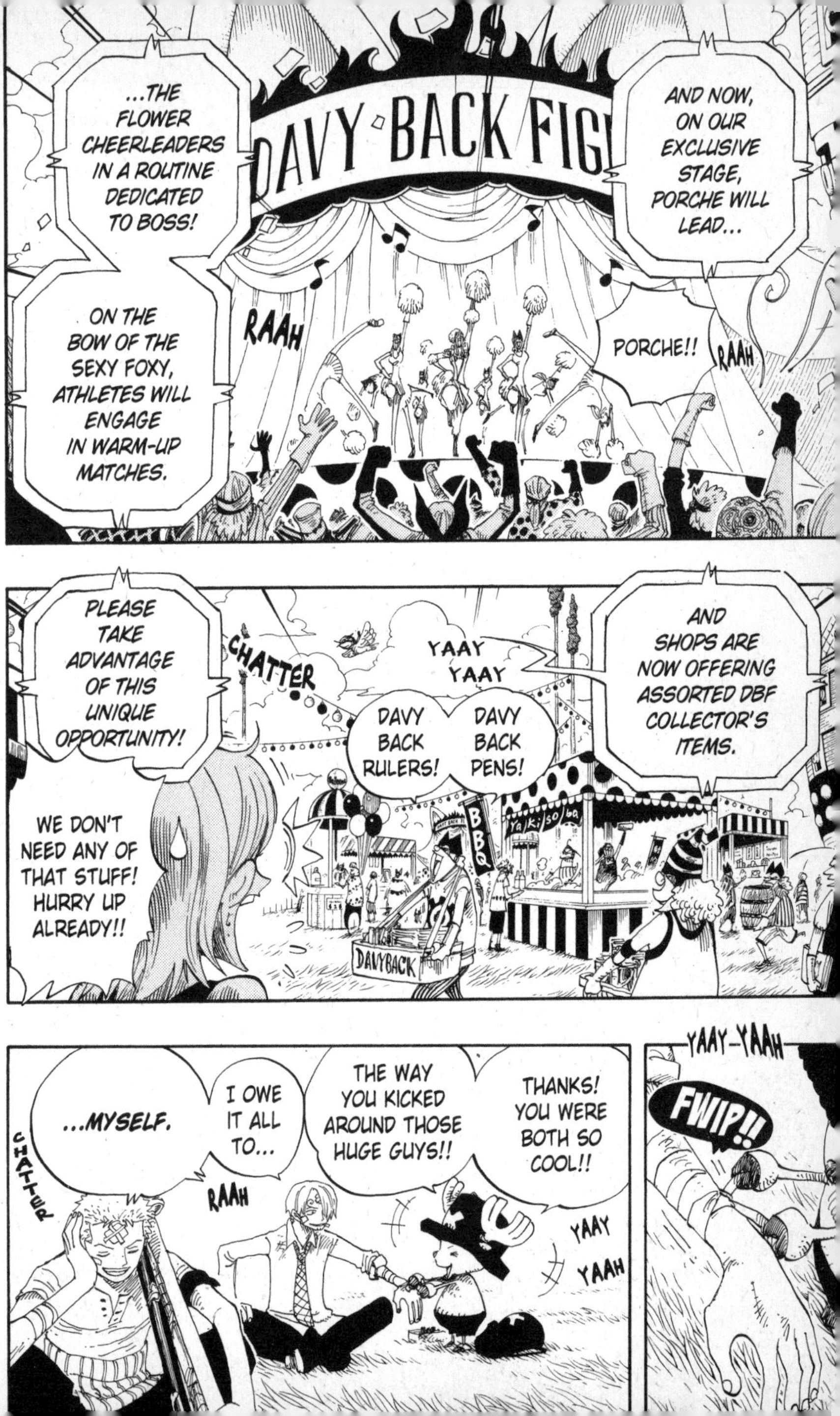
DAVY BACK FIG
AND NOW, ON OUR EXCLUSIVE STAGE, PORCHE WILL LEAD...
...THE FLOWER CHEERLEADERS IN A ROUTINE DEDICATED TO BOSS!
PORCHE!!
RAAH
RAAH
ON THE BOW OF THE SEXY FOXY, ATHLETES WILL ENGAGE IN WARM-UP MATCHES.
AND SHOPS ARE NOW OFFERING ASSORTED DBF COLLECTOR'S ITEMS.
YAAY YAAY
DAVY BACK PENS!
DAVY BACK RULERS!
CHATTER
PLEASE TAKE ADVANTAGE OF THIS UNIQUE OPPORTUNITY!
BBQ
Ya ki so ba
DAVYBACK
WE DON'T NEED ANY OF THAT STUFF! HURRY UP ALREADY!!
YAAY-YAAH
FWIP!!
THANKS! YOU WERE BOTH SO COOL!!
THE WAY YOU KICKED AROUND THOSE HUGE GUYS!!
I OWE IT ALL TO...
...MYSELF.
YAAY
YAAH
RAAH
CHATTER

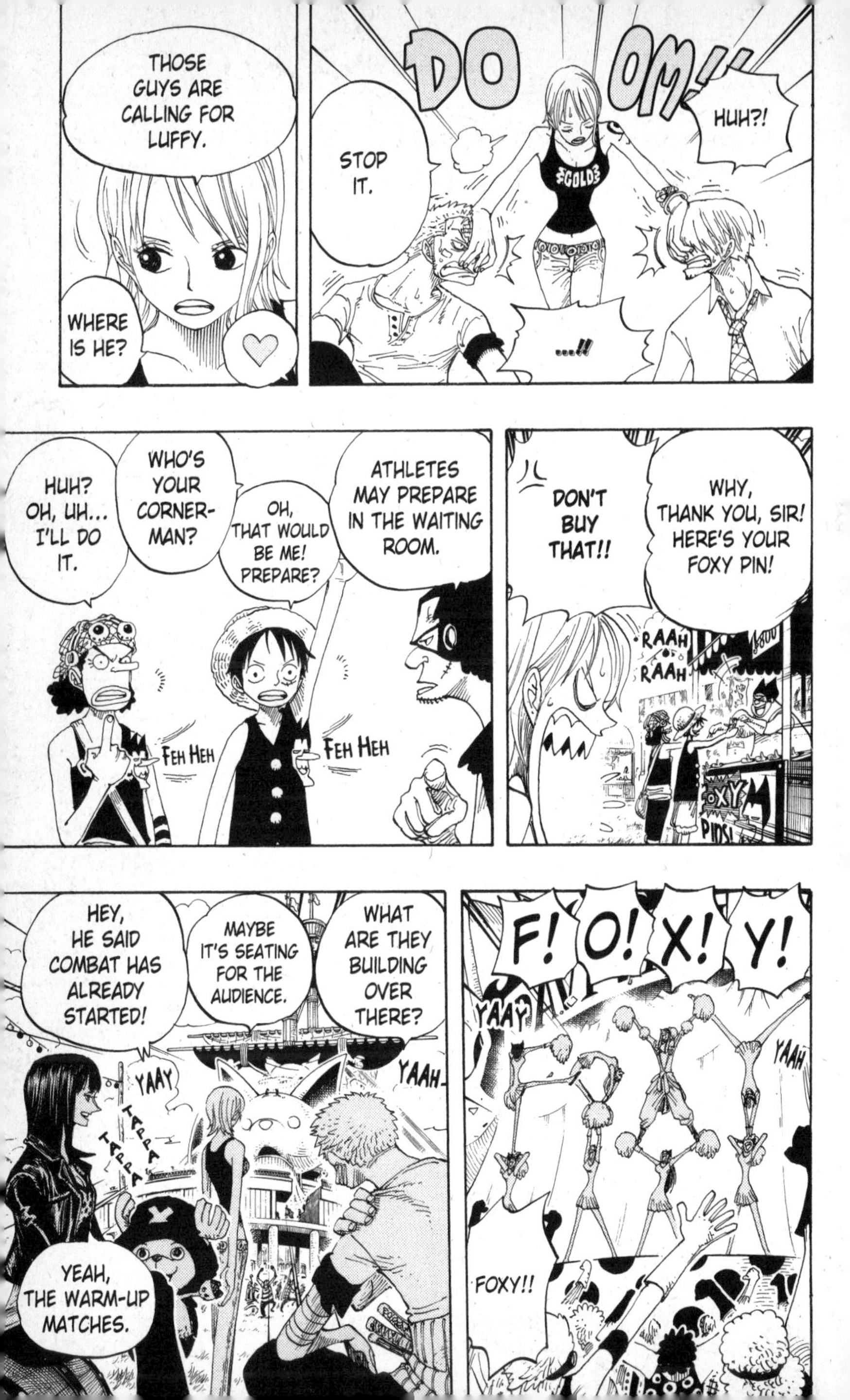
DOOM!!
HUH?!
STOP IT.
...!!
THOSE GUYS ARE CALLING FOR LUFFY.
WHERE IS HE?
WHY, THANK YOU, SIR! HERE'S YOUR FOXY PIN!
DON'T BUY THAT!!
RAAH RAAH
ATHLETES MAY PREPARE IN THE WAITING ROOM.
WHO'S YOUR CORNER-MAN?
OH, THAT WOULD BE ME! PREPARE?
HUH? OH, UH... I'LL DO IT.
FEH HEH
FEH HEH
F! O! X! Y!
YAAY
YAAH
FOXY!!
WHAT ARE THEY BUILDING OVER THERE?
MAYBE IT'S SEATING FOR THE AUDIENCE.
HEY, HE SAID COMBAT HAS ALREADY STARTED!
YAAH
YAAY
TAPPA TAPPA
YEAH, THE WARM-UP MATCHES.

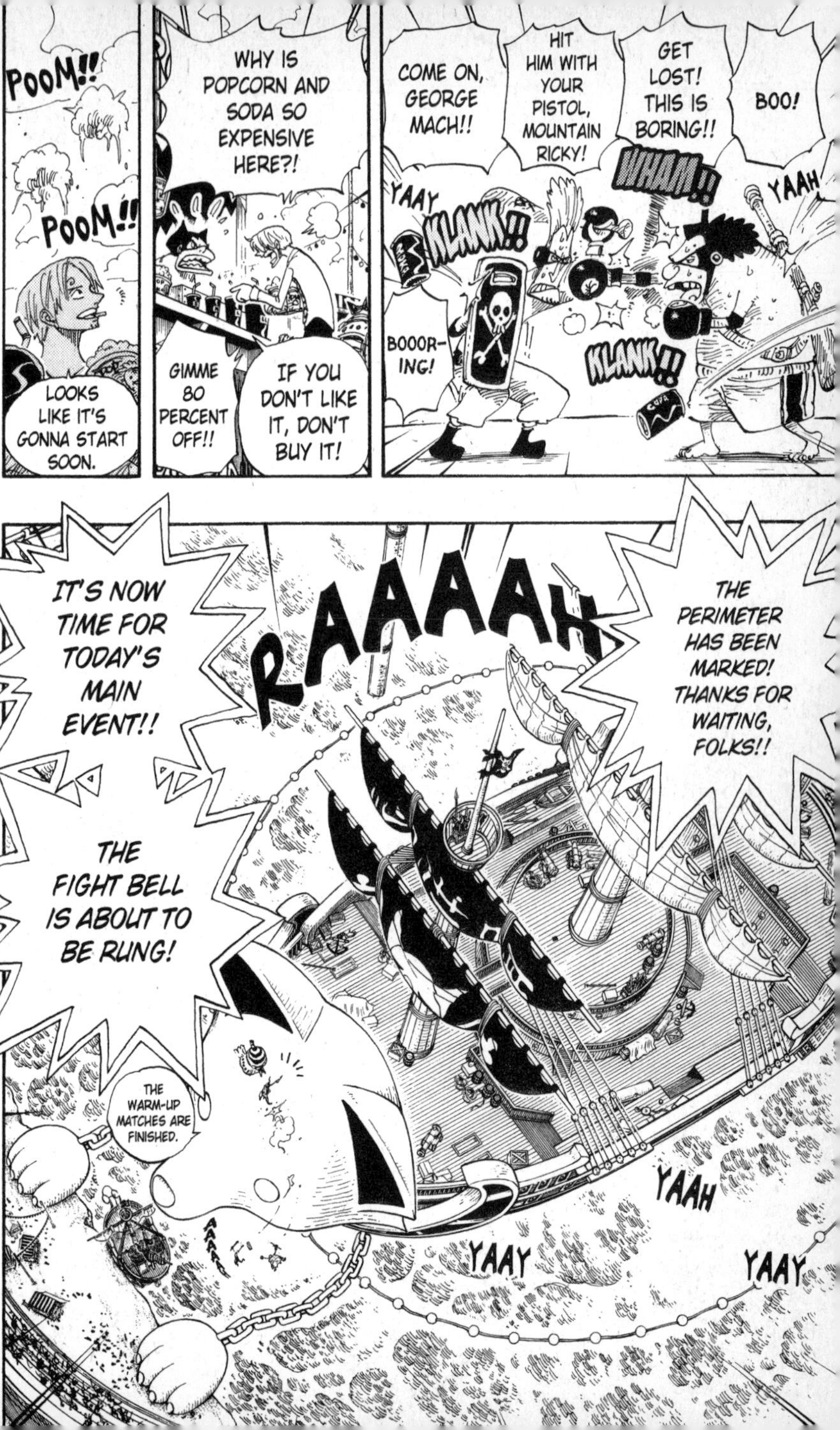
BOO!
GET LOST! THIS IS BORING!!
YAAH
WHAM!!
HIT HIM WITH YOUR PISTOL, MOUNTAIN RICKY!
COME ON, GEORGE MACH!!
YAAY
KLANK!!
KLANK!!
BOOOR-ING!
WHY IS POPCORN AND SODA SO EXPENSIVE HERE?!
IF YOU DON'T LIKE IT, DON'T BUY IT!
GIMME 80 PERCENT OFF!!
POOM!!
POOM!!
LOOKS LIKE IT'S GONNA START SOON.
THE PERIMETER HAS BEEN MARKED! THANKS FOR WAITING, FOLKS!!
RAAAAH
IT'S NOW TIME FOR TODAY'S MAIN EVENT!!
THE FIGHT BELL IS ABOUT TO BE RUNG!
THE WARM-UP MATCHES ARE FINISHED.
YAAH
YAAY
YAAY

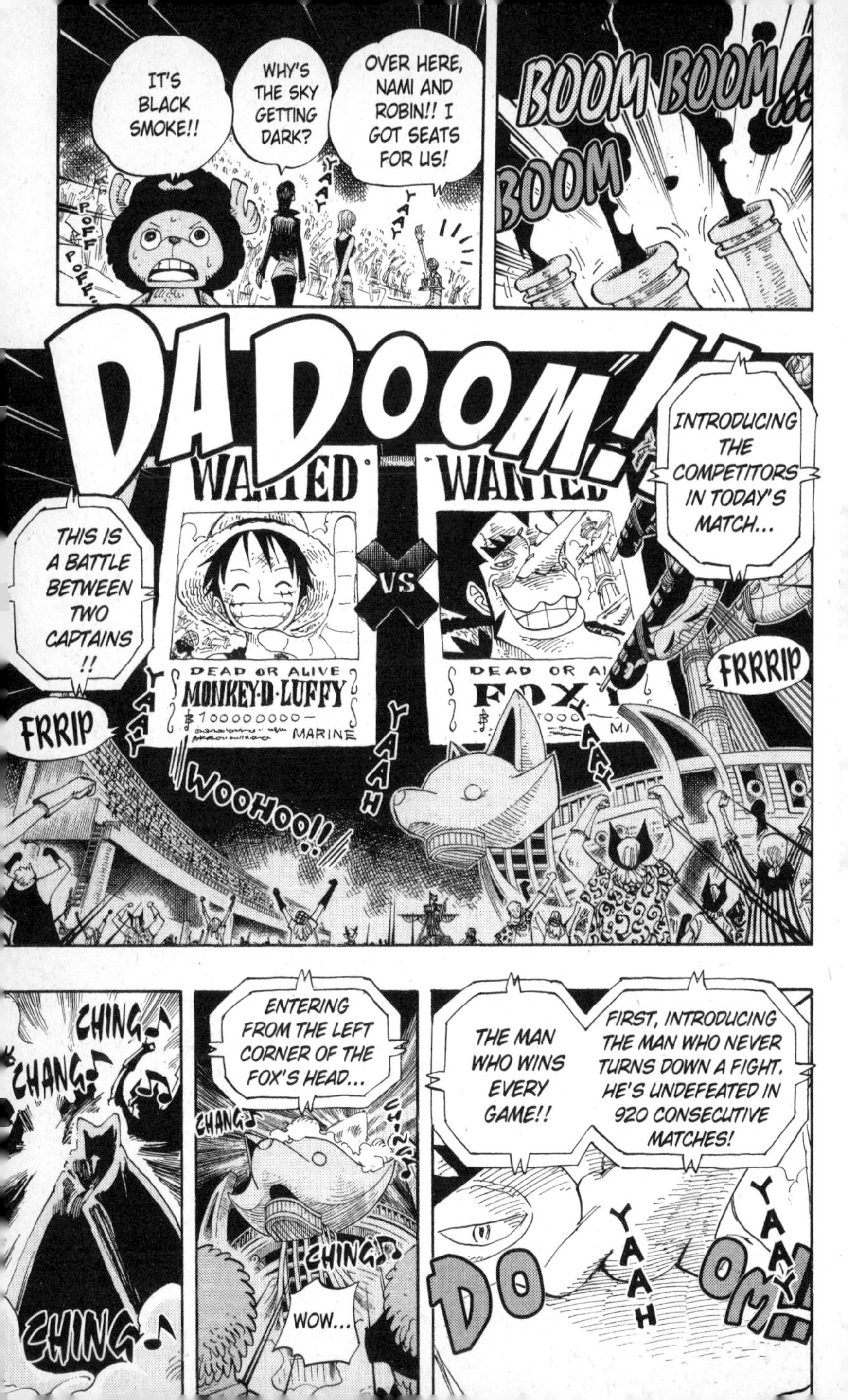
BOOM BOOM!!
BOOM
OVER HERE, NAMI AND ROBIN!! I GOT SEATS FOR US!
YAAAY
WHY'S THE SKY GETTING DARK?
YAAAY
IT'S BLACK SMOKE!!
POFF POFF...
DADOOM!!
INTRODUCING THE COMPETITORS IN TODAY'S MATCH...
FRRRIP
WANTED
DEAD OR AL
FOX
YAAAY
YAAAH
WOOHOO!!
WANTED
DEAD OR ALIVE
MONKEY·D·LUFFY
฿100000000—
MARINE
THIS IS A BATTLE BETWEEN TWO CAPTAINS!!
FRRIP
YAAAY
FIRST, INTRODUCING THE MAN WHO NEVER TURNS DOWN A FIGHT. HE'S UNDEFEATED IN 920 CONSECUTIVE MATCHES!
THE MAN WHO WINS EVERY GAME!!
YAAAY
YAAAH
DOOM!!
ENTERING FROM THE LEFT CORNER OF THE FOX'S HEAD...
CHING♪
CHANG♪
CHING♪
WOW...
CHING♪
CHANG♪
CHING♪

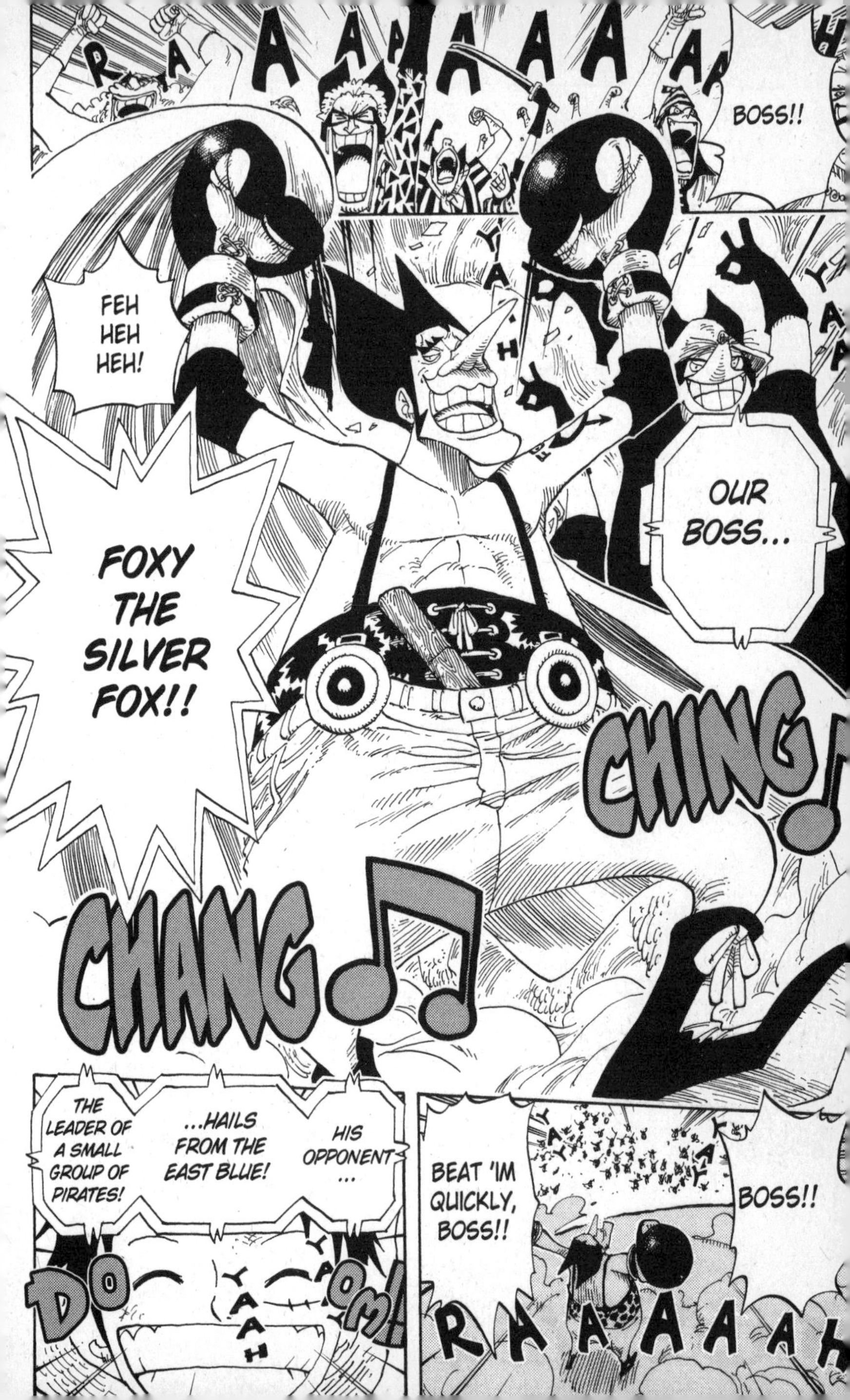
BOSS!!
RAAAAAAAAAH
FEH HEH HEH!
OUR BOSS...
FOXY THE SILVER FOX!!
CHING!
CHANG!
BOSS!!
BEAT 'IM QUICKLY, BOSS!!
RAAAAAH
HIS OPPONENT...
...HAILS FROM THE EAST BLUE!
THE LEADER OF A SMALL GROUP OF PIRATES!
POM!
YAAH
DO

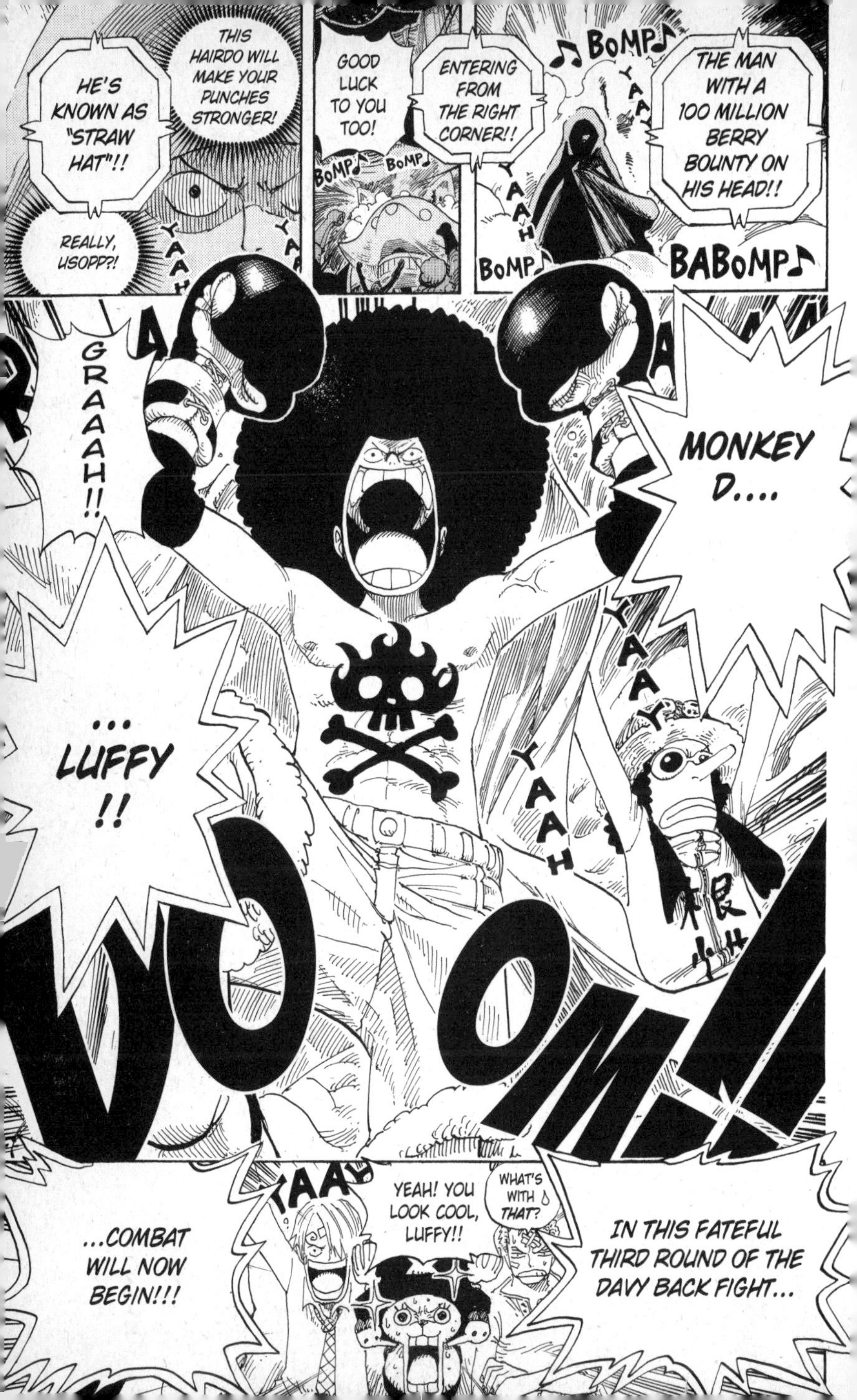

THE MAN WITH A 100 MILLION BERRY BOUNTY ON HIS HEAD!!
♪BOMP♪
BABOMP♪
BOMP♪
ENTERING FROM THE RIGHT CORNER!!
GOOD LUCK TO YOU TOO!
BOMP♪
BOMP♪
THIS HAIRDO WILL MAKE YOUR PUNCHES STRONGER!
HE'S KNOWN AS "STRAW HAT"!!
REALLY, USOPP?!
MONKEY D....
GRAAAAH!!
...LUFFY!!
YAAAAH
VOOM
IN THIS FATEFUL THIRD ROUND OF THE DAVY BACK FIGHT...
WHAT'S WITH THAT?
YEAH! YOU LOOK COOL, LUFFY!!
...COMBAT WILL NOW BEGIN!!!

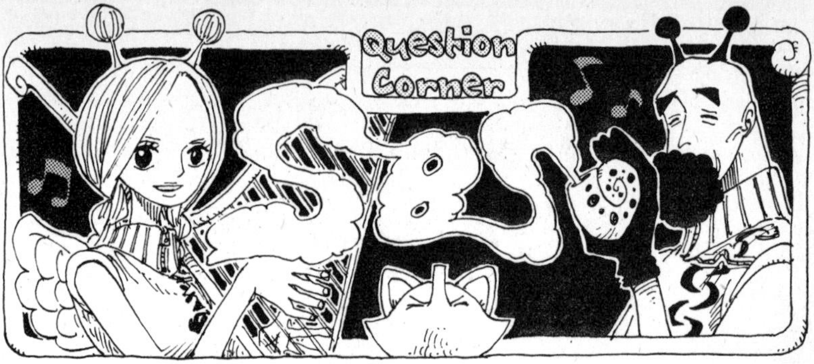
Question Corner
SBS

Q: Do Love Hurricanes just occur suddenly?

--Mikan Chips

A: YEP. Love strikes without warning and steals your heart.
↑ I sound pretty cool, huh?

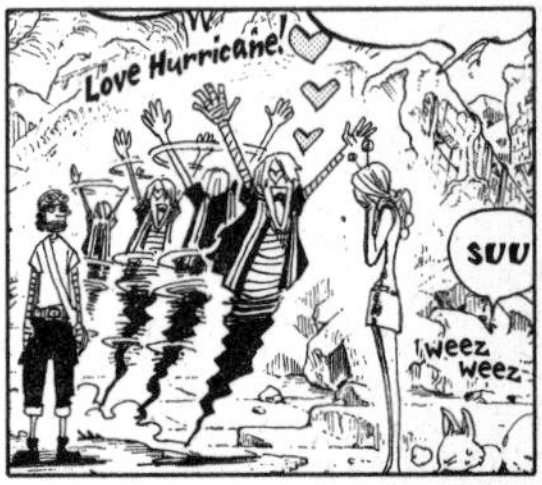
Love Hurricane!
SUU
weez weez

Q: Hello, Oda Sensei. A serious question came up, so allow me to ask you about it seriously. It's regarding the names of Eneru's special moves. It seems like many of them are the names of gods or spirits from Norse and Indian mythologies. Please explain in detail which gods and spirits you used.

--And Kin no Ho

A: Okay. Let's see... There were a lot of special moves around then. I don't know about "in detail," But here's a simple rundown.

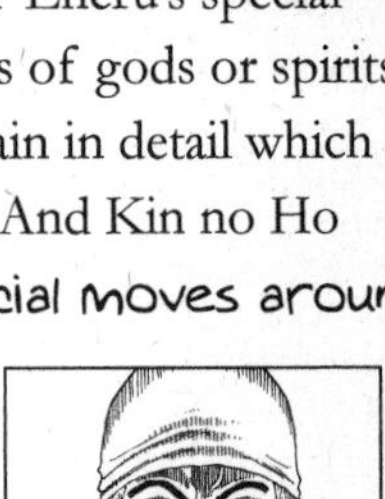

El Thor → Thor: God of Battle and thunder in Norse mythology

Hino → Hino: the Giant thunderBird of the Iroquois in North America

Kiten → Kiten: the Japanese thunder Beast

Lightning Dragon → This refers to Julungul: the thunder God of Australia's Arnhem Land

Mamaragan → Mamaragan: the central Australian thunder God

Amaru → Amaru: This means falls from Heaven, or thunderBolts in Japanese

Kari → Karei: Ancient thunder God of the Semang on the Malay Peninsula

And so on. Also, I decided on the name "Varie" Because thunder makes a sound like vaari vaari. In other words, it's all pretty made up. It's not any specific language.

Chapter 314: COMBAT!!

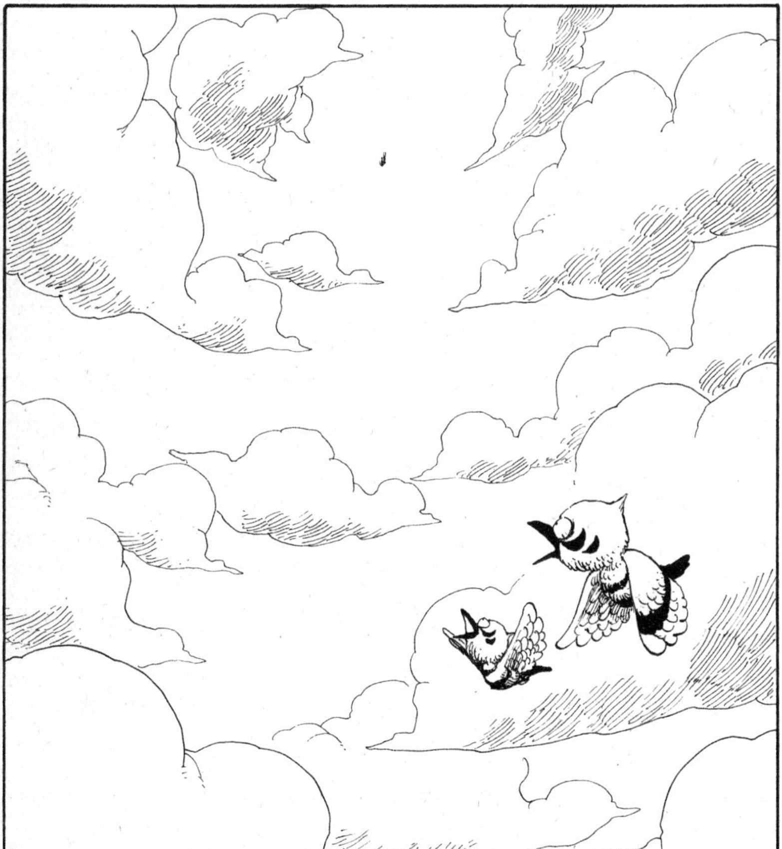

CHAPTER TITLE PAGE SERIES #7:
"AN ANGEL COMES DOWN FROM THE SKY"

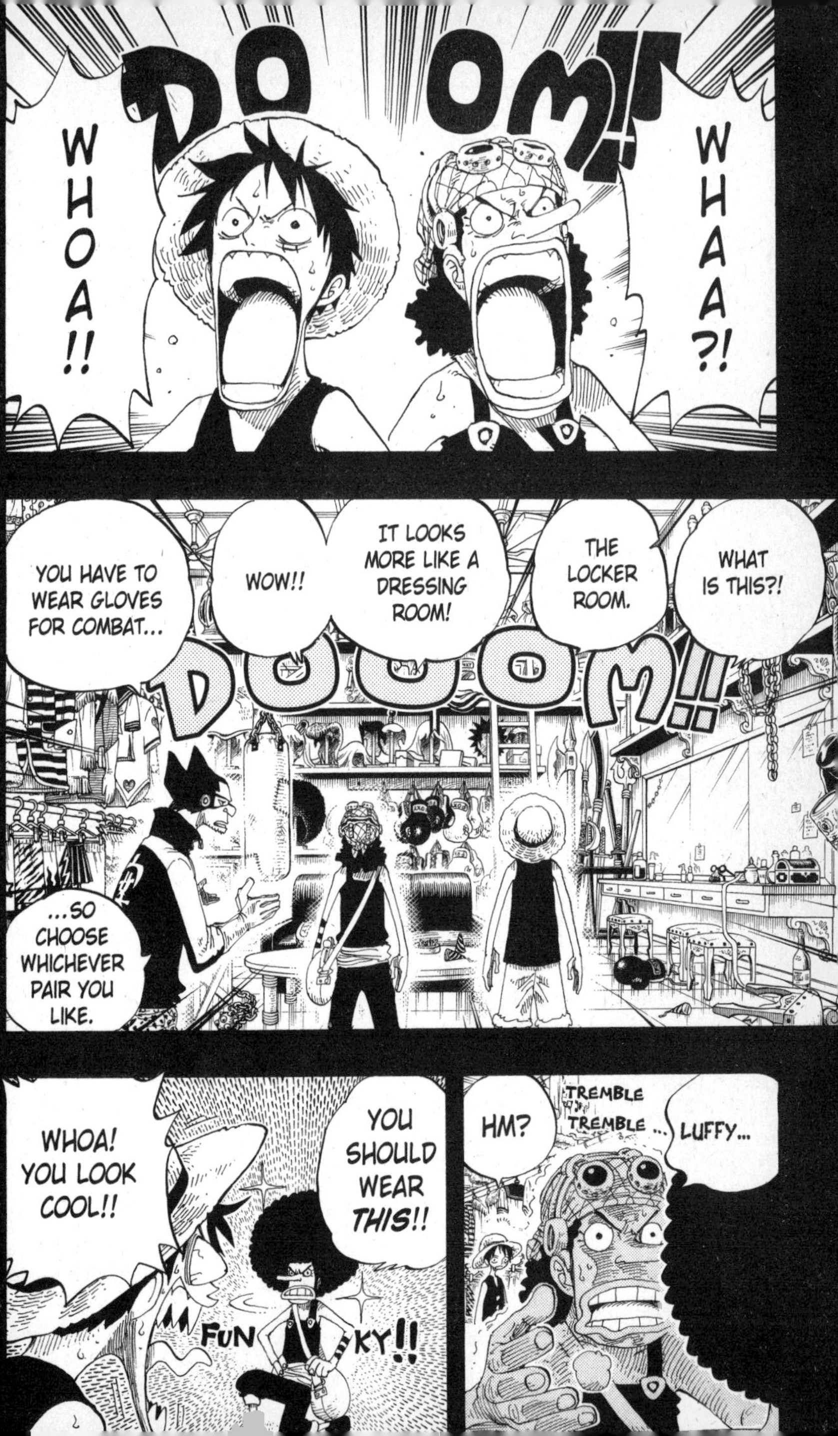
DOOM!!
WHAA?!
WHOA!!
WHAT IS THIS?!
THE LOCKER ROOM.
IT LOOKS MORE LIKE A DRESSING ROOM!
WOW!!
YOU HAVE TO WEAR GLOVES FOR COMBAT...
DOOOM!!
...SO CHOOSE WHICHEVER PAIR YOU LIKE.
LUFFY...
TREMBLE TREMBLE...
HM?
YOU SHOULD WEAR *THIS*!!
WHOA! YOU LOOK COOL!!
FUNKY!!

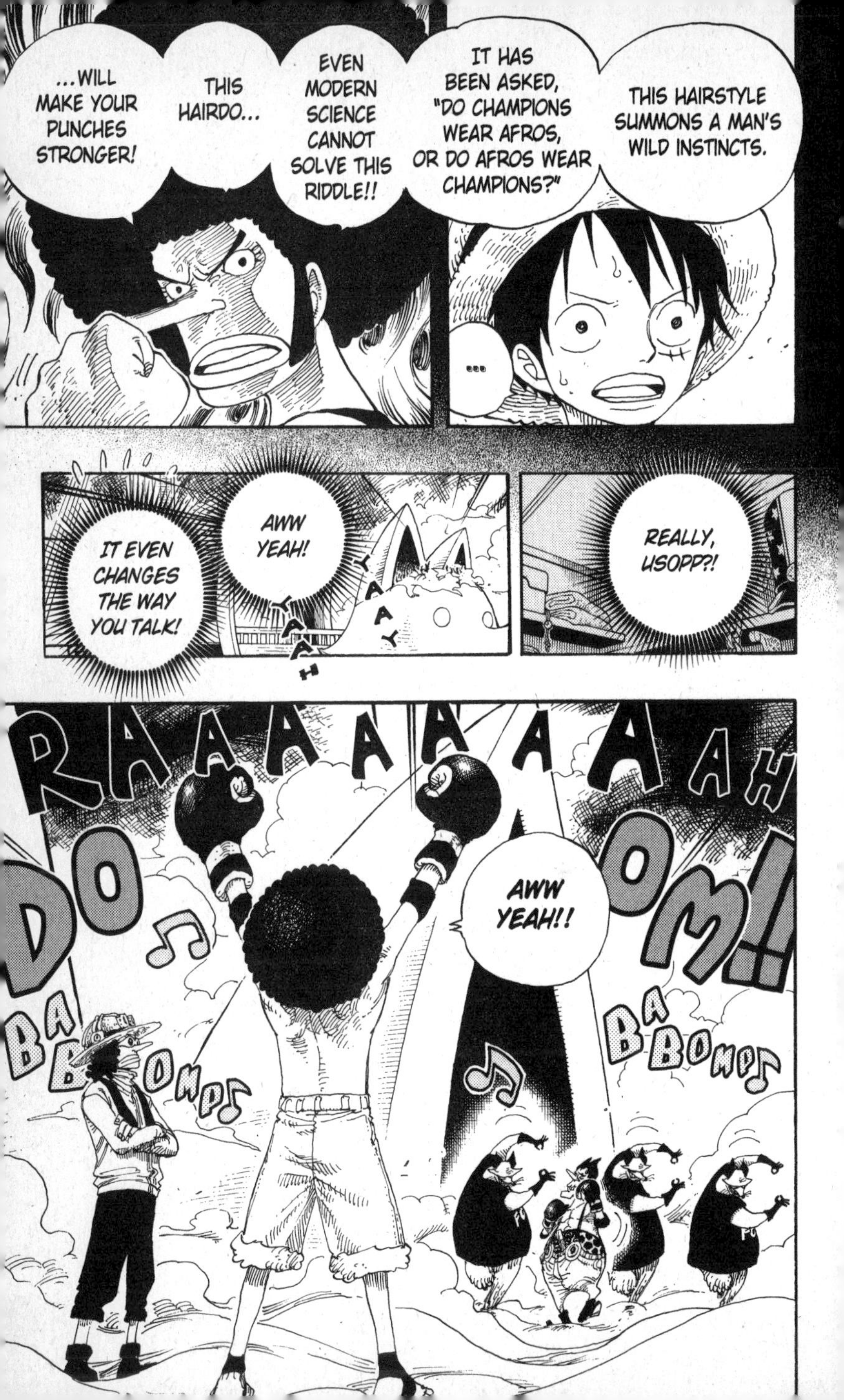
THIS HAIRSTYLE SUMMONS A MAN'S WILD INSTINCTS.
IT HAS BEEN ASKED, "DO CHAMPIONS WEAR AFROS, OR DO AFROS WEAR CHAMPIONS?"
EVEN MODERN SCIENCE CANNOT SOLVE THIS RIDDLE!!
THIS HAIRDO...
...WILL MAKE YOUR PUNCHES STRONGER!
...
REALLY, USOPP?!
AWW YEAH!
YAAY
YAAH
IT EVEN CHANGES THE WAY YOU TALK!
RAAAAAAAAH
DOOM!!
AWW YEAH!!
BA BOMP♪
BA BOMP♪

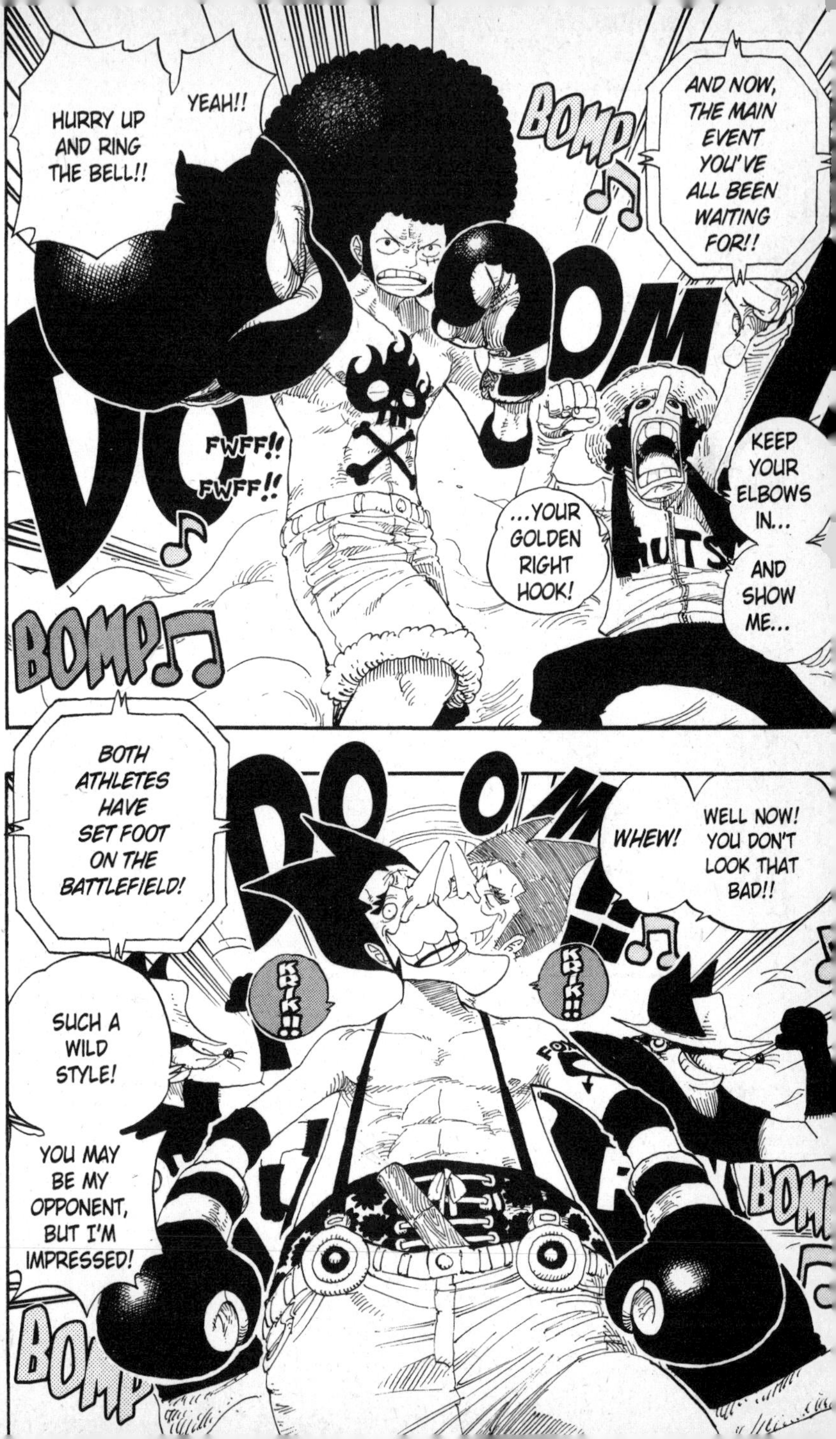
AND NOW, THE MAIN EVENT YOU'VE ALL BEEN WAITING FOR!!
BOMP
YEAH!!
HURRY UP AND RING THE BELL!!
KEEP YOUR ELBOWS IN...
AND SHOW ME...
...YOUR GOLDEN RIGHT HOOK!
FWFF!! FWFF!!
BOMP
WELL NOW! YOU DON'T LOOK THAT BAD!!
WHEW!
BOTH ATHLETES HAVE SET FOOT ON THE BATTLEFIELD!
KRIK!!
KRIK!!
SUCH A WILD STYLE!
YOU MAY BE MY OPPONENT, BUT I'M IMPRESSED!
BOMP

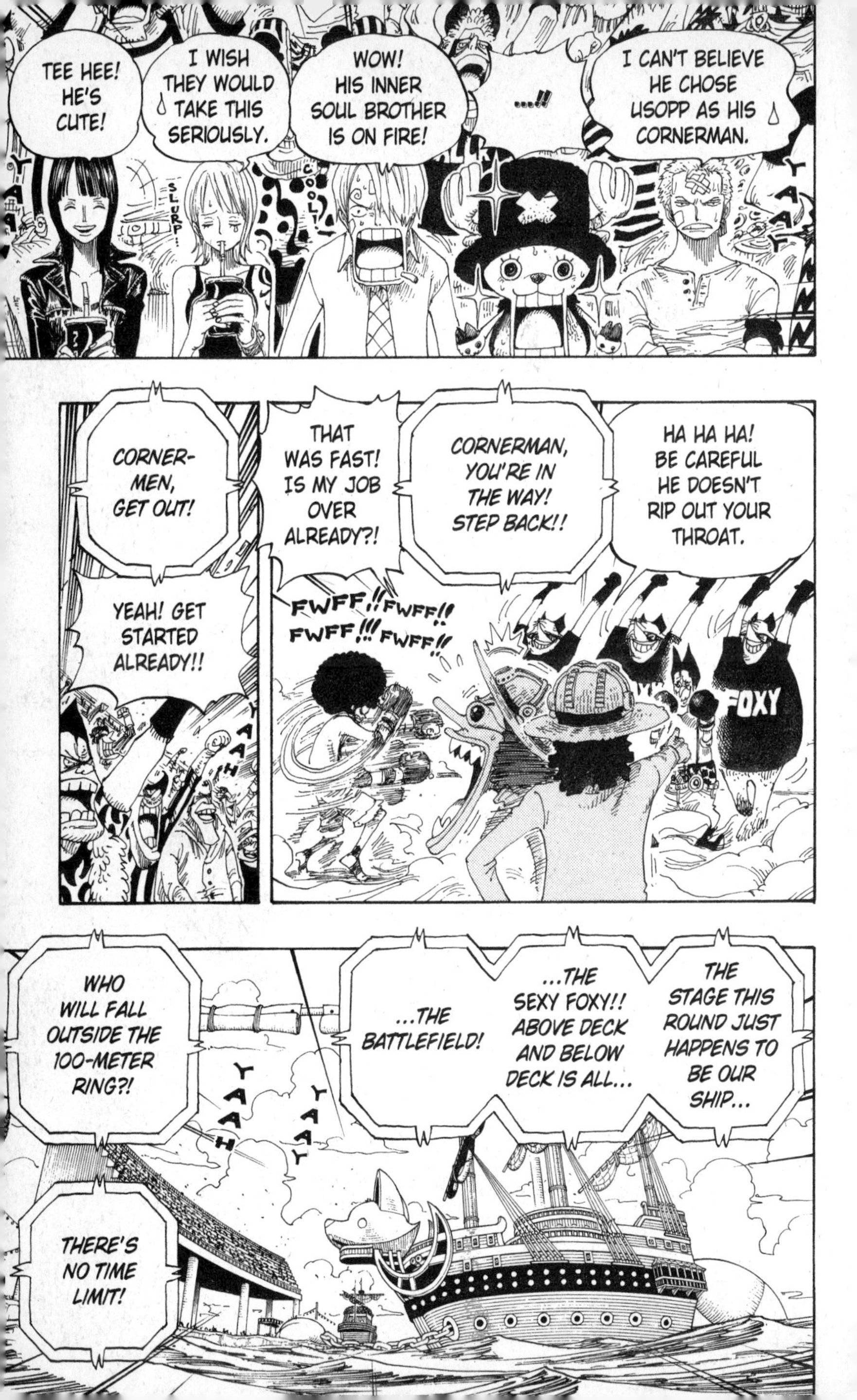
YAAAH
I CAN'T BELIEVE HE CHOSE USOPP AS HIS CORNERMAN.
...!!
WOW! HIS INNER SOUL BROTHER IS ON FIRE!
COOL!!
I WISH THEY WOULD TAKE THIS SERIOUSLY.
SLURP...
TEE HEE! HE'S CUTE!
YAAH
HA HA HA! BE CAREFUL HE DOESN'T RIP OUT YOUR THROAT.
CORNERMAN, YOU'RE IN THE WAY! STEP BACK!!
THAT WAS FAST! IS MY JOB OVER ALREADY?!
FWFF!! FWFF!! FWFF!!! FWFF!!
FOXY
CORNER-MEN, GET OUT!
YEAH! GET STARTED ALREADY!!
YAAAH
THE STAGE THIS ROUND JUST HAPPENS TO BE OUR SHIP...
...THE SEXY FOXY!! ABOVE DECK AND BELOW DECK IS ALL...
...THE BATTLEFIELD!
YAAAY
YAAAH
WHO WILL FALL OUTSIDE THE 100-METER RING?!
THERE'S NO TIME LIMIT!

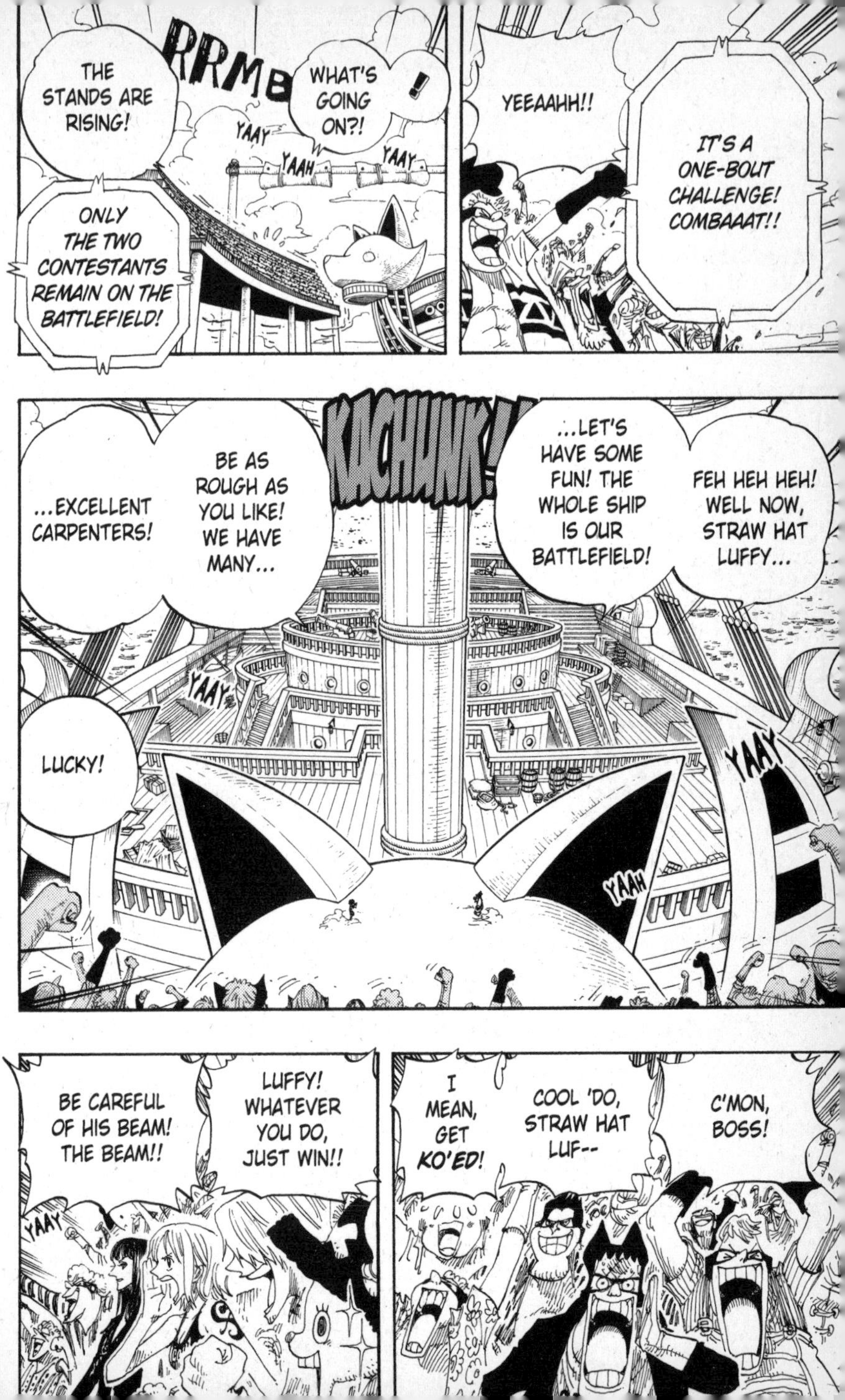
IT'S A ONE-BOUT CHALLENGE! COMBAAAT!!
YEEAAHH!!
WHAT'S GOING ON?!
!
RRMB
THE STANDS ARE RISING!
YAAY
YAAH
YAAY
ONLY THE TWO CONTESTANTS REMAIN ON THE BATTLEFIELD!
FEH HEH HEH! WELL NOW, STRAW HAT LUFFY...
...LET'S HAVE SOME FUN! THE WHOLE SHIP IS OUR BATTLEFIELD!
KACHUNK!!
BE AS ROUGH AS YOU LIKE! WE HAVE MANY...
...EXCELLENT CARPENTERS!
YAAY
YAAH
YAAY
LUCKY!
C'MON, BOSS!
COOL 'DO, STRAW HAT LUF--
I MEAN, GET *KO'ED*!
LUFFY! WHATEVER YOU DO, JUST WIN!!
BE CAREFUL OF HIS BEAM! THE BEAM!!
YAAY

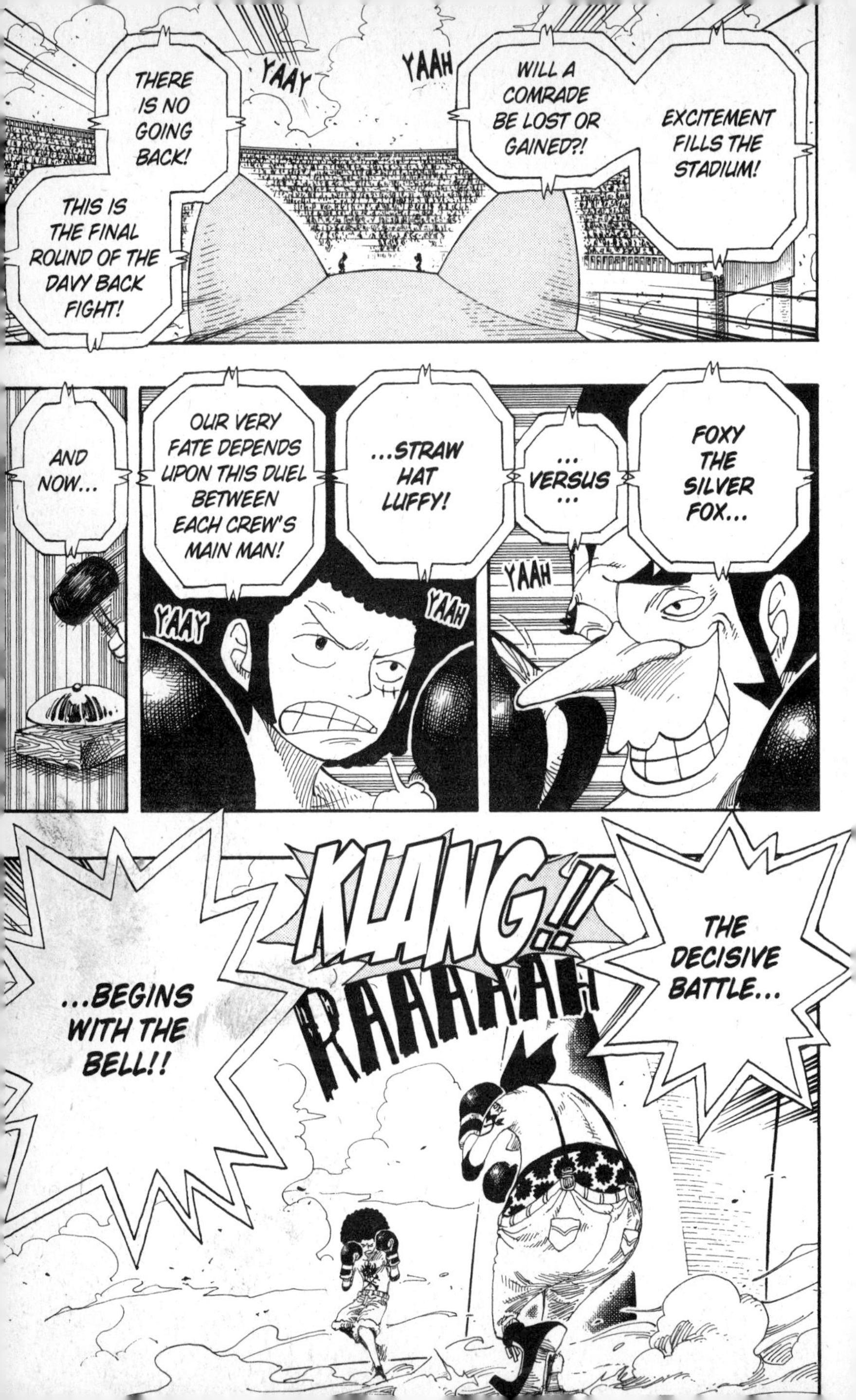
EXCITEMENT FILLS THE STADIUM!
WILL A COMRADE BE LOST OR GAINED?!
YAAH
YAAY
THERE IS NO GOING BACK!
THIS IS THE FINAL ROUND OF THE DAVY BACK FIGHT!
FOXY THE SILVER FOX...
...VERSUS...
YAAH
...STRAW HAT LUFFY!
OUR VERY FATE DEPENDS UPON THIS DUEL BETWEEN EACH CREW'S MAIN MAN!
YAAH
YAAY
AND NOW...
THE DECISIVE BATTLE...
KLANG!!
RAAAAAAH
...BEGINS WITH THE BELL!!

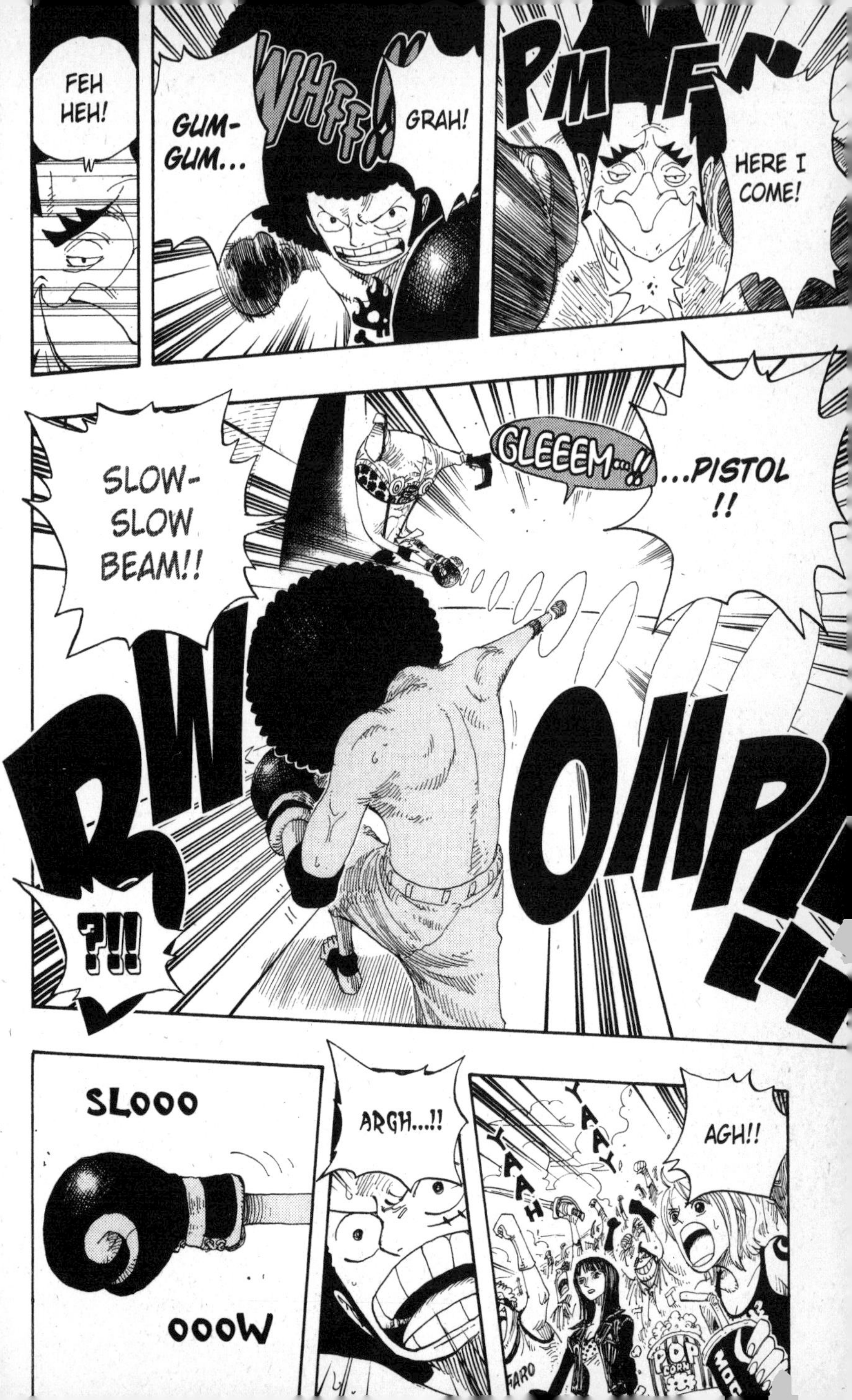
PMF
HERE I COME!
GRAH!
WHFF!!
GUM-GUM...
FEH HEH!
...PISTOL!!
GLEEEM...!!
SLOW-SLOW BEAM!!
RWOMP!!!
?!!
AGH!!
YAAAY
YAAAH
ARGH...!!
SLOOO
OOOW

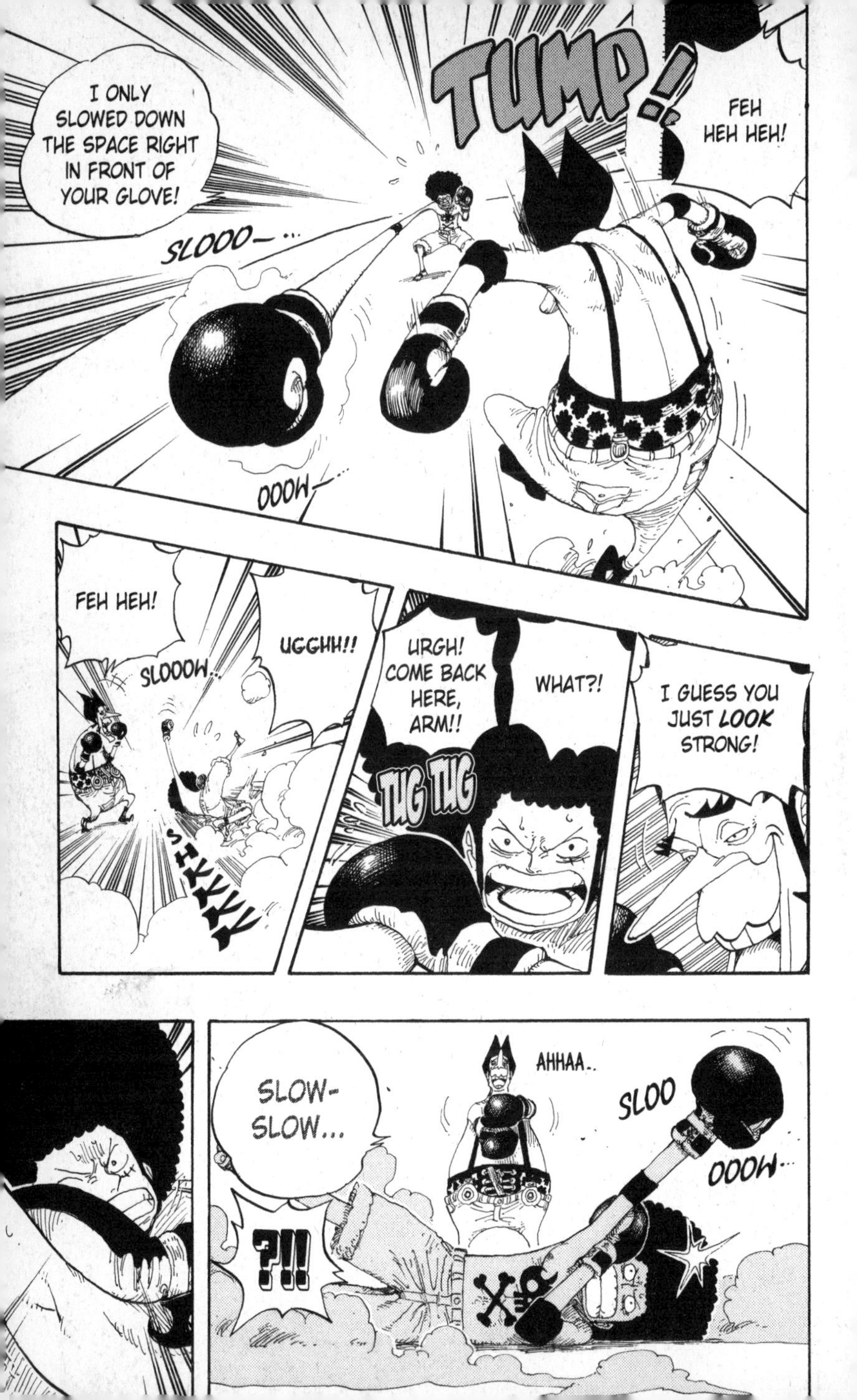
TUMP!!
FEH HEH HEH!
I ONLY SLOWED DOWN THE SPACE RIGHT IN FRONT OF YOUR GLOVE!
SLOOO—...
OOOW—...
I GUESS YOU JUST LOOK STRONG!
WHAT?!
URGH! COME BACK HERE, ARM!!
TUG TUG
UGGHH!!
FEH HEH!
SLOOOW...
SHKKKKK
SLOW-SLOW...
AHHAA..
SLOO
OOOW...
?!!

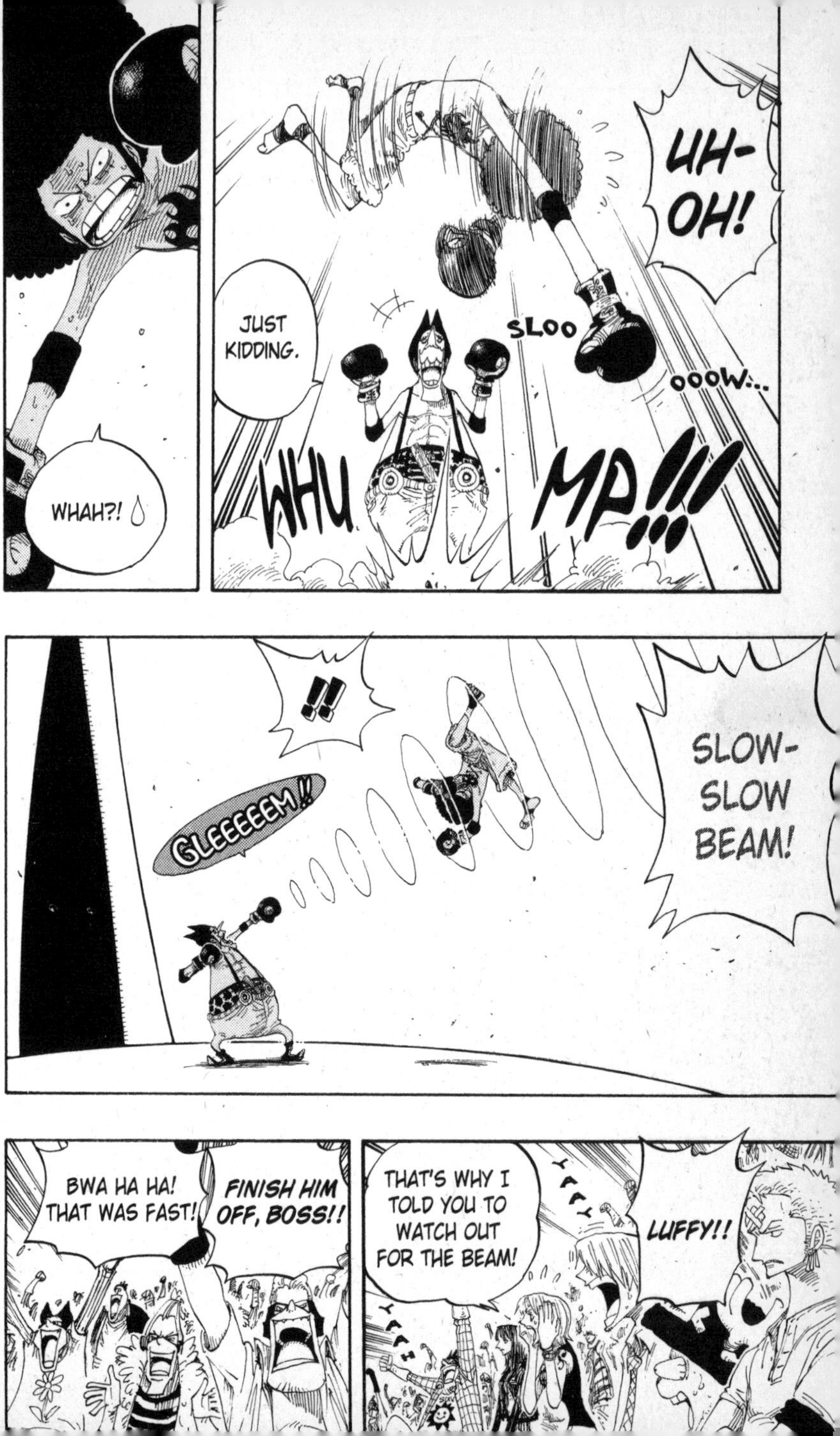
UH-OH!
SLOO
OOOW...
JUST KIDDING.
WHU
MP!!!
WHAH?!
SLOW-SLOW BEAM!
!!
GLEEEEEM!!
LUFFY!!
THAT'S WHY I TOLD YOU TO WATCH OUT FOR THE BEAM!
FINISH HIM OFF, BOSS!!
BWA HA HA! THAT WAS FAST!

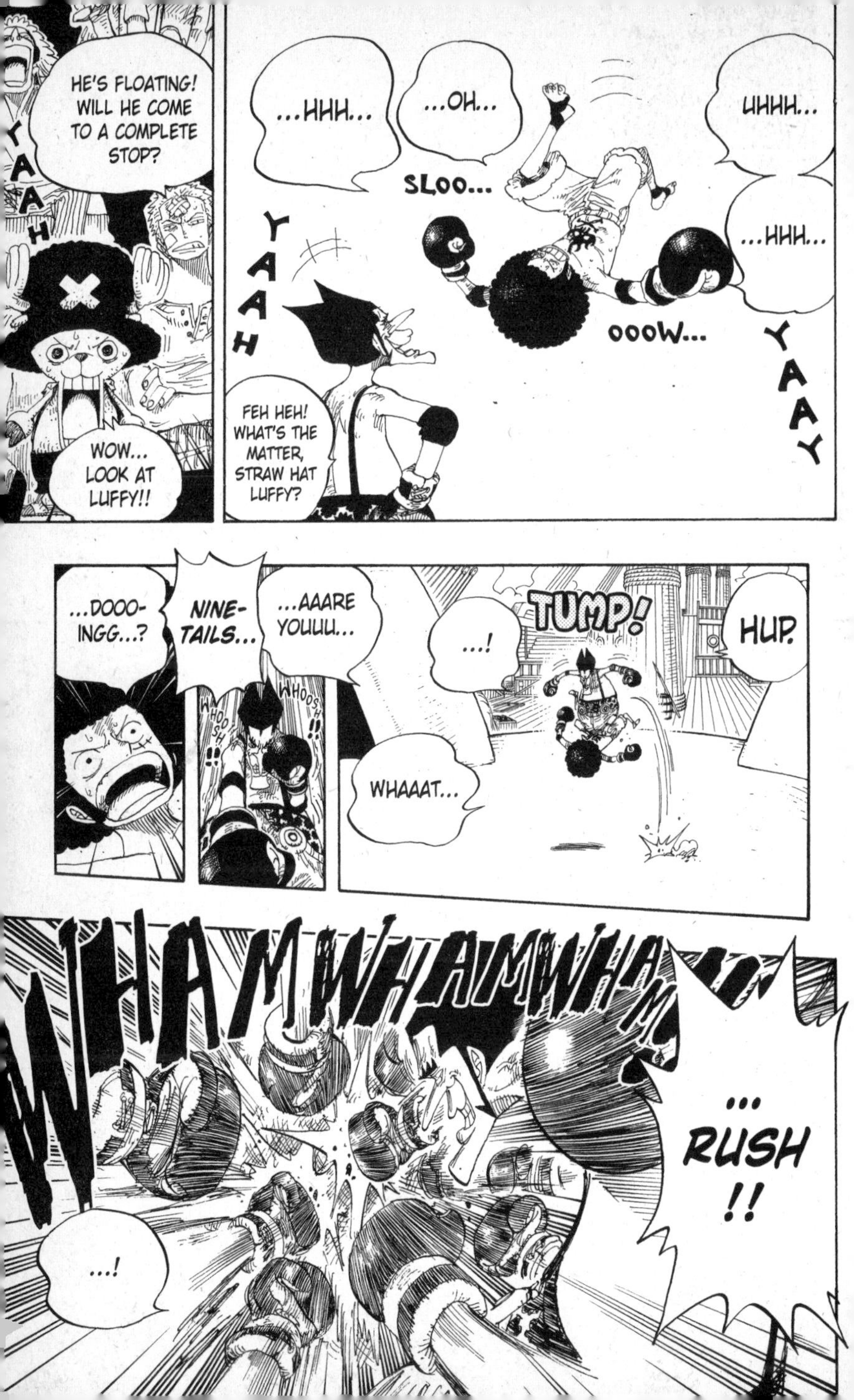
UHHH...
...HHH...
...OH...
...HHH...
SLOO...
OOOW...
YAAY
YAAH
FEH HEH! WHAT'S THE MATTER, STRAW HAT LUFFY?
HE'S FLOATING! WILL HE COME TO A COMPLETE STOP?
YAAH
WOW... LOOK AT LUFFY!!
HUP.
TUMP!
...!
WHAAAT...
...AAARE YOUUU...
WHOOSH!!
WHOOSH!!
NINE-TAILS...
...DOOO-INGG...?
WHAMWHAMWHAM
...RUSH!!
...!

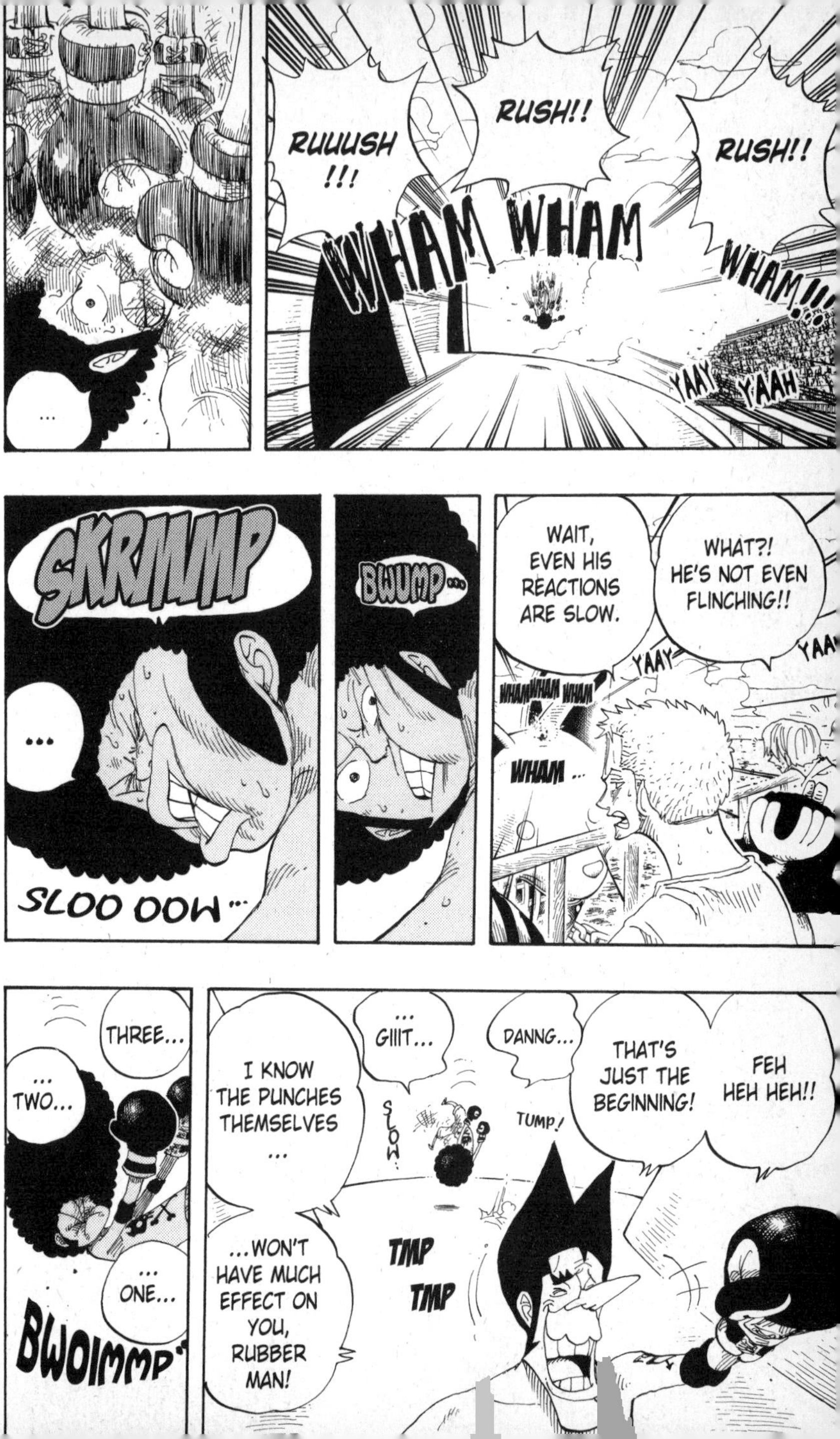
RUSH!!
RUSH!!
RUUUSH !!!
WHAM!!!
WHAM WHAM
YAAH
YAAY
...
WHAT?! HE'S NOT EVEN FLINCHING!!
WAIT, EVEN HIS REACTIONS ARE SLOW.
YAA
YAAY
WHAM WHAM WHAM
WHAM...
BWUMP...
SKRIMMP
...
SLOO OOW...
FEH HEH HEH!!
THAT'S JUST THE BEGINNING!
DANNG...
...GIIIT...
I KNOW THE PUNCHES THEMSELVES ...
TUMP!
SLOW...
...WON'T HAVE MUCH EFFECT ON YOU, RUBBER MAN!
TMP
TMP
THREE...
...TWO...
...ONE...
BWOIMMP

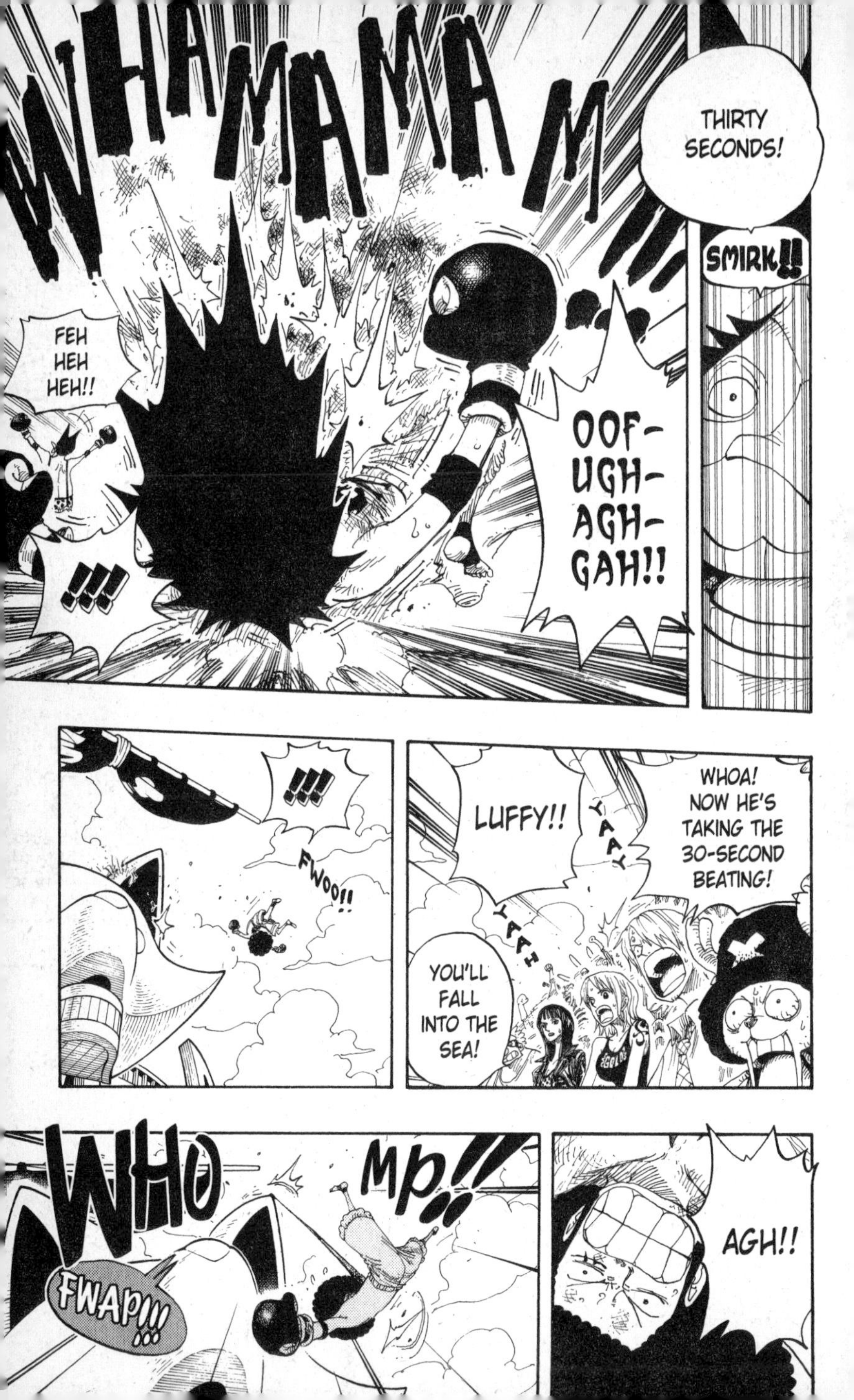
THIRTY SECONDS!
SMIRK!!
WHAMAMAM
OOF-UGH-AGH-GAH!!
FEH HEH HEH!!
!!!
WHOA! NOW HE'S TAKING THE 30-SECOND BEATING!
YAAAY
LUFFY!!
YAAAH
YOU'LL FALL INTO THE SEA!
!!!
FWOO!!
AGH!!
WHOMP!!
FWAP!!!

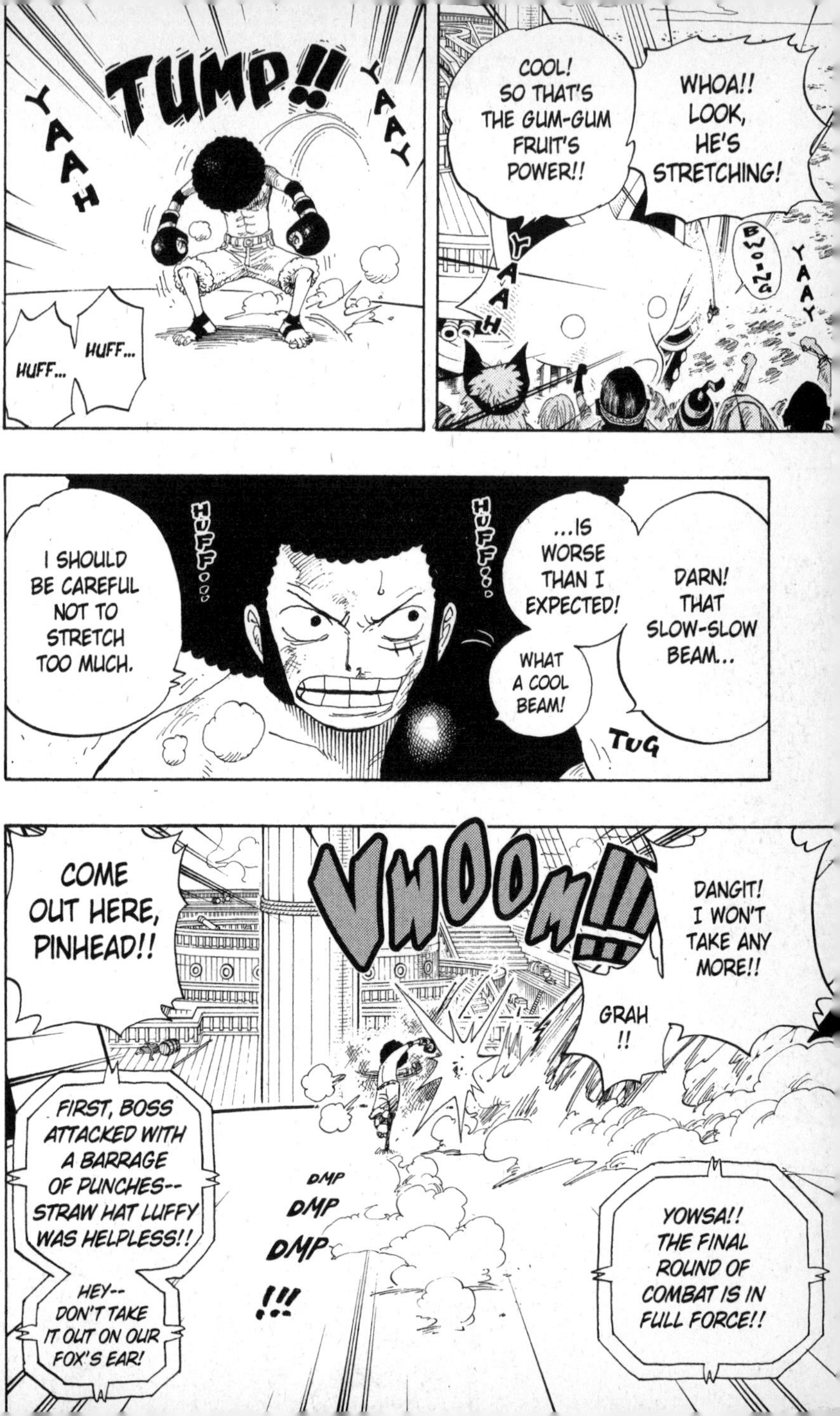
WHOA!! LOOK, HE'S STRETCHING!
COOL! SO THAT'S THE GUM-GUM FRUIT'S POWER!!
BWOING
YAAY
YAAAH
TUMP!!
YAAY
YAAAH
HUFF...
HUFF...
DARN! THAT SLOW-SLOW BEAM...
...IS WORSE THAN I EXPECTED!
WHAT A COOL BEAM!
TUG
HUFF...
HUFF...
I SHOULD BE CAREFUL NOT TO STRETCH TOO MUCH.
DANGIT! I WON'T TAKE ANY MORE!!
VWOOM!!!
GRAH!!
COME OUT HERE, PINHEAD!!
YOWSA!! THE FINAL ROUND OF COMBAT IS IN FULL FORCE!!
DMP
DMP
DMP
!!!
FIRST, BOSS ATTACKED WITH A BARRAGE OF PUNCHES-- STRAW HAT LUFFY WAS HELPLESS!!
HEY-- DON'T TAKE IT OUT ON OUR FOX'S EAR!

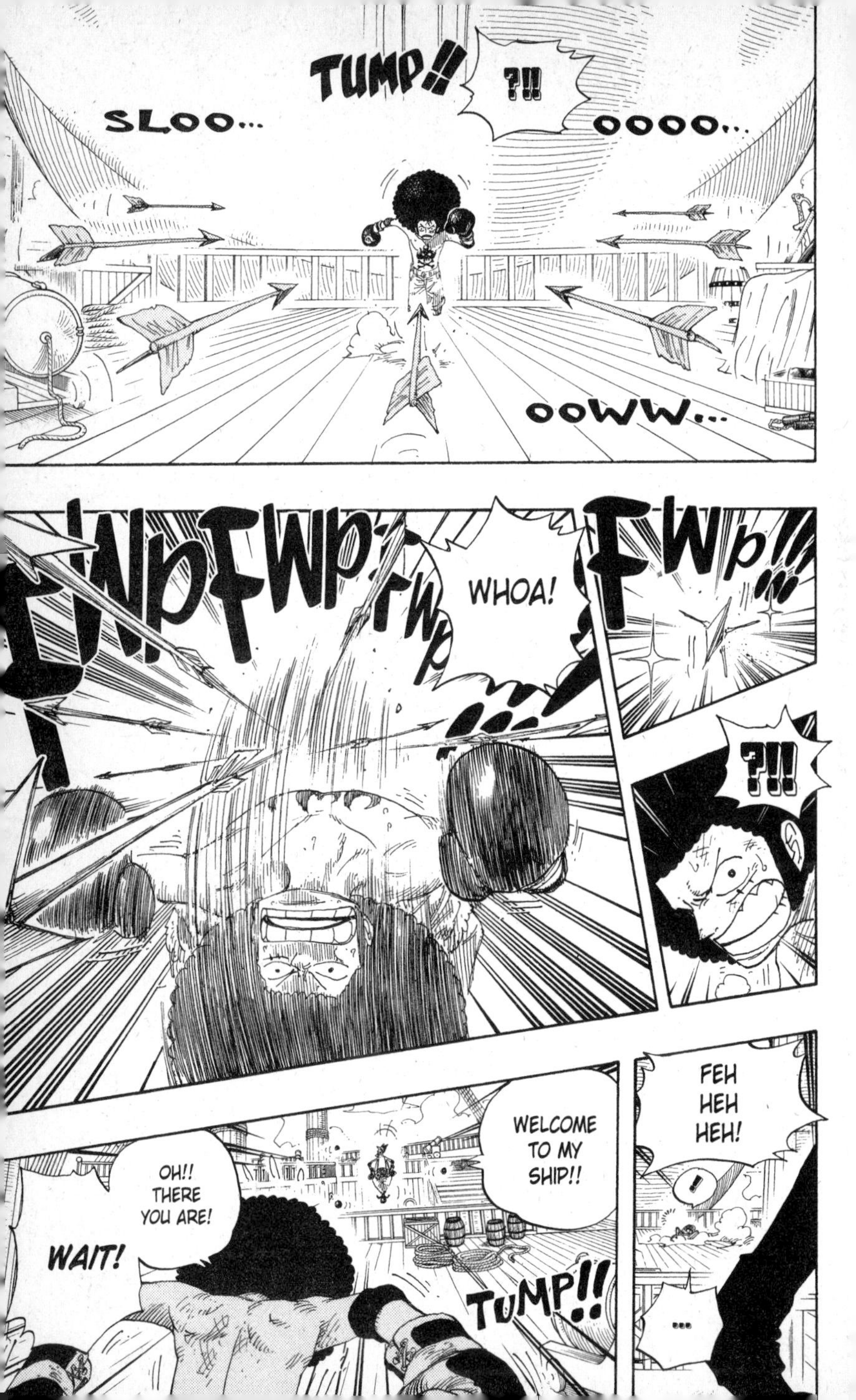
TUMP!!
?!!
SLOO...
OOOO...
OOWW...
FWP!!
FWPFWPFWP
WHOA!
?!!
FEH HEH HEH!
!
...
WELCOME TO MY SHIP!!
OH!! THERE YOU ARE!
WAIT!
TUMP!!

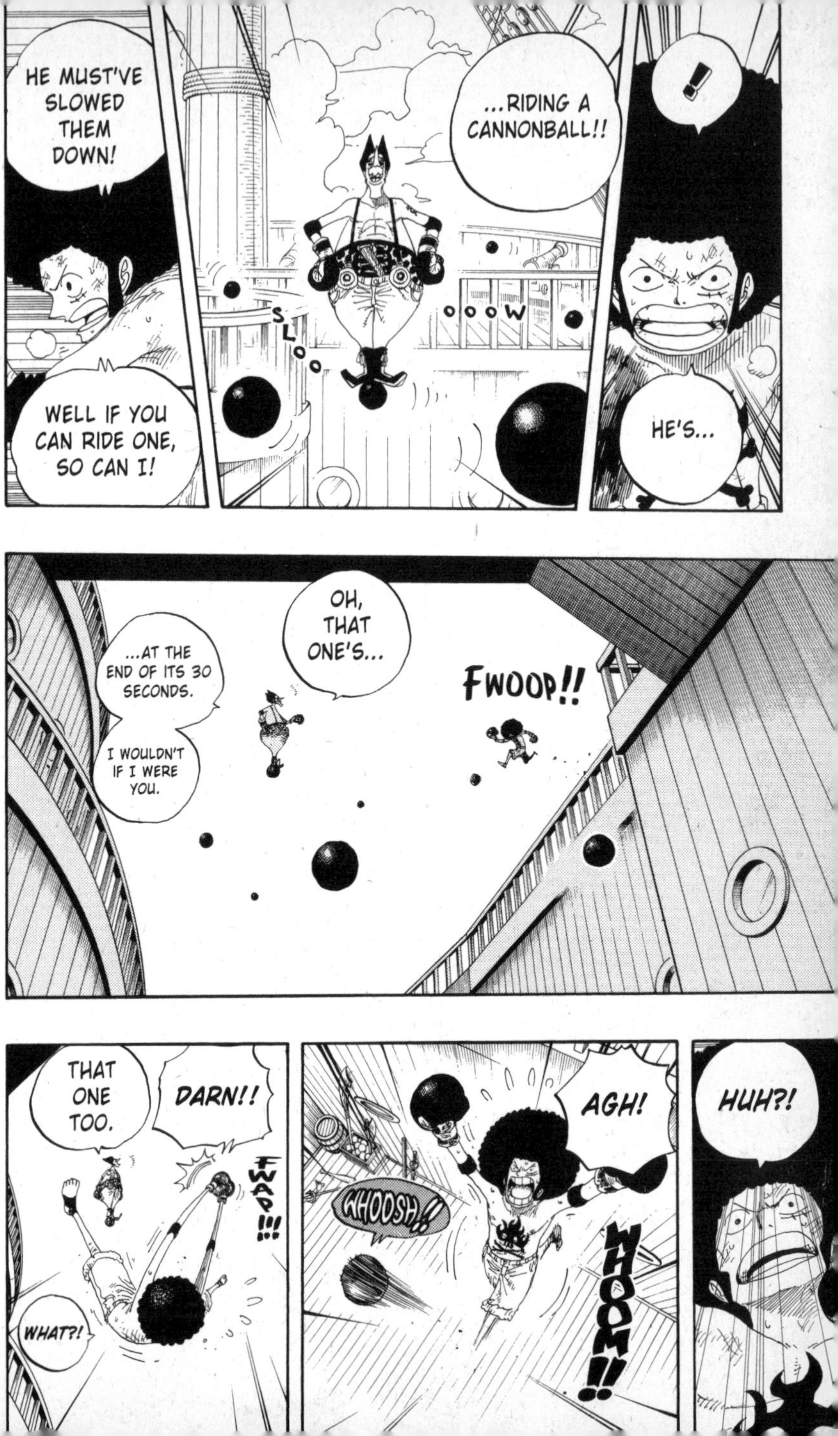
!
HE'S...
...RIDING A CANNONBALL!!
SLOOOOOW
HE MUST'VE SLOWED THEM DOWN!
WELL IF YOU CAN RIDE ONE, SO CAN I!
FWOOP!!
OH, THAT ONE'S...
...AT THE END OF ITS 30 SECONDS.
I WOULDN'T IF I WERE YOU.
HUH?!
AGH!
WHOOSH!!
WHOOM!!
DARN!!
THAT ONE TOO.
FWAP!!!
WHAT?!

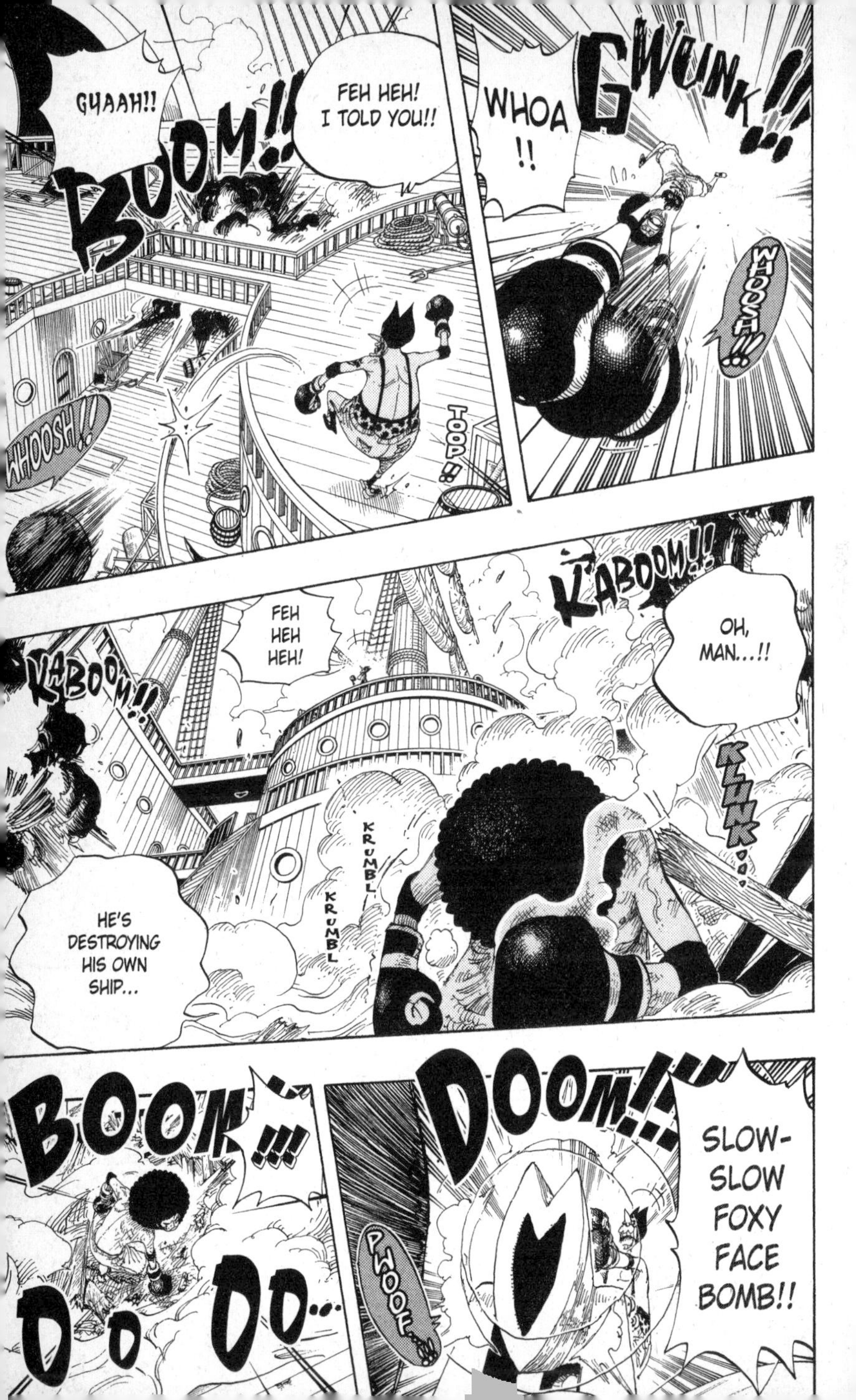
WHOA!!
GWUINK!!
WHOOSH!!
FEH HEH! I TOLD YOU!!
GUAAH!!
BOOM!!
WHOOSH!!
TOOP!!
KABOOM!!
OH, MAN...!!
FEH HEH HEH!
KABOOM!!
KLUNK...
KRUMBL
KRUMBL
HE'S DESTROYING HIS OWN SHIP...
SLOW-SLOW FOXY FACE BOMB!!
DOOM!!
PHOOF
BOOM!!!
DO DO DO...

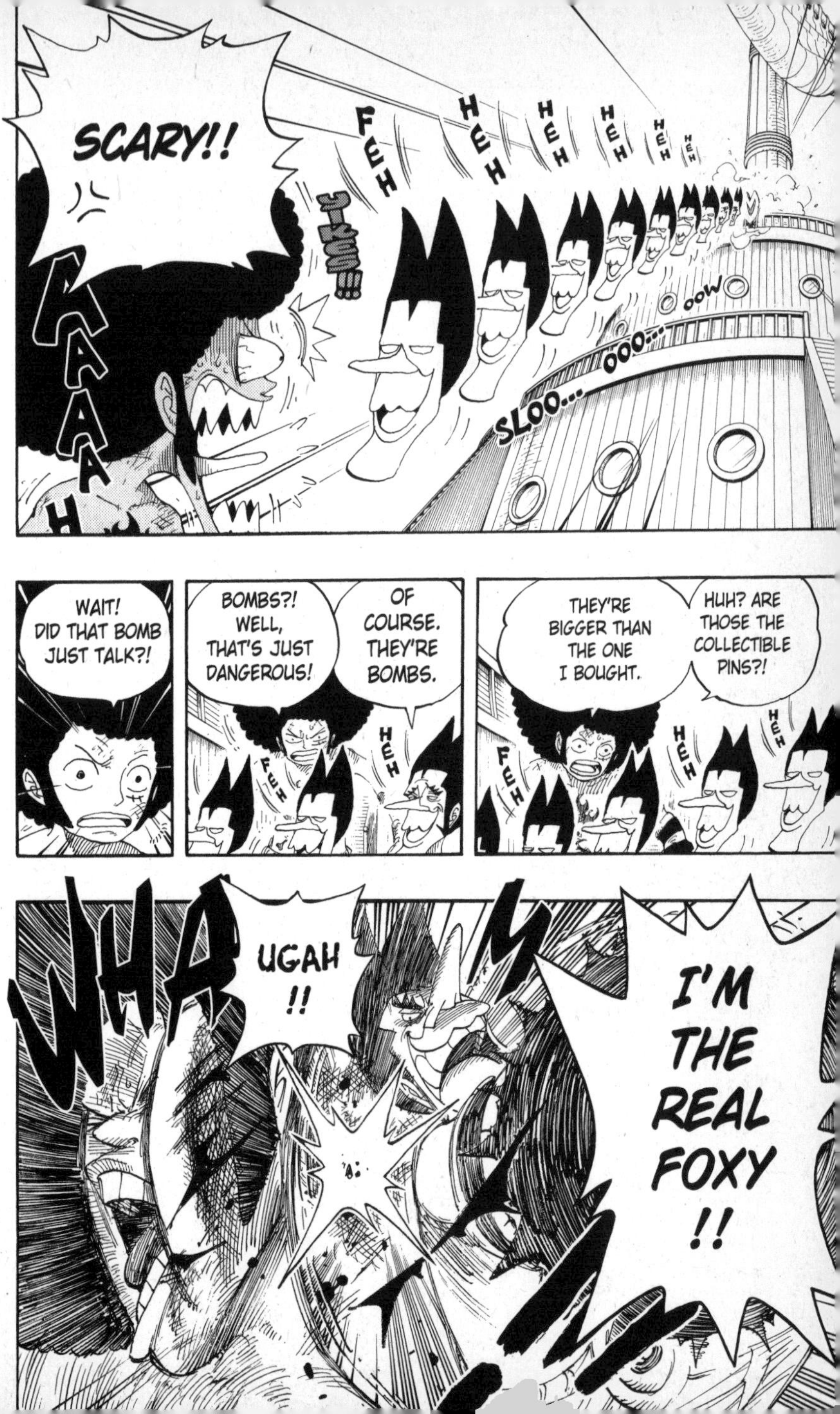
FEH HEH HEH HEH HEH HEH
SLOO... OOO... OOW
YIKES!!!
SCARY!!
KAAAAH
HUH? ARE THOSE THE COLLECTIBLE PINS?!
THEY'RE BIGGER THAN THE ONE I BOUGHT.
FEH HEH HEH
OF COURSE. THEY'RE BOMBS.
BOMBS?! WELL, THAT'S JUST DANGEROUS!
FEH HEH
WAIT! DID THAT BOMB JUST TALK?!
I'M THE REAL FOXY!!
UGAH!!
WHAM

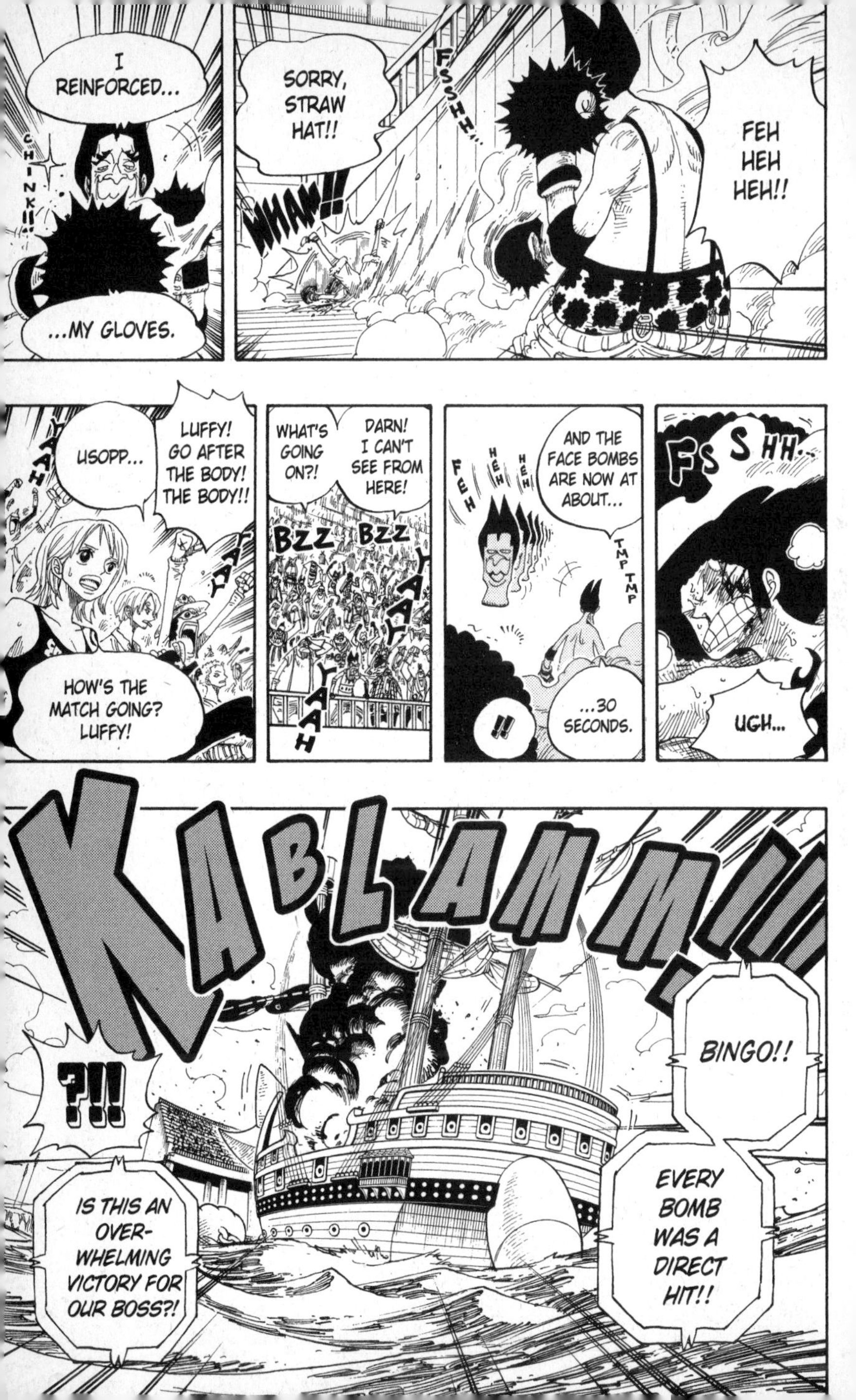
FEH HEH HEH!!
FSSHH...
SORRY, STRAW HAT!!
WHAM!!
I REINFORCED...
CHINK!!
...MY GLOVES.
FSSHH...
UGH...
FEH HEH HEH
AND THE FACE BOMBS ARE NOW AT ABOUT...
TMP TMP
...30 SECONDS.
!!
DARN! I CAN'T SEE FROM HERE!
WHAT'S GOING ON?!
BZZ BZZ
YAAAH
LUFFY! GO AFTER THE BODY! THE BODY!!
USOPP...
HOW'S THE MATCH GOING? LUFFY!
KABLAMM!!
BINGO!!
?!!
EVERY BOMB WAS A DIRECT HIT!!
IS THIS AN OVER-WHELMING VICTORY FOR OUR BOSS?!

Coloring Page

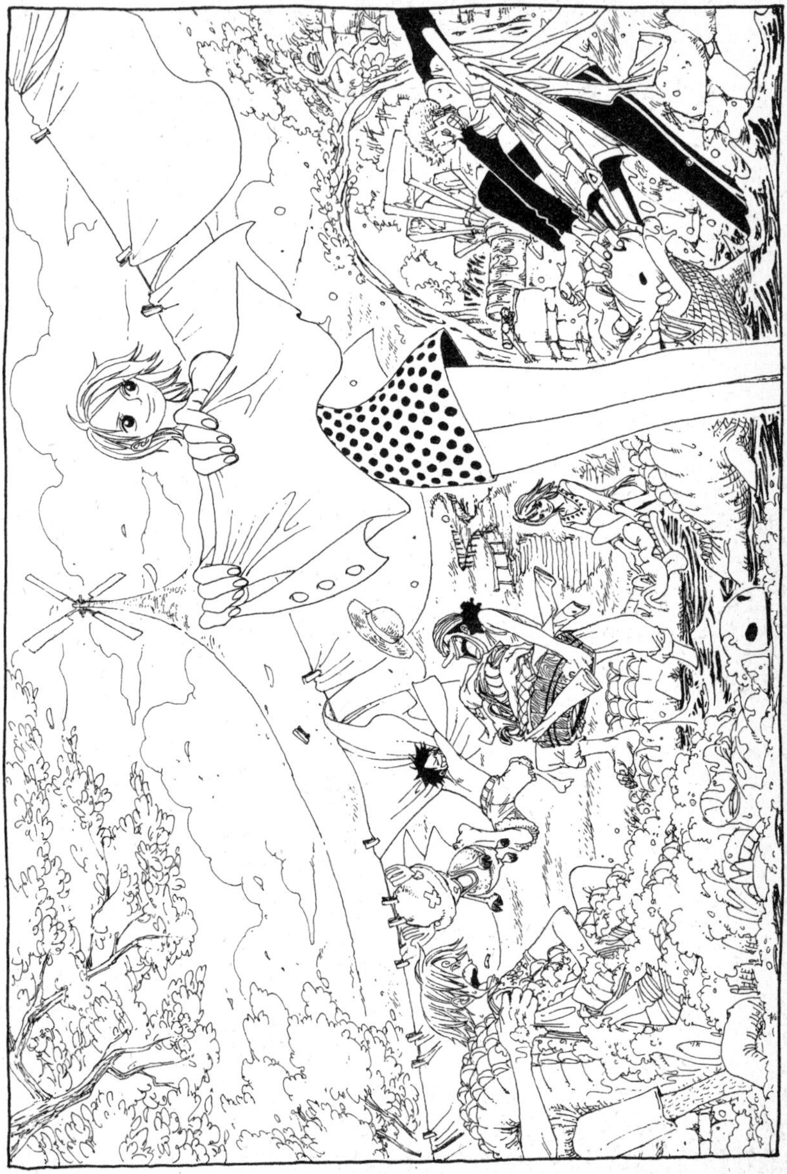

Chapter 315:
SECRET ROOM

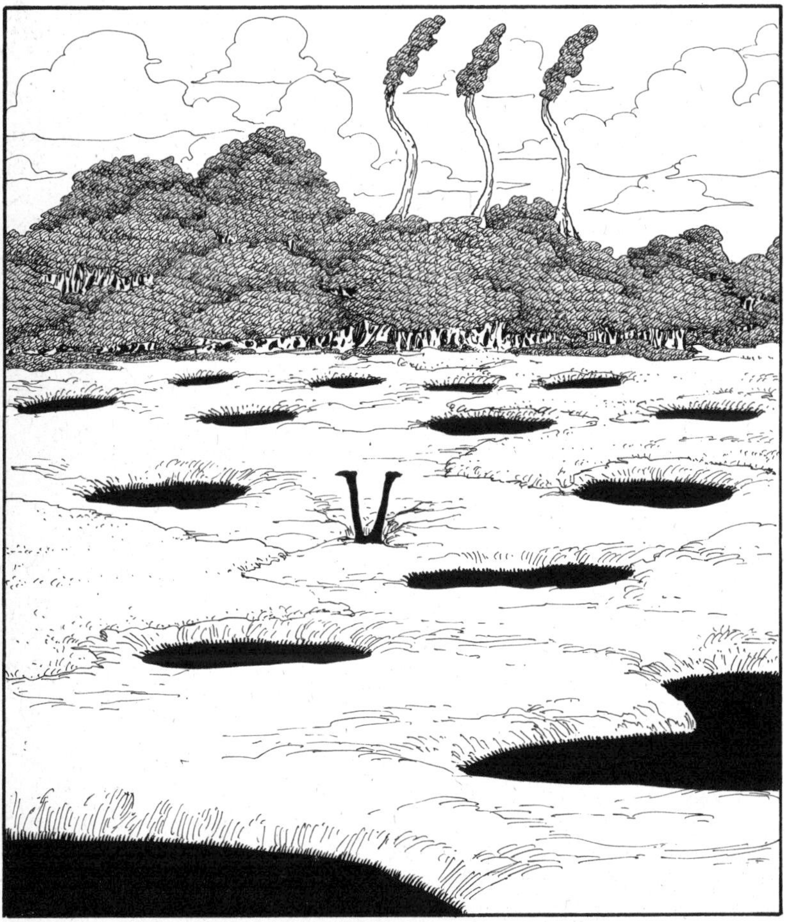

CHAPTER TITLE PAGE SERIES #7, VOL. 2:
"AN ISLAND FULL OF HOLES."

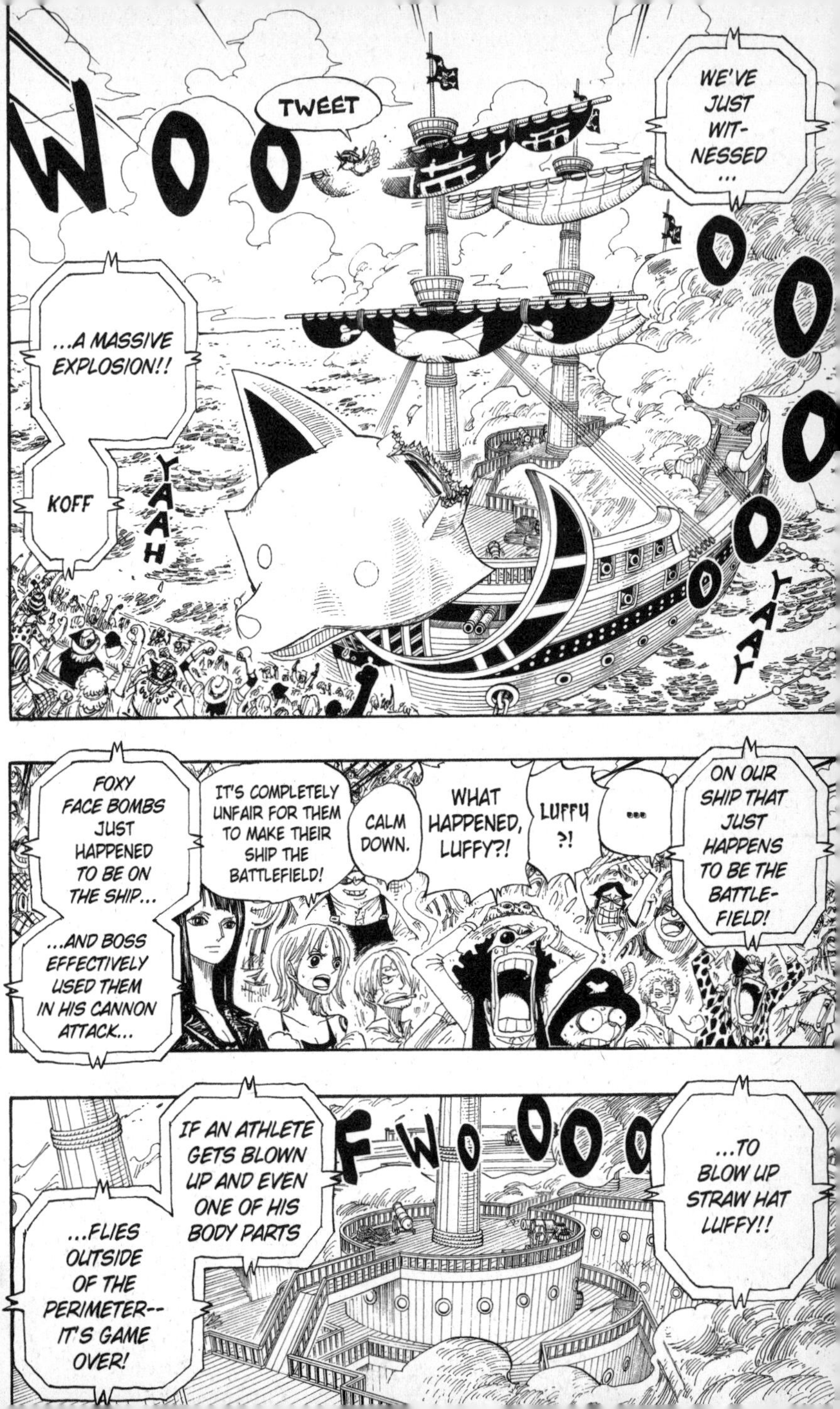
WE'VE JUST WIT-NESSED ...
TWEET
WOO
OOOOO
YAAY
...A MASSIVE EXPLOSION!!
YAAH
KOFF
ON OUR SHIP THAT JUST HAPPENS TO BE THE BATTLE-FIELD!
...
LUFFY ?!
WHAT HAPPENED, LUFFY?!
CALM DOWN.
IT'S COMPLETELY UNFAIR FOR THEM TO MAKE THEIR SHIP THE BATTLEFIELD!
FOXY FACE BOMBS JUST HAPPENED TO BE ON THE SHIP...
...AND BOSS EFFECTIVELY USED THEM IN HIS CANNON ATTACK...
...TO BLOW UP STRAW HAT LUFFY!!
FWOOO
IF AN ATHLETE GETS BLOWN UP AND EVEN ONE OF HIS BODY PARTS
...FLIES OUTSIDE OF THE PERIMETER-- IT'S GAME OVER!

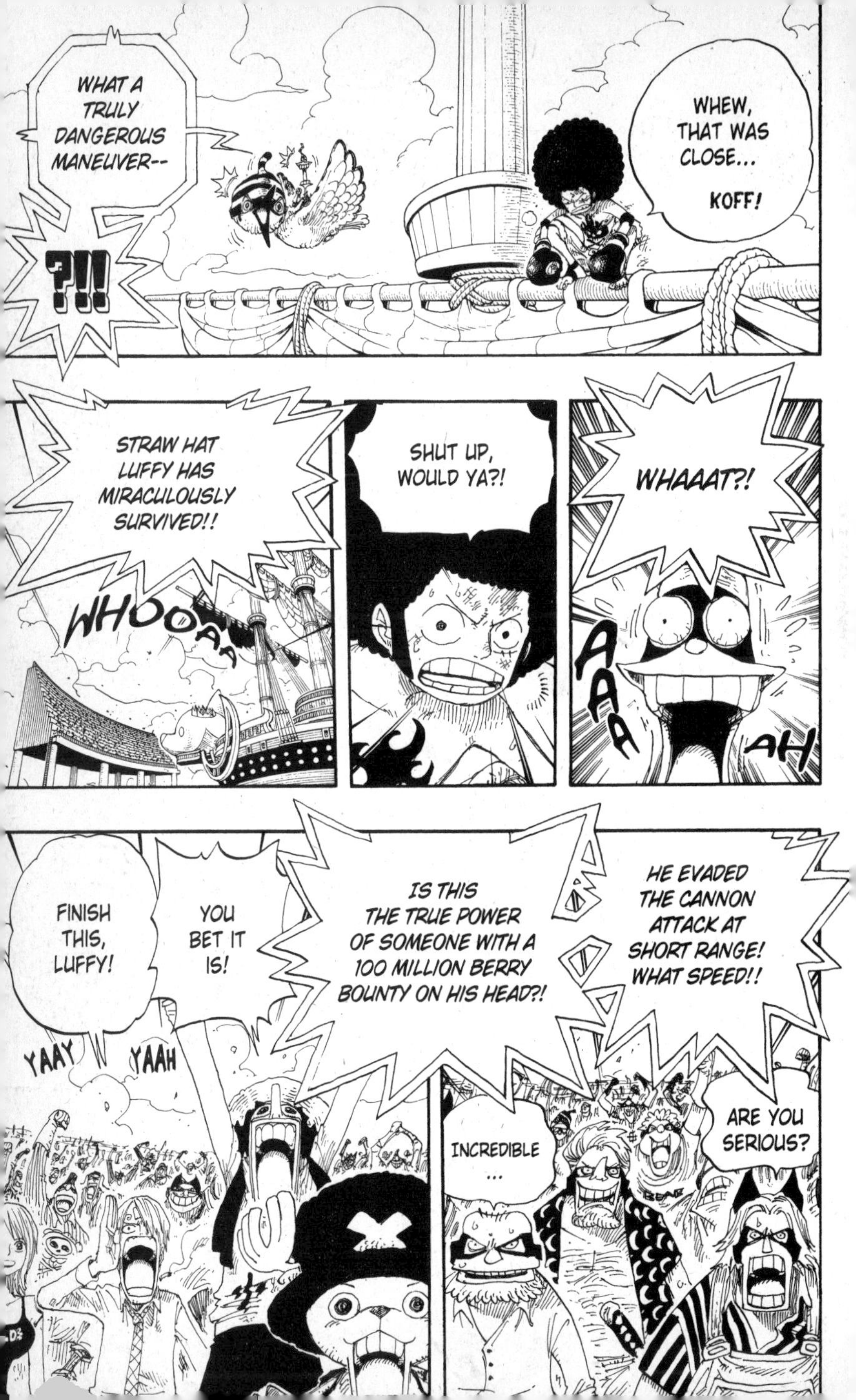

WHEW, THAT WAS CLOSE... KOFF!
WHAT A TRULY DANGEROUS MANEUVER--
?!!
WHAAAT?!
AAAAH
SHUT UP, WOULD YA?!
STRAW HAT LUFFY HAS MIRACULOUSLY SURVIVED!!
WHOOAA
HE EVADED THE CANNON ATTACK AT SHORT RANGE! WHAT SPEED!!
ARE YOU SERIOUS?
INCREDIBLE...
IS THIS THE TRUE POWER OF SOMEONE WITH A 100 MILLION BERRY BOUNTY ON HIS HEAD?!
YOU BET IT IS!
FINISH THIS, LUFFY!
YAAH
YAAY

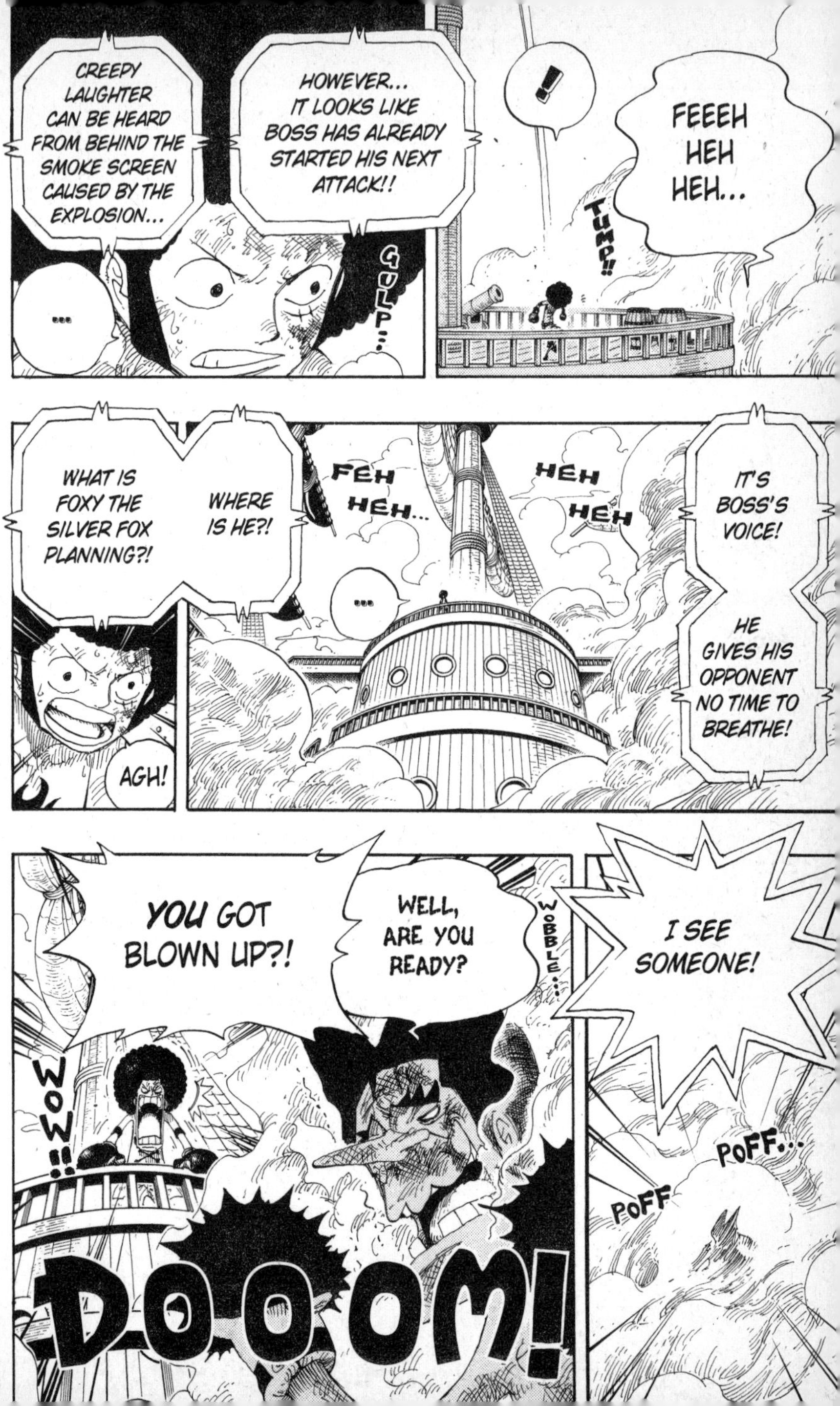
!
FEEEH HEH HEH...
TUMP!!
HOWEVER... IT LOOKS LIKE BOSS HAS ALREADY STARTED HIS NEXT ATTACK!!
CREEPY LAUGHTER CAN BE HEARD FROM BEHIND THE SMOKE SCREEN CAUSED BY THE EXPLOSION...
GULP...
...
IT'S BOSS'S VOICE!
HE GIVES HIS OPPONENT NO TIME TO BREATHE!
HEH HEH
FEH HEH...
...
WHERE IS HE?!
WHAT IS FOXY THE SILVER FOX PLANNING?!
AGH!
I SEE SOMEONE!
POFF...
POFF
WELL, ARE YOU READY?
WOBBLE...
YOU GOT BLOWN UP?!
WOW!!
DOOOM!

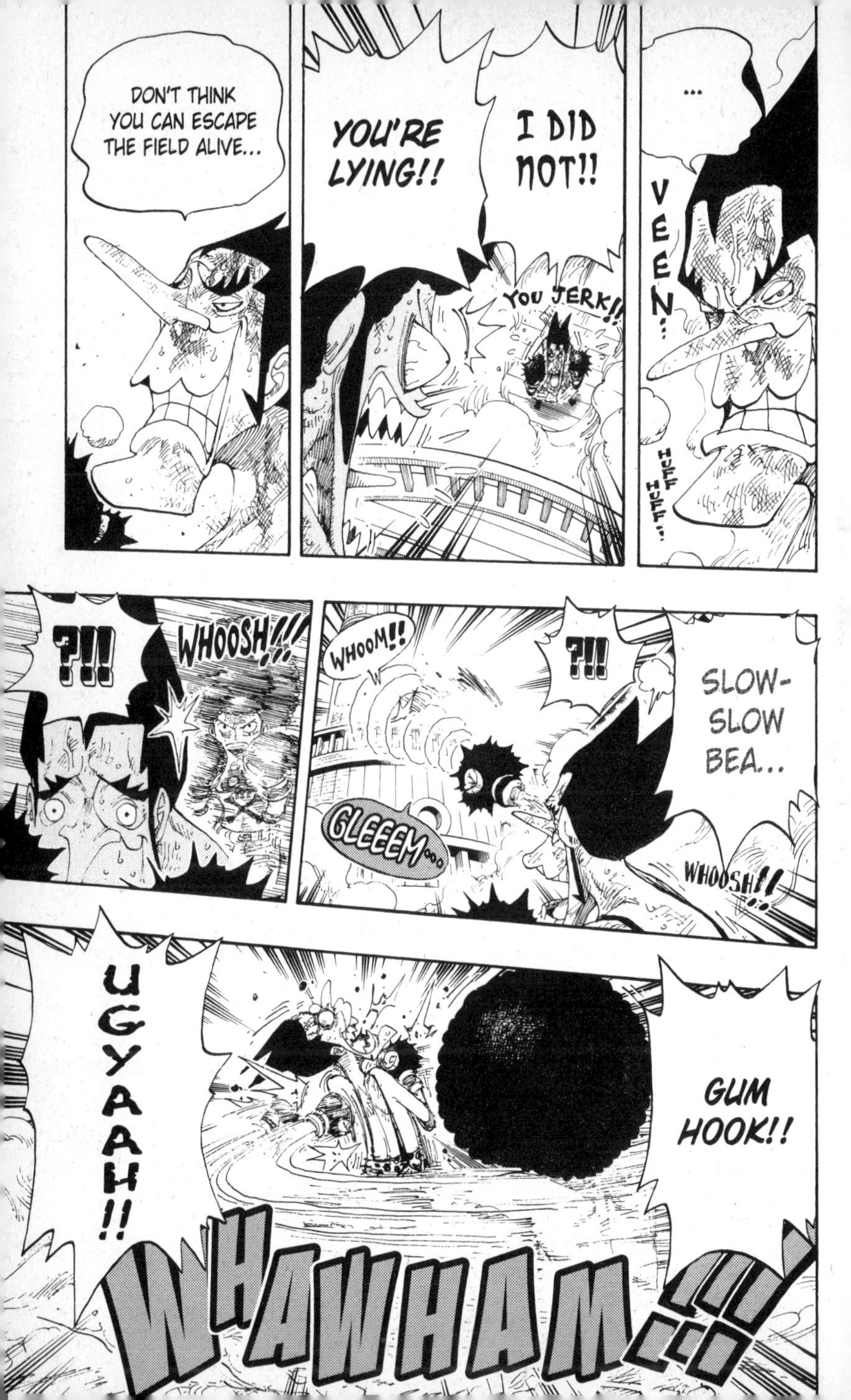
...
VEEN...
HUFF HUFF...
I DID NOT!!
YOU'RE LYING!!
YOU JERK!!
DON'T THINK YOU CAN ESCAPE THE FIELD ALIVE...
SLOW-SLOW BEA...
?!!
WHOOM!!
GLEEEM...
WHOOSH!!
WHOOSH!!!
?!!
GUM HOOK!!
UGYAAAH!!
WHAWHAM!!!

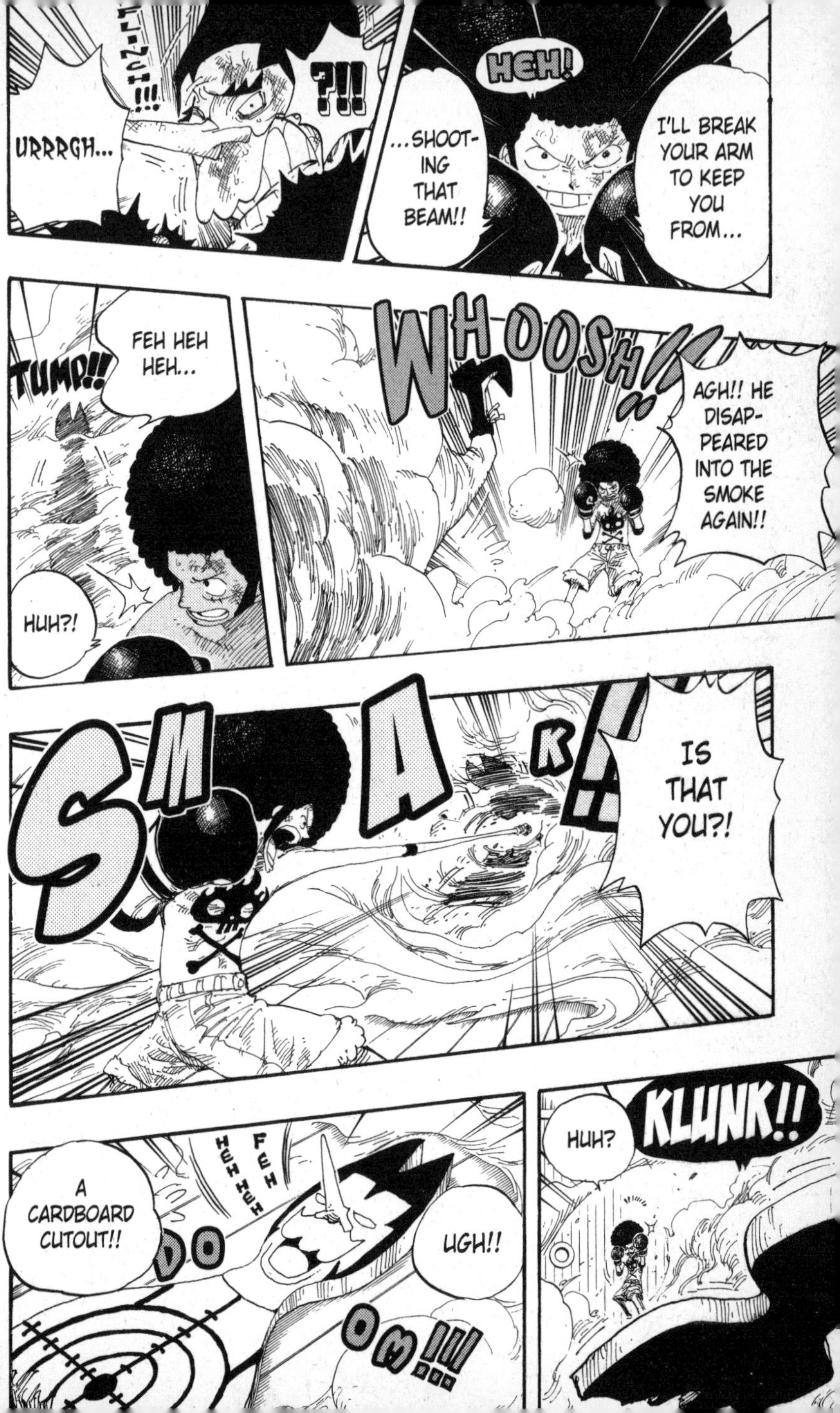
HEH!
I'LL BREAK YOUR ARM TO KEEP YOU FROM...
...SHOOTING THAT BEAM!!
?!!
FLINCH!!!
URRRGH...
WHOOSH!!
AGH!! HE DISAPPEARED INTO THE SMOKE AGAIN!!
FEH HEH HEH...
TUMP!!
HUH?!
IS THAT YOU?!
SMAK!!
KLUNK!!
HUH?
UGH!!
FEH HEH HEH HEH
A CARDBOARD CUTOUT!!
DOOM!!!

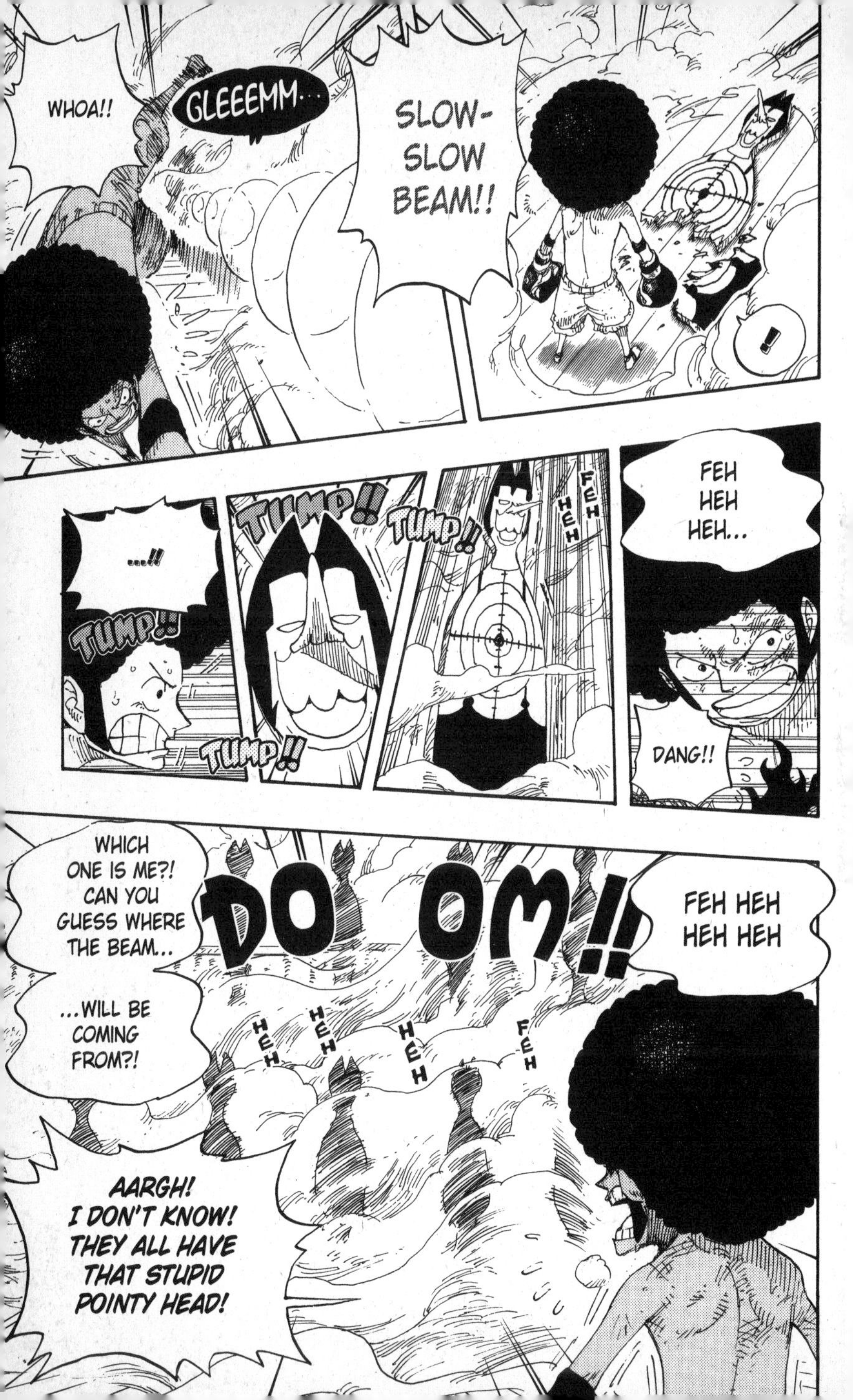
!
SLOW-SLOW BEAM!!
GLEEEMM...
WHOA!!
FEH HEH HEH...
DANG!!
FEH HEH
TUMP!!
TUMP!!
...!!
TUMP!!
TUMP!!
FEH HEH HEH HEH
DO OM!!
WHICH ONE IS ME?! CAN YOU GUESS WHERE THE BEAM...
...WILL BE COMING FROM?!
FEH HEH HEH HEH
AARGH! I DON'T KNOW! THEY ALL HAVE THAT STUPID POINTY HEAD!

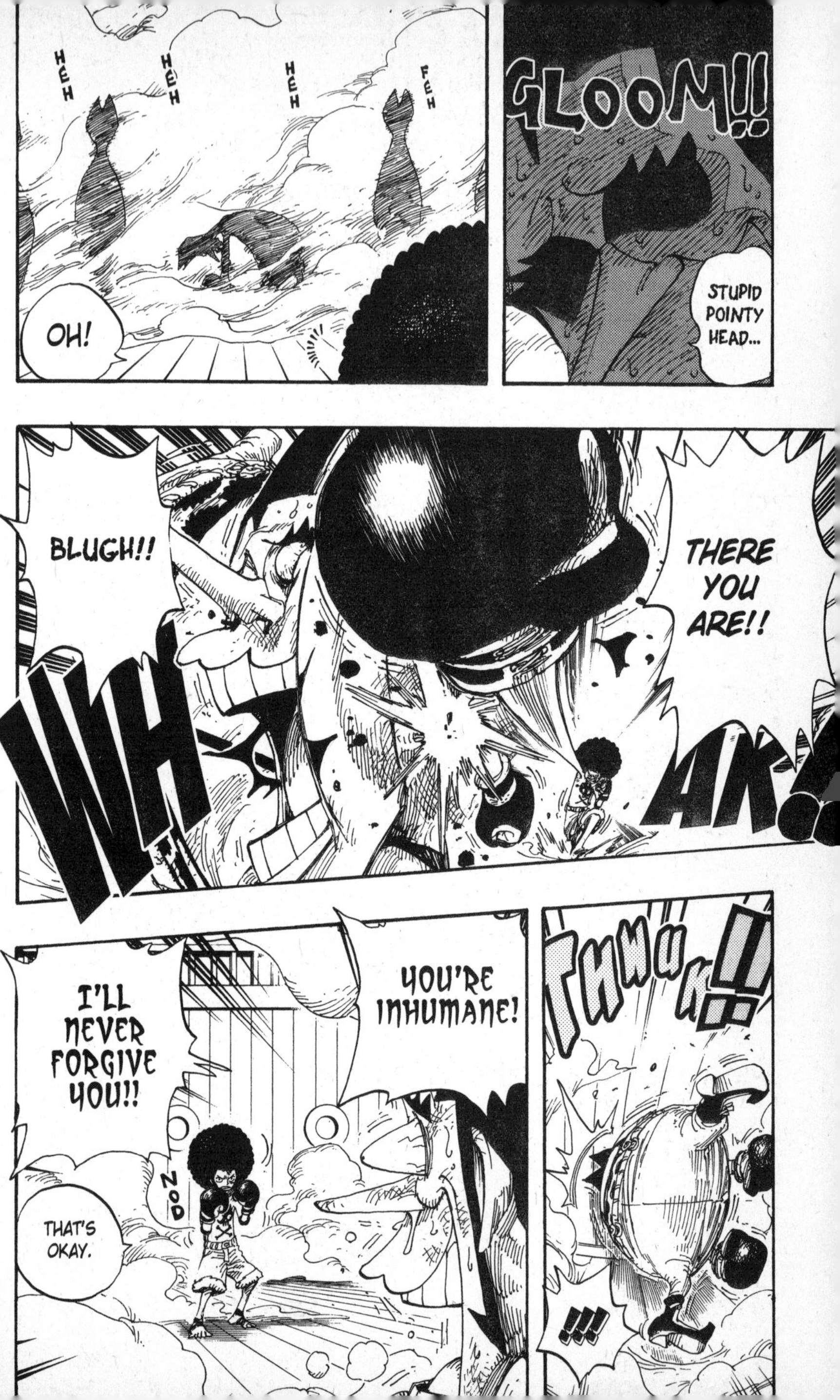
GLOOM!!
STUPID POINTY HEAD...
FEH
HEH
HEH
HEH
OH!
THERE YOU ARE!!
BLUGH!!
WHAK!!
THWUK!!
!!!
YOU'RE INHUMANE!
I'LL NEVER FORGIVE YOU!!
NOD
THAT'S OKAY.

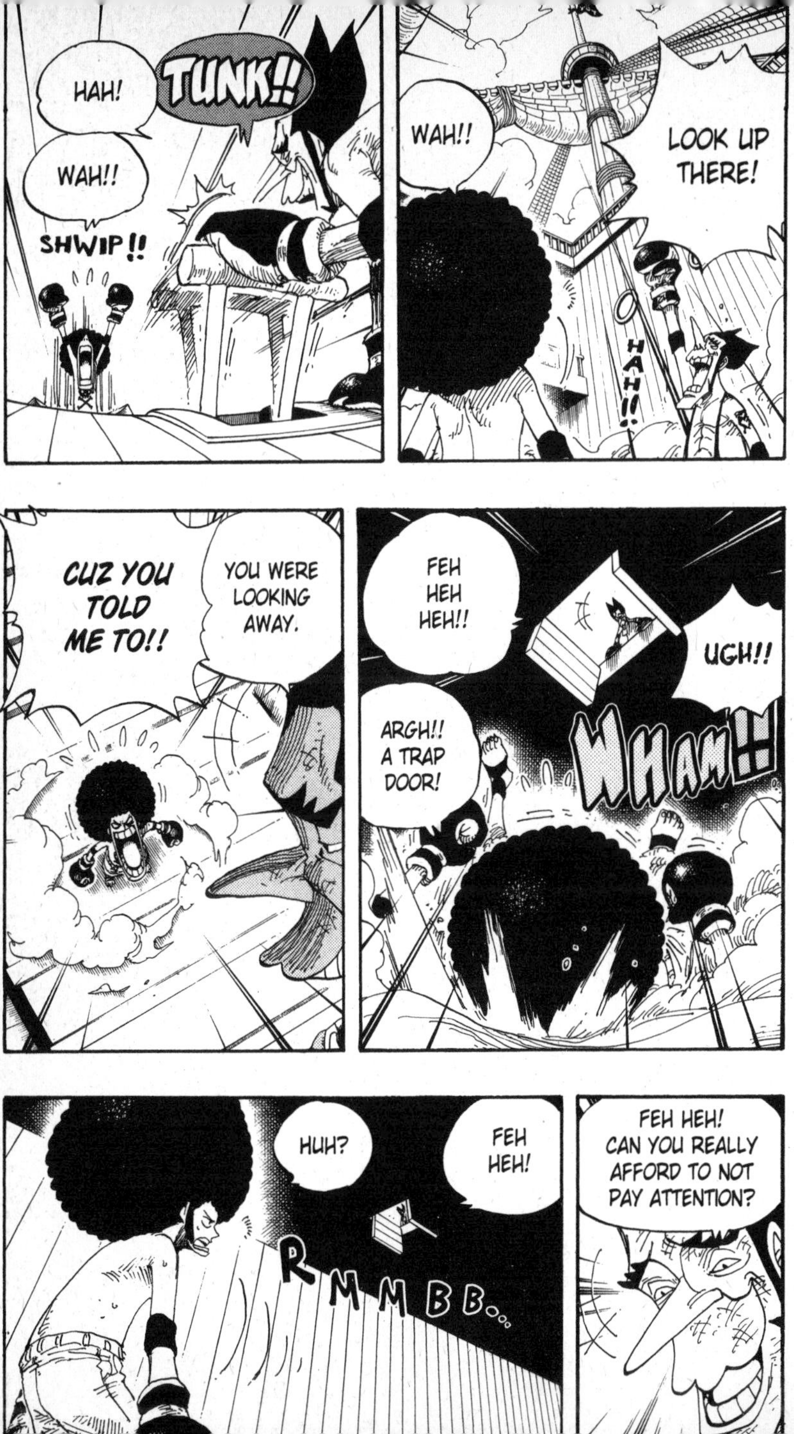
LOOK UP THERE!
WAH!!
HAH!!
TUNK!!
HAH!
WAH!!
SHWIP!!
FEH HEH HEH!!
UGH!!
WHAM!!
ARGH!! A TRAP DOOR!
YOU WERE LOOKING AWAY.
CUZ YOU TOLD ME TO!!
FEH HEH! CAN YOU REALLY AFFORD TO NOT PAY ATTENTION?
FEH HEH!
HUH?
RMMBB...

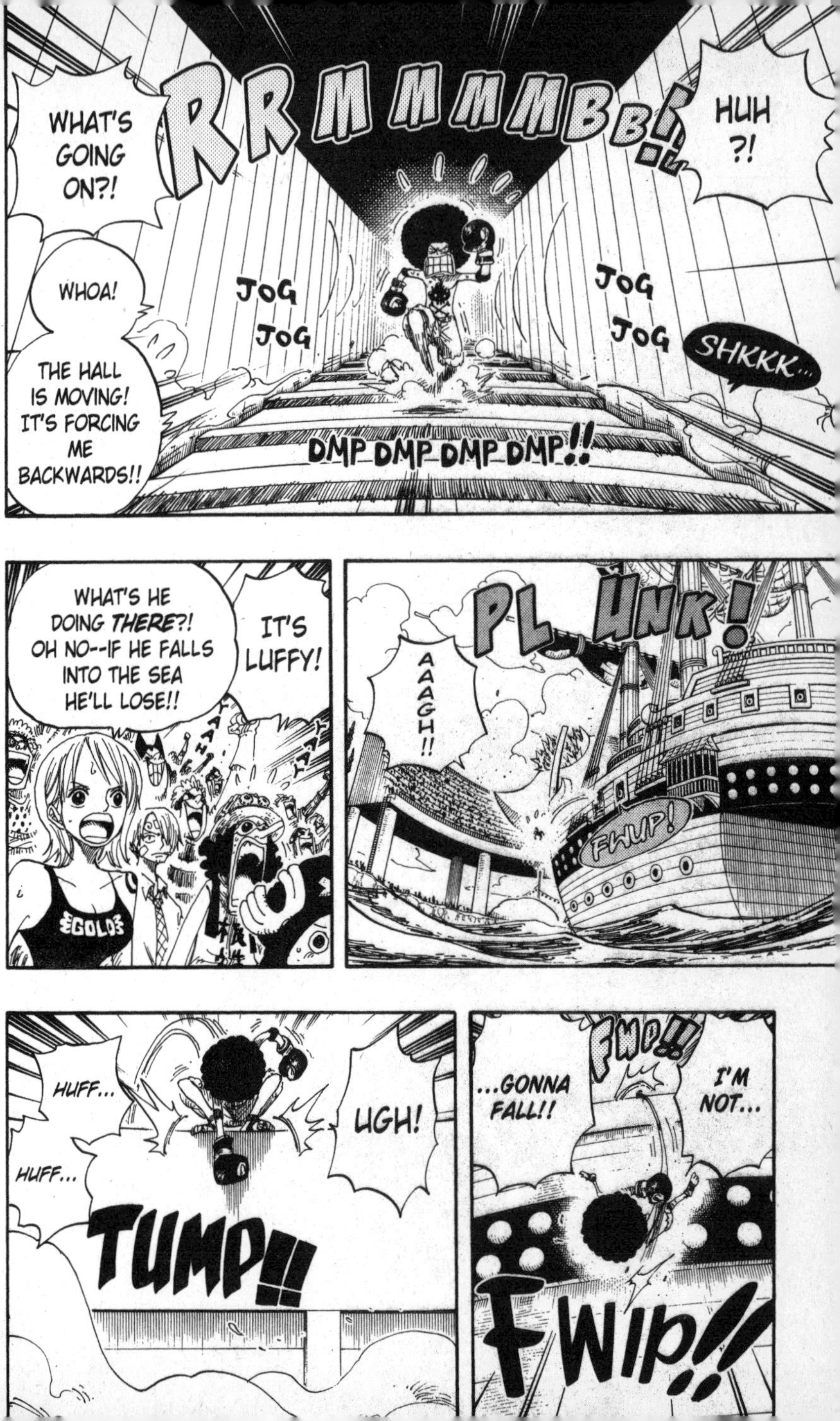
HUH ?!
RRMMMMMBB!!
WHAT'S GOING ON?!
JOG JOG
SHKKK...
JOG JOG
WHOA!
THE HALL IS MOVING! IT'S FORCING ME BACKWARDS!!
DMP DMP DMP DMP!!
PLUNK!
AAAAGH!!
FWUP!
IT'S LUFFY!
WHAT'S HE DOING THERE?! OH NO--IF HE FALLS INTO THE SEA HE'LL LOSE!!
GOLD
FWP!!
I'M NOT...
...GONNA FALL!!
FWIP!!
UGH!
HUFF...
HUFF...
TUMP!!

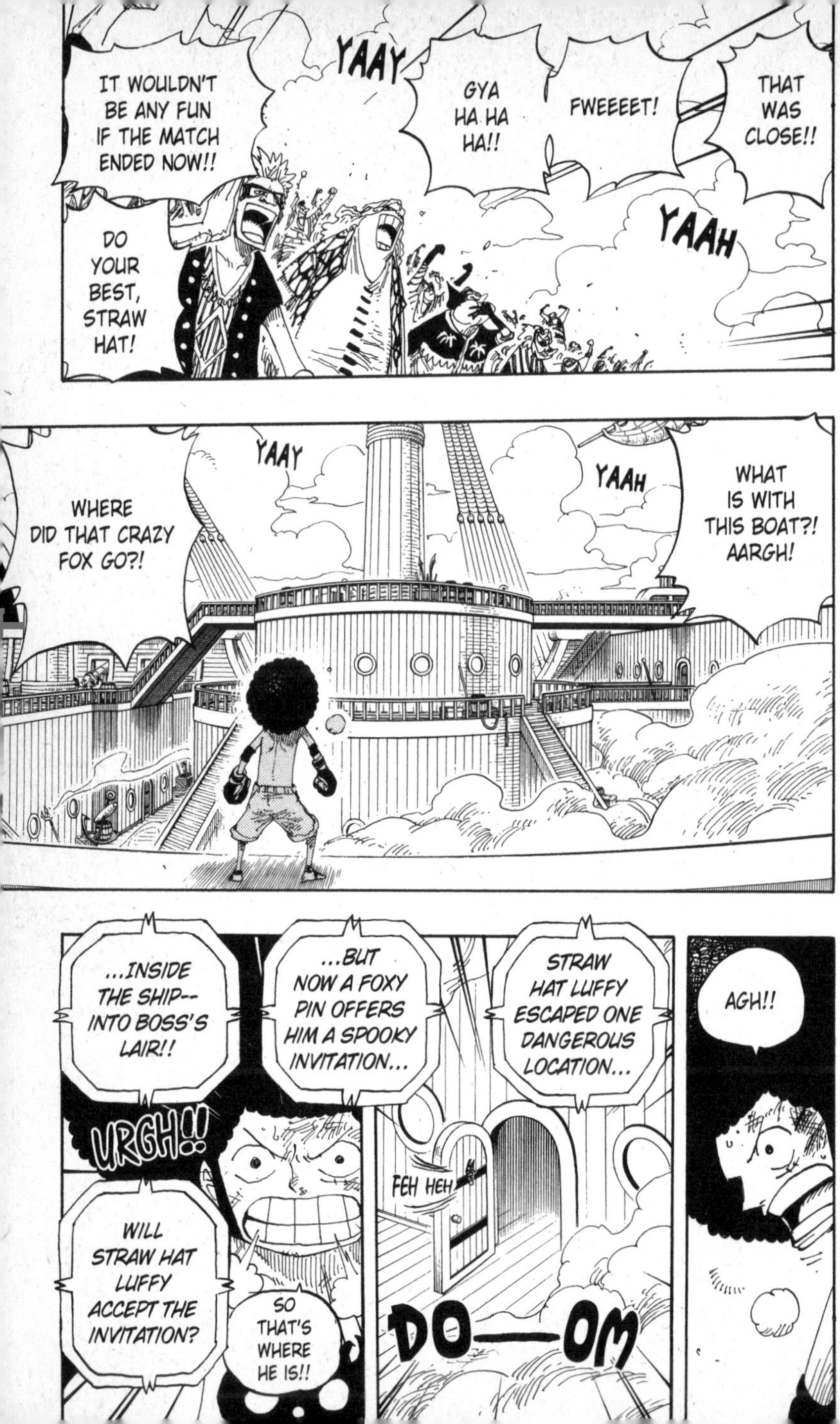
THAT WAS CLOSE!!
FWEEEET!
GYA HA HA!!
YAAY
IT WOULDN'T BE ANY FUN IF THE MATCH ENDED NOW!!
YAAH
DO YOUR BEST, STRAW HAT!
WHAT IS WITH THIS BOAT?! AARGH!
YAAH
YAAY
WHERE DID THAT CRAZY FOX GO?!
AGH!!
STRAW HAT LUFFY ESCAPED ONE DANGEROUS LOCATION...
FEH HEH
DO—OM
...BUT NOW A FOXY PIN OFFERS HIM A SPOOKY INVITATION...
...INSIDE THE SHIP--INTO BOSS'S LAIR!!
URGH!!
SO THAT'S WHERE HE IS!!
WILL STRAW HAT LUFFY ACCEPT THE INVITATION?

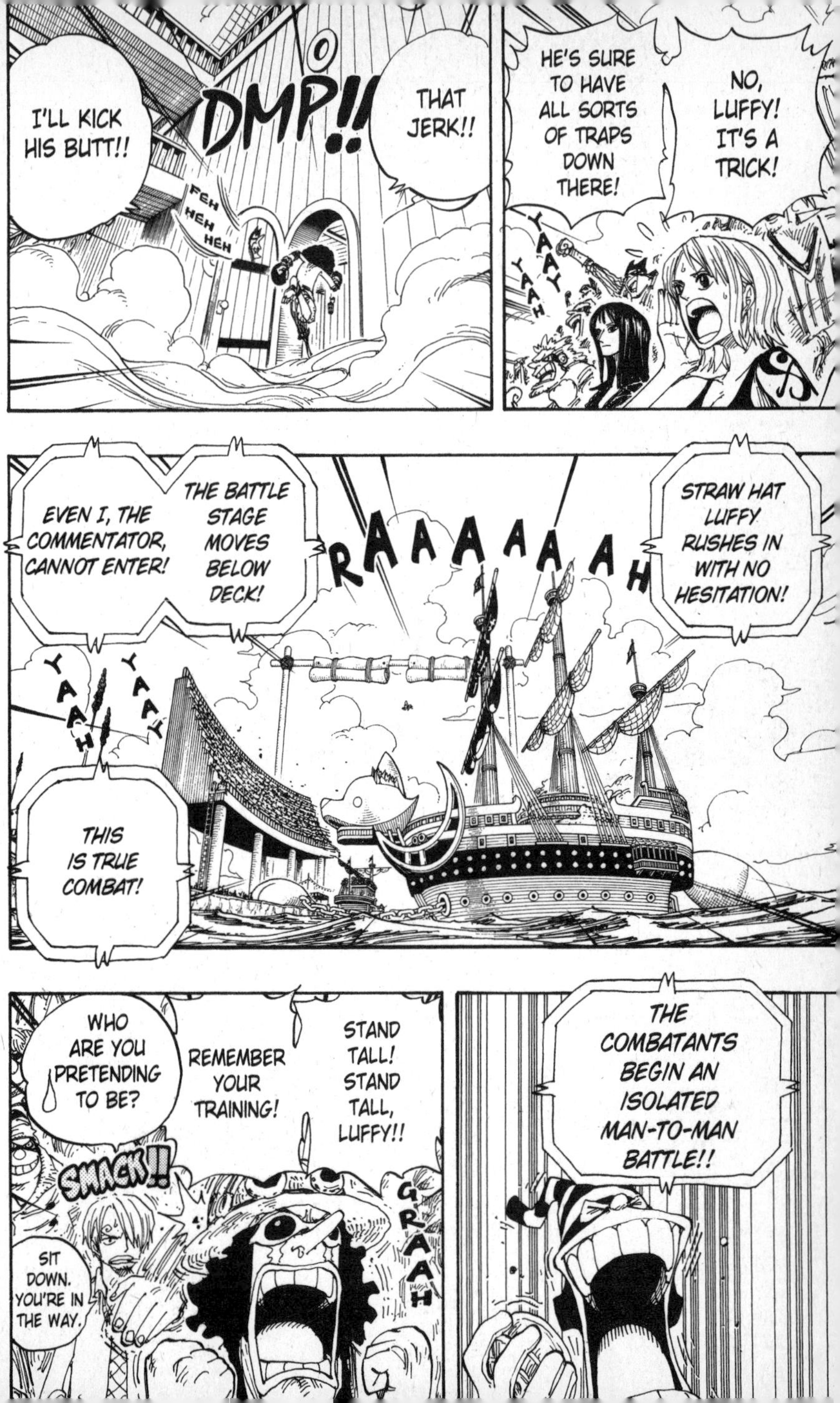
NO, LUFFY! IT'S A TRICK!
HE'S SURE TO HAVE ALL SORTS OF TRAPS DOWN THERE!
YAAAY
YAAAH
THAT JERK!!
DMP!!
I'LL KICK HIS BUTT!!
FEH HEH HEH
STRAW HAT LUFFY RUSHES IN WITH NO HESITATION!
RAAAAAAH
THE BATTLE STAGE MOVES BELOW DECK!
EVEN I, THE COMMENTATOR, CANNOT ENTER!
YAAAY
YAAAH
THIS IS TRUE COMBAT!
THE COMBATANTS BEGIN AN ISOLATED MAN-TO-MAN BATTLE!!
STAND TALL! STAND TALL, LUFFY!!
GRAAAH
REMEMBER YOUR TRAINING!
WHO ARE YOU PRETENDING TO BE?
SMACK!!
SIT DOWN. YOU'RE IN THE WAY.

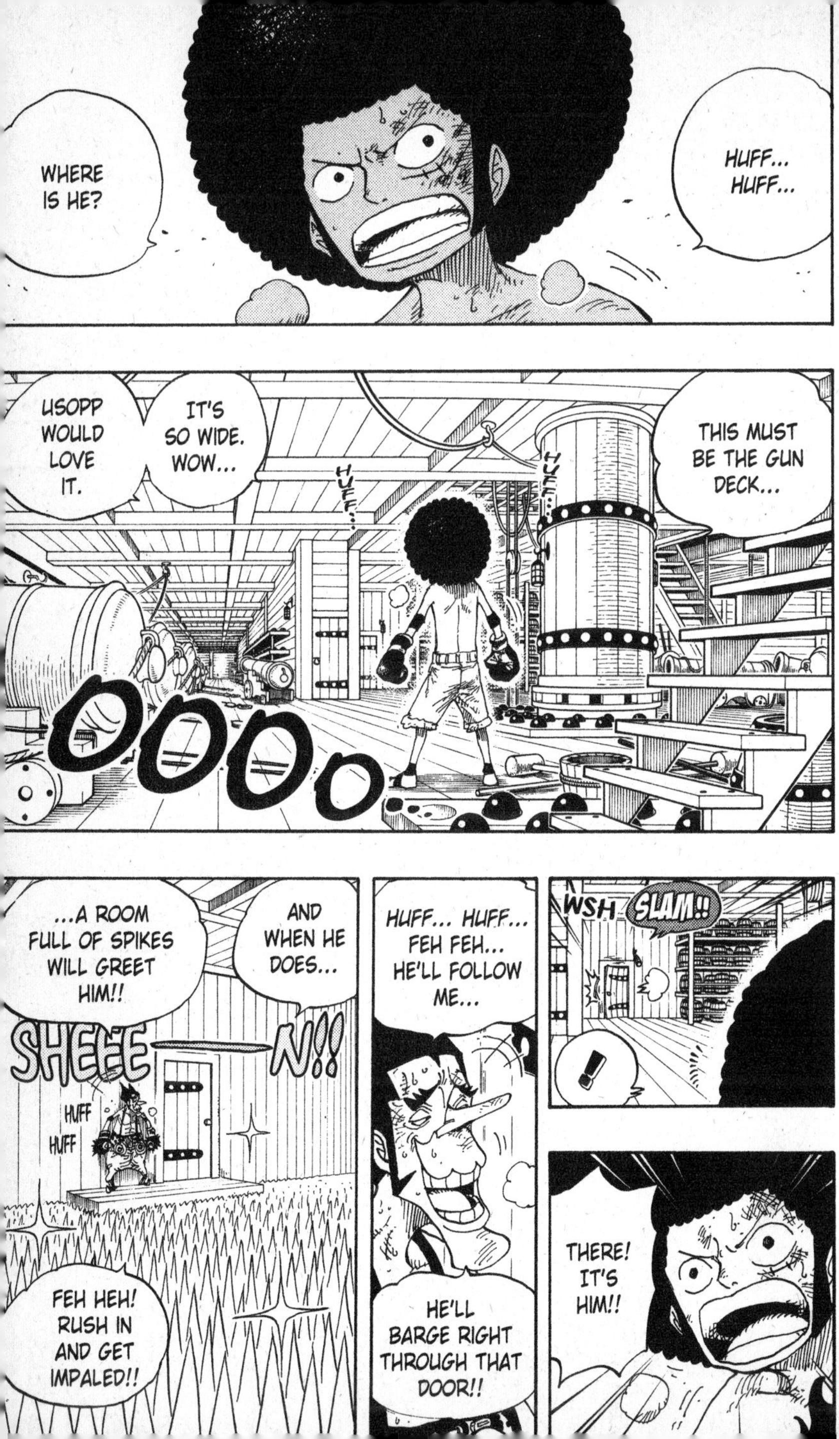
HUFF... HUFF...
WHERE IS HE?
THIS MUST BE THE GUN DECK...
HUFF...
IT'S SO WIDE. WOW...
USOPP WOULD LOVE IT.
OOOO
WSH
SLAM!!
!
THERE! IT'S HIM!!
HUFF... HUFF... FEH FEH... HE'LL FOLLOW ME...
HE'LL BARGE RIGHT THROUGH THAT DOOR!!
AND WHEN HE DOES...
...A ROOM FULL OF SPIKES WILL GREET HIM!!
SHEEE—N!!
HUFF
HUFF
FEH HEH! RUSH IN AND GET IMPALED!!

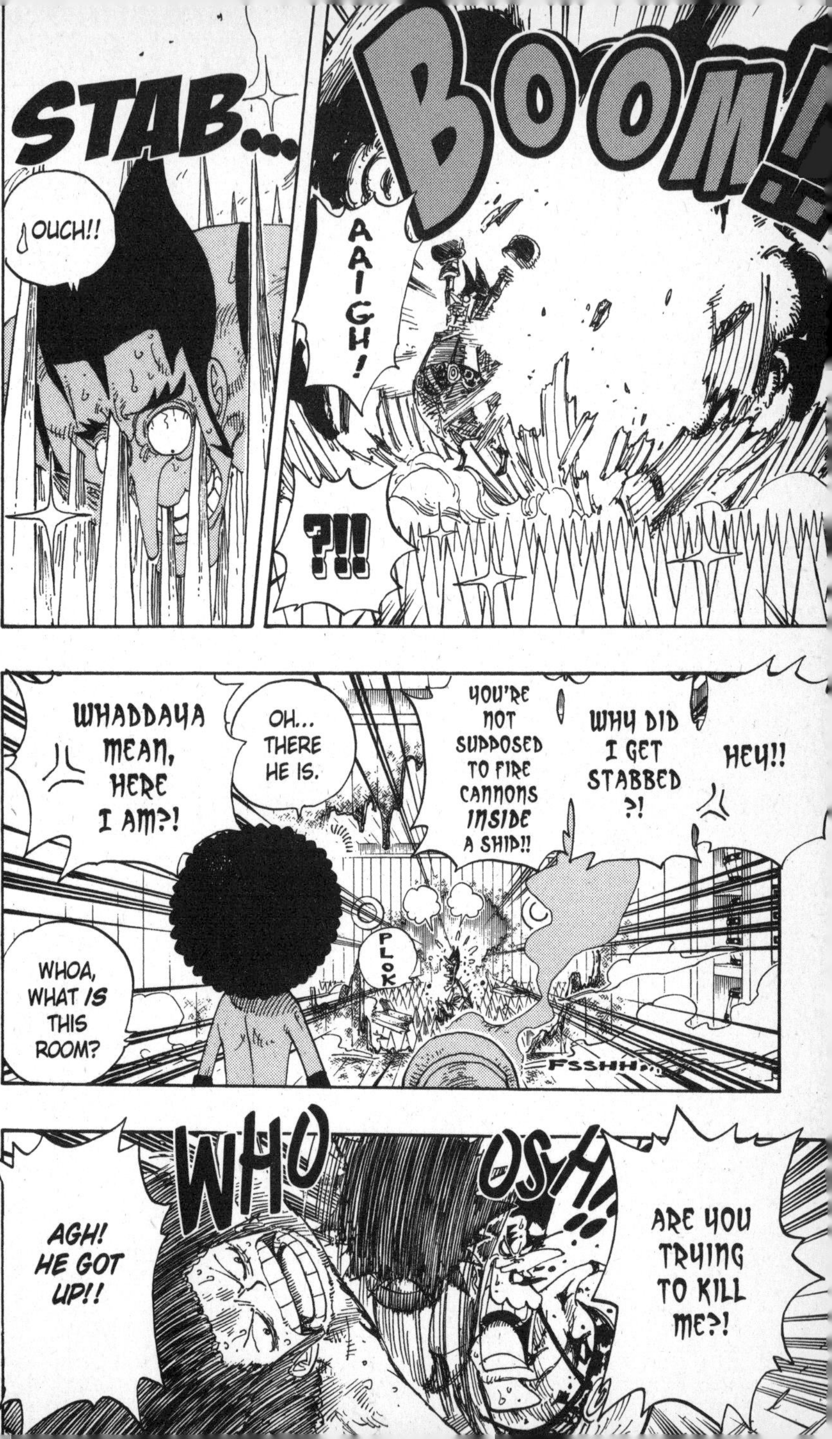
BOOM!!
AAIGH!
?!!
STAB...
OUCH!!
HEY!!
WHY DID I GET STABBED?!
YOU'RE NOT SUPPOSED TO FIRE CANNONS INSIDE A SHIP!!
OH... THERE HE IS.
WHADDAYA MEAN, HERE I AM?!
PLOK
WHOA, WHAT IS THIS ROOM?
FSSHH...
WHOOSH!!
ARE YOU TRYING TO KILL ME?!
AGH! HE GOT UP!!

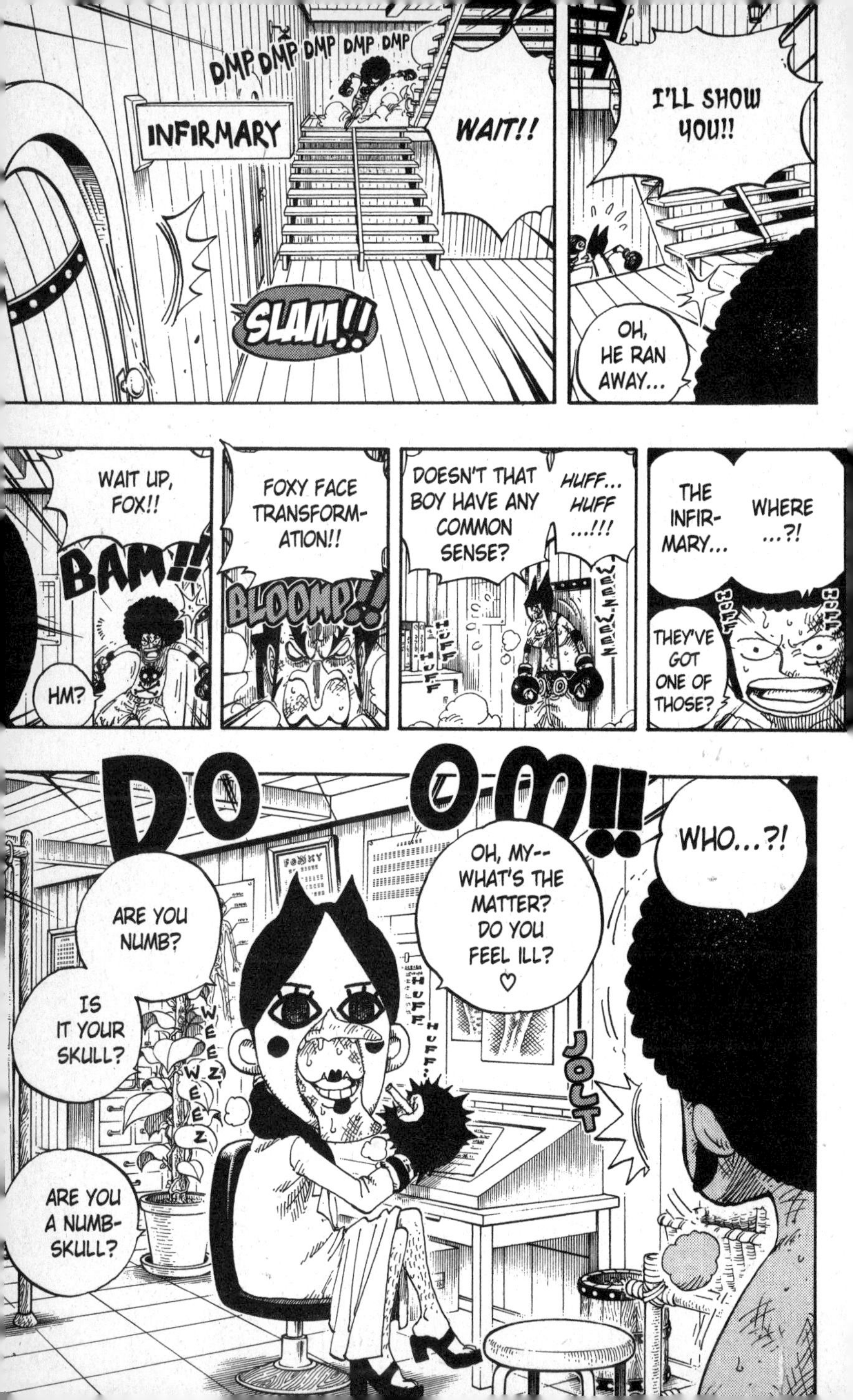
I'LL SHOW YOU!!
OH, HE RAN AWAY...
WAIT!!
DMP DMP DMP DMP DMP
INFIRMARY
SLAM!!
WHERE ...?!
THE INFIR-MARY...
HUFF
HUFF
THEY'VE GOT ONE OF THOSE?
HUFF... HUFF ...!!!
DOESN'T THAT BOY HAVE ANY COMMON SENSE?
WEEZ WEEZ
HUFF HUFF
FOXY FACE TRANSFORM-ATION!!
BLOOMP!!
WAIT UP, FOX!!
BAM!!
HM?
DO-O-M!!
WHO...?!
OH, MY-- WHAT'S THE MATTER? DO YOU FEEL ILL? ♡
JOLT
HUFF
HUFF
ARE YOU NUMB?
IS IT YOUR SKULL?
WEEZ WEEZ
ARE YOU A NUMB-SKULL?

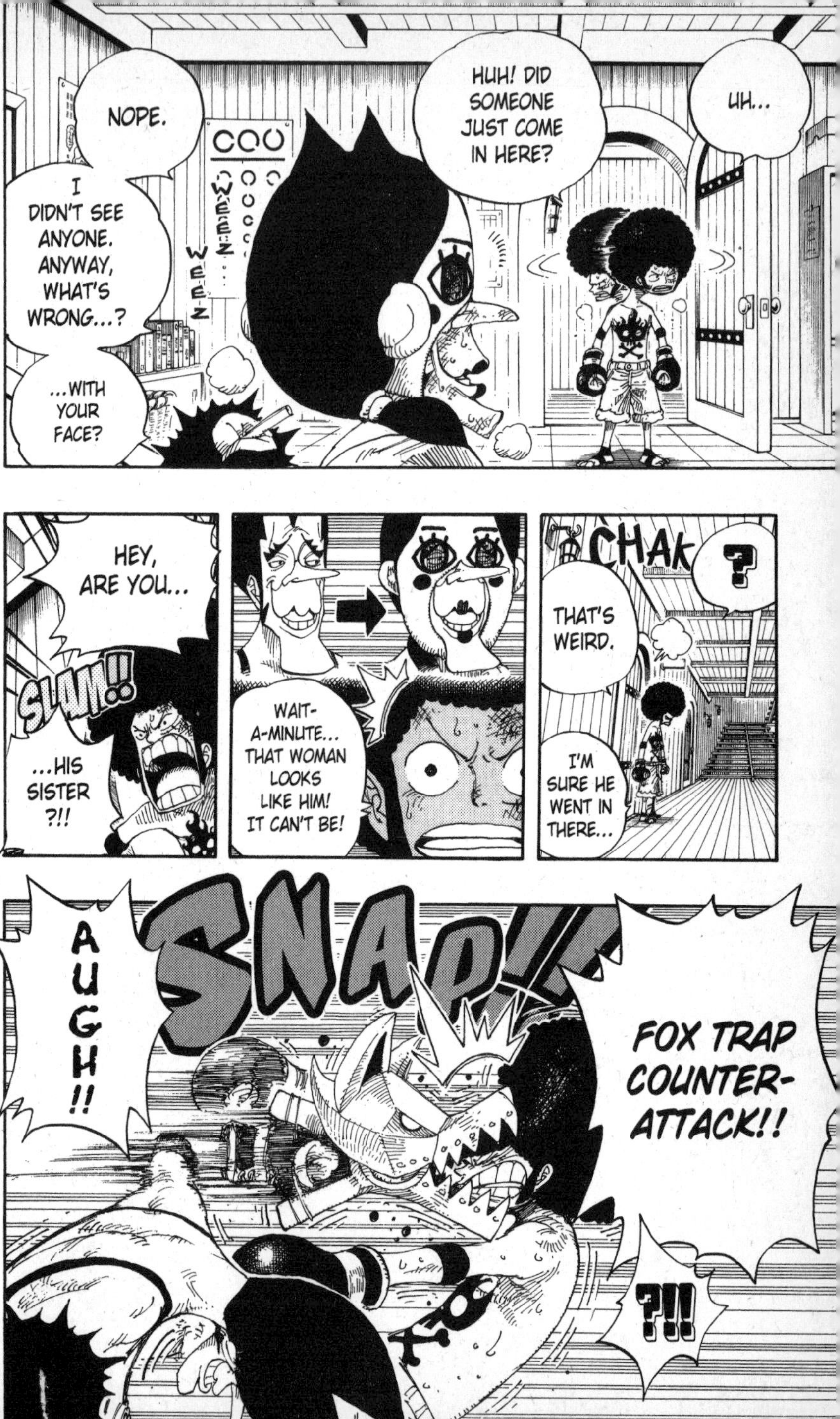
UH...
HUH! DID SOMEONE JUST COME IN HERE?
WEEZ...
WEEZ
NOPE.
I DIDN'T SEE ANYONE. ANYWAY, WHAT'S WRONG...?
...WITH YOUR FACE?
CHAK
?
THAT'S WEIRD.
I'M SURE HE WENT IN THERE...
WAIT-A-MINUTE... THAT WOMAN LOOKS LIKE HIM! IT CAN'T BE!
HEY, ARE YOU...
SLAM!!
...HIS SISTER ?!!
FOX TRAP COUNTER-ATTACK!!
SNAP!!
AUGH!!
?!!

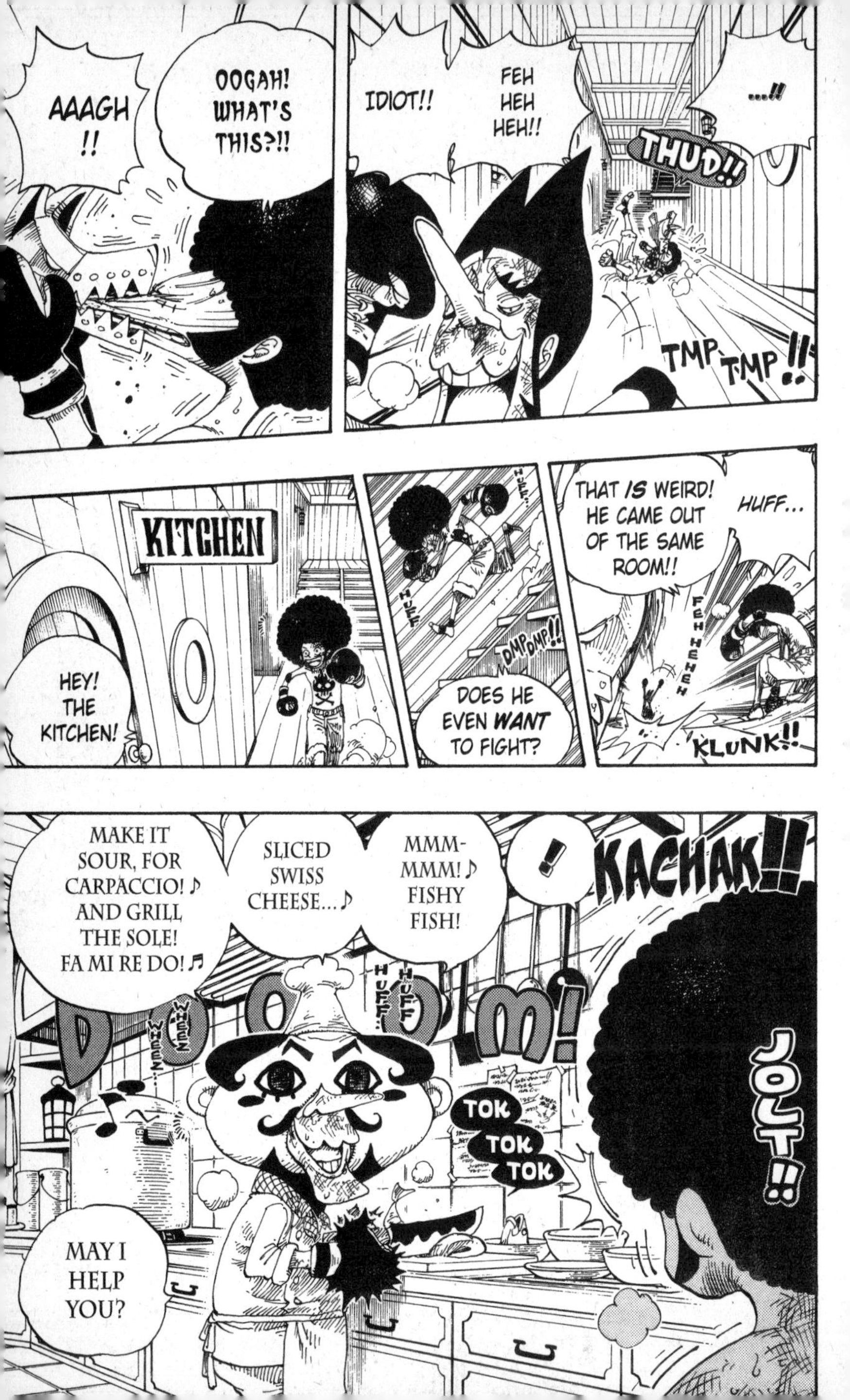
...!!
THUD!!
FEH HEH HEH!!
IDIOT!!
TMP TMP!!
OOGAH! WHAT'S THIS?!!
AAAGH!!
HUFF...
THAT *IS* WEIRD! HE CAME OUT OF THE SAME ROOM!!
FEH HEH HEH
KLUNK!!
HUFF...
HUFF
DMP DMP!!
DOES HE EVEN *WANT* TO FIGHT?
KITCHEN
HEY! THE KITCHEN!
KACHAK!!
!
MMM-MMM! ♪ FISHY FISH!
SLICED SWISS CHEESE... ♪
MAKE IT SOUR, FOR CARPACCIO! ♪ AND GRILL THE SOLE! FA MI RE DO! ♬
JOLT!!
DOOOM!
HUFF HUFF
WHEEZ WHEEZ...
TOK TOK TOK
MAY I HELP YOU?

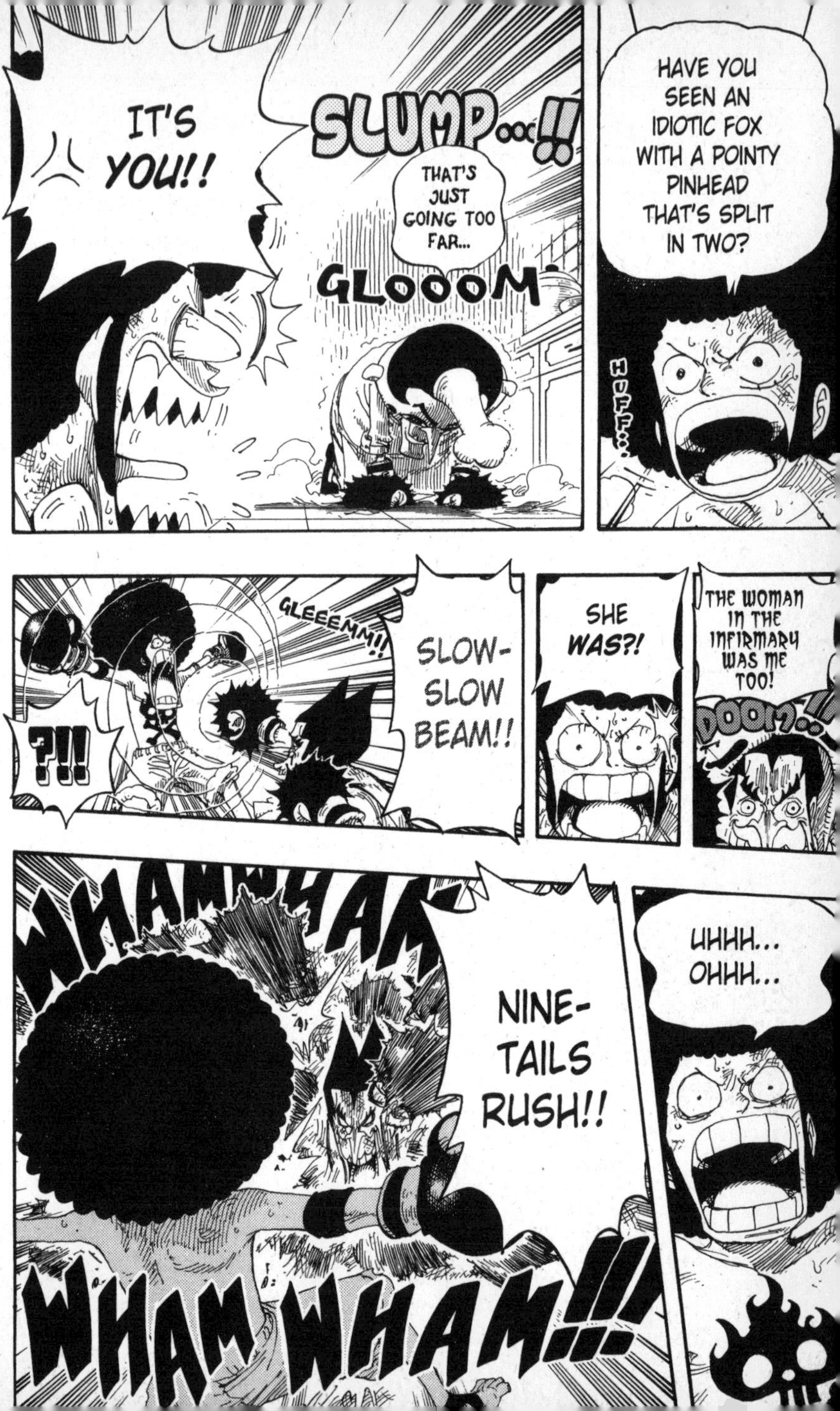
HAVE YOU SEEN AN IDIOTIC FOX WITH A POINTY PINHEAD THAT'S SPLIT IN TWO?
HUFF...
SLUMP...!!
THAT'S JUST GOING TOO FAR...
GLOOOM
IT'S YOU!!
THE WOMAN IN THE INFIRMARY WAS ME TOO!
DOOM..!!
SHE WAS?!
SLOW-SLOW BEAM!!
GLEEEMM!!
?!!
UHHH... OHHH...
NINE-TAILS RUSH!!
WHAMWHAM
WHAM WHAM!!

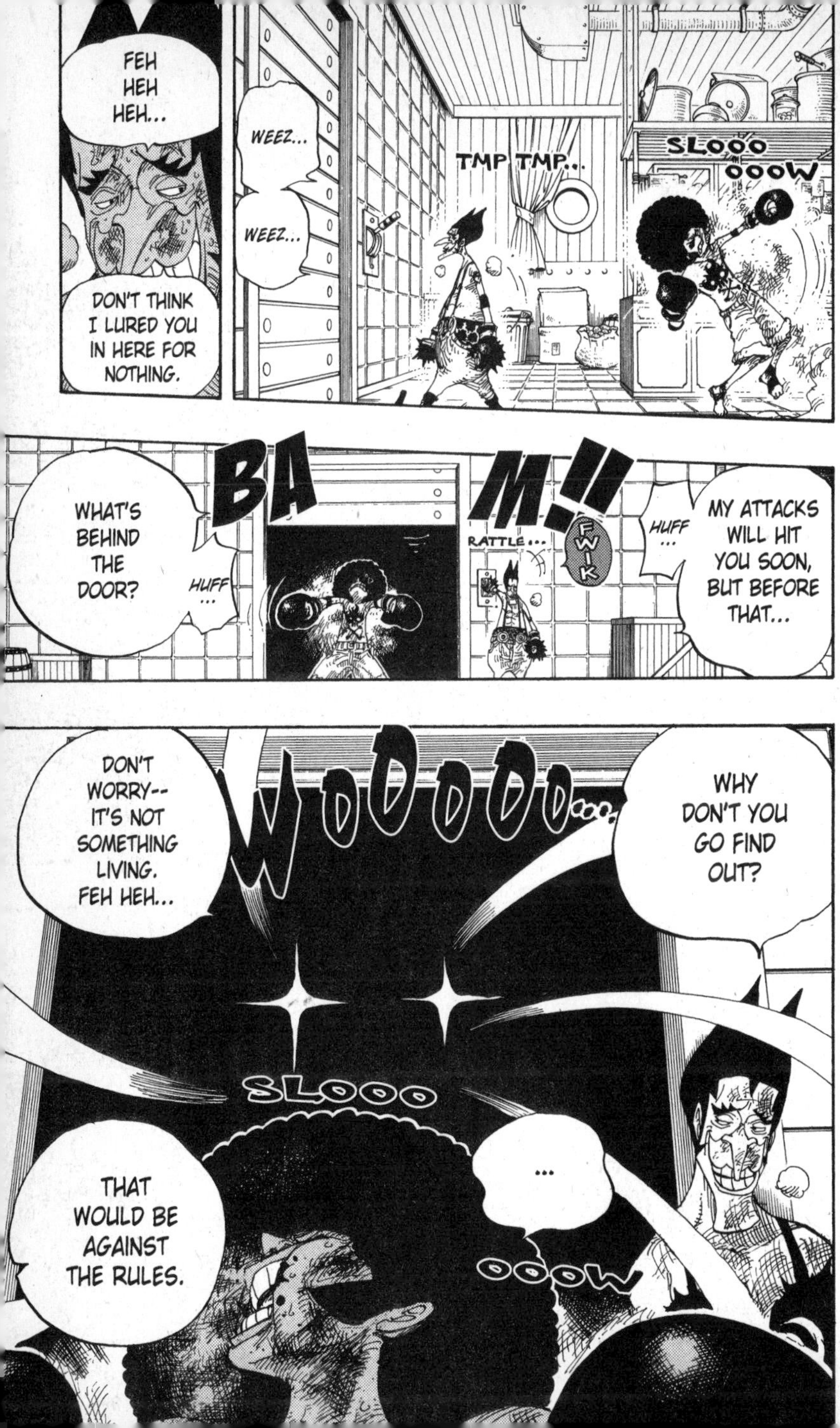
SLOOO OOOW
TMP TMP...
WEEZ...
WEEZ...
FEH HEH HEH...
DON'T THINK I LURED YOU IN HERE FOR NOTHING.
MY ATTACKS WILL HIT YOU SOON, BUT BEFORE THAT...
HUFF...
FWIK
BAM!!
RATTLE...
HUFF...
WHAT'S BEHIND THE DOOR?
WHY DON'T YOU GO FIND OUT?
WOOOOOO...
DON'T WORRY-- IT'S NOT SOMETHING LIVING. FEH HEH...
...
SLOOO OOOW
THAT WOULD BE AGAINST THE RULES.

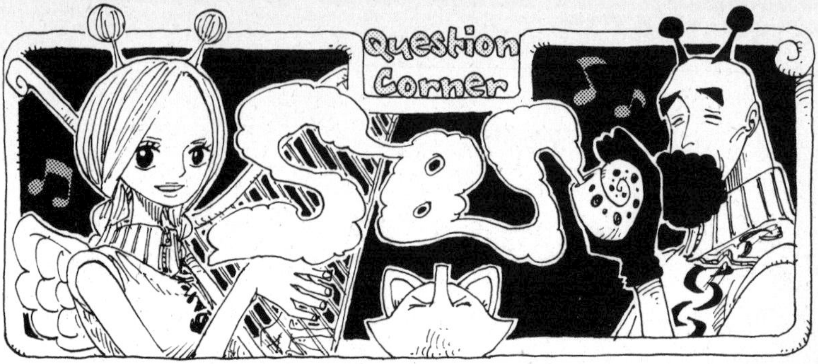
Question Corner
SBS

Q: I've got a question, Oda Sensei. On page 71 of Vol. 30, Conis says "I need to go back!!" and then says "Heso!"(Belly buttons) I think it's a little weird if Heso means hello… Would you explain it to me? I just couldn't stop thinking about it, so I finally decided to write you. Please respond. --Pen Name: Wanko

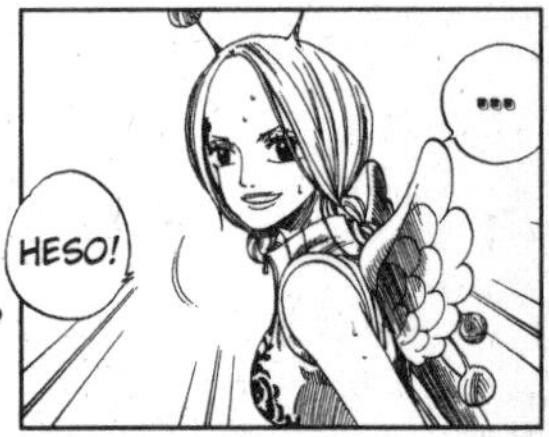
HESO!
...

A: You can think of it as an all purpose greeting on Sky Island. It doesn't correspond to any particular word in Japanese. It can, of course, mean "Good morning," "Hello" and "Good evening," as well as "How are you?" "Goodbye" and "Be careful," depending on the situation. You use it according to the context. If someone says "Heso" to you, you can respond "Heso." It just depends on the context.

Q: Hello. I'll jump right to my question! Tonjit was on stilts for ten years. How did he go to the bathroom?! S-Surely he didn't… Please respond in Tonjit's language.

--Pen Name: Mai 2

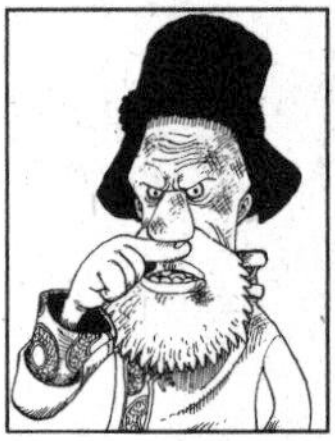

A: It just driiiiiiibbled down. Yep.

And I think that's a good place to wrap this up…

Q: NO!! THE QUESTION CORNER ISN'T OVER!! --Ko

A: OH YES IT IS!! See you next time!!

Chapter 316:
BROTHER SOUL

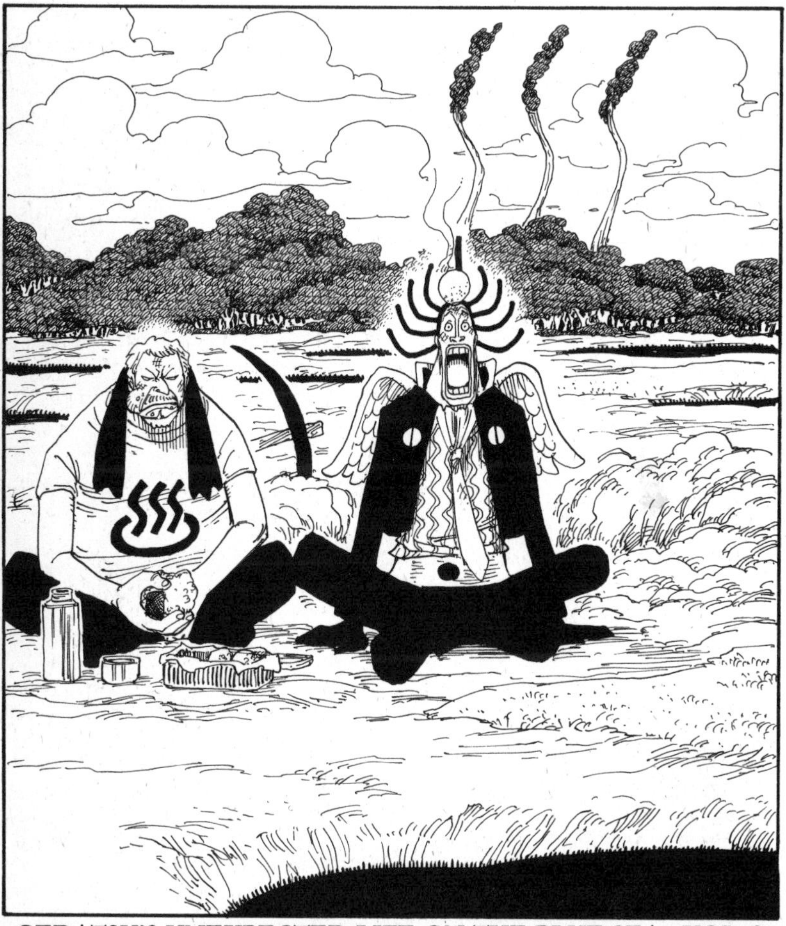

GEDATSU'S UNEXPECTED LIFE ON THE BLUE SEA , VOL. 3:
"UNEXPECTEDLY ALIVE"

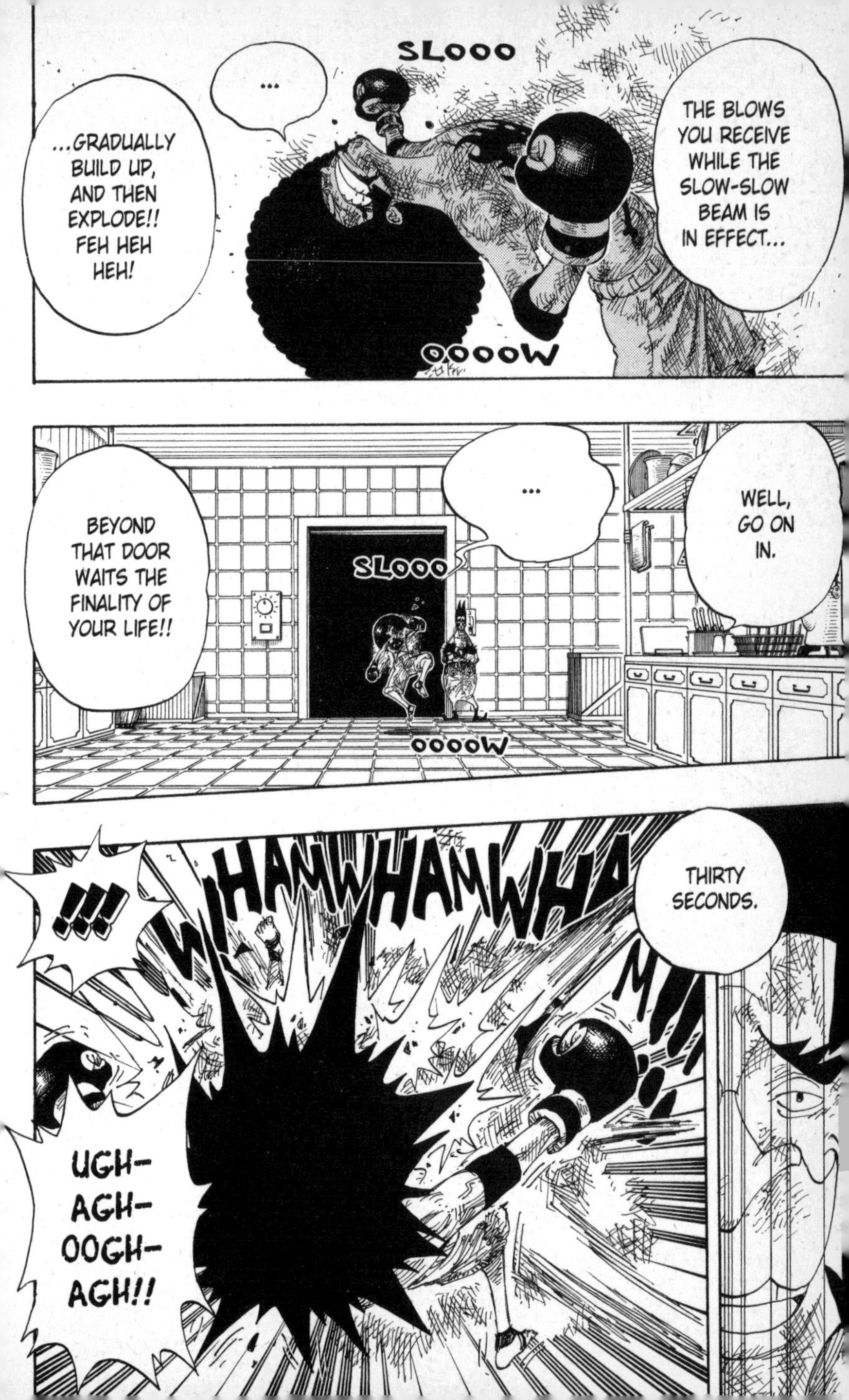
THE BLOWS YOU RECEIVE WHILE THE SLOW-SLOW BEAM IS IN EFFECT...
SLOOO
...
...GRADUALLY BUILD UP, AND THEN EXPLODE!! FEH HEH HEH!
OOOOW
WELL, GO ON IN.
...
SLOOO
OOOOW
BEYOND THAT DOOR WAITS THE FINALITY OF YOUR LIFE!!
THIRTY SECONDS.
WHAMWHAMWHAM!!!
!!!
UGH-AGH-OOGH-AGH!!

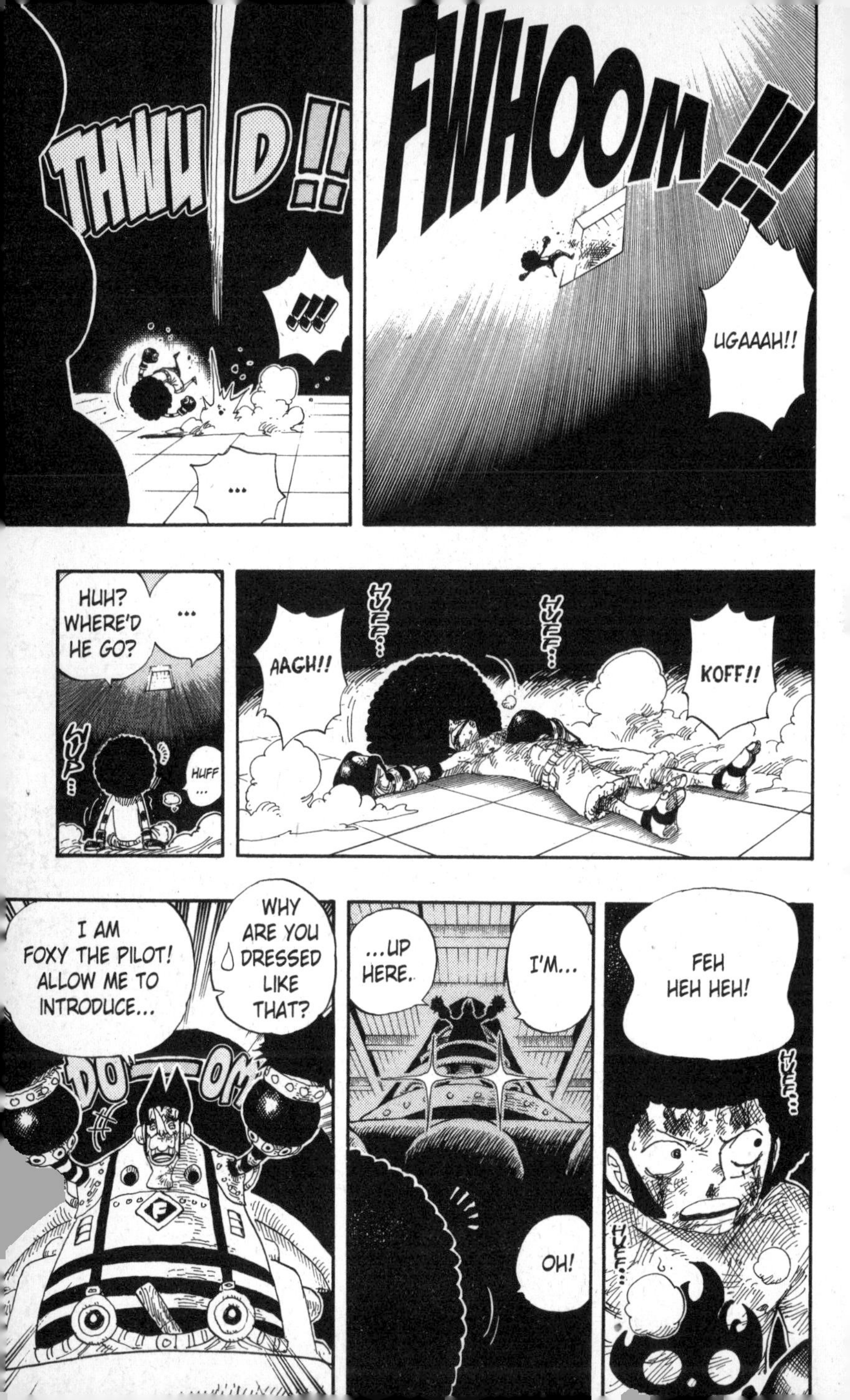
FWHOOM!!!
UGAAAH!!
THWUD!!
!!!
...
KOFF!!
HUFF...
HUFF...
AAGH!!
...
HUH? WHERE'D HE GO?
HUFF ...
FEH HEH HEH!
HUFF...
HUFF...
I'M...
...UP HERE.
OH!
WHY ARE YOU DRESSED LIKE THAT?
I AM FOXY THE PILOT! ALLOW ME TO INTRODUCE...
DO-OM

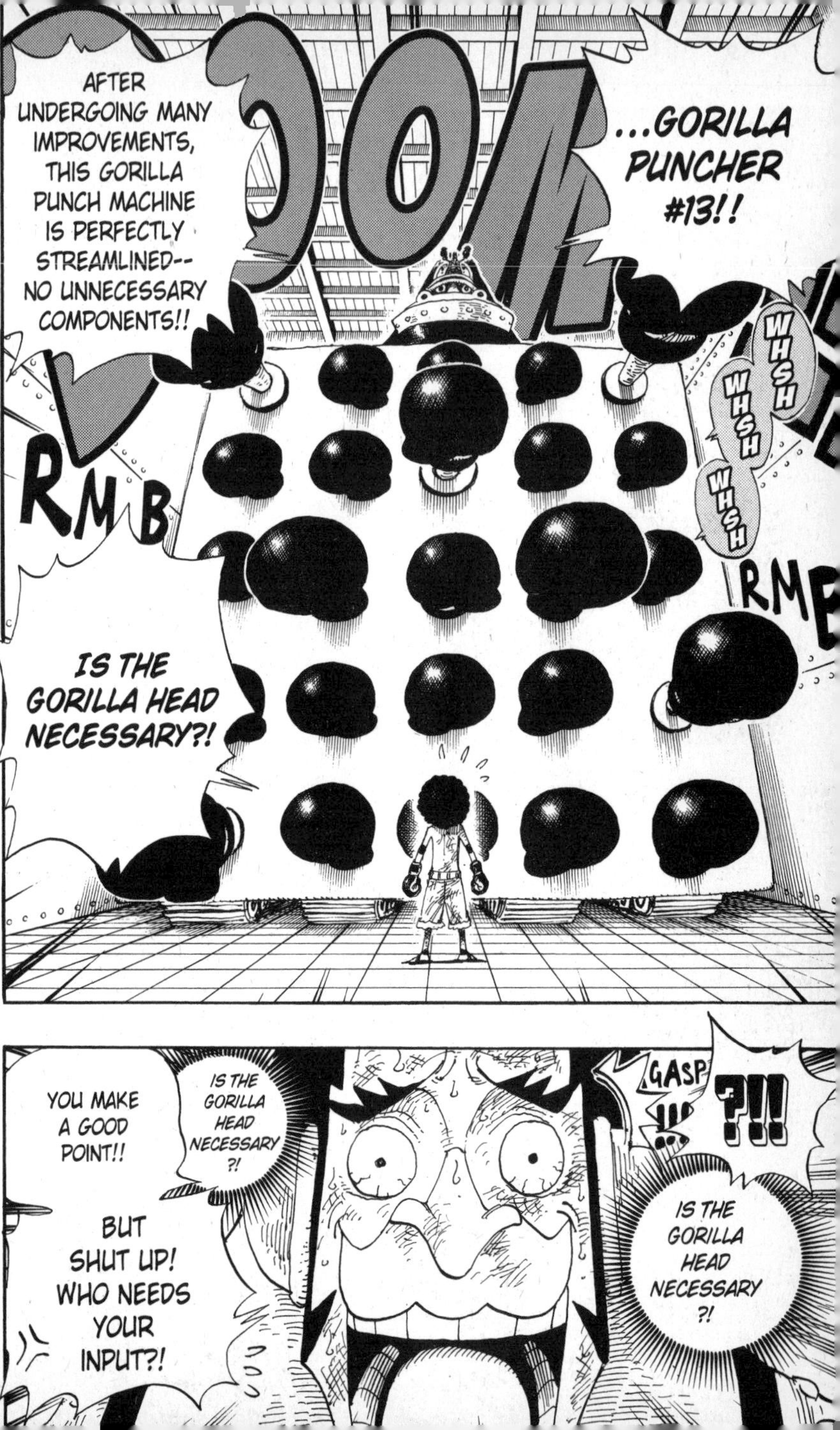
...GORILLA PUNCHER #13!!
AFTER UNDERGOING MANY IMPROVEMENTS, THIS GORILLA PUNCH MACHINE IS PERFECTLY STREAMLINED--NO UNNECESSARY COMPONENTS!!
WHSH
WHSH
WHSH
RMB
RMB
IS THE GORILLA HEAD NECESSARY?!
GASP!!
?!!
IS THE GORILLA HEAD NECESSARY?!
IS THE GORILLA HEAD NECESSARY?!
YOU MAKE A GOOD POINT!!
BUT SHUT UP! WHO NEEDS YOUR INPUT?!

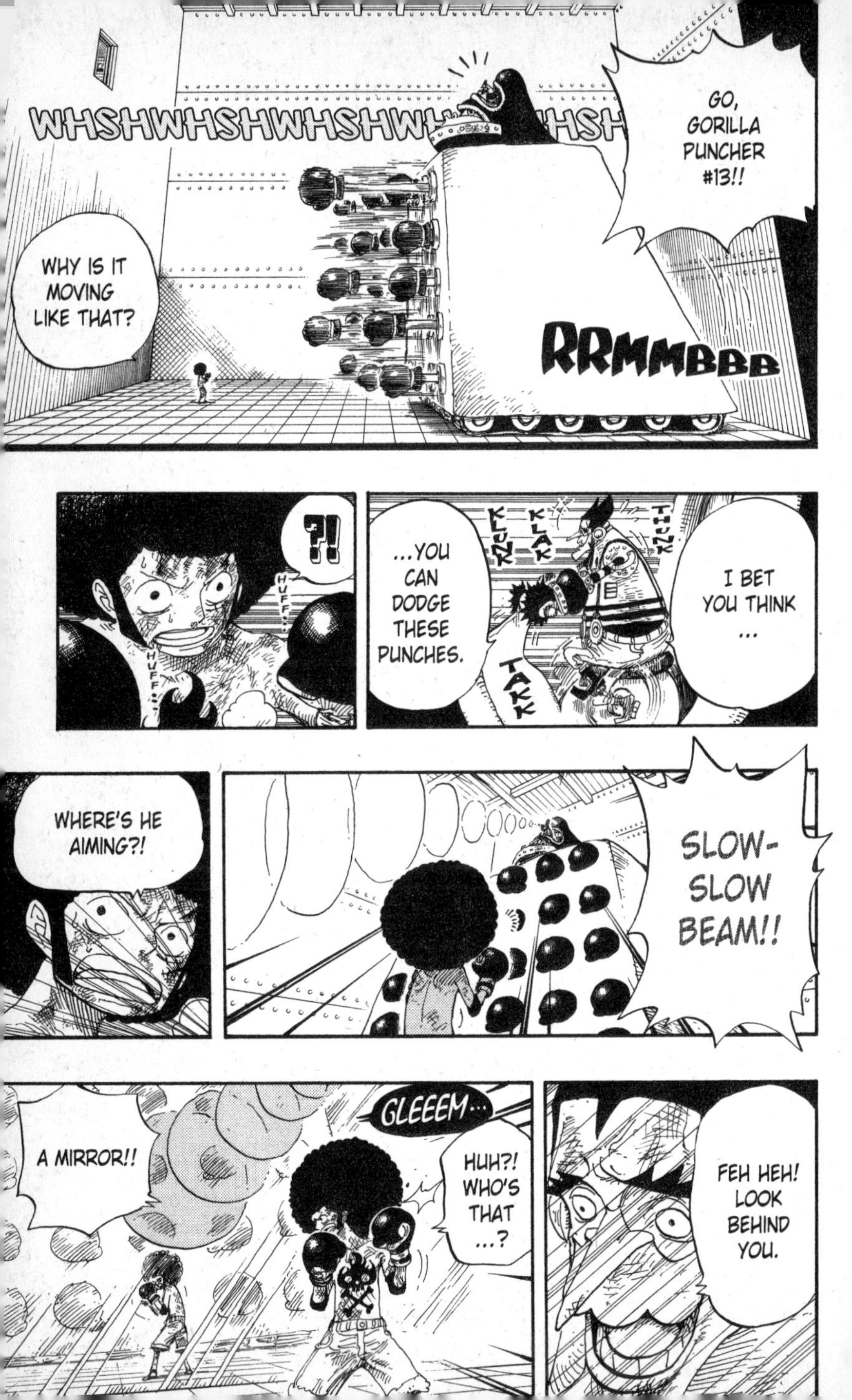
GO, GORILLA PUNCHER #13!!
WHSHWHSHWHSHWH...HSH
RRMMBBB
WHY IS IT MOVING LIKE THAT?
I BET YOU THINK ...
THUNK
KLAK
KLUNK
...YOU CAN DODGE THESE PUNCHES.
TAKK
?!
HUFF...
HUFF...
SLOW-SLOW BEAM!!
WHERE'S HE AIMING?!
FEH HEH! LOOK BEHIND YOU.
GLEEEM...
HUH?! WHO'S THAT ...?
A MIRROR!!

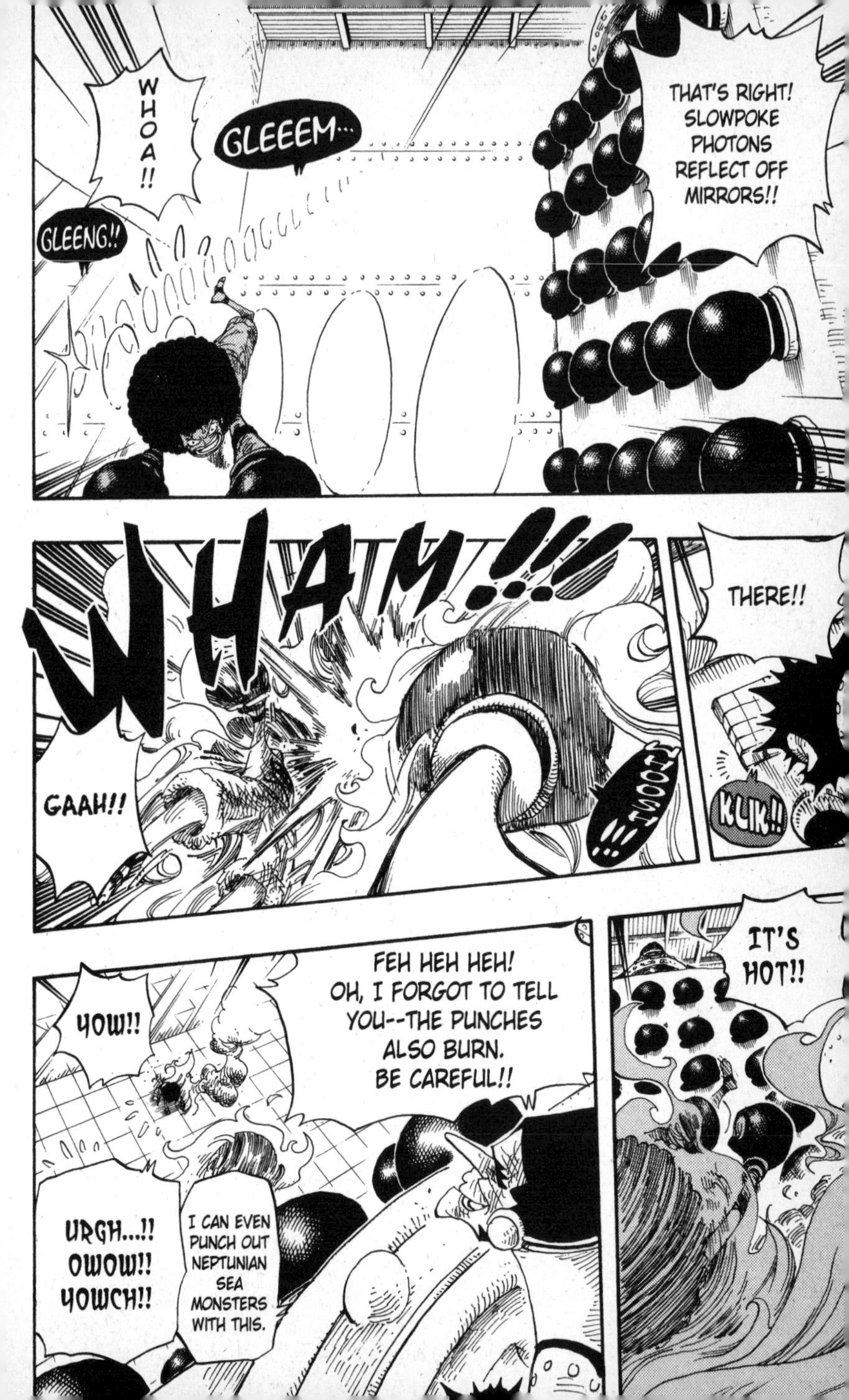
THAT'S RIGHT! SLOWPOKE PHOTONS REFLECT OFF MIRRORS!!
GLEEEM...
WHOA!!
GLEENG!!
THERE!!
KLIK!!
WHAM!!!
THOOSH!!
GAAH!!
IT'S HOT!!
FEH HEH HEH! OH, I FORGOT TO TELL YOU--THE PUNCHES ALSO BURN. BE CAREFUL!!
YOW!!
I CAN EVEN PUNCH OUT NEPTUNIAN SEA MONSTERS WITH THIS.
URGH...!! OWOW!! YOWCH!!

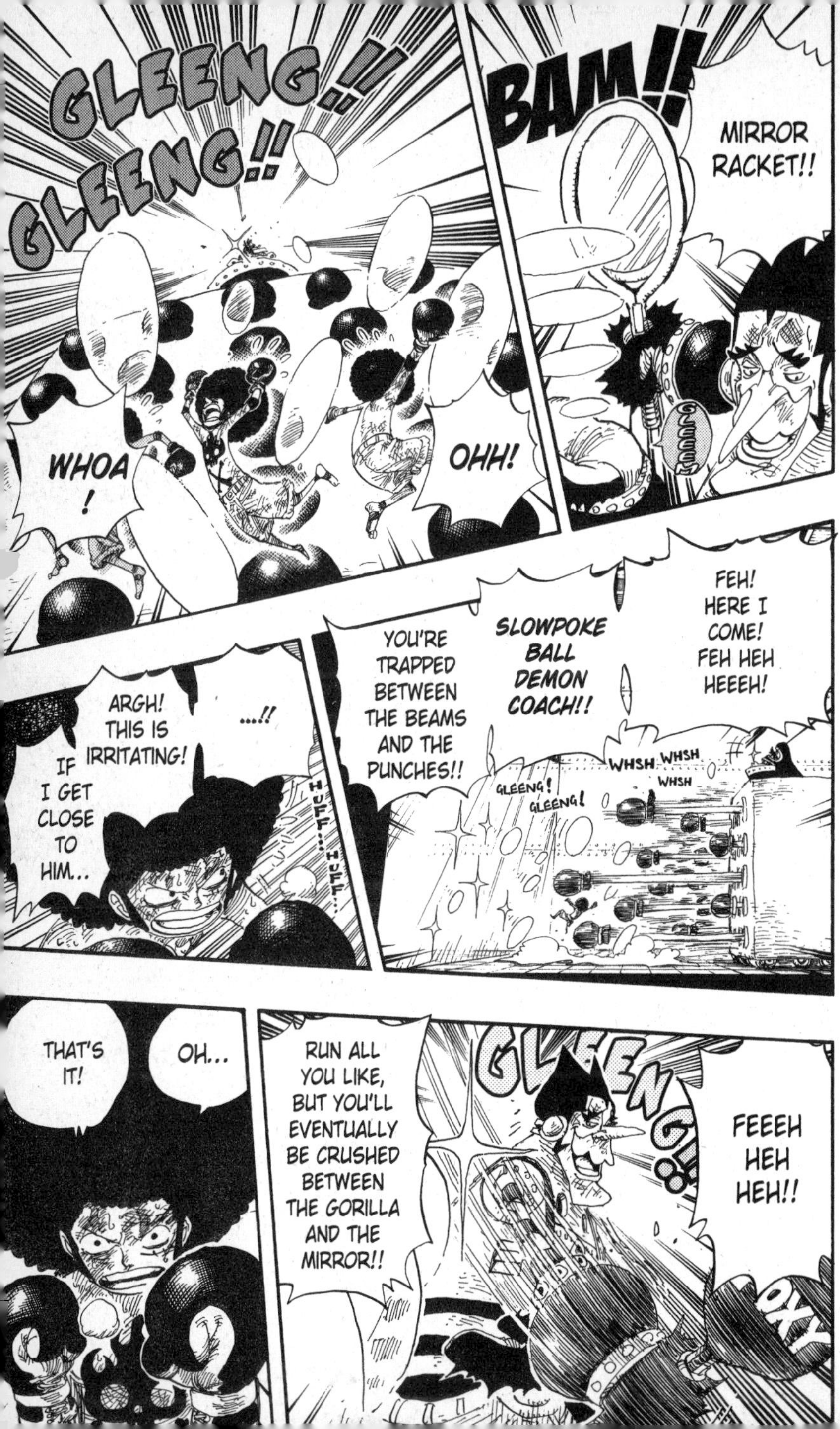
BAM!!
MIRROR RACKET!!
GLEENG!!
GLEENG!!
OHH!
WHOA!
FEH! HERE I COME! FEH HEH HEEEH!
SLOWPOKE BALL DEMON COACH!!
YOU'RE TRAPPED BETWEEN THE BEAMS AND THE PUNCHES!!
WHSH WHSH
WHSH
GLEENG!
GLEENG!
...!!
ARGH! THIS IS IRRITATING!
IF I GET CLOSE TO HIM...
HUFF... HUFF...
FEEEH HEH HEH!!
GLEENG!!
RUN ALL YOU LIKE, BUT YOU'LL EVENTUALLY BE CRUSHED BETWEEN THE GORILLA AND THE MIRROR!!
OH...
THAT'S IT!

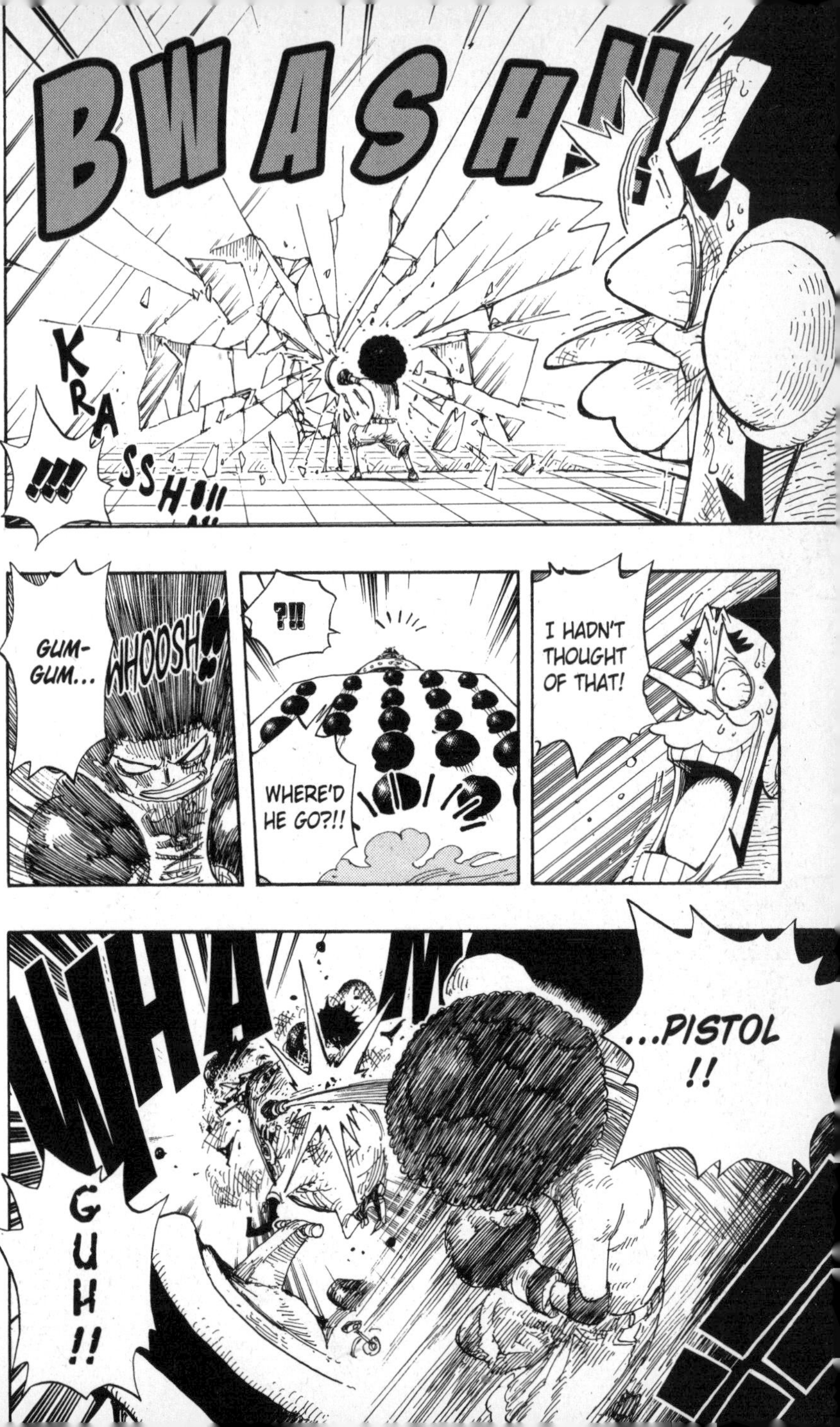

BWASH!!
!!!
KRASSH!!
I HADN'T THOUGHT OF THAT!
?!!
WHERE'D HE GO?!!
GUM-GUM...
WHOOSH!!
...PISTOL!!
WHAM
GUH!!

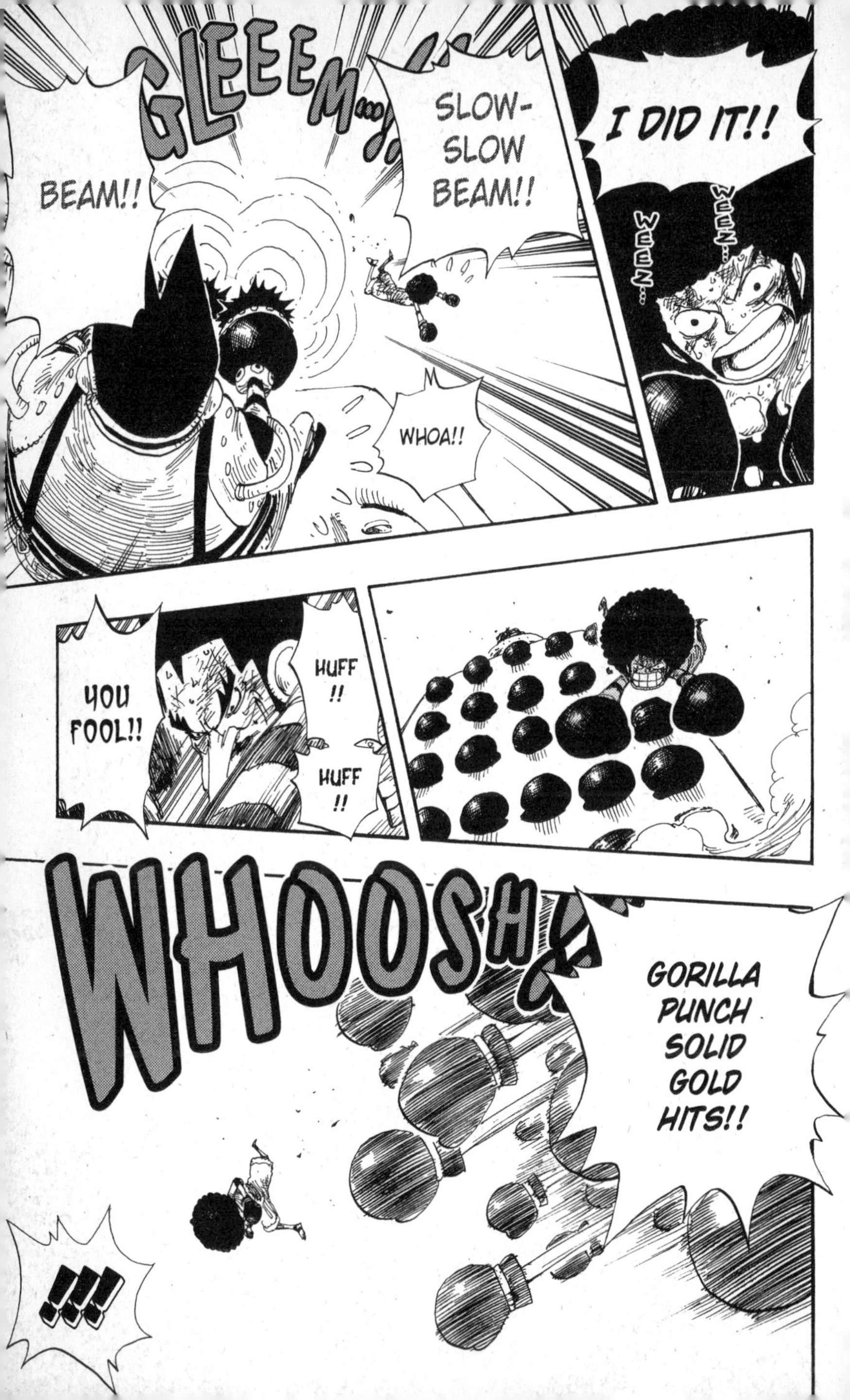
I DID IT!!
WEEN...
WEEEN...
SLOW-SLOW BEAM!!
GLEEEM...
BEAM!!
WHOA!!
HUFF!!
HUFF!!
YOU FOOL!!
GORILLA PUNCH SOLID GOLD HITS!!
WHOOSH
!!!

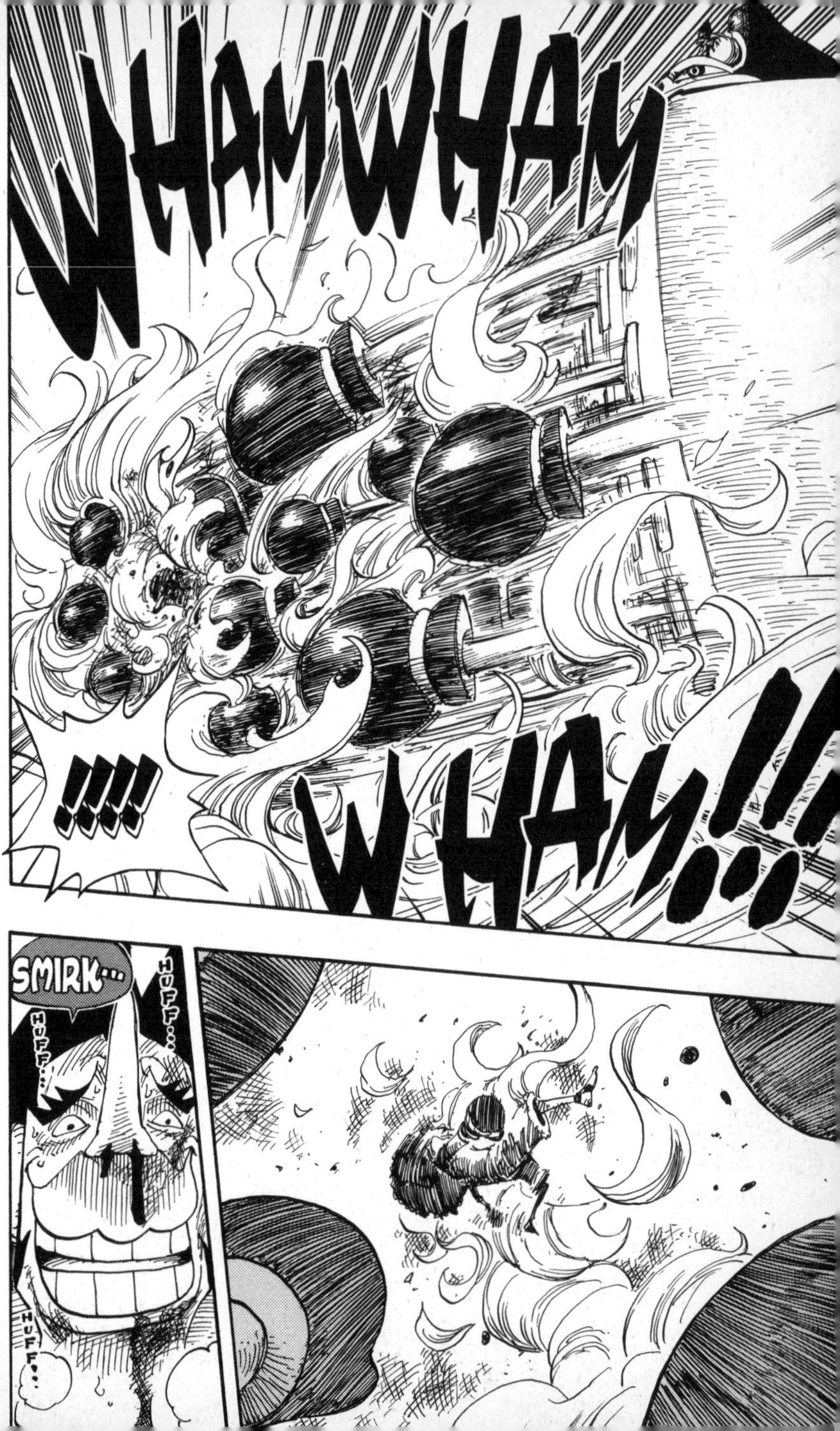
WHAMWHAM
!!!!
WHAM!!!
SMIRK...
HUFF...
HUFF...
HUFF...

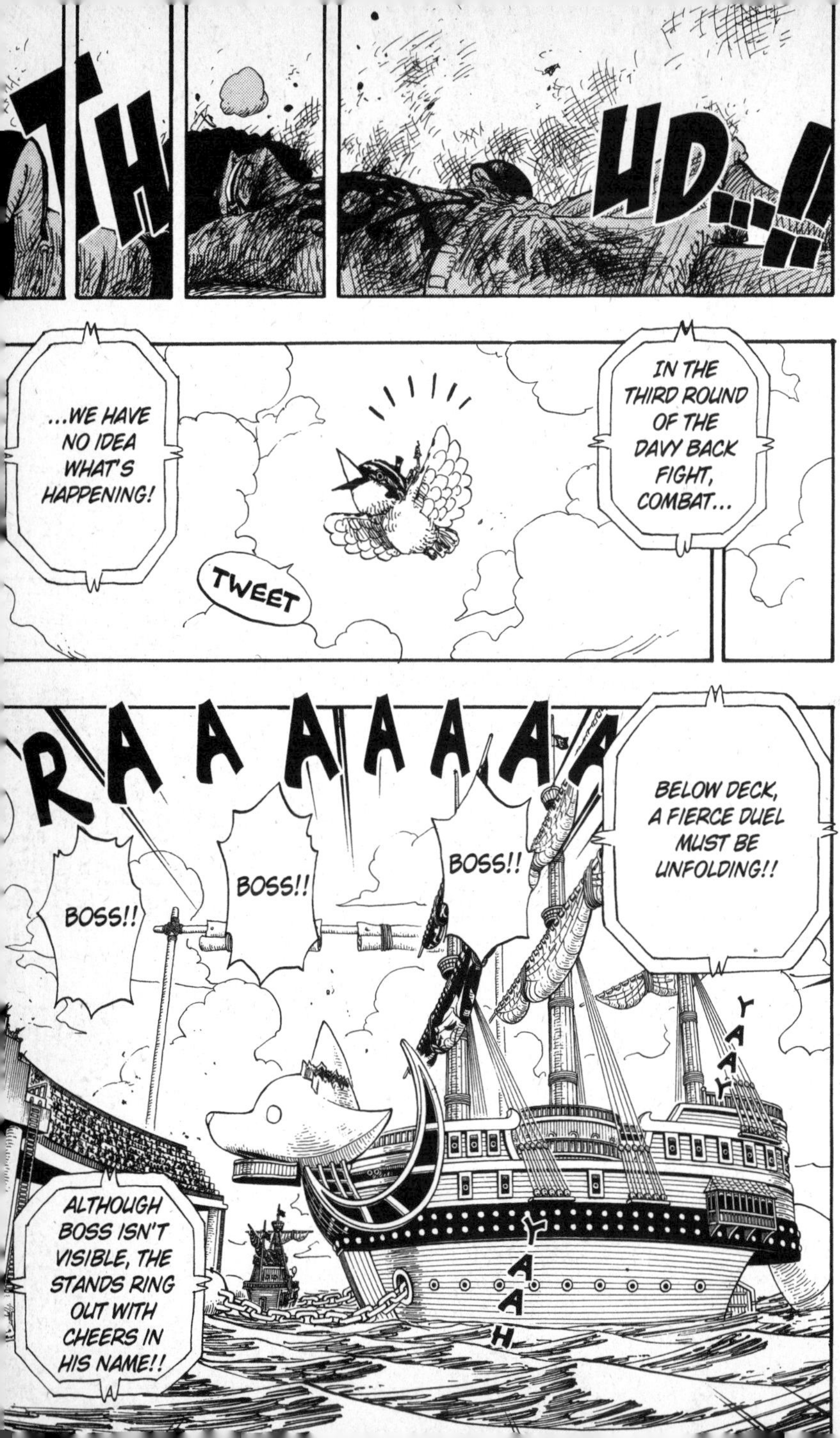
THUD..!!
IN THE THIRD ROUND OF THE DAVY BACK FIGHT, COMBAT...
...WE HAVE NO IDEA WHAT'S HAPPENING!
TWEET
BELOW DECK, A FIERCE DUEL MUST BE UNFOLDING!!
RAAAAAAA
BOSS!!
BOSS!!
BOSS!!
YAAAY
YAAAH
ALTHOUGH BOSS ISN'T VISIBLE, THE STANDS RING OUT WITH CHEERS IN HIS NAME!!

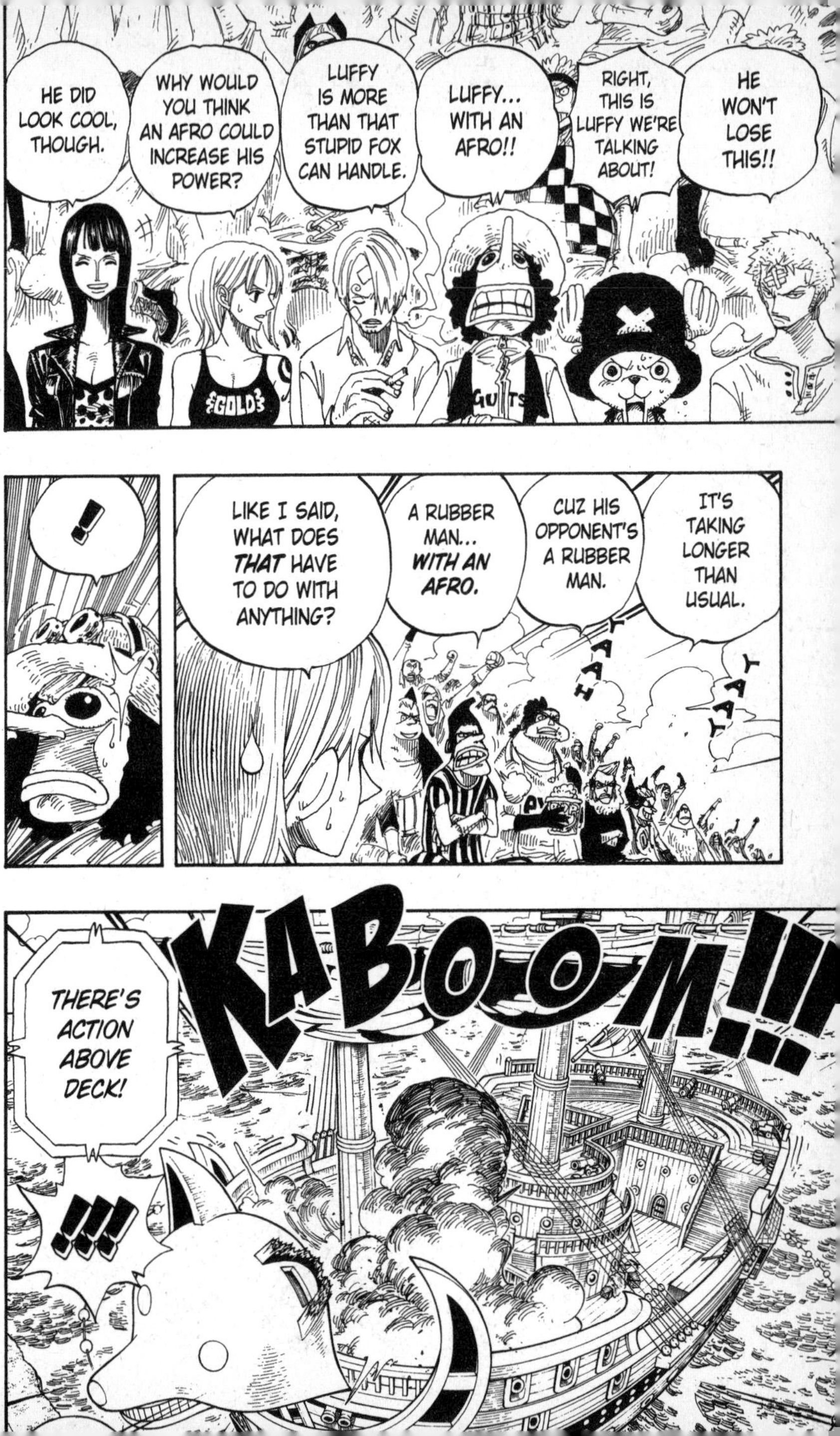
HE WON'T LOSE THIS!!
RIGHT, THIS IS LUFFY WE'RE TALKING ABOUT!
LUFFY... WITH AN AFRO!!
LUFFY IS MORE THAN THAT STUPID FOX CAN HANDLE.
WHY WOULD YOU THINK AN AFRO COULD INCREASE HIS POWER?
HE DID LOOK COOL, THOUGH.
IT'S TAKING LONGER THAN USUAL.
YAAY
CUZ HIS OPPONENT'S A RUBBER MAN.
YAAH
A RUBBER MAN... *WITH AN AFRO.*
LIKE I SAID, WHAT DOES *THAT* HAVE TO DO WITH ANYTHING?
!
KABOOM!!!
THERE'S ACTION ABOVE DECK!
!!!

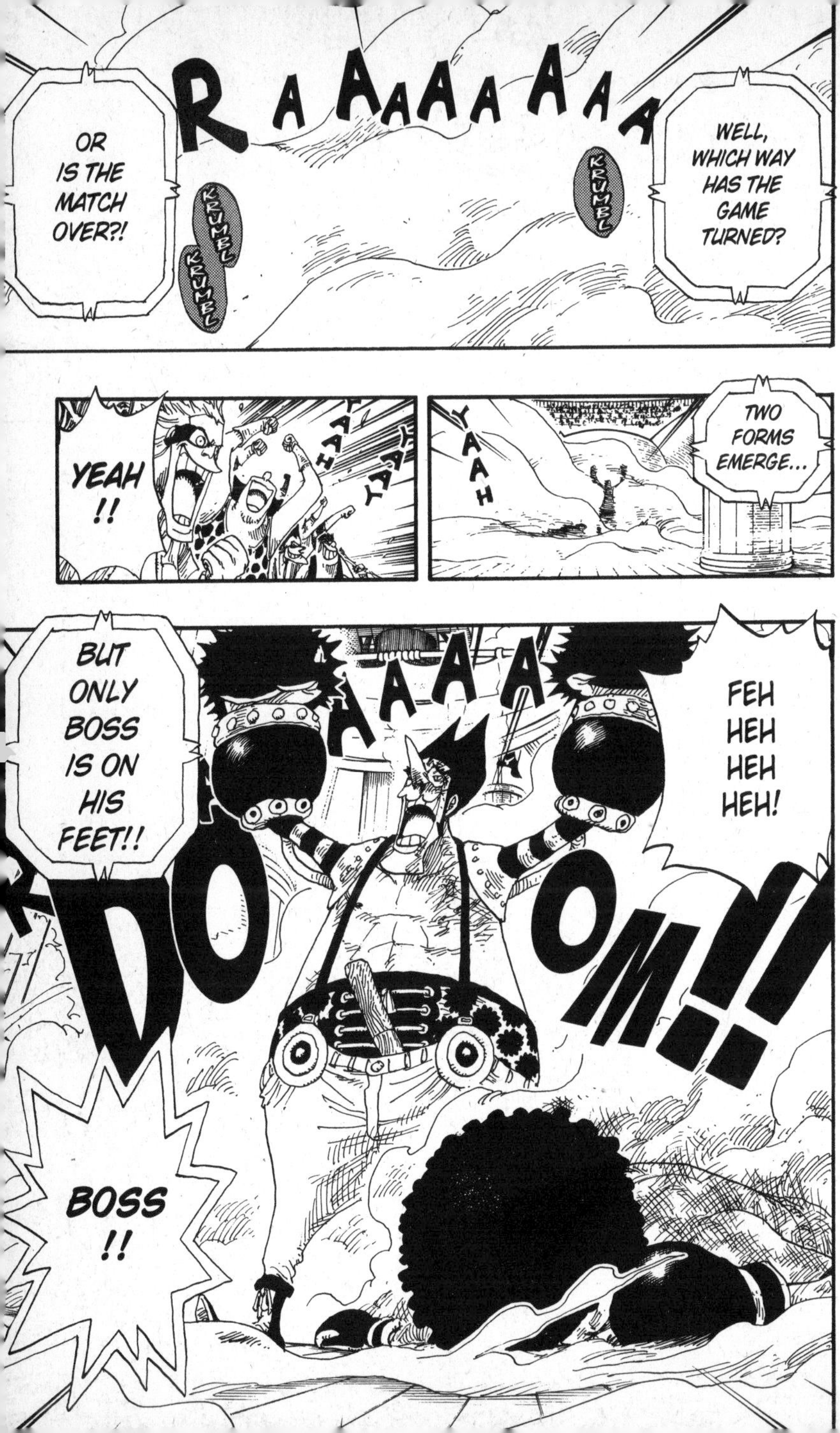
WELL, WHICH WAY HAS THE GAME TURNED?
KRUMBL
RAAAAAAAA
OR IS THE MATCH OVER?!
KRUMBL KRUMBL
TWO FORMS EMERGE...
YAAH
YAAAY
YEAH!!
FEH HEH HEH HEH!
AAAAA
BUT ONLY BOSS IS ON HIS FEET!!
DOOM!!
BOSS!!

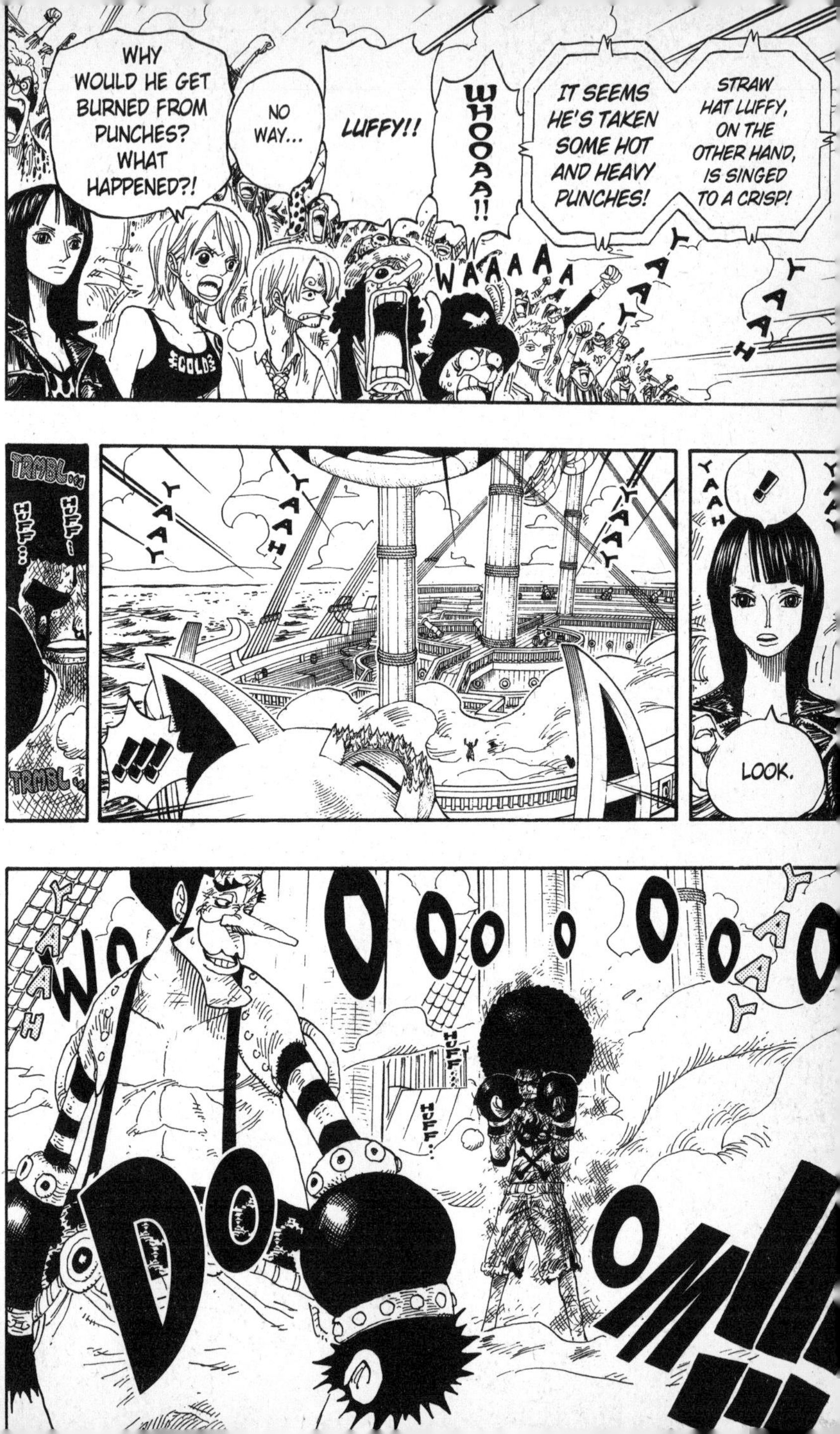
STRAW HAT LUFFY, ON THE OTHER HAND, IS SINGED TO A CRISP!
IT SEEMS HE'S TAKEN SOME HOT AND HEAVY PUNCHES!
YAAAH
YAAAY
WAAAAAA
WHOOAAA!!
LUFFY!!
NO WAY...
WHY WOULD HE GET BURNED FROM PUNCHES? WHAT HAPPENED?!
YAAAH
!
LOOK.
YAAAY
YAAAH
YAAAY
TRMBL...
HUFF...
HUFF...
TRMBL...
YAAAY
HUFF...
HUFF...
YAAAH

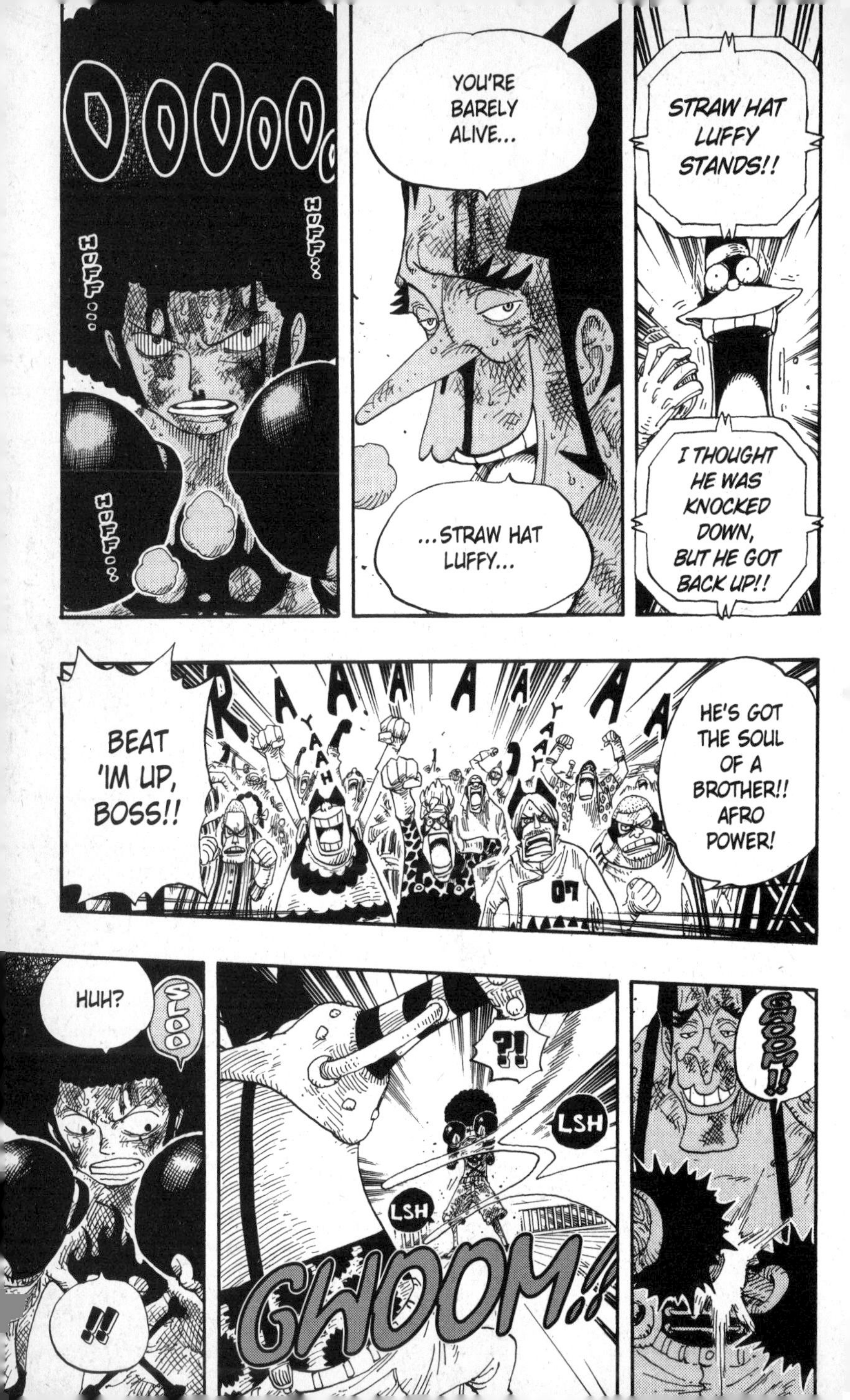
STRAW HAT LUFFY STANDS!!
I THOUGHT HE WAS KNOCKED DOWN, BUT HE GOT BACK UP!!
YOU'RE BARELY ALIVE...
...STRAW HAT LUFFY...
HUFF...
HUFF...
HUFF...
HE'S GOT THE SOUL OF A BROTHER!! AFRO POWER!
YAAAY
RAAAAAAA
YAAH
BEAT 'IM UP, BOSS!!
GHOOM!!
?!
LSH
LSH
GHOOM!!
HUH?
SLOO
!!

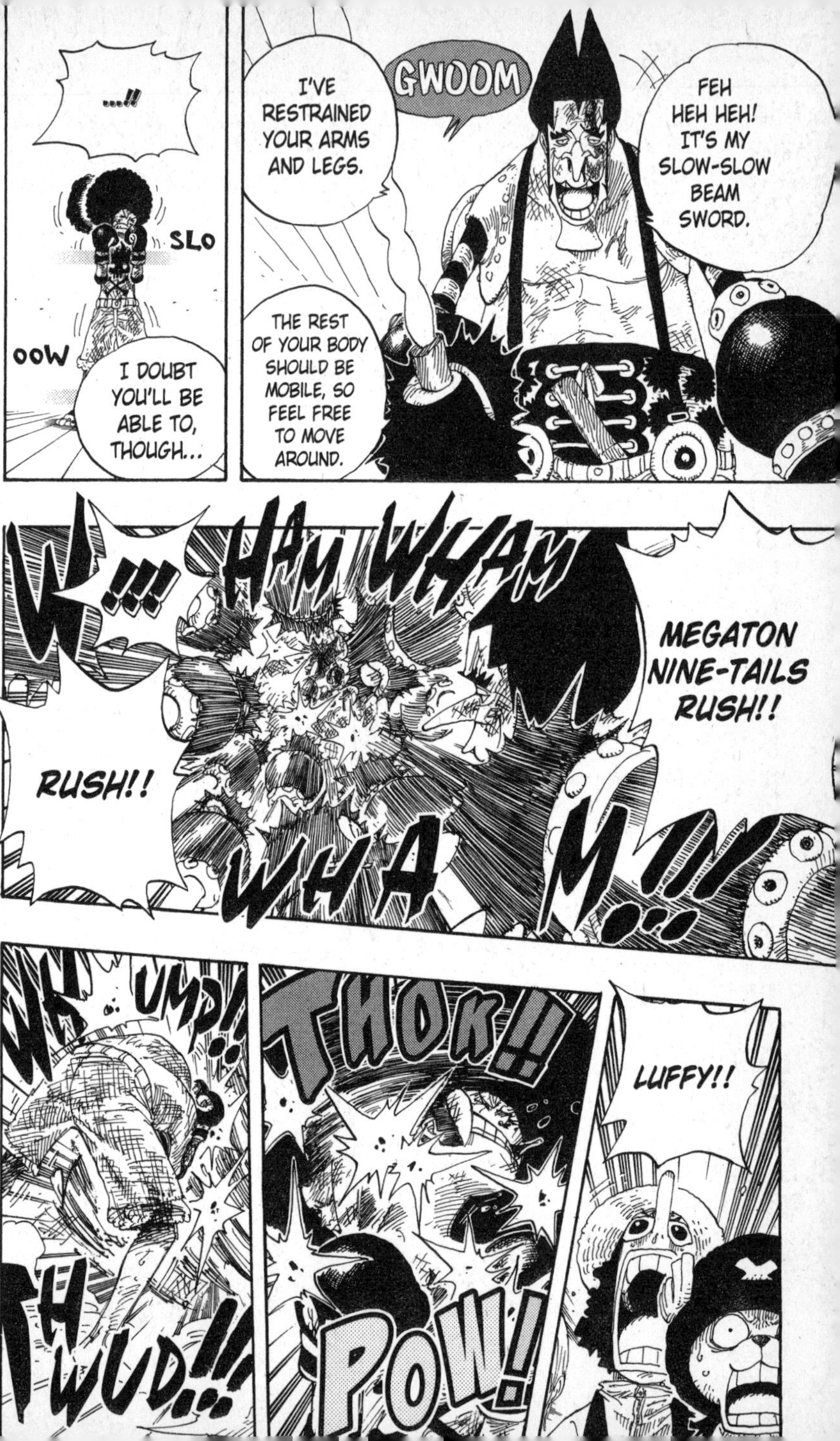
FEH HEH HEH! IT'S MY SLOW-SLOW BEAM SWORD.
GWOOM
I'VE RESTRAINED YOUR ARMS AND LEGS.
THE REST OF YOUR BODY SHOULD BE MOBILE, SO FEEL FREE TO MOVE AROUND.
...!!
SLO
OOW
I DOUBT YOU'LL BE ABLE TO, THOUGH...
MEGATON NINE-TAILS RUSH!!
WHAM
RUSH!!
LUFFY!!
THOK!!
POW!
THWUD!!!

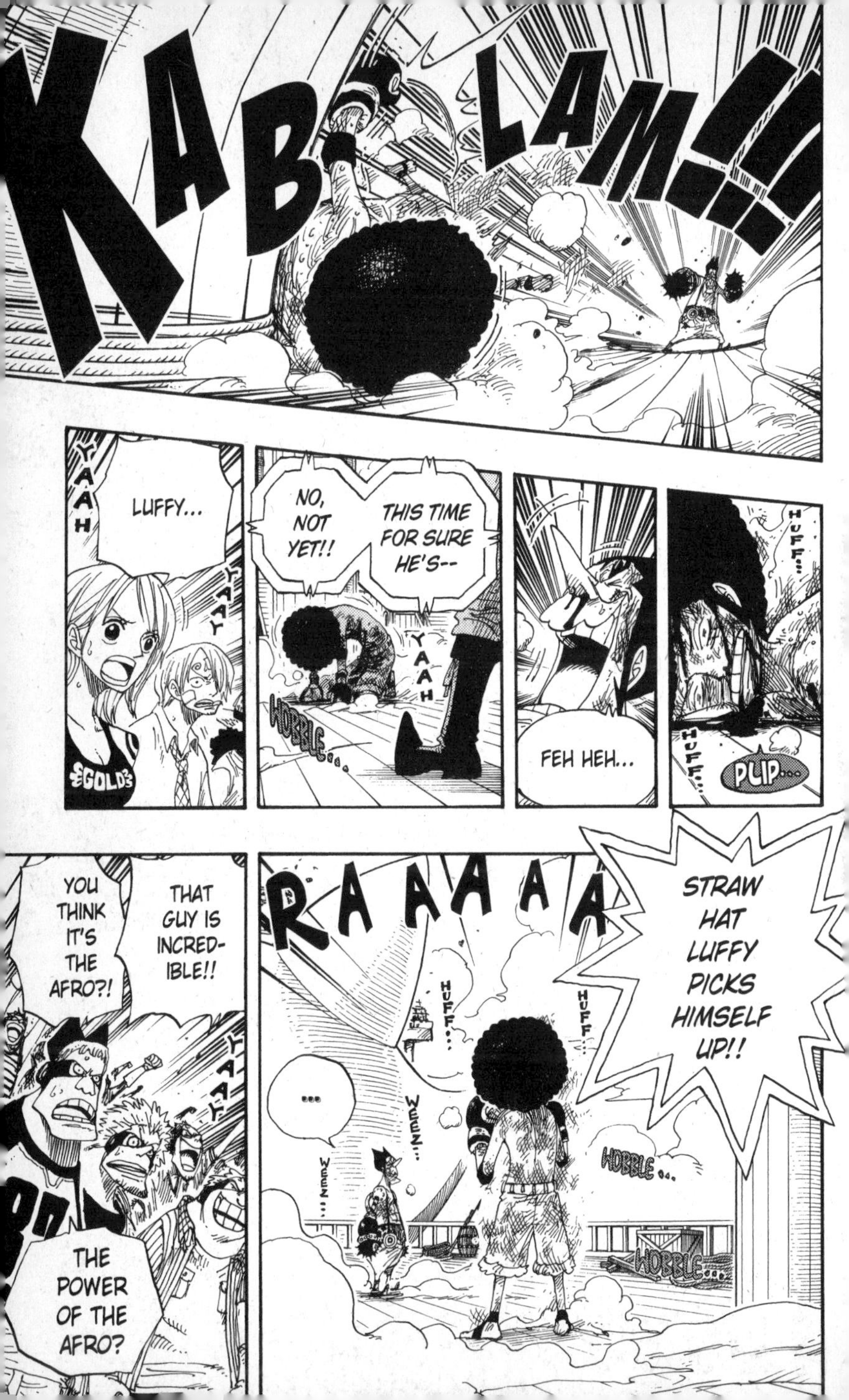
KABLAM!!!
HUFF...
HUFF...
PLIP...
FEH HEH...
THIS TIME FOR SURE HE'S--
NO, NOT YET!!
YAAH
WOBBLE...
YAAAH
LUFFY...
YAAY
STRAW HAT LUFFY PICKS HIMSELF UP!!
RAAAAA
HUFF...
HUFF...
...
WEEZ...
WOBBLE...
WEEZ...
WOBBLE...
THAT GUY IS INCREDIBLE!!
YOU THINK IT'S THE AFRO?!
YAAAY
THE POWER OF THE AFRO?

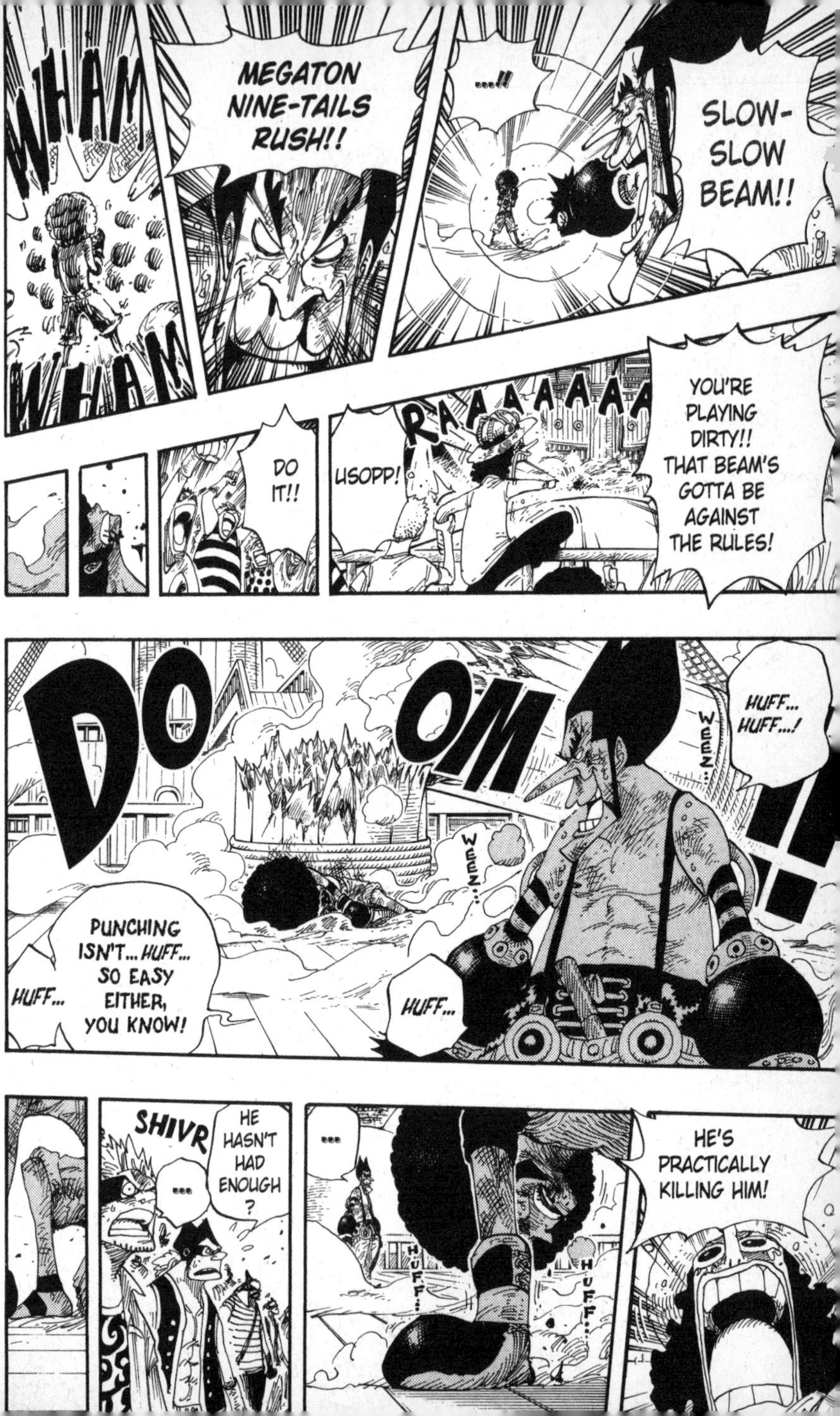
SLOW-SLOW BEAM!!
...!!
MEGATON NINE-TAILS RUSH!!
WHAM
WHAM
YOU'RE PLAYING DIRTY!! THAT BEAM'S GOTTA BE AGAINST THE RULES!
RAAAAAAA
USOPP!
DO IT!!
HUFF... HUFF...!
WEEZ...
DOOM!!
WEEZ...
HUFF...
PUNCHING ISN'T... HUFF... SO EASY EITHER, YOU KNOW!
HUFF...
HE'S PRACTICALLY KILLING HIM!
HUFF...
HUFF...
...
HE HASN'T HAD ENOUGH?
...
SHIVR

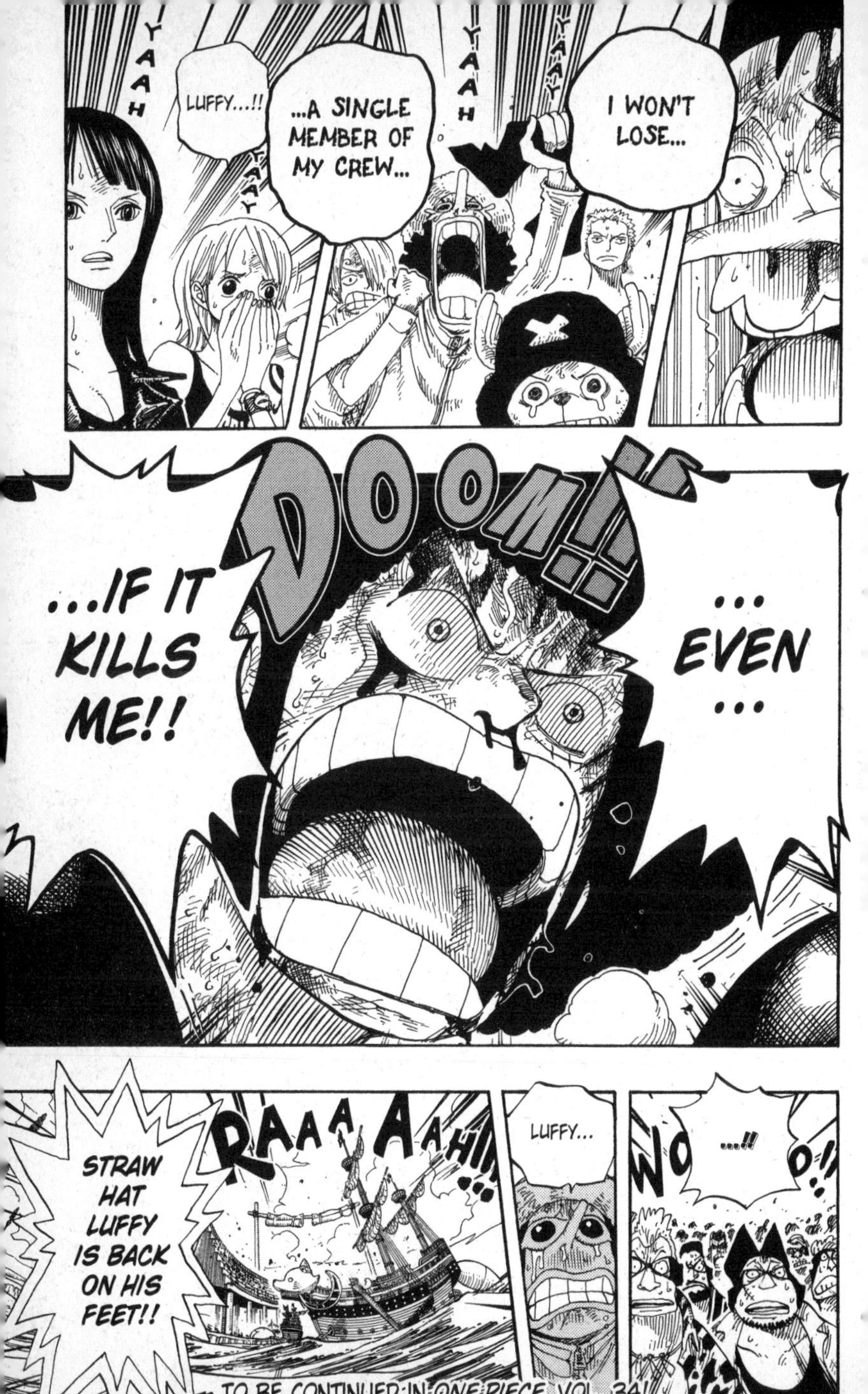
I WON'T LOSE...
YAAAY
YAAAH
...A SINGLE MEMBER OF MY CREW...
YAAAY
LUFFY...!!
YAAAH
DOOM!!
...EVEN...
...IF IT KILLS ME!!
WOOO!!
...!!
LUFFY...
RAAAAAH!!
STRAW HAT LUFFY IS BACK ON HIS FEET!!

TO BE CONTINUED IN ONE PIECE, VOL. 34!

COMING NEXT VOLUME:

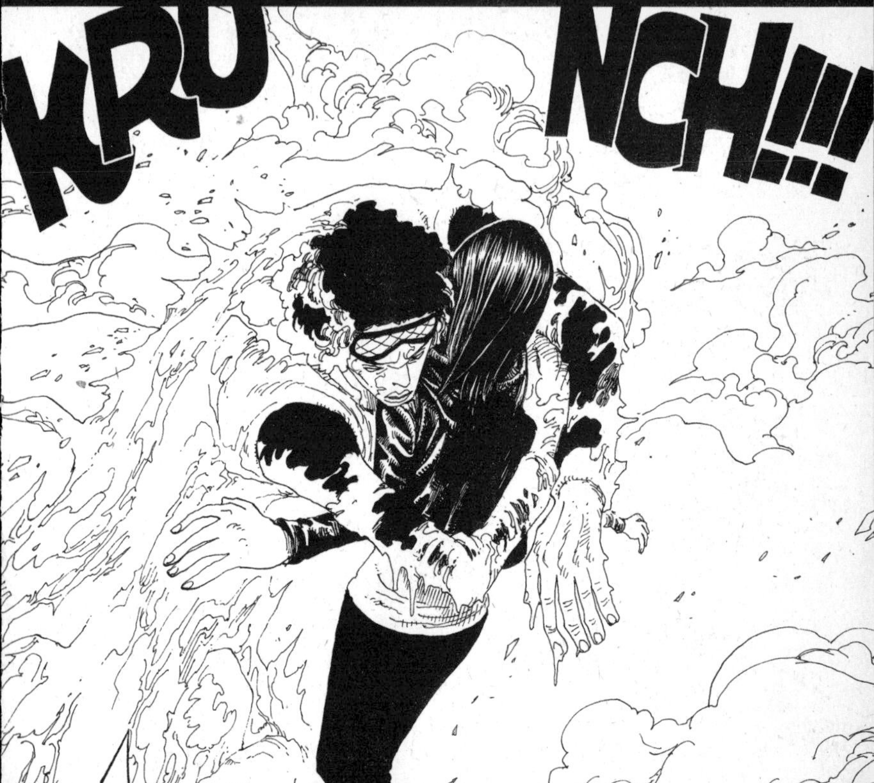
KRU
NCH!!!

The Davy Back Fight continues as Luffy struggles to get the upper hand against Foxy's tricks. Will Luffy's trump card be enough to get a knockout victory, or will the Straw Hat crew lose one of their valuable members? And when the scenery shifts to a new city, Water Seven, will the *Merry Go* finally be fixed?

COMING SOON!

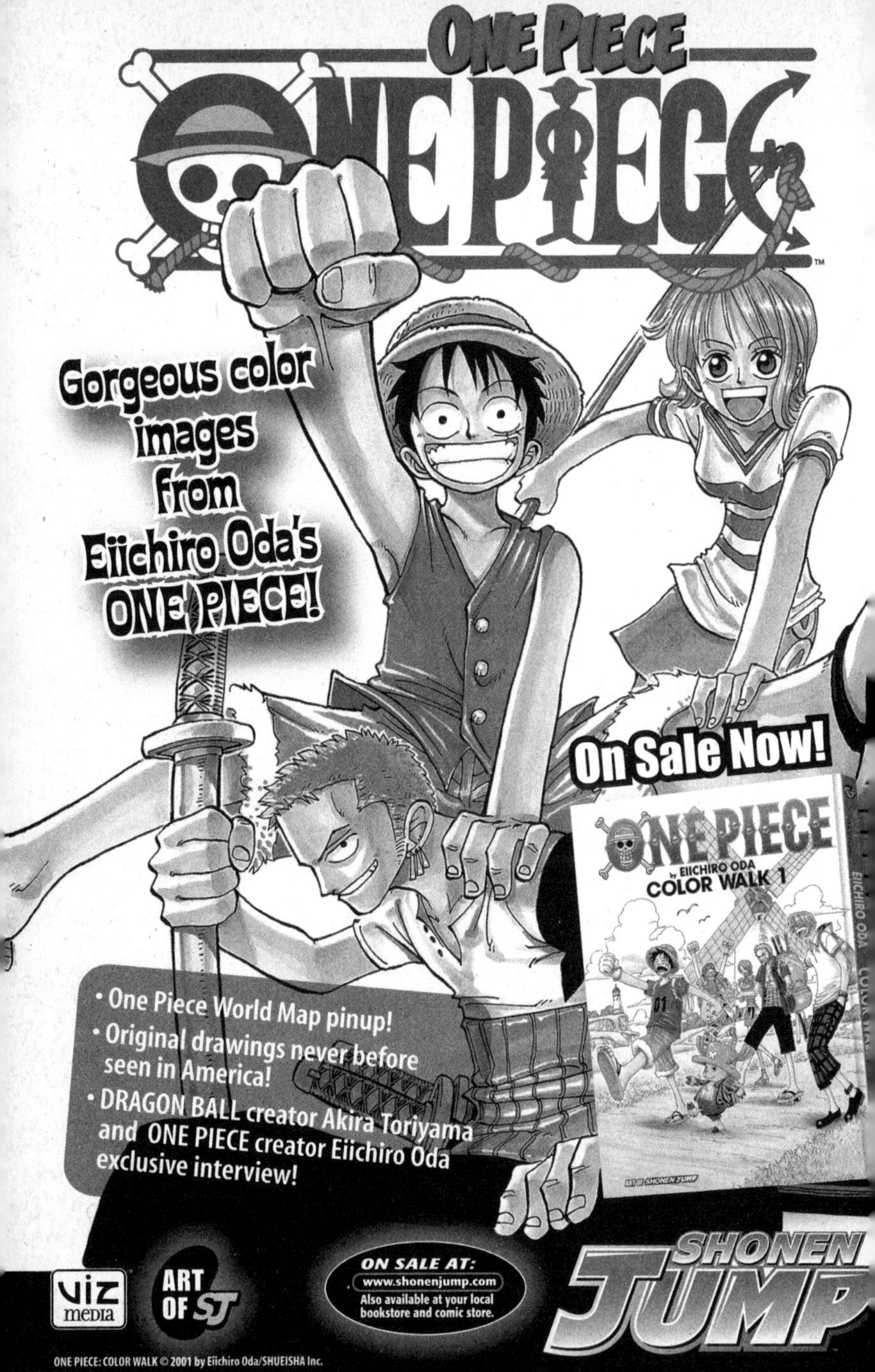
ONE PIECE
ONE PIECE
Gorgeous color images from Eiichiro Oda's ONE PIECE!
On Sale Now!
ONE PIECE
by EIICHIRO ODA
COLOR WALK 1
EIICHIRO ODA
ART OF SHONEN JUMP
• One Piece World Map pinup!
• Original drawings never before seen in America!
• DRAGON BALL creator Akira Toriyama and ONE PIECE creator Eiichiro Oda exclusive interview!
viz media
ART OF SJ
ON SALE AT:
www.shonenjump.com
Also available at your local bookstore and comic store.
SHONEN JUMP

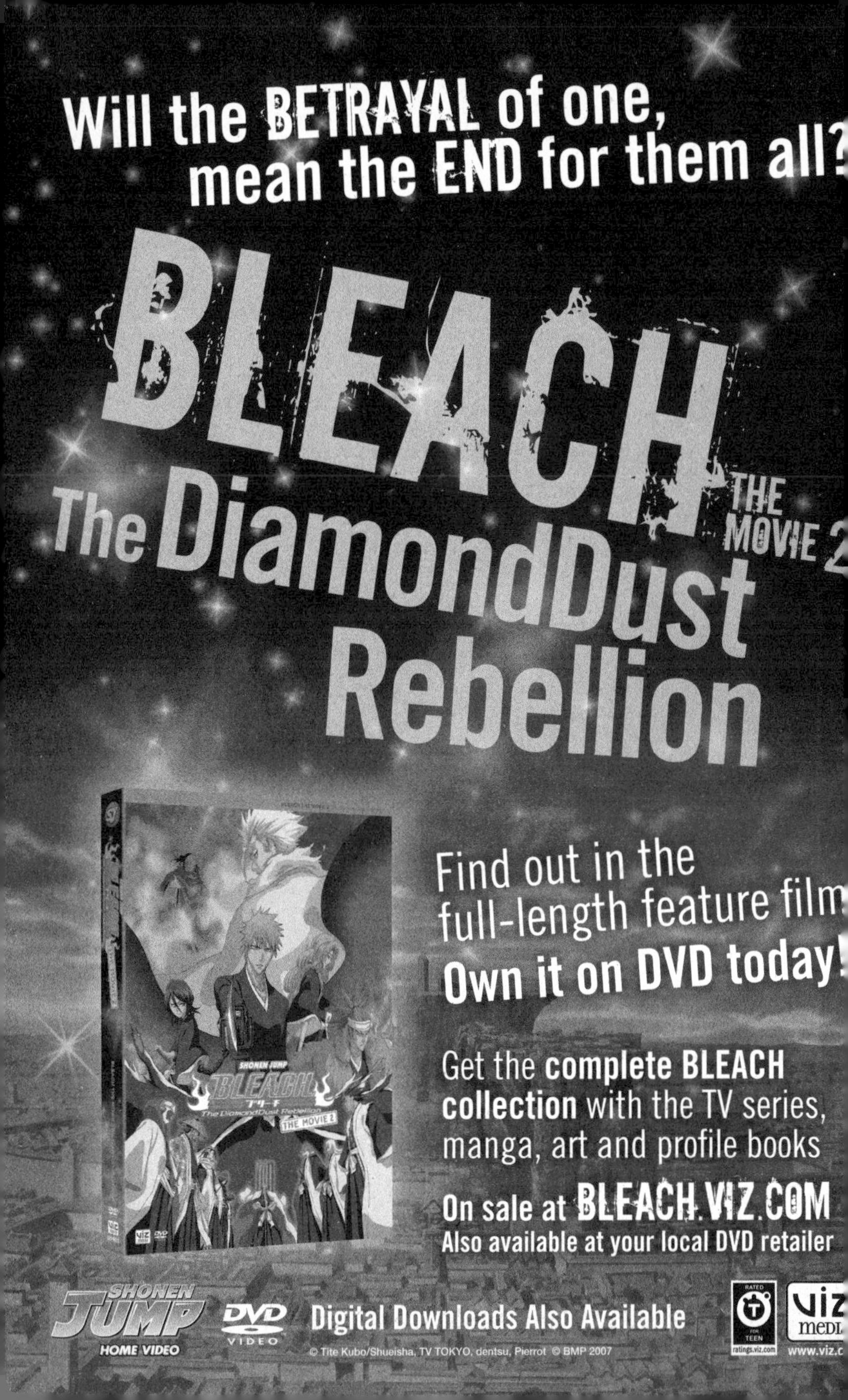
Will the BETRAYAL of one,
mean the END for them all?
BLEACH
THE MOVIE 2
The DiamondDust Rebellion
SHONEN JUMP
BLEACH
The DiamondDust Rebellion
THE MOVIE 2
Find out in the full-length feature film
Own it on DVD today!
Get the complete BLEACH collection with the TV series, manga, art and profile books
On sale at BLEACH.VIZ.COM
Also available at your local DVD retailer
SHONEN JUMP
HOME VIDEO
DVD
VIDEO
Digital Downloads Also Available
© Tite Kubo/Shueisha, TV TOKYO, dentsu, Pierrot © BMP 2007
RATED
T
FOR
TEEN
ratings.viz.com